David Hanlon

Remaking Micronesia

Discourses over Development in a Pacific Territory 1944–1982

University of Hawai'i Press

Honolulu

Printed in the United States of America
03 02 01 00 99 98 5 4 3 2 1

Library of Congress Cataloging-in-Publication Data
Hanlon, David L.
Remaking Micronesia : discourses over development in a Pacific territory, 1944–1982 / David Hanlon.
p. cm.
Includes bibliographical references and index.
ISBN 0–8248–1894–6 (cloth : alk. paper). —
ISBN 0–8248–2011–8 (pbk. : alk. paper)
1. Micronesia—Politics and government.
2. Micronesia—Economic conditions.
3. Micronesia—Social conditions. I. Title.
DU500.H35 1998
996.5—dc21 97–36316
CIP

University of Hawai'i Press books are printed on acid-free paper and meet the guidelines for permanence and durability of the Council on Library Resources

Maps by Manoa Mapworks, Inc.

Designed by Cameron Poulter

For my parents,

David Edward Hanlon, Jr., and Dorothy Mae Brock Hanlon,

who helped me travel from Hyde Park to Mānoa,

and for the people of the islands called "Micronesia,"

those very special places in between

Contents

Acknowledgments

I opt for an expansive definition of the term "acknowledgments" and so will begin these expressions of gratitude with the mention of two conversations that, in their own particular way, helped sustain this study of economic development in the former United States Trust Territory of the Pacific Islands. I spent the first six months of 1991 on Pohnpei, more particularly in Palikir, at the capitol complex of the Federated States of Micronesia (FSM) where I used the microfilmed archives of the Trust Territory government. Not too long after my arrival, I received an invitation to a Valentine's Day dinner hosted by the United States ambassador to the Federated States of Micronesia, Ms. Aurelia Brazeal. The dinner took place at her oceanside residence above Dolonier in Net municipality.

This was the time of the Gulf War, and a number of Micronesian young men and women were serving overseas in support of Desert Storm. The ambassador and her staff had been spending a good part of their days answering questions from concerned family about the welfare of these young people. Joining the table where I was seated with seven other guests, Ambassador Brazeal related one caller's strong dissatisfaction with the embassy staff's inability to provide more exact information on the whereabouts of Micronesians serving in the war. This individual wondered why the embassy staff seemed so indifferent to the situation. The ambassador resented the question and resented too the caller's additional statement that perhaps Americans did not care as deeply for their children as Micronesians did for theirs. The issue of family resurfaced later in the evening. Responding to the purposes for my presence on Pohnpei, the ambassador offered the opinion that there could be no real economic development in the islands until the hold of the extended family over its members was somehow loosened to allow for more unfettered individual initiative. I had come across those sentiments before. The ambassador's words struck me as very much a part of the long, tired history of colonialism in the region; they strongly echoed many of the prejudices in the reports, programs, plans, and correspondence generated during the Trust Territory administration's nearly forty years of efforts to develop the islands economically.

Two months later, I had a related conversation with Alibu Yamada. Alibu is a member of a large family from the south of the island with which my wife and I had lived during our early Peace Corps years. Alibu's branch of the family lives in Kolonia, the island's major town, which is in the north. Though about the same age, we had encountered each other only rarely. But now, in April 1991, we met at the Pohnpei airport, an appropriate place for a conversation on family, culture, and economy given the array of developmental pressures and influences that land there on any given day. Alibu was there on a job for the State Communications Office; I had come to Air Micronesia's cargo office to see if a print cartridge ordered from Guam had arrived.

Alibu noticed me seated and waiting for the office to open and came over to chat. As it had been years since we had last talked at any length, we each summarized recent events in our lives. Alibu then asked about my reason for being on the island. I explained to him my interests in differing cultures of economy and the politics of development. He listened intently. When I had finished explaining things as best I could, he commented on what he perceived to be one of the striking differences between Americans and Pohnpeians with regard to the use of money, goods, and other personal resources. Americans struck him as lonely, restless, isolated people, unable to enjoy the present because of their fears about the future. They could be generous, but only to a point. Pohnpeians, on the other hand, could give or *kihla* until there was literally nothing left to give. Family honor and social obligations took precedence over an individual's wealth or possessions. For an individual to hold back or keep something in reserve was considered greedy and selfish. Of course, no one ever became truly impoverished because there was the extended family to fall back upon. Alibu conceded that things were changing, that Pohnpeians were becoming more like Americans in their attitudes toward money; still, he felt the differences remained significant and helped explain why Micronesians in general and Pohnpeians in particular had failed to develop the kind of economy Americans thought they should.

I cite the comments of Alibu and the American ambassador to highlight not only the kinds of themes with which I am dealing in this study, but the fact that, for me, the issues around development have been first personal and experiential rather than academic or intellectual. I was a part of the program of development in Micronesia long before I ever thought to write about or against it. Over a ten-year stretch of time on Pohnpei beginning in 1970, I served as a Peace Corps volunteer, a liaison officer for a community road project, and an advisor to the Pohnpei State Historic Preservation Program. If Gayatri Chakravorty Spivak is correct, however, an acknowledgment of complicity offers a space from which to produce not only counter histories, but a critique of the larger system of which they are undeniably a product. This strategy does not come without risk and the possibility of further complicity no matter how unwitting. I hope that readers will indulge my eclecticism and my penchant to ground theory in ways that, to borrow Teresia Teaiwa's words, help "loose rather than lose" indigenous perspectives. I am not unmindful, for example, of the criticisms surrounding the practice of ethnography in Micronesia and have even added my voice to them. In this study, however, I have called upon what I consider to be some of the more insightful, critically conscious ethnographic works to suggest alternative understandings of development. This study, then, marks an attempt to revisit critically a process with which I was once directly involved.

Other kinds of acknowledgments need to be made. I want to thank first Kathy Hanlon, whose limitless patience, support, and understanding made possible the absences from home and family necessitated by the research for this project. Maikel, Emma, and Alyna O'Hanlon put up not only with their father's physical absences, but also his mental distraction during the actual writing of this history. I wish to acknowledge as well the receipt of a Fulbright-Hays grant that allowed me to carry out six months of research at the FSM capitol complex in Palikir, Pohnpei. Jones George, the director of the FSM's Administrative Services Office, is one of the most generous men I have ever met. His professional support and personal kindnesses during my stay on Pohnpei were overwhelming.

While on Pohnpei, I also enjoyed the warm hospitality of Carlos Villazon and his young family, who opened their Kolonia home to me. I should mention too Carlos' father, Julio, who listened to my initial plans to commute daily to Palikir from Wone in the south of the island. It was Julio Villazon, known more properly by his Pohnpeian title of Noahs Kiti, who pronounced my plans impractical and proceeded to make arrangements for me to stay with his son, Carlos. I owe a great deal to Noahs, Carlos, and all of the Villazons of Daini and Kumwonlaid. Many of my weekends were in fact spent at Wone; there, I stayed with Benno Serilo or Souroko en Tirensapw Kiti at Pahnkomou in the hills of Ohlipel; Sau's graciousness and concern for my well-being never ceased, even during the illness and passing of his wife, Mihla. During these visits to the south, I also spent time with many old and dear friends among whom are the Miguel, Ladore, and Eperiam families. I wish to thank Fr. Joseph Cavanagh of the Pohnpei Agriculture and Trade School (PATS) in Madolenihmw for his encouragement. Returning to Honolulu via Guam, I visited several days with Dirk Ballendorf, Francesca Remengesau, and Dirk's late mother, Mercedes Ballendorf, at their home on Barrigada Heights.

I wrote a good part of this book in Canberra, Australia, between May and August 1995. My time there was made possible by a fellowship from the Australian National University's Research School of Pacific and Asian Studies. I wish to thank Prof. Merle Ricklefs, the director of the RSPAS, for providing me with a wonderfully quiet and supportive work environment. Prof. Donald Denoon of the Division of Pacific and Asian History took time from his own scholarly pursuits to handle most of the logistical relationships associated with my visit; he and Mary Mortimer proved to be marvelous hosts. I also benefited from the camaraderie of Professors Brij Lal and Hank Nelson and the consideration shown by the support staff of the division whose ranks include Dorothy McIntosh, Julie Gordon, and Jude Shanahan. In remembering my time in Australia, I would be remiss if I didn't mention two special trips: one to visit with Greg Dening and Donna Merwick in Melbourne and the other to see Stewart Firth and Kate Hannan in Sydney.

Back in Hawai'i, I have had the constant support of Prof. Robert C. Kiste, the director of the University of Hawai'i's Center for Pacific Islands Studies here at Mānoa. As usual, Dr. Karen Peacock, the curator for Hamilton Library's Special Pacific Collection, has been most generous in responding to my research queries. I am grateful for Tom Brown's assistance with the reproduction of photographs and for permission from Giff Johnson, the United States Navy, and the Bernice P. Bishop Museum in Honolulu to borrow from their collections. I cite Bill Cummings for carefully reading an earlier version of this manuscript; helpful also were the comments offered by two anonymous readers for the University of Hawai'i Press. Pam Kelley of the press was at all times professional and encouraging in directing this manuscript into print, while Joanne Sandstrom proved a most able copy editor. I thank as well the University of Hawai'i Press, the University of Melbourne's Department of History, and the Pacific History Association for permission to reproduce material in this manuscript first published under their auspices. Jane Eckelman of

Manoa Mapworks ably drafted most of the maps reprinted in this volume. Finally, there are friends, colleagues, and students whom I have encountered during my years at Mānoa. They have reminded me at critical moments about the value of scholarship and about the courage that its promotion sometimes requires. Among these very special people are Vince Diaz, Louise McReynolds, Teresia Teaiwa, David Chappell, Jonathan Osorio, Joakim Peter, Kanalu Young, Momiala Kamahele, Rainer Buschmann, Anne Hattori, Amanda Morgan, Bernardo Michael, and Pete Wilcox.

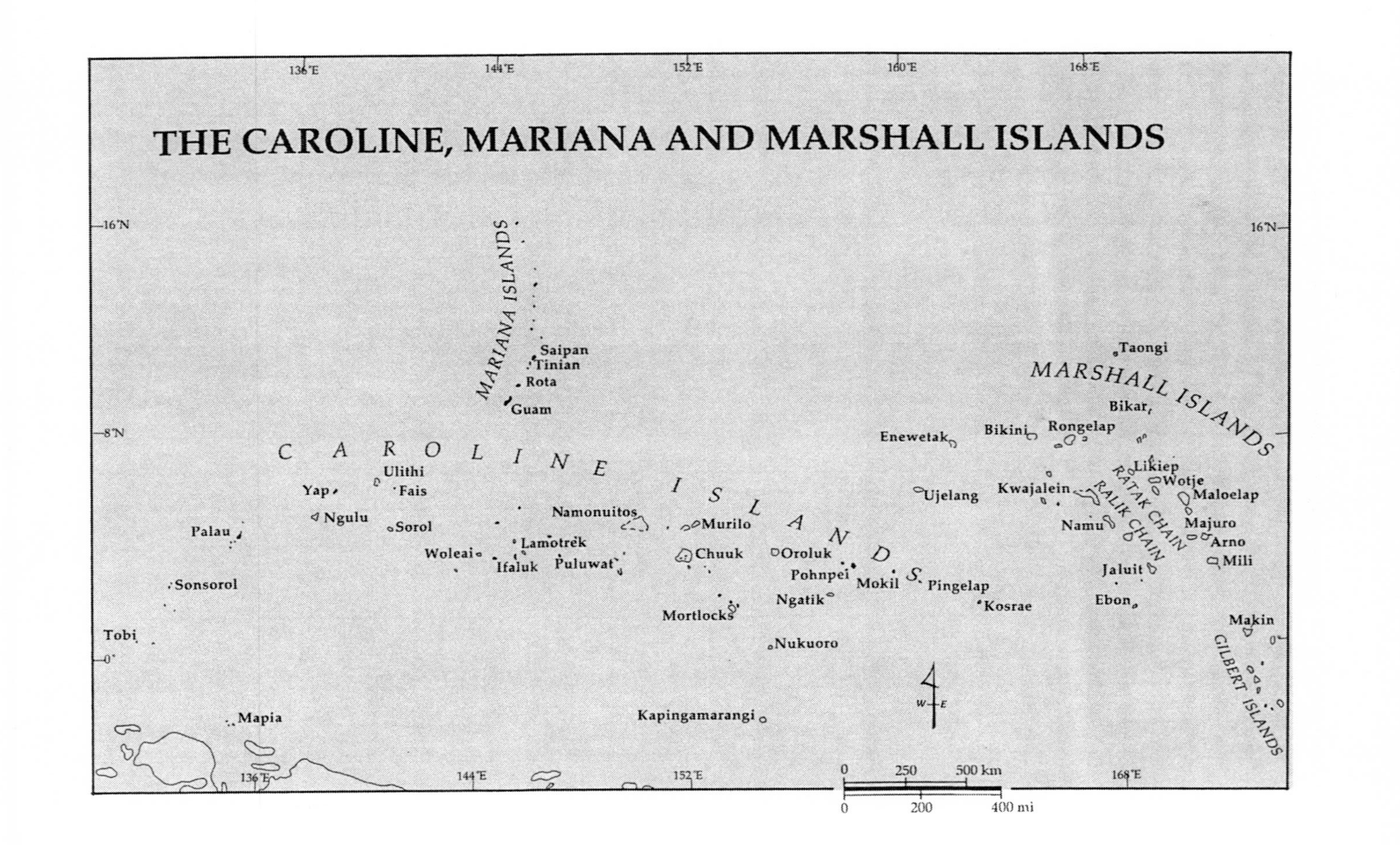
THE CAROLINE, MARIANA AND MARSHALL ISLANDS
136°E
144°E
152°E
160°E
168°E
16°N
8°N
0°
MARIANA ISLANDS
Saipan
Tinian
Rota
Guam
CAROLINE ISLANDS
Ulithi
Yap
Fais
Ngulu
Palau
Sorol
Namonuitos
Murilo
Lamotrek
Woleai
Ifaluk
Puluwat
Chuuk
Oroluk
Pohnpei
Mokil
Pingelap
Ngatik
Mortlocks
Nukuoro
Kosrae
Sonsorol
Tobi
Mapia
Kapingamarangi
Enewetak
Ujelang
Bikini
Rongelap
Kwajalein
Taongi
MARSHALL ISLANDS
Bikar
Likiep
Wotje
Maloelap
RATAK CHAIN
RALIK CHAIN
Namu
Majuro
Arno
Mili
Jaluit
Ebon
Makin
GILBERT ISLANDS
W
E
0
250
500 km
200
400 mi

Chapter 1

As the Frigate Bird Flies

They lie spread across a vast expanse of ocean in the western Pacific. Their total land area amounts to little more than a thousand square miles. Geographers locate the vast majority of these islands and atolls as being north of the equator and west of the international date line. Considered by some to be among the most peripheral of peripheries, these island bodies nonetheless have been at the center of several of the more historically prominent events of this century. Tarawa, the Truk (now Chuuk) Lagoon, Guam, Saipan, Angaur, and Peleliu served as sites for some of the most vicious, destructive battles fought between Japanese and American military forces during the Second World War. Tinian, Bikini, Enewetak, and Kwajalein are important in the earliest chapters of the planet's nuclear history.

World war and nuclear testing are but part of a deeper history of colonialism in the region, a history that in its broadest dimensions goes back centuries to Magellan's 1521 landing on Guam and that is encapsulated in the very word "Micronesia." The traditions of scientific discovery in an expansionist-minded Europe stipulated that new information about the world be officially incorporated into the existing corpus of knowledge by the use of appropriate, sanctioned designations in the classical languages.[1] With Polynesia and Melanesia already bounded and labeled on European maps, there remained to be named the many small islands in the western Pacific described by the French voyager Jules Dumont d'Urville and earlier explorers. In 1831, the geographer Gregoire Louis Domeny de Rienzi asked for and received official approval from La Société de Géographie in Paris to call these islands "Micronesia."[2] The term, derived from the Greek and meaning "tiny islands," marked in the minds of Domeny de Rienzi and others the most essential, distinguishing characteristic of the islands. Being more metaphorically blunt, a later European observer likened them to a "handful of chickpeas flung over the sea."[3]

Its more pejorative features notwithstanding, the designation "Micronesia" also evidenced the European world's need to order, locate, name, and know these islands.[4] The names of particular island groups within this area—the Carolines, Gilberts, Marianas, and Marshalls—represented not more indigenous conceptions of time, place, or identity, but existed rather as markers of earlier, more localized European activities that commemorated the names of Spanish royalty or British sea captains. Underneath all of these names lay still more local histories for which imperial travelers had little time, interest, or need. Having been named "Micronesia," the islands would be further distinguished by proper adjectives that reflected more than three centuries of formal, varied, and changing colonial rule. Between 1668 and 1986, the islands, at different times, would be described as Spanish, British, Australian, German, Japanese, and American. British annexation in 1902 gave a different colonial history to the Gilberts or Kiribati, while Nauru passed from German to Australian control in 1914. Beginning in 1899, successive waves of German, Japanese, and American colonialism provided the Caroline, Marshall, and Northern Mariana Islands with a shared or bound-together experience. In each of these separate colonial possessions, there would be attempts to remake and re-present Micronesia in the images of its different colonizers, for purposes that had to do with national needs and global rivalries and through means that were essentially violent, exploitative, and racist.

I concern myself in this study with America's attempts to remake Micronesia—more specifically, the Caroline, Marshall, and Northern Mariana Islands—in ways that reflected, served, and affirmed its particular national ideology. No clearer physical representation of this attempted domination exists than a map of the islands upon which is superimposed an outline of the United States map. Employed to make intelligible to North American audiences the vast distances over which the islands of Micronesia are spread, the map also suggests a dominance designed to be total. It is the extent and character of this dominance with which I am concerned in this book.

There has been no lack of criticism of America's administration of Micronesia. In many ways, the explicitly political dimensions of America's colonial relationship with the islands has proven the topic of greatest concern for academic experts and professional observers. These writers have emphasized the primacy of American strategic interests in the area and the ways in which those interests subverted America's commitment, under the 1947 Trusteeship Agreement with the United Nations, to promote the political, economic, social, and educational development of the islands. These critics charge that the islands, rather than being developed, were bought off or made over by overwhelming, crippling amounts of American largesse. "Americanized" is the gloss employed to indicate this supposed history of total abject colonization.

Dissatisfied by the limitations of this criticism and by the conventional, highly ethnocentric assumptions and tropes through which it has been delivered, I opt for a different tack. The focus of my research is not political issues per se but rather development, more particularly economic development, as a strategy of domination. A seemingly more benevolent, well-intentioned program of rule, the promotion of economic development presented a process of change no less disruptive and destructive than other colonial initiatives in its effects upon the peoples, places, and cultures of the area called Micronesia. If successful, the many and varied plans for development would have resulted in a total remaking of Micronesia.

There is, however, a rich, deeply entangled history in the gap between intent and effect over efforts at economic development in the area that

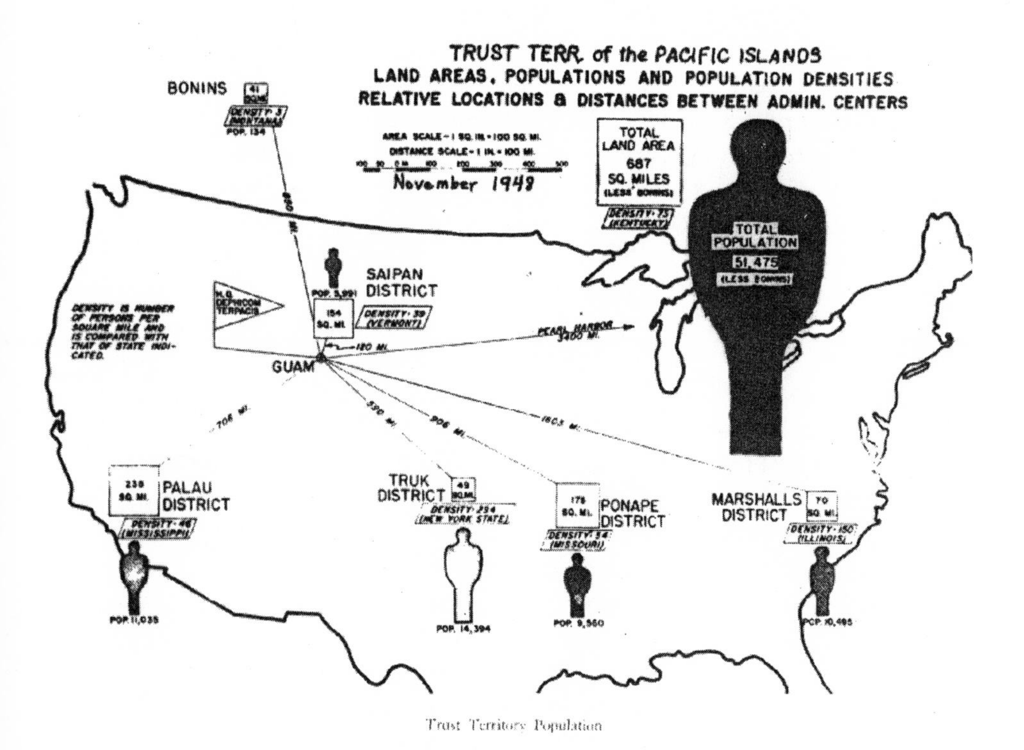

Mapping hegemony (Richard III, 1957; US Navy).

came to be officially known after 1947 as the United States Trust Territory of the Pacific Islands. I would like to lift a bit the blanket of American domination to see what else lies under it. We will find revealed not only the extent to which representatives of the United States government, in not always coordinated, consistent, or successful ways, sought to promote a transformation of life in the islands, but also local responses and understandings that took the agenda of development and applied it to more locally meaningful purposes and arrangements. My approach in this study, then, is to get beyond the liberal rhetoric that has surrounded the term "development," to examine what it actually entailed, and to chart some of the ways in which it was appropriated and applied—often in multiple, complex, layered, and even conflicting ways—by local groups of island people. Much like the flight of the frigate bird, this study provides an overview of a distinctly American colonial process that sought to transform yet again a diverse collection of islands into a single administrative entity that served the interests of certain offices and agencies of the United States government. Such a summary approach admittedly comes at the expense of a fuller investigation into island histories and epistemologies. Hopefully, this study will encourage more local ethnographies of development among the islands called Micronesia. As further preface, I offer introductory comments on four key frames of analysis that inform this work: American ideology in the postwar period, economics as culture, development as discourse, and the counterhegemonic dimensions of what has been called "underdevelopment."

American Ideology in the Postwar Period

Following Karl Marx and Friedrich Engels, Raymond Williams defines ideology as "an articulated system of meanings, values and beliefs" that can be abstracted to serve as a worldview for any social group.[5] This definition will serve our purposes well enough, especially as we amend it to account for the historically specific circumstances of American colonialism in Micronesia. It is perhaps one of the functions of a national ideology to mask the crude objectives of self-interest and to deny the violence of conquest that precedes and makes possible the colonial act. In 1945, representatives of the United States government would behave no differently in their public pledges to provide for the welfare of a people who inhabited an area of prime strategic concern just seized from Japan through violent struggle. While recent and much needed attention to matters of division and diversity have problematized the meaning of the word "American" in the late twentieth century, it remains possible, I think, to speak of a dominant, subsuming American ideological identity in the post–World War II period. Whatever their motivations and objectives, most white Americans believed deeply in the superiority of their way of life and in its essential appeal to others; assumptions about its inherent worth, goodness, and desirability all worked to justify America's position of global primacy and to obscure the disruptive, even destructive consequences of that exercise of power on others.

Historian Thomas G. Paterson has written that Americans crafted from a consciousness of their historical experience a national ideology that integrated political and economic tenets into a "peace and prosperity" view of life. Through the Cold War period, Americans believed they were prosperous because they were democratic, and democratic because they were prosperous.[6] In an extension of this view, American ideology held that peace and stability in the larger world were dependent upon economic prosperity and political democracy. Poverty, on the other hand, led to injustice, chaos, violence, and abusive political systems. Despite the hard counterrealities that disturbed the equation in terms of race, class, and gender relations, this dominant national ideology was used to justify and promote American interests and activities in the larger world. Thomas Gladwin, an anthropologist working in the islands during the first years of American rule, offered an earlier, more locally focused version of Paterson's contention:

> Americans have long been noted for their conviction that their political, social and economic philosophy is the best ever developed, not only for Americans but for everyone. This is nowhere so evident as in the administration of dependent peoples. It is sometimes extraordinarily difficult to persuade people that the institutions which have made the United States great may not fit Micronesian society at all.[7]

Ernest Renan has written that "getting its history wrong is a part of being a nation."[8] It could be added, I think, that a nation's misrepresentation of the past to its citizens, subjugated peoples, and a larger world audience constitutes an important prerequisite for and justification of colonialism.

Economics as Culture

The linking of peace, prosperity, and democracy in American minds concerned more than a simple matter of dollars and cents. It involved something deeper, something we might characterize as "cultural." Other scholars have written about the essentially economic interests and metaphors that lie at the heart of American society. Charles Beard viewed the United States' most fundamental political document, the Constitution, as an essentially economic program designed to ensure the commercial interests of its creators and their like-minded heirs. Adding an anthropological perspective to an idea borrowed from Marx and Engels' *The German Ideology,* Marshall Sahlins argues that all production is ultimately concerned with the reproduction of a "definite mode of life." In the West, most particularly the United States, there has emerged an essentially bourgeois capitalist ethic that places economic values and activities at the core of American life. American society, writes Sahlins, sees itself as logical, practical, rational and work-oriented, as a society in which individuals pursue through unfettered economic activities the satisfaction of their perceived needs and induced wants. We have, then, what Stephen Gudeman has called "economics as culture."[9]

In the immediate postwar world, this very particular cultural bias toward the assumed virtues of productive economic activity carried over into American views of and dealings with the larger world, especially those non-Western areas of the globe whose beliefs and practices were informed by very different and localized ideologies about living in this world. Historian Greg Dening has written that cultures in their exposure to one another assert their structures of law and morality, present their rationalizing myths, and perform symbolic rituals expressive of their most fundamental beliefs about themselves.[10] American efforts at economic development in Micronesia would reveal what it meant to be productive, prosperous and free, what it meant to be American. The need to assert this presentation as dominant precluded any possibility of understanding counterperformances presented by the various and distinctive groups of people who inhabited the area called Micronesia.

Involved in the presentation of this dominant ideology was the threat of hegemony, the obliteration or total make-over of other resident and indigenous systems of being. This fact was brought home to me in a very curious, initially puzzling way during the course of my research. While moving slowly through the 2,169 reels of microfilm on which are preserved the United States Trust Territory archives, I came across "How to Plant Coconuts," a pamphlet produced by the Department of Agriculture on Saipan.[11] The pamphlet, published in 1964 through the auspices of the South Pacific Commission as Agricultural Extension Circular 7, struck me as an odd document. The coconut tree has been a longstanding part of the physical environment in Micronesia; its uses remain many and varied, its place in the lore and material cultures of the islands deep and intimate.

Surely, even the most narrow-minded of colonial officials would know that the coconut was one crop of which Micronesians possessed a strong understanding and knowledge. It soon came to me, however, that the pamphlet was offering suggestions on the coconut as something other than a subsistence crop. Timing, spacing, access to sun and water, pruning, fertilization, and harvesting schedules were all a part of a process of commercializing this tree. The coconut, once a relatively ready and abundant natural resource with multiple uses and purposes that were cultural as well as economic, symbolic as well as material, was now being made into a commodity. By the norms expressed in Agricultural Extension Circular 7, coconuts were no longer available for the taking and using as they had once been. Their use became a strictly economic matter measured in terms of tonnage, shipping schedules, and prices. The pamphlet, written by two staff members of the Trust Territory Department of Agriculture, indicated, then, something of the major transformations in the everyday uses and perceptions of the physical and cultural environment that economic development would bring. In its own peculiar way, "How to Plant Coconuts" underscored the idea that economic development in Micronesia was also about more than the enhanced income to be earned from prudent planting, harvesting, and spacing of crops; it was about basic changes in the established way of doing things, about a major transformation in peoples' relationships with their environment and with each other. It was about being made to become something else and other.

Development as a Discourse of Domination

Given the limitations of conventional political analysis and understandings of development, the question becomes how to approach colonialism differently in America's Micronesia. Michel Foucault has written extensively about the ways in which the production of knowledge both reflects and supports the interests of the dominant, powerful, and governing groups in a society—more specifically, the state. The things with which government is concerned, wrote Foucault,

> are men, but men in their relations, in their links, their imbrication with those other things which are wealth, resources, climate, irrigation, fertility, etc.; men in their relation to other kinds of things which are customs, habits, ways of doing and thinking, etc: lastly, men in their relation to that other kind of things [*sic*] which are accidents and misfortunes such as famine, epidemics, death, etc.[12]

Disciplinary or managing technology, drawn from the empirical sciences and with a strong statistical orientation, is employed to reshape the populace into a docile body that can be monitored, controlled, transformed, and directed toward the purposes of the state. Since Western society has become largely capitalist in character, the concerns of the state focus on the methods and profits of production, and with considerable effect. From the history of capitalism in the West emerges "homo economicus," a normalized, controlled subject who produces under certain conditions to satisfy perceived needs and imposed requirements.[13] The lives of economic men and women of the West are now mediated by the constructs of the market and the process of production. Economization has touched almost all aspects of life, including personal relationships, human biology, and even dealings with the natural world.

Although Foucault did not concern himself specifically with issues of imperialism and colonialism, the extension of his ideas into these areas would seem a natural and desirable undertaking. I am suggesting, then, an analytical approach that borrows selectively from Michel Foucault and that treats development and its accompanying arsenal of tropes not so much as a measurable or quantifiable endeavor, a question of econometrics if you will, but rather as discourse that possesses the power to create or recreate reality in colonized settings through acts of representation and prescription. With reference to American efforts at economic development, I use the word "discourse," then, to include all of the recorded speeches, conversations, and debates as well as books, reports, plans, studies, and policy statements through which various individuals, offices, and agencies sought to make another, assumedly better, and more familiar Micronesia. In analyzing development as a discourse, I draw heavily on the works of Gustavo Esteva and Arturo Escobar.

Esteva has begun a more critical reexamination of development as discourse by providing a genealogical history of the word itself that documents the changes in its meanings and applications over time. Originally referenced to a pre-Enlightenment conception of the movement of nature to a more appropriate form of being, the term "development" came to assume a more modern meaning heavily affected by nineteenth-century ideas of evolution and history. Development now meant transformation toward an ever more perfect state that reflected the influence of both the Hegelian concept of history and the Darwinian notion of evolution. Marx employed the term as a keyword in his historical analysis of capitalism, giving it a decidedly pronounced political character. Applied to colonial situations of the nineteenth century, development became a conceptualizing tool for measuring native peoples against the standards of Western civilization. By the early decades of the twentieth century, the word "development" was most often employed to refer to the productive capabilities of a colonized population that could be employed in the establishment of a modern market economy.[14]

The tensions and rivalries of the post–World War II world made economic stagnation and backwardness a threatening, dangerous condition for the capitalist West, particularly the United States. The program of modernity or development for those areas of the world now characterized as "underdeveloped" is seen as lying at the core of President Harry S. Truman's "fair deal" speech before the United Nations on 20 January 1949. Esteva describes the general reception to Truman's speech in the following words:

> Never before had a word been so universally accepted on the very day of its political coinage. A new perception of one's own self, and of the other, was suddenly created. Two hundred years of social construction of the historical-political meaning of the term "development" were successfully usurped and transmogrified. A political and philosophical proposition of Marx, packaged American style as a struggle against communism and at the service of the hegemonic design of the United States, succeeded in permeating both the popular and intellectual mind of the rest of the century.[15]

Esteva holds the legacy of that speech and its ideas to be a lifetime of subordination and betrayal, of discrimination and subjugation, for two-thirds of the world's people.[16] The island peoples of Micronesia certainly would come to experience the power and politics behind Truman's plans for the underdeveloped world.

The power of development as a discursive force capable of both interpreting and controlling much of the non-Western world is demonstrated convincingly in Arturo Escobar's *Encountering Development: The Making and Unmaking of the Third World.* Escobar writes of Truman's "fair deal" for all as a call for development, a development concerned with replicating the features that distinguished the more advanced nations of the capitalist, postwar West the world over. These distinguishing features included industrialization, urbanization, high levels of technology, an affluent material culture, and specific, value-laden structures of education and cultural expression. What this particular vision of the world really entailed, believes Escobar, was but another, albeit more totalizing and global colonization of reality.[17]

The discourse of development coming out of the West constituted a form of Orientalism in which the underdeveloped world of the postwar period came to be known and controlled through the writing, describing, interpreting, and teaching of it and by experts whose tools of measurement reflected the rationality and logic of their own very privileged, powerful world. Escobar writes that the alleged desirability of development contributed significantly to a process of institutionalization that included the appearance of international funding agencies, foreign aid bureaucracies, career specialists, and programs of study that offered degrees in developmental studies. Development's assumed necessity helped justify a multiplicity of governmental interventions into areas of life deemed in need of more accelerated modernization. There evolved a "devspeak" or "devthink" that showed itself universalizing and Eurocentric in its presumptions about the ease with which poor countries could follow the path to development. Development, however, was about far more than figures, graphs, tables, statistics, and equations. Its ultimate significance lay in its power as discourse to create a reality through the representing of it. Development, then, offered the prospect of a more effective hegemony in its discursive homogenization and systemization for knowing and hence controlling the "Third World."[18]

Understanding development as discourse offers, I believe, a more insightful approach to the study of American colonialism in Micronesia. The end of World War II would bring the islands directly under the control of the world's then reigning superpower. Because the area was so deeply identified by military planners as being an integral part of American defense concerns and, by projection, world capitalism, the United States government, more particularly the Department of War, possessed a totalizing concern for Micronesia. By promoting the process of development, military and later civilian leaders were able to address certain humanitarian concerns about progress and betterment while at the same time ensuring that Micronesia would be remade in ways that served the strategic interests of the larger American state. This normalization of the islands and their people made possible the identification of anomalies, anomalies that theoretically could be isolated and then controlled through the corrective and therapeutic technology that was economic development. Economic development would be one of the techniques of power, one of the dividing practices, employed to rationalize American domination of the islands. Micronesians would indeed have a reason to fear what Max Weber termed the "mighty cosmos of the modern economic order . . . the iron cage [in which] specialists without spirit, sensualists without heart [are] caught in the delusion that [they] have achieved a level of development never before attained by mankind."[19]

The Counterhegemonic Dimensions of Underdevelopment

As Esteva and Escobar both acknowledge, a discursive approach to development and its hegemonizing potential risks relegating the "peoples of the periphery" to the role of passive victims or mute witnesses to the gross commodification of their way of life. Foucault's work, on the surface at least, seems to acknowledge little or no possibility of resistance or counterhegemonic discourses. This concern over the denial of engagement on the part of colonized or affected people is shared by James Scott, who finds Antonio Gramsci's highly influential theory of hegemony equally wanting because of the assumptions it makes about the submission, acceptance, and complicity of subordinated classes in their own domination.[20] In like critical voice, Jean Comaroff and John Comaroff note that the essence of colonization is now assumed to lie

> less in political overrule than in seizing and transforming "others" by the very act of conceptualizing, inscribing, and interacting with them on terms not of their choosing; in making them into the pliant objects and silenced subjects of our scripts and scenarios; in assuming to "represent" them, the active verb itself conflating politics and poetics.[21]

But where, the Comaroffs ask, does such a total, Gramscian-like conceptualization of colonialism allow for a consideration of the consciousness of the colonized? The question is certainly germane to our study of economic development in American Micronesia. There were Micronesians who engaged the discourse of development, and, in some instances, countered that discourse with visions of their own. Through a reading of correspondence, reports, minutes of meetings, and transcribed debates, we can learn something of the discourses of educated, elected, or otherwise elite Micronesian males over programs of development. There must be other discursively sensitive methodologies, however, that will allow us broader insights into on-site encounters with development, including the spaces for resistance or local appropriation that are created by less-than-complete or -successful projects of economic transformation.

The Comaroffs' answer to their own question rests with a particular concept of culture, a concept that takes culture to be the contested space of signifying practices or semantic ground on which human beings "seek to construct and represent themselves and others—and, hence, society and history." The Comaroffs, then, offer a historically attuned notion of culture that includes others as well as selves, actions as well as signs, creativity as well as mimesis, and empowerment as well as subjugation. This empowerment, they hasten to add, shows itself at different times and in varied ways that often defy simple romanticized Western notions of colonial resistance.[22]

Marshall Sahlins, a colleague of the Comaroffs at the University of Chicago, makes many of the same points for the Pacific, and with specific reference to the issue of economic development. Sahlins describes a local Pacific variant to development—namely, "develop-man," meaning both the material and social enrichment of local lifestyles.[23] Sahlins defines the term "develop-man" as capturing the spirit behind indigenous ways of coping with capitalism. Pacific peoples are neither awed nor overwhelmed by external systems beyond their control. Their response is rather to appropriate. Such pragmatic behavior lies at the heart of every cultural scheme known to history. The impulse of local people in the Pacific and elsewhere, writes Sahlins, is not to become like us, but to become more like themselves. Living in cultural systems still concerned with the relationships of kith and kin, Pacific peoples employ Western goods to aid in the fulfillment of the obligations these social arrangements entail.

Playing with Hegel a bit, Sahlins writes that the "cunning of culture" thus mediates the invisible hand of the market economy. Modern economic rationality is transformed by a different cultural rationality that can show itself in extravagant traditional ceremonies replete with all manner of Western goods ranging from rolls of cloth to bags of rice, basins of canned goods, cases of beer, and money trees.[24] Local culture, then, displays itself on an exaggerated, more materially and symbolically enriched scale; what development specialists or economists might call "waste" or "backwardness" is actually a form of cultural enhancement determined by local values and logic. Such an interpretation is not to deny the more pragmatic or utilitarian aspects of consumption; people do seek advantage, utility, and satisfaction in their commerce. These transactions, however, cannot be wholly or simply measured in terms of dollars and cents or judged apart from the local histories, politics, and cultural systems that add meaning, significance, and value to the process.[25]

There are then, as exemplified in Sahlins' concept of develop-man, different systems of logic and rationality that allow for the emergence of other local discourses about development. Stephen Gudeman says much the same thing in his ethnographic analysis of house economics in Colombia. Gudeman examines the cultural and historical contexts that have made the house a site of convergence where local economics interact with capitalist modes of thought and production. The result is a "thick combination" where culturally informed innovations occur in remarkably effective, reasonably profitable, and socially appropriate ways.[26] Escobar, Esteva, Gudeman, and Sahlins all encourage us to look for other models of economy that "are no less scientific because they are not couched in equations or produced by Nobel laureates."[27] The global capitalist system, then, is really the expression of a relative and particular cultural logic, whose distinguishing features lie deeply embedded in the European past. Although advocates of a world systems approach might reduce all history to stages of capitalism, a more ethnographic study of encounters that concerns itself with local concepts of status, kinship, labor, productivity, exchange, and consumption would suggest other, more nuanced and diverse interpretations.[28] Against a simple history of world capitalism, Sahlins writes of encounters involving "cosmologies of capitalism" in which the modern global order is engaged in many and complex ways by so-called peripheral peoples and their persisting systems of distinctive cultural logic.

An important qualification—one that Sahlins and other writers cited in this introduction readily acknowledge—needs to be appended to the argument of cultural persistence as political resistance. Encounters with modernity do not always end successfully or even in compromise. Apart from the efforts at domination by colonial or neocolonial forces are the structural and historical entanglements created by increasingly involved, even dependent relations with the system of world capitalism.[29] Efforts at appropriation by the parties involved in an encounter may be mutual, but they are also unequal given the factors of wealth and power that privilege the global. Moreover, inequalities within local systems resulting from specific histories and practices work to the advantage of some and not others. Witness the disturbance and suffering caused by nuclear testing in the Marshall Islands and the more recent efforts of the Marshallese government to capitalize on them; or consider the efforts from both within and beyond Palau to subvert the antinuclear provisions of the Palauan constitution. A history of colonialism in American Micronesia must account for these sad conflicts as well; there is no simple story that is only about external efforts at domination and local means of resistance.

A Different Plan for Examining Economic Development in Micronesia

I contend that the history of economic development in American Micronesia is not to be found solely in the shrill statistics of Trust Territory administrators, federal officials, or United Nations Development Programme (UNDP) specialists. I begin my task by examining the politics of representation that permeate descriptions of the wartime occupation of the islands and the first years of American military government. I review the artificiality of the colonial and neocolonial construct that was and is Micronesia, and the inability of Americans to give credence or even consideration to the vitality and distinctiveness of local island worlds, their unique systems of social organization, and the cultural principles that shaped and directed them. Detailed also are the effects of war and the massive infusion of men, technology, and war goods on indigenous orders where exchange tended to be expressive of social relations and political hierarchies and where the presence of foreigners and foreign goods involved complicated, stressful negotiations with existing systems of power, hierarchy, and status. In this chapter, I rely on Dorothy Richard's official history of the United States Navy's occupation and administration of the islands. Richard's three-volume text is instructive not only for the facts and figures it relates, but for its inadvertent display of the attitudes, assumptions, and prejudices that informed the navy government and its efforts at economic development.

In these first formative encounters between Americans and the people they called Micronesians, images were formed and set, given an almost canonical legitimacy that would explain at once the necessity for economic development in the islands and the reasons for the failure of those efforts. Micronesians were described as quaint, happy, but backward people who no longer could afford to enjoy the luxury of living apart from the larger global order. The irony was that Americans created dependency, or what seemed to them to be dependency, through the imposition of programs calculated to make Micronesians economically self-reliant. A paradox also showed itself in this earliest literature on American rule; namely, a recognition of the impossibility of creating a viable, local, Western-style economy, and yet the need, for purposes of domestic and international legitimization, to make the effort. Distance, isolation, climate, the calumnies of previous colonial regimes, the lack of exploitable resources, and, most important, the perceived unwillingness and inability of the different island peoples came to constitute a litany that would be articulated by many among the succeeding generations of administrators, planners, visitors, and developmental specialists from 1944 to 1982. This litany expressed both frustration and consolation for those who enunciated it—frustration at the many failed efforts at development and consolation that, in the end, these failures resulted from factors involving local environments and peoples.

Chapter 3, dealing with the U.S. Navy's administration of the islands under the 1947 Trusteeship Agreement, underscores the close, admitted link between security and economic development that was obscured but remained nonetheless salient in subsequent decades. The navy's efforts at a variety of economic development projects are examined, with special attention given the rationale for the efforts and the explanations for their failure. Chapter 4 examines three prescriptions or texts for economic development: the political motivations that inspired them, the very distinct and particular assumptions about living and being in this world that they embraced, and the highly ethnocentric, powerfully discursive notion of planning itself. International consultants, Trust Territory officials, and on-site administrators often paid verbal homage to the need for cultural sensitivity; at the same time, these individuals often cited the word "culture" to explain the failure of development efforts in such fields as fishing, tourism, and agriculture. Making use of local stories and selected ethnographic studies, I also attempt in chapter 4 to suggest something of the historical and cultural realities that confronted and confounded development initiatives in these areas.

Chapter 5 focuses on Micronesian discourses surrounding the issue of economic development; here, I draw heavily from the records of the Congress of Micronesia in the late 1960s and early 1970s. Although Micronesian reservations are expressed at least officially in English and using theories, metaphors, examples, and references that seem to have a decidedly liberal American character to them, I argue, borrowing from the work of Ranajit Guha and his subaltern studies program, that these expressions of reservation, doubt, and grievance reflect in part attempts to co-opt the language, ideas, and principles of the hegemonizer for more local purposes.[30]

As noted previously, one of the tropes of recent Pacific studies has been the tendency to slip into Manichean representations that presume a stark opposition in the encounters between islands and continent. Chapter 6 concerns the debate, largely within Micronesia and among Micronesians, about increased levels of U.S. federal assistance and their effects on Micronesian societies and political aspirations. Through an examination of the debates in and around these federal assistance programs, the complexity, variety, and even ambiguity of Micronesian responses begins to emerge. Chapter 7 pursues this issue by examining the history of nuclear testing in the Marshalls and the disruption and division it caused within Marshallese society. In the Marshalls, the dominant discourse of development took on a decidedly different character. Rather than a seductive, misleading advertisement for a better future, development proved to be a belated, condescending, grossly insufficient form of compensation for the social, physical, and environmental havoc caused by an American nuclear testing program that would not wait for any tomorrows. As conclusion, chapter 8 considers the ways in which the compacts of free association between the American and different Micronesian governments have sought to sustain American dominance in the region through the continuing discourse of development and developmental funding. This chapter also uses the review of a recent book on Micronesia, *The Edge of Paradise,* to reveal the gulf between liberal despair over the course of economic development in the islands and more locally determined efforts to manipulate developmental projects for very different purposes.

In bringing this introduction to a close, I should add a few qualifying statements about my relationship to certain words and topics. As I implied earlier, the terms "Micronesia," "Micronesian," and "Micronesians" are far more reflective of colonizing forces than of ethnographic realities. Nonetheless, their usage is difficult to avoid in a study that concerns itself in part with colonial knowledge, policy, and administration. The employment of these words, however, can also hint at other understandings. These normalizing labels were at times appropriated by the very people upon whom they were imposed to speak of shared colonial histories and common developmental dilemmas. The subjugated thus addressed their rulers through the referents of colonization, but with purposes that could at times be countercolonial in nature. My decision to use the words "Micronesia," "Micronesian," and "Micronesians" results, then, from a desire to acknowledge local manipulations as well as from more pragmatic stylistic concerns.

Similarly, I have been somewhat relaxed in my use of the word "American" and the phrase "American colonialism." These words obscure a complexity and variation in the American colonial presence in Micronesia that needs to be noted. In an enthusiasm to discover local responses to Western domination, we too quickly reduce and simplify that which, despite a seemingly coherent agenda of possession and control, is not easily reduced or simplified. In *Colonialism's Culture,* Nicholas Thomas writes against a perception of colonialism as monolithic in character, purposes, personalities, and efficiency. He argues for a recognition of colonialism that is more sophisticated, localized, and also nuanced regarding the diverse, often conflicting agendas and approaches advanced by different groups from a single colonizing nation.[31]

Thomas' caution is well taken. In this account of the history of economic development in American Micronesia, I strive to represent the diversity, debate, and contentiousness among different groups of Americans involved in the economic development of the islands. Military administrators, missionaries, educators, Trust Territory officials, Peace Corps volunteers, expatriate businesspeople, and representatives from U.S. governmental agencies in Washington, D.C., were not one in their attitudes and opinions toward Micronesians and toward economic development within Micronesia. A good history of economic development in Micronesia, then, needs to heed Greg Dening and Paul Rabinow in their calls for studies that provide ethnographic perspectives on the colonizers as well as the colonized.[32] At the same time, and this I believe is testament to the power of the word "development" and the ideas behind it, almost all groups of Americans expressed a belief in the need to promote a better life for Micronesians. This paradox of unanimity within diversity is one of the more striking features of the colonizing discourse of development in Micronesia.

It is important also to note the decidedly patriarchal, sexist character of development. More than two decades ago Ester Boserup showed how programs of development directed from metropolitan sites have worked to deny the extent and significance of women's economic roles.[33] Reflecting the pronounced male bias of Western colonial regimes toward women's roles, this denial did not necessarily end or even diminish women's local economic obligations; they continued amidst a host of new economic pressures and expectations. More often than not, women's work was at once increased and denigrated by policies that encouraged employment in the more menial areas of developing economies.

Micronesia would prove no exception to this pattern. Francis X. Hezel, S.J., writes about the overwhelmingly "masculine and mechanical" feel to the makeshift towns of quonset huts that sprang up around American military bases in the months immediately following the seizure of the islands from Japan.[34] These same adjectives would characterize America's later civilian administration of the islands and the process of economic development it sought to engender. Beginning in 1947, the U.S. Department of State's annual reports to the United Nations Trusteeship Council asserted the equality of women with men under the law. At the same time, these reports often pointed to persisting "traditional patterns" that relegated women to subordinate positions in Micronesian societies. To read these documents, the blame for discrimination against women belonged solely to Micronesian societies.

Employment statistics provided by the territorial administration, however, belied these claims of equality and equal opportunity; women worked as nurses, secretaries, clerks, and teachers and at levels of compensation considerably below the earnings of men in like or related categories of employment. As employment opportunities for Micronesians increased over the course of the Trust Territory administration, positions of leadership and responsibility went almost exclusively to men. Development in Micronesia, then, proved a largely sexist project that sought to replicate a patriarchal capitalist economy among colonized island peoples. Still, we need to remind ourselves of the long-standing centrality of women in these island economies, the continuing if not expanding significance of their economic contributions, and the increasingly more public profile being exhibited by women over a host of development-related issues.[35] I have endeavored where possible to indicate something of Micronesian women's responses to development and development-related issues, including the successful efforts of women in Chuuk to address the serious problem of alcohol abuse there in the late 1970s.

I should mention here other decisions involving more practical and stylistic matters. Throughout this study, I have employed the more modern orthographic renderings of major Micronesian islands or island groups. I use Chuuk, Kosrae, and Pohnpei rather than Truk, Kusaie, and Ponape, respectively. My use of quotations from historical documents and my references to the large body of literature produced on the islands over the last century or so make the elimination of the older spellings impossible, however. Given the temporal, geographic, and thematic sweep of this study, I have also had to make decisions about parameters. I have elected, for example, not to include an examination of the mid-1970s debate over the construction of a superport in Palau[36] designed to facilitate the transshipment of crude oil from the Middle East to Japan. The central issues around the superport involved not struggles over colonially directed policies of development but struggles with more global forces of capitalism that sought not the remaking of people but the pursuit of profit and the direct exploitation of the natural environment.

The time period under consideration also requires some explanation. I open this study in 1944, when the United States began its violent seizure of the area from Japan. The possessing of these islands through war provided a necessary preface for the establishment of formal colonial rule.

The choice of 1982 as the concluding date for this study might strike some as perplexing (or odd). After all, the formal termination of the Trust Territory government's jurisdiction over the Caroline and Marshall Islands did not occur until November 1986, when the United States declared operative the compacts of free association with what are now the Federated States of Micronesia (FSM) and the Republic of the Marshall Islands. The Republic of Palau did not emerge as a self-governing entity under its own agreement of free association until October 1994, and this after a long, confounding, tortuous, and sometimes violent process of ratification that endeavored to reconcile continuing American strategic interests with the antinuclear provisions of Palau's constitution. Despite the logic of extending this study to accommodate the approval and implementation of the compacts, I believe that the actual terms of free association, finalized in 1982 through separate negotiations between representatives of the United States and the different Micronesian governments, display in striking relief the past and future purposes of economic development in the islands.

Finally, I find myself compelled to say something about the larger significance of this work. There are those who would think a history of economic development in American Micronesia from 1944 to 1982 is "micro" indeed—"micro" in its relation to larger issues and events in the world. But there is, I argue, a broader, wider-reaching relevance to this study. Efforts at economic development in the area called Micronesia were ultimately about transforming in dramatic and total fashion a people who occupied real estate deemed vital to American strategic concerns. As inhabitants of islands with many, varied, and different cultural systems, they were discovered to be "other"; their otherness came to be seen as inconsistent with, even threatening to American interests. And so economic development became a strategy designed to provide a new, more comfortable, malleable, and reassuring identity for the inhabitants of this prime piece of strategic real estate. Underneath the liberal rhetoric that surrounded arguments, proposals, and programs for economic development was a deeper purpose: dominant interests in American society would be made more secure, reaffirmed in their privilege and dominance, and sustained in their self-image by the remaking of these islands into places that had the look, feel, sound, speed, smell, and taste of America about them. The remaking of Micronesia and Micronesians is, in part, about the way dominant systems of power preserve themselves. Micronesians have much in common, then, with other groups of people who have had modernity thrust upon them and who have experienced the consequent normalizing, controlling pressures behind programs of capitalist cultural development that seek at once to indict and obliterate difference in favor of efficiency, conformity, and gain.

It is not only present conditions in "underdeveloped" worlds such as Micronesia that are found wanting. The imposition of development also involves the denial of history as well as the remaking of contemporary physical and cultural landscapes. As Fredric Jameson has noted, development does not allow for a history outside that of the West; development seeks to complete the colonial project by defining non-Western areas solely in terms of the experience of colonialism.[37] History as practiced in and by the West becomes a part of the colonizing process in its sacrifice of other peoples' pasts to the demanding god of progress.[38] Getting beyond development as a discursive strategy of domination and control entails a recognition of other ways of knowing, being, and living. Recognizing development as part of a larger colonial project that disavows racial, cultural, and historical difference invites an anticolonial discourse that "requires an alternative set of questions, techniques and strategies in order to construct it."[39] I offer, then, this study in support of future histories and ethnographies that are more locally ordered and meaningful.

Chapter 2

Beginning to Remake Micronesia

It would not be too extreme an interpretive extrapolation to argue that Americans' encounters with Micronesians drew their informing precedents from earlier confrontations with native peoples on the North American continent. In a still persuasive piece of literary criticism that foreshadowed more contemporary concerns with the issues of texts, contexts, and representation, Roy Harvey Pearce has written of the interplay between the ideas of savagism and civilization on the expanding frontier of the American West.[1] Civilized peoples from Europe regarded as savages the indigenous inhabitants of the continent they sought to claim. In their confrontation with these "Indians," European settlers, argues Pearce, were forced to consider what it meant to be civilized and what civilizing the savage might require. In the person of the savage, these Europeans saw all that they had evolved from and all that they still had to overcome. Initial efforts to change and to convert the Indian were ultimately abandoned. By 1850, the colonizers had come to realize that the spread of civilization necessitated the destruction of all that stood as different and thus opposed to the principles of private property, manifest destiny, and the general ethic of progress. Pearce concludes, "Studying the savage, trying to civilize him, destroying him, in the end they had only studied themselves, strengthened their own civilization, and given those who were coming after them an enlarged certitude of another, even happier destiny—that manifest in the progress of American civilization over all obstacles."[2]

The history of economic development in American Micronesia involves, in many ways, an extension of the same patterns evidenced in the encounters between Americans and others on an earlier continental stage. For American officials dealing with Micronesia, the word "underdeveloped," it seems, served as a twentieth-century synonym for "savage." Like "Indian," the term "Micronesian" would prove no less invented, manipulable, or self-serving an image for imperial interests.

People identifying themselves as Americans began reaching Micronesia in the first half of the nineteenth century. Salem traders, Yankee whalers, beachcombers, and the occasional government vessel constituted the first American presence in the islands. The American Civil War even touched the area in the form of a naval engagement between the Confederate raider *Shenandoah* and four northern whalers in the harbor of Pohnatik along the southeastern coast of Pohnpei Island in the Eastern Caroline group. Among the different groups of nineteenth-century Americans who labored among, fought in, or passed through the islands, none were more persistent in their purposes than the Congregationalist missionaries of the Boston-based American Board of Commissioners for Foreign Missions. These men and women, with the help of Hawaiian evangelists they called "assistants," established mission stations in the Caroline and Marshall Islands beginning in 1852. Their admitted objective was not just conversion to Christianity, but the total "reconstruction" of life in the islands.[3]

One of the missionaries working on Pohnpei, Rev. Albert A. Sturges, bemoaned the socialism, communalism, and general lack of individual responsibility that he saw as inhibiting progress on the island. Sturges felt that only a strong popular acceptance of the notion of private ownership could better the people's lives. To this end, Sturges and his colleagues built Christian villages, complete with elected sheriffs and a quasi-republican form of democratic government, and sustained by the ethics of Christian work, trade, and commerce. At least they tried. By their own admission, things did not proceed as planned. "Many seem to think their only duty is to take what we have to give and the more worldly goods the better," declared one American missionary in 1876; "the idea of gratitude for the Gospel or services done seems not to trouble their minds." Four years later another missionary wrote, "Pohnpei is not where we hoped it would be."[4]

The efforts of American missionaries on Pohnpei and elsewhere in the Caroline and Marshall Islands groups revealed just how integrated Christianity had become into a national cultural system at whose core lay capitalist values and practices. In a real sense, these missionary efforts anticipated the objectives of a later, more formal, encompassing American presence in the islands that promoted a similar social reconstruction that went by the more secular name of "development."

War and Its Representations

As it had in 1899 and 1914, war would bring a change in colonial administrations for Micronesia. Unlike the Spanish-American conflict or World War I, whose major battlegrounds lay elsewhere, the islands of the area called Micronesia saw some of the most violent encounters between Japan and the United States as they struggled for supremacy in the Pacific. Referring directly to the battles fought on Micronesian islands, Fletcher Pratt, the author of *The Marines' War*, wrote that "never in the history of human conflict had so much been thrown by so many at so few." With 36,000 shells dropped on it, Kwajalein endured the most concentrated bombing of the Pacific War. Other Micronesian islands experienced similar devastation. Some 127,000 American troops, supported by 535 ships, invaded Saipan on 15 June 1944. Caught between the armies of the two major combatants and surrounded by Japanese and Korean civilian populations of more than eleven thousand, some twenty-three hundred Chamorros and nine hundred Carolinians struggled to survive in a home become a strange and terrifying land. The battle for Saipan created, in the words of Japanese colonial historian Mark Peattie, "unbounded horror." Major islands or island groups not invaded experienced the terror and destruction of American bombing; Kosraeans, Palauans, Pohnpeians, and residents of the Chuuk Lagoon area all came to fear the drone of bombers that arrived with the dawn during the middle months of 1944. The fighting and bombing transformed the once verdant physical environments of many Micronesian islands into ravaged, potted, desolate landscapes. Douglas Oliver's general characterization of World War II in the Pacific as "catastrophically disturbing" the lives of island peoples spoke directly to local experiences of global war in Micronesia.[5]

Written texts that seek to describe war and its effects can carry, in their own ways, themes that are themselves destructive and dangerous. Homi Bhabha, Patrick Brantlinger, Anthony Pagden, Mary Louise Pratt, and Edward Said, among others, remind us of the subliminal, politically charged messages that can lie embedded in the simplest, most seemingly straightforward narratives.[6] While not meaning to deny or diminish the tragedy of war, I begin this chapter with a consideration of how representations of war-devastated societies in Micronesia ultimately worked to sustain American efforts to rehabilitate and develop the islands in ways that at once disguised, served, and promoted American strategic interests. In essence, the project called "economic development" would become part of the rhetoric used publicly and internationally to help explain America's extended presence among the islands. The devastation of war and the powerful images used to describe it served as justifying preface for the efforts at social reconstruction that would follow. There would be an official history written to see to it.

Published in 1957, Lt. Cmdr. Dorothy E. Richard's three-volume history looms as the officially commissioned record, indeed canon, on the United States Navy's occupation and administration of Micronesia from 1944 to 1951. Its sheer size, the extensive detail embedded in its chronological narrative, and the inclusion of numerous tables, figures, charts, lists, and reproductions of primary documents give Richard's history an intimidating quality. The geographical foci of Richard's text are the Mariana and Marshall Islands, where the earliest American fighting had taken place and where wartime relief efforts and postwar administrative concerns proved most prominent. Richard represents most of the Marshall Islands as totally devastated by the effects of the war. She cites accounts from American landing forces that described the people as "ill, dazed, hungry and clad in tatters. Even the sails of their canoes were threadbare. . . . Their economy was ruined and they had no trade goods nor money. Their diet was barely a subsistence one. There was no market for their copra and their coconut trees were deteriorating from lack of care."[7] Other Micronesian island groups touched directly by combat are represented in similar language.[8] In the logic of Richard's text, the destructive effects of the war on Micronesian islands necessitated the reconstruction of island life, a major effort that would have a particularly American character to it.

Americans expected that their role as liberators would secure a welcome reception and an extended period of goodwill from grateful, needy, debilitated local populations. Micronesians were said to be awed by the landing craft that brought ashore crate after crate of relief supplies and by the generosity of American troops who gave away candy, cigarettes, and canned goods.[9] Eight hundred Nauruans, moved to Chuuk as wartime laborers by the Japanese in 1943, are described as having rehearsed the Star Spangled Banner for days before the arrival of American occupying forces.[10] In the printed pages of Richard's history, the people of Kwajalein behave "much as we do," enjoying democracy and being especially appreciative of the antics and adaptations of American troops "who do not know how to think in terms of racial condescension."[11] Richard records the speech of a King Tomeing of Wotje in the Marshalls on the repatriation of his people to their home atoll by American forces. Thanking his liberators profusely, Tomeing, in Richard's account, found deep metaphoric lessons in the American flag:

> The bars are telling us to be true and brave, and to be loyal to our country; the stars are bright that the people can see by their light and understand their message of freedom. The message of

> the stars we have heard for the last eighty-eight years, but the skies were overclouded and we did not get to see them. Now the sky is clear and the stars are shining brightly over our head, over the whole world.[12]

American liberation of Micronesia did not, however, result in the immediate transfer of the peoples' loyalty or allegiance. More recent ethnographic investigations into the war and immediate postwar periods suggest alternative, variant understandings among different island peoples. The brightness of the stars, to use Tomeing's metaphor, was not readily perceived by all. The earliest American naval officials in the area acknowledged the alienation of islanders toward a nation whose bombs, bullets, and blockades had caused injury or death to many of their friends and relatives. One Pohnpeian elder remembered hoping for a Japanese victory.[13] When asked why, he replied that he knew the Japanese and felt comfortable with them. He feared the Americans because of what the Japanese had said about them.

A Marine Corps combat correspondent on Kwajalein realized the futility of asking the people of that atoll to choose between a new colonizer recently arrived amidst a hail of exploding shells and the just-displaced Japanese regime that had held sway over the atoll for the past forty years.

> Overt cruelty was not part of the official Japanese policy on Kwajalein. They must have cultivated some favorites who would stand to lose by the Japanese departure. Among the younger native people must be others who will wait to see how they like the Americans before they decide how they liked the Japanese and some who would be too courteous to express a liking for your enemy.[14]

There was also the matter of intense personal feelings of attachment and affection. Marriage between Japanese men and Micronesian women added depth, sentiment, and emotion to the relationship between colonizers and colonized, a fact not easily forgotten or overcome by American liberation of the islands.[15]

An oral history of the period from Enewetak describes the people of that atoll as impressed with American military might but distressed by the attitudes and behaviors of their new overlords. Americans were seen as powerful, intelligent, wealthy conquerors who had little need for the people of Enewetak. Remembering war from a badly disturbed, nuclear-affected present, one resident of the atoll stated,

> We are like shit to these foreigners (Americans). They give us a new way of governing and take off, because they do not need us. We will never become like Americans. Now we quarrel like cats and rats because this new way of law is unsuited. We need someone to help us and to straighten us out because we are not like Americans, we are still uneducated, crazy like children.[16]

The American homeland came to be regarded as the "source of a force" to be celebrated and feared, a force that was ultimately indifferent to but disruptive of Marshallese society.[17] Conquest and philanthropy were not the compatible combination that Americans thought them to be, especially in Palau. Palauans sang mournfully to those Japanese and Okinawans being repatriated from Babeldaob:

> We won't forget you good Japanese people
> Who were our teachers for thirty years.
> My favorite sakura.
> Our relationship with you has ended
> We don't know which direction to go next.[18]

One young Palauan man continued to wear his Japanese military cap defiantly even after an American officer told him to discard it; one elderly Palauan woman, apparently unimpressed by the distinctions that separated the United States from the United Nations, later said to a member of an early UN Visiting Mission, "The next time you have a war, please don't have it here."[19]

The Politics of Relief and Restoration

Dorothy Richard tells us that the relief of native populations and the restoration of island economies in the war zone constituted the most immediate task facing American naval forces in Japan's former Mandate Islands. The greatest war-caused destruction occurred in the population centers of the larger islands and among communities contiguous to Japanese military installations—namely, Rota, Saipan, and Tinian in the Northern Marianas; Angaur, Koror, and Peleliu in the Western Carolines; Kosrae, Pohnpei, and Chuuk in the Eastern Carolines; and Jaluit, Kwajalein, Mili, and Wotje in the Marshalls. All experienced considerable devastation as the result of invasion or aerial bombardment. From a military perspective, the immediate relief needs of local populations on war-affected islands did not tax the supplies or manpower of the invading American forces. Troops carried with them as a matter of general policy enough supplies and equipment to "insure that the civil population is fed at not less than a minimum subsistence level and clothed in accordance with at least minimum needs." The military defined relief supplies as "those things required for health and sustenance of the population in the absence of other means of local supply or production—e. g., food, medicine, tools or equipment normally utilized and required for their self-support."[20]

Foreign trade goods had been crossing Micronesian beaches for centuries before the outbreak of World War II. From the late seventeenth century to 1815, Guam had served as a provisioning depot for the Manila galleon trade that linked the colonies of Spanish America with Asia via the Philippines. Most island societies had demonstrated both enthusiasm and imagination in their selective appropriation of Euro-American material goods. Although the people of Yap remained largely indifferent to Western trading practices through the nineteenth century, the commercial acumen of the Marshallese, Palauans, and Pohnpeians had earned generally favorable comment from many European voyagers and traders working among the islands. No historical precedents, however, had prepared the people of Micronesia for the speed and relative enormity of relief supplies brought ashore by American soldiers during time of war.

The numbers could be overwhelming. The 462 evacuees from the Japanese-held island of Maloelap in the Marshalls received an initial allotment of 1,368 pounds of corned beef, 660 pounds of vegetable stew, 720 pounds of meat and vegetable hash, 480 pounds of beans, 5,000 pounds of salmon, 2,880 pounds of biscuit, 600 pounds of spaghetti, 3,000 pounds of flour, and 1,600 pounds of freshwater soup among their relief supplies. At Saipan's Camp Susupe, where Chamorro refugees were joined by large numbers of Japanese and Korean civilians waiting for repatriation, 3,950,000 pounds of relief food were distributed between April and October 1945.[21]

Military commanders and later naval historians were little concerned about how island peoples understood and accepted relief supplies. Although the navy's historical record and even more recently collected oral histories of the period are generally silent on the matter, the cross-cultural negotiations involved in the distribution and acceptance of foreign relief supplies deserves a reflective comment. A long and critical tradition within anthropology has identified the culturally specific contexts in which gifts are proffered and received.[22] Although generalizations for an area as diverse as Micronesia run the risk of essentializing economic practices that are complex and varied, it can be argued that relief supplies, perceived as gifts or forms of assistance, established social relationships between givers and receivers and created expectations of future obligations among the involved parties. The humanitarian principles governing the dispensing of what was held to be simply relief supplies ignored these entanglements, and could and did conflict with local hierarchies that expected acknowledgment and participation in the distribution of this new, foreign, potentially challenging form of wealth and power.

An account from Pohnpei provides a glimpse of the dilemma.[23] There, a hundred pairs of green navy work trousers were to be distributed to the most needy; in this instance, the most needy were identified as widows, orphans, and "people with no pance." The American officer in charge of distribution decided it appropriate to give a new pair of these navy trousers to Oliver Nanpei, a wealthy landowner and holder of one of the three major ruling titles of the chiefdom of Kiti, located along the island's western shore. Appearing at the administration building in the town of Kolonia the next day in his new trousers, Nanpei was confronted by the island's executive officer who reprimanded him with the question, "Are you needy? Have you no pants that you must wear these?" The description of the encounter provides meager ethnographic detail; nonetheless, at its most elemental level, the story underscores conflicting notions of need, protocol, and propriety that would haunt America's efforts at economic development in the islands for decades to come. To the executive officer, a relief item in the possession of a prominent, relatively privileged man made a mockery of American standards of relief. A more ethnographic read of the situation might have recognized the local negotiations of status and power involved in the introduction of these highly charged, symbolically potent goods.

American occupation of the islands was piecemeal and gradual. The seizure of the islands began with Kwajalein in January 1944 and concluded with the capture of Peleliu in the Western Carolines in November 1944. The war in Micronesia ended formally with Japan's surrender on 2 September 1945 aboard the battleship USS *Missouri,* anchored in Tokyo Bay. Based in Honolulu, Hawaii, the U.S. Navy's Commander in Chief for the Pacific Ocean Areas (CINCPOA) was given responsibility for occupation and relief efforts in Micronesia; on military command charts, the islands were divided into two major groups, designated as the Marianas and Marshall-Gilberts Areas. Temporary administrative units staffed by naval officers managed each of the captured islands. Policy guidelines for the occupied islands had been defined in a January 1944 memo issued by the joint chiefs of staff. In particular, the memo committed occupation forces to the development of the islands, a condition marked by a return "to their normal degrees of self-sufficiency."[24] This policy showed a decidedly flawed understanding of the just-ended period of Japanese colonialism in the islands.

In the distribution of relief supplies, Americans were concerned not to "spoil" the people. The navy held dependence to be ultimately corrupting of any and all efforts to restore productive economic activity in the islands. To this end, the navy arranged for income-generating activities so that islanders would be able to purchase trade items. The readily apparent enthusiasm of occupation troops for the purchase of local handicrafts provided an instant infusion of cash, thereby allowing the navy to establish local trade stores stocked with salvaged Japanese goods and later with consumer items supplied through military requisition. Most of these trade stores were in the Marshalls. To encourage the manufacture and sale of handicrafts, CINCPOA created a special fund of $250,000 to stock these early trade stores; this amount was later increased to $750,000. In August 1944, for example, the sale of handicraft on the atolls of Majuro, Arno, and Aur amounted to $4,220.23. Items sold included woven mats, shell necklaces, and model canoes. With the withdrawal of American troops from the islands, however, sales dropped sharply. Where there had once been tens of thousands of occupying troops, military forces in the islands totaled 1,041 in October 1945. By the end of 1946, about 58 officers and 119 enlisted men constituted the American military presence in the islands.[25]

Efforts to expand the local handicraft industry through export also foundered against a June 1945 decision by the United States Department of the Treasury's Bureau of Customs; the bureau ruled that the islands' status as a foreign territory could not be waived to allow for the duty-free importation of Micronesian handicraft into the United States.[26] The imposition of import duties upon Micronesian handicraft added costs to the production and marketing process that precluded the possibility of profits from sales in the United States.

Before the formal end of hostilities, the military had turned over its trade store operations to the Foreign Economic Administration (FEA). On 21 April 1945, an agreement between the navy and the FEA, successor to the ominously named Office of Economic Warfare (OEW) in Washington, D.C., established procedures for the requisition, transport, and distribution of merchandise by the FEA to trade stores on occupied islands. The FEA's ability to supply these stores depended heavily on the availability of naval shipping. On occasion, island communities would stretch American abilities and conceptions of appropriate and needed trade goods;

Marshallese requests for shoes struck military officials as excessive and unnecessary in light of more pressing requirements.[27] The success of the first trade store confirmed in military officials' minds the desirability of promoting a market economy in the islands. More important, the collaboration between the FEA and the navy evidenced early on, albeit in modest dimensions, the intimately entwined relationship between domination and development, a relationship that would show itself more clearly and dramatically at later periods in the more than forty-year period of formal American rule over the islands.

The use of islander labor in support of occupation forces provided another source of income through which the navy hoped to revive local markets.[28] In determining the nature of and compensation for local labor, the navy adopted the policy first set forth in the Hague Convention of 1907 and the Rules of Land Warfare. These regulations stipulated that native labor would be voluntary, to be commandeered only in an emergency. Compensation, which could include rations, was to be commensurate with prewar scales of 70 sen to 2 yen per day. In a gesture toward local sources of authority, CINCPOA ordered that all native labor was to be recruited through village headmen or recognized leaders. The number of islanders to be hired fell to the discretion of island commanders, who were to weigh their labor needs against the costs and the possible disruption to native economies caused by the large influx of relief supplies and the displacement of hired labor away from vital traditional activities. In truth, however, the navy drew heavily on other sources of labor to clear and restore island landscapes ravaged by war. The military government used more than a hundred thousand Japanese nationals, the vast majority of them soldiers waiting for repatriation, as laborers. A long, drawn-out process, repatriation of these nationals, whose numbers included a goodly number of Okinawans and some Koreans, was largely completed by mid-1946.[29] Some five thousand Japanese troops were held an extra six months, however, to assist with clearing operations in Chuuk, Palau, and Yap.[30]

Trade stores, the purchase of local handicraft, and wage compensation for employed islander labor proved only temporary strategies designed to revitalize the most basic functions of a still nascent market economy. As early as 1942, the navy had contracted with the Office of Economic Warfare to plan a broader agenda for more extensive development of the island economies.[31] The plan called for the expansion and diversification of vegetable, fish, and lumber supplies to help meet the needs of American troops stationed or temporarily billeted in the islands. The Northern Marianas proved the principal focus of these efforts. In September 1944, CINCPOA, now using FEA personnel and resources, inaugurated a vegetable-growing program on Guam, Saipan, and Tinian. The purpose behind the program was to supplement the rations of the locally stationed armed forces and to provide work for native peoples that would contribute to the economic rehabilitation of the Northern Marianas.

Despite its initial promise, the FEA vegetable project in the Marianas did not meet the navy's expectations. Limited shipping space aboard naval vessels for goods associated with civilian projects meant delays in the procurement and transportation of necessary equipment and supplies. Nonetheless, the military government advertised the farming project as a significant achievement in restoring pride and confidence to the islands' peoples. Secretary of the Navy James Forrestal credited the program with bearing fruit; it had begun as a "nebulous and ungrateful task" that had achieved success because of the patience and determination of those who saw it through. Morale, said the naval officials in the Marianas, was enhanced by the income earned and by the "illusion of ownership."[32]

The "illusion of ownership," however, proved less than sustaining. A petition later presented to the United Nations Trusteeship Council in 1950 by the High Council of Saipan complained about the general uncertainty among farmers caused by the navy's failure to give them deeds to the land they farmed.[33] The possible revocation of their permits proved a constant source of anxiety and severely inhibited the development of a more modern economy for Saipan. On behalf of the farmers, the High Council of Saipan requested legal deeds to the government land which, it was argued, should be offered as replacement for private lands destroyed or made unusable by war or war-related activities.

By the cessation of hostilities in Micronesia, the United States Navy was proclaiming that the January 1944 directive of the Joint Chiefs of Staff "to restore the islands to their normal degree of self-sufficiency" had been honored and with considerable success.[34] What exactly naval officials understood to be a "normal degree of self-sufficiency" was unclear. Moreover, in touting its success, the navy failed to mention that most of its efforts had been focused on the Northern Marianas, the area of Micronesia assumed to be the most historically and culturally disposed toward economic initiatives because of its nearly three centuries of direct colonial rule. Similar projects elsewhere in Micronesia were considerably smaller in terms of both scope and results; here the "restoration of self-sufficient economies" came more accurately to mean clearing and salvage.

Other and Earlier Histories of Economic Development

Efforts at economic development were nothing new in the colonial history of Micronesia; earlier colonizers of the area had employed development as a strategy of domination through transformation.[35] To the end of the German colonial period in 1914, these earlier efforts at development and transformation involved foreign trading firms, a fledgling copra industry in the Marshalls, and the mining of phosphate on Nauru and also on Angaur, Fais, Peleliu, and Tobi in the Western Carolines. Local responses to German efforts at development elicited a variety of responses not the least of which were violent rebellion on Pohnpei, vigorous protests in Chuuk against the exploitation of islander labor in the mining of phosphate, and defiance in Palau against colonial policies designed to bring about the elimination of cultural practices and institutions deemed wasteful and immoral. Beginning in 1914 and lasting until 1944, Japan's colonization of the islands proved to be more overwhelming in its dimensions and effects than that of either Spain or Germany. By 1935, there were 50,000 Japanese nationals in the islands, the majority of whom were from Okinawa.[36] In 1940, the total Japanese population had climbed to 77,000; two years later, it reached 96,000. By the outbreak of hostilities between Japan and the United States, there were almost twice as many Japanese in Micronesia as Micronesians, with Saipan and Koror, Palau, serving as the major residential centers for this colonial prewar population. Micronesians became increasingly marginalized spectators in the development of their islands; indeed, their cultural survival seemed doubtful.

An examination of the financial ledger of Japan's Micronesian colony reveals dramatically the extent of economic development.[37] In 1922, the islands were a drain on the imperial treasury, with administrative expenditures required to compensate for the lack of local revenues and the failure of the very first development projects. By the late 1920s, a combination of private initiative and government support, especially in the areas of sugar and phosphate production, had generated revenues that began to reverse this imbalance. In 1932, local revenues were such that grants from the Japanese national government were no longer necessary. By 1937, the colonial government in Micronesia had a reserve of close to a million yen. Within the larger context of the Japanese empire, the economic standing and contributions of the Mandate Islands, as they were now internationally known, were quite small. The tiniest of Japan's colonies, the Mandate Islands provided only 1 percent of the total value of goods produced by the empire in 1939. More than offsetting these seemingly insignificant trade figures, however, was the fact that Japan's ultimate strategic interests in the islands could be served by a relatively active, vibrant local economy that paid for the cost of its own administration. War with the United States would bring an end to all of this.

War, it might be argued, had more than ravaged the landscapes of the islands and atolls of Micronesia; it had obliterated in the minds of the victors themselves any consciousness or understanding of the area's prior colonial history and of the varying strategies employed by earlier colonizers to direct Micronesian people and their resources toward the service of larger metropolitan interests. Indeed, the American military seemed determined at times to remove all traces of the Japanese presence. An embittered American military official on Palau wanted no trace left of Japan's presence in the islands; he thus ordered his construction battalion to raze and remove all structures built by the Japanese.[38] The extensive remains of the Japanese settlement on the island of Toloas in Chuuk Lagoon were similarly treated. American efforts at reconstruction would not be carried out on foundations laid by Japan or any other of Micronesia's earlier colonizers.

Naval commanders, it seems, had hoped that the destructive fury of war would sweep away all memories and traces of the colonial past. They had done what they could to begin the total make-over of the islands. There were neither ears to hear nor eyes to read histories of earlier efforts at development that carried within them voices of Micronesian resistance and protest. American naval officials believed that time, their ways, and their manifest humanitarianism would win the people over. Totally overlooked, however, were persisting links to deeper, precolonial pasts that included a hierarchy of island relations that stretched across the Central Carolines from Yap in the west to the Namonuitos in the east. Little attention was given to the ways in which nebulous, erratically applied strategies for economic development in Micronesia might conflict with surviving systems of varied but still powerful chiefly rule throughout the Caroline and Marshall Islands. The sociodemographic strategies employed by atoll populations, the important role of clan lineages in the allocation of land and distribution of wealth, the very meaning of value and exchange, and the well-established locally informed practices of cultural adaptation and appropriation all failed to register in the minds of Micronesia's newest colonial rulers. Naval officials expended little worry over how wages for labor might be understood; how trade goods might be contexted differently in the minds of people who, by themselves, carried on exchange that was still largely expressive of social relationships; how practices involving capital, credit, finance, loan, and budgets might disturb social environments more concerned with obligations toward kin, clan, or chiefs. To American military personnel charged with the first efforts at reconstruction on islands ravaged by war, the phrase "economic development" may well have implied the promise of a desirable, necessary, more materially comfortable life that would advance the interests of Micronesians and Americans alike. For the people of the islands, those two words would lie at the heart of yet another brand of colonialism. The future history of economic development would prove far more complicated and disturbing than what navy planners envisioned.

Military Government: September 1945 to July 1947

It came as no surprise to anyone when, in September 1945, President Harry S. Truman awarded the navy responsibility for the interim postwar government of the islands. The decision had been anticipated and planned for two years earlier. Before the formal end of hostilities with Japan, the navy had decided that the Mandate Islands would have to be governed by naval personnel. The points put forth to promote the argument evidenced a curious blend of paternalism and bias. Responding to calls for civilian government, the officer in charge at the Department of the Navy, in a memorandum dated 23 April 1943, argued that the paramount strategic concerns that imbued the area with significance would necessitate a continuation of naval rule over the area.[39] The cumbersome restrictions of civilian bureaucracy were not what was needed in the tense, confused environment of the immediate postwar island world. Civilian government was to be desired and worked toward, but at a deliberate, gradual pace. The greatest threat to the establishment of democratic forms of government was not navy rule, but rather the premature introduction of those democratic forms.

The perceived backwardness of the people of the islands added further justification to the need for military government. In making its case for a formal structure of military government to replace the departing occupation forces, the navy characterized social traditions and indigenous forms of political government as primitive, feudalistic, and revolving around family, clan, and village. Island peoples were said to seldom comprehend or respond rationally to political federations or to other features of Euro-American government. "All in all," wrote the officer in charge, "the interest of the inhabitants (and incidentally, the best interests of the United States) would be best served by establishing in most of these islands a strong but benevolent government—a government paternalistic in character, but one which ruled as indirectly as possible (i.e., one which made minimum interference with local family and organization and custom)."[40] "Government from a distance" is the way one historian has termed the navy's tenure in the islands.[41] The word "distance" would come to refer to more than just miles of ocean.

From its Hawaiian base, CINCPOA now held responsibility for the governing of the region. Local military governments were established for each of the major islands. These island governments were headed by a commanding officer under whom served an executive officer and a group of civil administrators. These civil administrators were actually junior naval officers fresh from their training in military government at Stanford University's School of Naval Administration (SONA). Reaching their assigned islands, they headed smaller individual offices or departments responsible for personnel matters, public health, public safety, legal affairs, field operations, economics, public works, and education. The title of these men as civil administrators, along with their civilian style of dress, was intended to blunt the more martial features of military government in the islands and thus deflect some of the criticism of naval government emanating from certain government agencies in Washington, D.C.

The United States Navy defined its immediate objectives for administration of the islands in both strategic and economic terms, a conflation of categories that suggested the ways in which domination might be achieved to serve American interests and a stated objective often forgotten or overlooked by those who see only the crassly political dimension of America's agenda in the islands.[42] The military's first formal statement of economic policy for the postwar period appeared in the Pacific Charter, a document issued on 12 December 1945. In addition to the physical rehabilitation of the islands and the restoration of educational, health, and local political systems, the document committed the military government in the postwar period to the economic development of trade, industry, and agriculture "along lines that will insure that the profits and benefits thereof accrue to the native inhabitants and which will assist them in achieving the highest possible level of economic independence."[43]

Civil administrators who headed an island administration's economic office were ordered to survey the copra, handicraft, and livestock industries; conduct studies on all possible marketable and exportable items; develop private enterprise; promote the creation of local trading companies on the major islands and island groups of the area; teach the making of soap; and keep accurate records on the presence of pests detrimental to economic activities in the islands. Ostensibly to protect the islands and their resources against the rapaciousness of opportunists, the navy closed the area to all private enterprise. This ban on foreign investment, including entrepreneurial capital from within the United States, also indicated American possessiveness regarding the islands. As had the phrase "self-sufficiency" during the occupation period, the words "economic independence" seemed self-evident in meaning to those who employed them. The preclusion of a more exact definition would soon prove a problem for the colonizers as well as the colonized.

On 1 November 1945, the United States Commercial Company (USCC) assumed the direction for all commercial development from the FEA. Although administratively an independent federal agency, the USCC was "in effect, a direct agency of the U.S. Navy." Its internal organization was its own, but its chain of command closely paralleled that of the navy. Honolulu was the headquarters for all USCC activities in the Pacific. A chief representative or liaison officer from the USCC was attached to the staff of the commander of the Marianas area, who now had sole jurisdiction for all of Micronesia, including the Marshalls; from this location, the USCC liaison officer supervised all company activities in the field. USCC personnel in the islands consisted of agriculturists, animal husbandry specialists, entomologists, trade specialists, economists, and accountants. In February 1947, there were twenty-nine USCC agents in the islands, with Pohnpei and Saipan possessing the largest contingents, seven each.[44]

As successor to the FEA, the USCC assumed management of the trade store program. Although initially successful, the trade store program in the Marianas, Marshalls, and Carolines was hindered both by the difficulty of procuring trade goods on schedule and by the shortage of naval shipping to transport those goods. Problems with shipping delays were sometimes compounded by the type of merchandise provided to the USCC stores. The commanding military officer at Yap noted the arrival in May 1947 of a shipment that included medical supplies, steel wool, sugarcane, work gloves, woollen drawers, leggings, pins, rubber boots, picks, and 3,100 toothbrushes.[45] The officer added sarcastically that toothbrush sales on Yap averaged about six per month. The problems with shipping and supply notwithstanding, most naval officials assumed that these stores provided training in business methods and created a firm basis on which to expand indigenous trading activities.

The USCC also assumed responsibility for small-scale development projects such as the vegetable farms established in the Marianas during the immediate occupation period.[46] Despite the joint efforts of the navy and the USSC, the agricultural program in the Caroline and Mariana Islands proved of little consequence in terms of acres tilled or crops harvested. Land problems, lack of supplies, environmental pests, and what was termed "native apathy" all worked to impede what Americans held to be acceptable levels of progress. Joint endeavors by the navy and the USCC to revitalize other areas of economic activity disrupted by the war proved equally unsuccessful. Island communities' preoccupation with rebuilding homes and replanting subsistence gardens had seriously hindered the earlier attempts to restore the prewar commercial production of copra. The purchase of copra at $40 a ton, a price set—it was said—to protect against inflation and promote parity among the different islands, attracted little local interest. In late 1946, the price was raised to $80 a ton, a figure only one-third that of the world price.[47] Not surprisingly, islander responses to such an incentive remained lukewarm.

The drive to restore the islands' livestock populations proved no more successful than efforts to revitalize copra production. Livestock sold through the USCC's trade stores or directly to individuals was butchered quickly. The desire of local peoples to obtain poultry and hogs reflected the use of such stock as immediate sources of food or as cultural items that had little to do with simple commercial or economic values promoted by the navy. Failed attempts to revive the once vibrant but Japanese-manned fishing industries in Chuuk and Palau quickly demonstrated that Micronesians still viewed fishing largely in terms of subsistence.[48]

Micronesians' material well-being during the interim period of military government compared badly with the prewar days of Japanese colonial rule. Annual family income for Micronesians in 1946 stood at between a half and a third of what it had been in 1939.[49] Under the Japanese, Micronesians had been required to deposit a portion of their earnings as postal savings. The United States' reluctant and delayed redemption of these postal savings at one-fifth their original value resulted in considerable losses for individual Micronesians. Assessing the navy's efforts at economic development, one USCC employee in the islands wrote, "We have destroyed a twentieth-century economy, and are now trying to put it back with bailing wire and splintered boards."[50] Given these failures, the navy developed a more discriminating sense of which island groups within the region held the most promise and potential. Consequently, special programs were devised to enhance the prospects of development in the Northern Marianas. Expectations for the remainder of the islands were significantly reduced; military officials now expressed the cautious, very guarded hope that the Caroline and Marshall Islands could become "practically self-sustaining at a satisfactory subsistence level."[51]

The final statement on general economic policy promulgated during the military government period was contained in the "Joint Chiefs of Staff Interim Directive for Military Government in the Central Pacific Islands."[52] Approved in April 1947, the document revealed a sense of continuing responsibility now tinged by frustration, even exasperation. As had the directives and policies that preceded it, this latest statement committed the naval administration to the development of a balanced economy through the full utilization of natural and other resources. To ensure basic subsistence, the military government pledged itself to supplementing local produce, when necessary, with daily food rations. The government continued to bolster agricultural development efforts through the distribution of tools, seeds, fertilizers, and insecticides. Monies continued to be set aside for the revival of local fishing industries and for enhanced handicraft and copra production. The directive authorized price controls and selective rationing to provide for a fair distribution of all material goods and supplies. The military command considered it essential that all medical care and school supplies be furnished free of charge "for some time to come."[53] These paternal subsidies showed the frustration that began to characterize American efforts at creating in the islands the foundations of a viable economy; impatience resulted as distance, environment, and culture interrupted the rhythms of progress the navy brought to the islands. The inclination to intervene in behalf of people who seemed unable to work hard enough or fast enough in their own and also American interests had the look of precedence about it.

Belaboring Micronesians

The navy listed the impediments to its local development projects as many and varied: geography, isolation, distance, the weather, the lack of natural resources, the presence of environmental pests, and the priorities of a larger postwar world itself concerned with reconstruction and development. As time passed, however, official reports came to focus more and more on the alleged inadequacies and failings of Micronesians as laborers. Islanders' sense of time, or rather their lack of it, struck naval administrators as being at the root of all labor problems in Micronesia. Frederick Cooper has written that colonizing space is one thing, colonizing time another.[54] Economic development requires, argues Cooper, an adaptation to rhythms of industrial capitalism and a submission to the idea that work has to be steady, regular, and controlled. In a capitalist society driven by concerns for production and profit, the clock serves as a panopticon of sorts that observes, segments, and directs peoples' lives. It ticks away as an omniscient presence, commanding people's attention through its intimate link to the productivity it measures, the rewards it promises, and the penalties it threatens. It is perhaps the most fundamental and determining of capitalist technologies. Greg Dening has also written of the importance of the concept of time to the "civilizing mission." Referring specifically to the people of the Marquesas Islands but with words that strongly evoke histories of colonialism elsewhere in the Pacific, Dening comments,

> Civilizing them in its essence was giving them a different sense of time. . . . This new sense of time was not just a concern for regularity, although that was important. Making seven days in a week and one of them a sabbath, making meal-times in a day, making work-time and leisure-time, making sacred time and profane time laid out time in a line, as it were. . . . It removed the cyclical time of rituals in which a legendary past was re-enacted to legitimate and prolong the present. Most important in the new sense of time was a notion of progress and a break-out from the present. . . . Their present was not without change, but the fundamental mode of their existence was continually to re-establish their land in its metaphors. To become civilized, they needed an emptiness in their souls that left room for the future.[55]

Remaking Micronesia, then, would necessitate first remaking time. The various peoples of Micronesia, however, had persisted in living according to a very different sense of time through three previous colonial regimes. Sensing this resistance early on, the Japanese had consigned the island peoples to the margins of economic activity during the years of their mandate. A report on conditions during Japanese times had noted that "native labor as a factor in the agricultural and industrial future of the islands will play a very insignificant part. . . . Even at its best, it is valued, both in efficiency and in wage, at less than half the value of imported Japanese labor."[56] Having worked to obliterate all semblance of the Japanese presence, Americans now endeavored to persuade Micronesians to live by the clock; they sought to teach Micronesians the material advantages and pleasures of living for themselves rather than for each other. Forty years of colonial rule would seem a long time to American government officials committed to the agenda of development; it would not be long enough, however, to change, at least totally, more indigenous conceptions of time.

In the immediate period following the cessation of hostilities, the naval military government had made extensive use of Japanese, Okinawan, and

Korean laborers marooned by the war. With their eventual repatriation, a gradual and encumbered process not completed until December 1946, the naval administration was forced to rely almost exclusively on Micronesians. As it had during the earlier occupation period, the navy now decreed that employment would be voluntary, with payment for all labor performed and with no forced separation from home or family. For purposes of compensation, wage earners were divided into six general categories ranging from apprentices, domestics, and unskilled workers to clerical, professional, and administrative workers.[57]

Wages varied from island group to island group and tended to reflect the military's geographical priorities and prejudices regarding different groups of Micronesians. The lowest pay scale, that for the Caroline Islands, ranged from $0.15 to $0.65 per hour for laborers, higher of course for administrative and professional employees. Pay scales for corresponding categories of workers in the Marshall Islands were approximately double those in the Carolines. Saipanese, ostensibly on the grounds that their cost of living was higher, received wages one-third greater than those paid in the Marshalls. Islanders employed on Guam earned $0.80 per day and were provided quarters, sustenance, and clothing. Upward adjustments were quickly made in these initial compensation schedules. By February 1947, the base minimum salary for the islands ranged from $0.40 to $0.90 per day for laborers and from $15 to $70 a month for administrative and governmental employees.[58]

An important component of the military government's labor policy was training. Instruction in the operation of equipment and machinery constituted a prime part of the naval administration's on-the-job training program. The navy wanted to turn Micronesians into stevedores, plumbers, carpenters, ship fitters, radio operators, typists, and seamen.[59] Although sex discrimination was expressly forbidden, women were usually employed in lower-paying jobs that required fewer skills; they worked as clerks, secretaries, and domestics, thus earning considerably less than men. In September 1947, Saipan had the largest number of women employed with forty-four; figures for the other islands ranged from a high of thirty-eight on Chuuk to none on Yap. Economic development, it seems, was largely the work of men.[60]

The naval government's efforts at rehabilitation and development now opened up considerable opportunity for Micronesian laborers. The most pressing need for labor proved to be on Saipan, Guam, and select areas within the Marshalls. Saipan had a large enough labor pool to meet immediate reconstruction and rehabilitation needs, but Guam and the

Marshalls were forced to rely on imported labor. By the fall of 1945, camps for Marshallese laborers from other areas of the atoll complex had been established at Kwajalein, Roi, and Majuro. In March 1946, 113 Pohnpeians were working on Enewetak. The most pressing need for islander laborer, however, existed on Guam. The naval government of that island requested a thousand workers from the Carolines but settled for three hundred when its initial figure proved unobtainable.[61]

Despite the willingness of Micronesians to travel for work, the military's assessment of Micronesians as laborers quickly showed itself to be a decidedly negative one. Drawing from the naval records of the interim military government period, Dorothy Richard conceded the congeniality that pervaded Micronesians' work ethos; they worked in groups rather than as individuals, and with the line between work and play often obscured.[62] Nonetheless, against American expectations of work, they looked lazy, unenterprising, improvident, and both unable and unwilling to work at regular, sustained labor. The eight-hour workday kept by Americans lay beyond Micronesians' capacities. The problem with islander labor, according to Richard, was not only a difference in definition and attitude toward work, but also an inability to work away from home. Marshallese and Yapese exhibited a decided preference for home, while Pohnpeians proved just slightly more venturesome. Only Palauans and Chuukese demonstrated a capacity for labor in a distant land, but their numbers were not sufficient enough, said Richard, to satisfy the labor needs of the military government. In short, the navy, as evidenced in Richard's text, concluded that Micronesians, because of their natural inclinations and cultural orientations, lacked the basic skills and attitudes necessary for the successful development of their islands' economy.[63]

Richard's history offered a pictorial as well as textual vision of development. I refer to the powerful, thematically reinforcing photographs that accompany Richard's words. Subliminal, politically charged messages can be conveyed graphically well as textually. While the photographs employed in the earlier sections of Richard's study underscore a war-inflicted devastation that requires American beneficence and protection, later pictures play upon the trope of a highly romanticized but ultimately untenable primitivism.[64] We see photographs of idyllic lagoons, beautiful beaches, quaint thatched-roof structures, outrigger sailing canoes, bare-breasted women, naked children, tattooed chiefs, and a variety of cultural practices that at first glance seem to work against Richard's themes.

By themselves or in different contexts, these photographs could be taken as evidence of cultural survival, persistence, and pride. In Richard's

Above and right: Editorializing development through pictures. (Richard I, 1957; US Navy).

text, however, these photographs work in conjunction with negative assessments about Micronesians' skills and abilities as laborers. The concept of the primitive that informs the deliberate, editorializing placement of these middle photographs is employed to indict the very subjects being imaged on film. Text and photograph combine to argue that these differences cannot be sustained in a modern world that requires regular, timed and managed work to create self-sufficient and sustaining economies.

Later photographs tend to depict women beating clothes in island rivers, bathing their crying children in shallow tidal pools, cooking with converted ship biscuit tins over open-air fires, or engaging in other domestic routines amidst dilapidated, makeshift structures. The attractiveness of the primitive thus dissolves against the hardships and difficulties of life in a beautiful but badly underdeveloped area of the world. The last pictures in Richard's three-volume study depict collaborative projects in which Micronesians labor, listen, or learn under the colonial gaze of the American presence. The overall effect is a highly edited, visually and textually coordinated argument for American colonialism in Micronesia and the program of development that accompanies it.

Development Aside

While the navy wrestled with the problems that plagued its interim government, intense debates about the ultimate disposition of the islands were occurring elsewhere. Away from the area called Micronesia, platitudes for the development of the islands and their people dissolved to reveal the crasser, more self-serving aspects of America's presence—but not until after the outcome of the war had been decided. As early as 1941, the United States and its allies, through the Atlantic Charter, had disavowed any interests in territorial aggrandizement or acquisition. This pledge was renewed three years later as part of the Cairo Declaration. With victory assured, however, other sentiments began to be expressed.

At Yalta in 1945, Secretary of War Henry Stimson insisted that the

United States must have the absolute power to rule and fortify the islands.[65] What was involved, argued Stimson, was not annexation or colonization, but the simple acquisition of bases needed by the United States to meet its global defense commitments in a threatening, unsettled postwar world. Evidencing more of a sense of history, United States Senator Thomas Hart, himself a former admiral, remembered with chagrin how the United States had stood by and allowed the islands to pass to Germany in 1899 and later to Japan in 1914. The consequence of that abdication of national self-interest, preached Hart, was the unnecessarily long and costly war just concluded. Admiral Thomas King spoke even more bluntly in a speech given in April 1945: "these atolls, these island harbors, will have been paid for by the sacrifice of human blood."[66] King did not mention the numbers that sustained his assertion, but others would: 7,353 dead and 32,375 wounded. King would later add that Micronesia was as important as Hawaii to the United States.[67] King's words evidenced the navy's position of annexation, a position supported by former president Herbert Hoover who stated that the development of air power necessitated the westward extension of the American defense periphery in the Pacific. Hoover went on to insist that the former Mandate Islands most assuredly fell within the geographical area covered by this extension.[68] Apparently assuming that economic exploitation constituted the sole criterion for measuring imperialism, Hoover argued that American annexation of the islands could not be construed as imperialistic because the United States held no commercial interests in the area.

Some agencies within the United States government, however, were opposed to any outright annexation of the islands. The civilian-run Department of State spoke for an internationally recognized agreement that promoted the eventual institution of self-government for the islands. While the military sought the establishment of American sovereignty over the islands to facilitate the construction of naval bases and air stations necessary for what were perceived to be global security responsibilities, the Department of State advanced a minimal American presence consistent with the general climate of decolonization in the postwar period and America's commitment to the United Nations as an international organization dedicated to the promotion of world peace.

It soon became apparent that the ultimate disposition of the Caroline, Mariana, and Marshall Islands would involve the United Nations. In his broadcast summation of the Potsdam Conference on 6 August 1945, President Truman stated,

> Though the United States wants no territory or profit or selfish advantage out of this war, we are going to maintain the military bases necessary for the complete protection of our interests and world peace. Bases which our military experts deem to be essential for our protection and which are not now in our possession, we will acquire. We will acquire them by arrangements consistent with the United Nations Charter.[69]

With regard to the islands of Micronesia, Truman's words spoke to the highly calloused, semantically self-serving position that the islands were not to be considered annexed or colonized territory, but rather prospective military bases. Within the United States, the debate now focused not on the continuation of American power over the area, but rather on the specific institutional vehicle for the exercise of that power.

Given its occupation and later military government over the area, the navy looked to be the logical choice. Strong dissenting voices opposed to the continued naval administration of the islands, however, arose within the government. Vociferous opposition to the continuation of naval rule emanated most strongly from competing quarters of the United States government that believed the islands more appropriately placed under their jurisdiction—namely, the Departments of State and the Interior. Secretary of the Interior Harold L. Ickes criticized the general record of naval administration in the Pacific, more particularly in Guam and American Samoa. At an address before a joint gathering of the Institutes of Ethnic Affairs and Pacific Relations in Washington, D.C., on 29 May 1946, Ickes accused the navy of running the islands like a battleship while ignoring the true problems of those striving toward democracy. The secretary decried the navy's particular brand of absolutism, which sneered at constitutional guarantees and was arbitrary, dictatorial, racist, and utterly disregarding of civilian rights. The navy, insisted Ickes, had no intention of leading the island peoples toward self-government or democracy or racial equality. The navy's submission in August 1946 of a report to the United Nations on its government of the islands intensified the debate. An editorial in the 24 August edition of the *New York Times* praising the navy's report was rebutted seven days later by Mr. John Collier, president of the Institute of Ethnic Affairs. Collier accused the navy of providing information that was inaccurate, misleading, and "in a good many cases, glaringly false." On 2 September 1946, the *New York Times* published an article that itself criticized the navy's record in Guam and American Samoa for not adequately ensuring the democratic rights of the affected island peoples. Secretary of the Navy James Forrestal endeavored to counter these criticisms by arguing in a 24 September letter to the *New York Times* that the preservation of the inhabitants' democratic rights was the "exact objective of naval civil government and, for that matter, of military government as well" and that the navy's record in Guam and American Samoa needed no defense.[70]

Tensions abated with the achievement of a compromise reached at a December 1946 meeting involving representatives of the Departments of War, State, and the Navy.[71] Extensive negotiations at this meeting produced the idea of a strategic trusteeship that allowed for the primacy of American security interests while according some recognition to international concerns for the development of self-government among the islands. The United States Navy would administer the islands in trust, but with the right to maintain military bases and to carry out activities in support of its international defense interests. Truman announced the plan on 6 November 1946; the United Nations Trusteeship Council gave its approval in April 1947. Implementation of the strategic trusteeship agreement followed on 19 July 1947. The face of domination now hid behind the stamp of an international imprimatur of sorts. The particulars of this arrangement will be taken up in the next chapter.

"Mild Benevolence" as Strategic Denial

A particularly revealing reflection on the navy's first three years among the Caroline, Mariana, and Marshall Islands was provided by Rear Adm. Carleton H. Wright in a 1947 article for the *Saturday Evening Post,* a popular American weekly at the time.[72] Wright had served as deputy commander for the Marianas area during the navy's occupation government and would eventually become deputy high commissioner under the Pacific naval commander-in-chief following the United Nations' award of a trusteeship. Wright's text reveals the irony, contradictions, and ulterior purposes that underscored American colonial rule over the area.

In his argument, Wright expressed paternal affection for the people of the island. Borrowing from classical mythology, Wright thought that Micronesia approached the Greek idea of "Islands of the Blessed." He described the Micronesian temperament as being tranquil and of good cheer; this serenity, he believed, derived from a minimum of government, a simple economy, and an idyllic, paradise-like environment. Reflecting further, Wright felt the islanders' enviable happiness, contentment, and self-sufficiency were in inverse proportion to the standards of "Occidental civilization." If civilization were measured by flush toilets, ice cubes, machine guns, and sewing machines, then Micronesians were indeed savages. If, however, civilization meant an economic system in which there was no relative poverty, but rather adequate food, shelter, physical security, and a social system in which all participate equally and actively in the material and aesthetic standards of community life, then the people of Micronesia were indeed civilized and had much to teach the rest of the world.

Wright wrote not unmindful of the ills wrought among the islands by colonizers from both the East and West. The imposition of alien notions of economy, politics, and morality upon the Pacific Islands had created, he wrote, squalor, discontent, endemic diseases, and "poor imitations." But Wright perceived a resilience among the people that had allowed them to persevere and survive. He saw in the continued use of Yapese stone money a metaphor of survival, an indigenous measure of worth that persisted while varying forms of colonial currency passed in and out of use with the comings and goings of their sponsors. Wright worried, however, about the latest threat posed by "brisk missionaries of modernism, the bureaucrats, the sentimentalists, and the busybody do-gooders."[73] He asked who would protect the island people from the military autocrat, the ideology-ridden bureaucrat, and the theological dogmatist.

Wright hoped for the mitigation of the overwhelming forces of change that seemed poised to overwhelm the islands. To be sure, the admiral acknowledged the importance of the islands for American strategic interests. The question became whether or not the satisfaction of those interests would drastically alter the tone and tenure of established patterns of life in the islands. Wright proposed education in basic technical skills that would allow the island peoples to build better houses and ocean-going craft. Wright admitted to a certain remorse at promoting skills and technology that would lead to tin rather than thatched roofs for Micronesian houses, but all in all, he reasoned, a tin roof would provide a drier, cleaner, insect-free environment.

Schools with native teachers trained not to impose alien cultural values but to perfect indigenous ones were another of Wright's objectives. He argued that these schools should teach English as a second but common language to compensate for the language diversity within the island territory. Islanders, in Wright's scheme, would not be taught to want radios or jukeboxes or button shoes. Instruction in elementary tree surgery, for example, would be a useful effort that would help the breadfruit and other food trees of the area to bear more lavishly and to suffer less from disease or neglect. Wright, in short, endeavored to create a school system that would not disrupt islanders' social, aesthetic, or economic standards and that would allow them to be left alone.

Wright's words on education stood in stark contrast to the then-current realities surrounding yet another formidable aspect of the development agenda—namely, education. By mid-1947, the navy had opened 152 elementary schools. Local teachers were hired and paid by the communities in which they taught. Although Wright and other officials professed a commitment to instruction in native Micronesian languages, the navy supplied the schools with only secondhand primers written in English. According to Francis Hezel, the curriculum content of these schools was bluntly, almost exclusively, American: "the geography of the United States, dialogues on snowmen and machine guns, Stephen Foster folk songs, and John Philip Sousa marches."[74] A directive on education dated 12 December 1945 from CINCPOA stated bluntly that the schools were intended "to inculcate respect for and loyalty to the United States by teaching the history, customs and beliefs of the United State and its people."[75]

"Mild benevolence" was the wistful term employed by Wright to characterize his policy toward the area and its people. It was a strategy ostensibly designed to place the tools and techniques of self-help and self-development within the islanders' reach to use as they wished and as they saw fit. This, according to Wright, should be the beginning and end of America's contribution. Such enlightened restraint would save these island folk from the ills visited upon other indigenous peoples in earlier contact with the West. Wright closed his piece by noting that if the dire predictions of global destruction through intercontinental atomic warfare were to come true, the meek of these islands might well come to inherit the earth.

The admiral's commentary placed a benign, even benevolent mask on America's domination of the islands. His paternal concern and prescriptions for Micronesians served ultimately to blunt or obscure the dominant reality that, as the admiral himself admitted elsewhere, the islands were "ours."[76] Indeed, American nuclear testing in the Marshalls, more particularly the detonation of two atomic devices in July 1946 on Bikini Atoll, gave lie to the contention that these "happy, contented people" might survive a global nuclear holocaust to inherit the earth. Even before the publication of Wright's piece, groups of Marshallese had begun to experience the disease, displacement, and disruption of the nuclear age.

A different prescription for America's administration of the islands—

a different kind of denial of the real costs and effects of that imposed administration—found expression in the words of Prof. Benjamin O. Wist, dean of the University of Hawai'i's School of Agriculture. In an address delivered on 2 December 1947 before an advisory committee on education created by Adm. Louis E. Denfield, the first high commissioner for the newly awarded trusteeship, Wist acknowledged that there were those who worried about the effects of Westernization upon non-Western peoples. Wist conceded that the Micronesians might well have been better off and happier if they had been left alone, but the fact was they had not. They already differed materially from their forbearers in their social practices, hopes, and aspirations. Wist went on:

> We cannot, therefore, in his interest or ours leave him to his own devices. . . . We can, on the other hand, demonstrate that we have a genuine faith in American democratic precepts by assisting him to achieve self-government, to develop social institutions and practices in harmony with his needs and desires, and to attain the self-respect which can result only from economic self-dependence. None of these will result from exploitation, paternalism, or restrictive socio-educational opportunities.[77]

Expressed in quite sexist language, West's denial of any exploitative dimension to America's presence in the area aligned itself with the dominant strain of American national ideology in the postwar period. The blood shed on island shores by American combatants during World War II and the assumed primacy of American strategic interests in the area led to the conviction that the islands must remain under American rule. The general development of the islands was seen as a process that would serve American strategic interests and, at the same time, lead to a better quality of life for America's island charges. But as we will see in subsequent chapters, other realities were at work in the crosscultural encounters between Americans and different groups of island people called Micronesian.

The public prescriptions of the admiral and the dean, though different in character, both represented attempts to rationalize and make palatable the exercise of American power in Micronesia. In a sense, their words were at once different and the same. In the efforts at economic development in the period of naval occupation and military government were revealed patterns that would persist over the next four decades. Representations of war emphasized a destruction that was cultural as well as physical in its dimensions and that made plausible the massive social change and redefinition that economic development entailed. Geographical isolation, the logistical dilemmas of administration and supply in so widespread an island area, the lack of resources, and what was termed the general apathy and ineptitude of a "happy, contented" people constituted a litany used to explain the first failures at economic development during the navy's time. Nonetheless, efforts would continue. The replacement of the interim military government with an internationally sanctioned trusteeship would not seriously alter a program of radical social change and transformation that went by the name of "development."

Chapter 3

Strategic Developments

The award of a trusteeship, one of eleven granted by the United Nations in the immediate postwar period, did not drastically alter the nature of naval government in the islands called Micronesia. What it did do was sanction a program of major social transformation that operated under the obfuscation provided by the seemingly benign term "trust territory." "Making them like US" is another way of describing the flawed, considerably less than successful agenda of development imposed during the occupation and postwar years. With its eventual replacement as administering authority by the United States Department of the Interior in July 1951, the navy would leave behind, in the words of its critics, not a trust territory but a "rust territory."[1]

Underneath the veneer of trust that had turned to rust, different groups of island people struggled in their encounters with the concept of development and its larger strategic purposes. This chapter includes an examination of efforts on Angaur in the Palau group to confront the destructive, divisive forces of American dominance that revolved around the mining of phosphate. From the Chuuk Lagoon area emerges a second example of a local encounter with development. There, in the last year of the navy's administration of the Trust Territory, people engaged the Western economic concept of savings. Their culturally informed negotiations, as we will see, added new layers to imposed economic practices, layers whose textures and meanings involved more than the simple accumulation of money and material goods. I turn first, however, to the formal chartering of American colonialism over the islands and to the navy's efforts at government and development under that charter.

The Navy's Trust Territory

The veil of legitimization provided by internationally sanctioned treaties or arrangements often can be used to hide or even help promote the subordination of others. The 1947 Trusteeship Agreement between the United States and the United Nations over the postwar status of the Caroline, Mariana, and Marshall Islands served just this purpose. Conventional critics have often pointed to the failure of the United States to satisfy its obligations under the Trusteeship Agreement, but a closer scrutiny of the document's terms and conditions reveals just how extensive was America's license to control and direct. The Trusteeship Agreement granted to the United States

> full powers of administration, legislation, and jurisdiction over the territory subject to the provisions of this agreement and gave it the authority to apply to the trust territory, subject to any modifications which the administering authority may consider desirable, such of the laws of the United States as it may deem appropriate to local conditions and requirements.[2]

The dimensions of America's dominance showed themselves clearly under Article VI, which "committed" the United States to fostering the political, economic, social, and education advancement of the islands. Indeed, the United States government received license not only to foster but to define the very nature of development in categories or areas of activity that encompassed, under a Western scheme of being at least, every major aspect of life and living. Further indicative of American control over the territory was Article XV of the Trusteeship Agreement, which stipulated that no alteration, amendment, or termination of stipulated sections could be effected without the consent of the administering authority. Article XII allowed the United States to withhold from the United Nations information on any matters directly relating to American security interests. At the insistence of representatives from the Soviet Union during the UN Trusteeship Council's review of the agreement, a telling reference to the Trust Territory of the Pacific Islands as "an integral part of the United States" was deleted.[3]

In its governance of the territory, the United States secured the right to incorporate the islands into customs, fiscal, and administrative unions or federations with other territories and to enter into membership with various regional bodies, organizations, and institutions in the satisfaction of its obligations under the Trusteeship Agreement. To ensure that the Trust Territory, in accordance with the charter of the United Nations, played its part in the maintenance of international peace and security, the United States was entitled to establish military bases and to construct fortifications. The stationing and deployment of armed forces was permitted as was the construction of facilities to promote international peace and to maintain law and order in the territory.

With the commencement of the trusteeship on July 1947, the identification of specific administrative policies became the navy's first major task. Some months later, on 15 January 1948, the navy issued the basic policy objectives for its administration of the islands, objectives said to be in total accord with its responsibilities to the United Nations. The document evidenced the qualified commitment to self-government that opponents of naval rule had feared. Micronesians, it was written, were to be guided toward "the highest degree of self-government which they were capable of assimilating"; playing on shades of meaning and semantic distinctions within a distinctly self-serving colonial vocabulary, Adm. Leon S. Fiske, the deputy high commissioner for the Trust Territory who replaced Rear Admiral Wright, later added that "we advocate self-government, not necessarily democracy."[4] From his office at Pearl Harbor some 2,000 miles distant from the Trust Territory's easternmost border, Fiske declared that the American pattern of self-government could not be forced upon people as varied in cultural institutions as the Micronesians. The hereditary class structure of rule by chiefs provided the best foundations for a more appropriate pattern of native government. Indirect rule, then, was to be the way the navy administered the Trust Territory.

As defined in the *Handbook of the Trust Territory* put out by the navy for 1948, indirect rule meant the use of existing indigenous structures of government; such a strategy, in the minds of its employers, allowed for a minimum of intervention and also reduced the likelihood of manipulation by local competing groups, factions, or individuals. Indirect rule, it was argued, helped overcome the foreign and arbitrary features of imposed colonial administration while permitting the involvement of native peoples in the actual process of government. To guard against the abuse of power by local chiefly leaders, the navy at the same time committed itself to training younger persons of ability, regardless of rank.

As it had since its earliest occupation of the islands, the United States Navy continued to stress economic development as mandatory preface to advancement in any and all other fields of social activity. Adm. Arthur W. Radford, who by virtue of his position as commander in chief of the navy's Pacific Forces also served as the Trust Territory's high commissioner, had made this relationship explicit in a letter to the chief of naval operations in Washington, D.C. Radford conceded that the granting of the trusteeship "did not represent the will of the indigenous people." He went on to note, however, that the peoples' sovereignty was being withheld from them temporarily

> that they might be educated, induced, and assisted to cope better with the impact of Western civilization. . . . Certain policies and details of their advancement, determined by the Western World as desirable are imposed upon them, notably in the several fields: organization of municipalities, requirements for safety and health, taxation, and elementary education. The Administering Authority has a grave responsibility that the steps taken are well adapted to the state of acculturation of the inhabitants and their environment and, if possible, tactfully imposed in order that the maximum progress can be effected without deleterious consequences.[5]

For Radford, economic development constituted a necessary prerequisite for the return of sovereignty to the people of Micronesia. Economic development, believed the admiral-cum-high commissioner, had to be regulated carefully to create a sufficient number and variety of enterprises, to exploit fully the natural resources of the area and abilities of the people, to improve the general standard of living, and to attain the maximum degree of self-sufficiency. Thus were the paternal and self-serving strategic politics of economic development articulated.

The Island Trading Company

Things had not gone as planned for the United States Commercial Company during the period of the interim military government. The costs of operating in the islands, compounded by the serious differences that had developed with navy officials over the future direction of development in the islands, led to the company's decision to terminate its operations in Micronesia, effective 31 December 1947. After some consideration, the navy created the Island Trading Company (ITC) as a replacement for the USCC.[6] Its main office on Guam, the ITC opened branch operations on Kwajalein, Majuro, Pohnpei, Yap, Weno, and Koror.

Trade stood as the first priority and most successful area of operation for the Island Trading Company. Staples such as rice, flour, canned milk, cigarettes, sugar, salt, biscuits, canned meat and fish, matches, and cooking utensils stocked the shelves of the island stores. Despite the problems of procurement and distribution for such a large area as the Trust

Territory, the ITC did well by its own measure. As a result of its careful efforts and accounting practices, the ITC, on 30 June 1951, reported assets of $2,998,930.21 against liabilities of $2,149,240.77, of which $1,801,713.58 represented the amount technically owed the navy for its shipping and other subsidies.[7]

Other areas of the ITC's effort to help develop the islands economically proved much less successful than its trade store operations.[8] The whims of the world market defeated the development of the copra industry in the Trust Territory. A variety of small-scale development projects that included a duck farm and bee project on Majuro, a marine railway on Chuuk, an experimental coir fiber farm on Pohnpei, a coffee project on Saipan, a cacao plantation in Palau, and several small boat-building projects dispersed throughout the islands all foundered against a series of environmental, logistical, and cultural impediments.[9]

Efforts to exploit fish stocks and other marine resources such as trochus shell suffered from fluctuations in world prices and the logistical difficulties of doing business amidst the vast watery expanse that was Micronesia. The considerable investment in scientific studies and training programs apparently could not convince islanders to fish for commercial profit instead of subsistence. In her assessment of the failure of marine resource development, Richard concluded that the waters around Micronesia had little value for Micronesians except as a source of subsistence food and as a pleasant place to sail: "The greatest number of sea creatures in the world might inhabit those waters but they were safe from molestation by the natives."[10]

The Colonial Culture of Agriculture

While the ITC engaged in commercial trade and small-scale development projects, the naval administration concerned itself with what it held to be more potentially significant areas of economic advancement. Operating on the assumption that a formal system of agriculture constituted a precondition for the growth of modern economies and oblivious to the constraints of the physical and cultural environments about them, naval personnel embarked upon a program of agricultural development in the islands. In its efforts, the naval government solicited the assistance of the United States Department of Agriculture (USDA). The Department of Agriculture responded with an elaborate proposal that included the establishment of an agricultural vocational school, the construction of a main experimental institute with branch stations on the major islands, and a program of agricultural extension courses throughout the Trust Territory, all at a cost of approximately $500,000 a year and under the supervision of the Department of Agriculture itself.[11]

Then Deputy High Commissioner Carleton Wright opposed the USDA's plan because it involved too little participation by the peoples of Micronesia. Instead, the deputy high commissioner requested Dr. Harold A. Wadsworth, dean of the College of Agriculture of the University of Hawai'i, to suggest an alternative plan for the general improvement of the agricultural situation in the Trust Territory. Wadsworth, in his report dated 8 September 1949, recommended basic scientific studies in insect and disease problems, investigations into the agricultural economics of the Trust Territory, preparation of basic data leading to more effective land use policies, improvement in subsistence food production, appropriate agricultural courses in the schools and the communities, and revitalization of the old Japanese agricultural demonstration station on Pohnpei.[12]

The Wadsworth Report's call for further study had the feel of precedent about it: much of the history of economic development in the Trust Territory would involve the production of studies and reports that called for further studies and reports. Nonetheless, the Wadsworth Report became the basis for an agricultural policy during the navy's administration of the Trust Territory. It made little difference, however. Dorothy Richard remarked with an insight tinged by pessimism that all of the agriculturists, quarantine experts, and entomologists could not succeed in making agriculture a source of income for Micronesians. The seeming absurdity that at times could characterize the navy's economic program can be glimpsed in the plans for the commercial exploitation of the islands' few small forest lands. With funding from the Hawaii-based Pacific Science Board, Mr. Colin Marshall, conservator of forests in Fiji, conducted a survey of forest land in the Trust Territory during July 1950. From his survey, Marshall concluded that the islands "have no forests which in the immediate future can be developed to provide lumber either for export as a cash crop or for local use."[13] This fact, however, did not stop the eventual establishment of a Department of Forestry for the Trust Territory.

The Colonizing Politics of Conservation

During its tenure in the islands, the United States Commercial Company had conducted an extensive economic survey of the islands for the interim military government. Based on this survey, the USCC had put forth a comprehensive development plan for the islands. This plan, considered in the following chapter, went largely ignored and proved to be a major part of the friction between the company and the military government. Dissuaded by the sweeping dimensions of the plan and by its own failed efforts at agricultural development, the navy eventually opted to pursue a far more modest program that involved the continuation of local development projects and the inculcation of basic market economy concepts through the ITC's trade store program. This relatively cautious, now go-slow approach to economic development was mirrored in the navy's attention to the conservation of the natural and human environments within Micronesia. It was a conservation program that reflected the deeper strategic concerns that infused the navy's view of development in the Trust Territory.

The naval administration sought to preserve the limited natural resources of the area by rigid conservation laws and interim regulations.[14] The indiscriminate exploitation of natural resources and profiteering by foreign-owned businesses were expressly prohibited. To prevent the further alienation of land, the navy reaffirmed its policy to refuse commercial licenses to foreign individuals, companies, and associations whose activities were deemed abusive of local populations and the natural environment.[15] Other conservation regulations concerned measures designed to control the outbreak of fires and eradicate such environmentally harmful pests as the rhinoceros beetle, the Giant African snail, and the banana root borer. The specific means employed to implement this early environmental conservation program, as well as its operating assumptions, had a heavy colonial tinge to them as these imposed regulations, restrictions, and general practices reflected very alien assumptions about the environment and human beings' relationships with it.

A program of human or social conservation, called by its critics the "zoo theory," complemented the navy's efforts at ecological protection, or rather applied the concept of conservation to the human as well as natural environment. Concerned in the larger postwar world with the containment of world communism, the navy in Micronesia practiced a different form of containment that served equally well its global strategic concerns. In October 1947 Deputy High Commissioner Carleton H. Wright, reiterating sentiments expressed in his *Saturday Evening Post* article, proclaimed the navy's intention to avoid upsetting the "natural and, I might add, superbly happy existence of these natives by endeavoring to introduce into their lives an overdose of what you and I are pleased to call 'civilization.'" Wright went on to affirm the American belief in helping the islanders to help themselves, but without unduly interfering in their "simple, happy life." To Wright's mind, the rights of individuals were being protected, the economic independence of the residents was being established, and a government by and for island peoples was being created. Speaking directly to the criticisms of navy government in the islands made by academics, Wright concluded that a visit to the islands would confirm in anyone's mind that "these contented islanders . . . are being bound to us by ties of mutual cooperation as well as friendship."[16]

Attempts to transform islanders into skilled, reliable workers also continued during the Trust Territory period. The navy issued its general policy for labor practices in the Trust Territory on 22 March 1949. Consistent with the United Nations Charter and the Trusteeship Agreement, these guidelines stipulated equal opportunity for all comparably qualified individuals, equal pay for men and women engaged in the same or equivalent work, and advancement in pay and rank based on demonstrated proficiency, length of service, and the successful completion of on-the-job training programs designed to enhance job skills. Classifications for workers applicable throughout the Trust Territory were established in March 1949; these classifications ranged from apprentices through categories of unskilled, semiskilled, and skilled workers to specialists, administrators, and professional staff.[17]

Government employees proved the largest but not necessarily the most secure group of workers in the Trust Territory government. Government employment had dropped from 2,300 in 1948 to 1,517 by June 1951. Throughout the navy's administration of the Trust Territory, the overwhelming number of government employees were male. On the eve of the navy's departure, Saipan had the largest number of female employees with 43 and also the highest percentage of females in the work force with 17 percent. The Marshalls, for the same period, reported 5 female workers out of a government labor force of 205.[18] Prejudices on all sides of the cultural divide worked to limit the number of indigenous women employed by the government. While most Micronesian societies viewed work in offices, stores, or foreign households as antithetical to the role and responsibilities of women, the United States Navy's seemingly more liberal attitude masked the deeper patriarchal bias of the society from which it had come. Women were offered a place in the workforce but in lesser, often demeaning jobs and at considerably lower pay than what men earned.

Wages continued much as they had during the navy's interim government, privileging administrative and skilled labor over other workers and revealing the regional, sexist, and strategic prejudices of the navy presence.[19] Modest increases during the navy's administration of the Trust Territory did not disturb the prejudices of the wage scale. Workers employed away from their home islands were provided medical care and recreation facilities at no cost, and housing and meals at cost. Such provisions did not preclude problems and misunderstandings, however. As a result of recruitment by the navy, Palauan women journeyed to Guam to accept work as domestics in the households of naval personnel. While on Guam, many of them became pregnant and were thus forced to return to the care of their families in Palau. Before leaving, however, they requested from the navy severance pay and money to cover the cost of their return travel to Palau. The navy apparently regarded their pregnancies as seditious. In a perverse defense of culture, officials identified the women as members of a larger dissatisfied group bent upon the deliberate violation of traditional Palauan customs. Consequently, the civil administrator's office in Palau directed that henceforth no woman was to travel to Guam unless accompanied by her husband.[20] The navy could also manipulate as well as indict Micronesian societies and their social practices. No system of social security was created for island workers because "in their society none was necessary."[21]

In her section on labor relations during the navy's administration of the Trust Territory, Dorothy Richard wrote that there were no trade unions in the Trust Territory because there were no labor problems. In fact, the Trust Territory did have a fundamental labor problem, and it involved the very nature and meaning of work. Other words written by Richard revealed the chasm that separated naval expectations from local definitions of work. Reiterating her assessment of Micronesian labor at the close of the interim military government period in mid-1947, Richard concluded that the naval administration found it a struggle to persuade island laborers to observe regular working hours and stay on their jobs over an extended period: "The Micronesians were accustomed to work where and if they desired and a five day week and an eight hour day of specific hours was beyond their ability to understand and appreciate. It was a problem the Navy never resolved."[22]

Very Telling Stories

"Blaming the victim," a practice often employed in Richard's three-volume history of the navy in Micronesia, is certainly nothing new to the histories of colonialism in the region. As had previous colonizers, naval officials often indicted island people for the perceived ignorance, indifference, and primitive logic with which they approached the modern world. The navy's exasperation sometimes showed itself in the form of humorous stories that sought to call attention to the seemingly odd, hilarious ways in which Micronesians confronted the novel and the strange.[23] These funny stories, however, did little to mask the dynamics of a larger exploitative process that was not funny at all. In effect, these colonizing tales mocked island people for their assumed inabilities to cope with, adjust to, or understand the most rudimentary of market practices. In so doing, these stories conveyed a not-so-subtle and continuing justification for American colonialism in Micronesia.

Richard's history of the naval administration relates stories that credit Micronesians with no sense whatsoever of the economic forces that effect supply, demand, and price. Moreover, this assumed basic ignorance is compounded in these stories by the allegedly bizarre, irrational preferences that Micronesians exhibited toward Western goods. Yap provided the setting for a number of these tales. There, the people were described as having a peculiar desire for red and blue cloth, which they unfortunately used to further enhance the distinctions in their primitive caste system. Another story recounts the enthusiastic response of Yapese women to the sale of navy T-shirts; they were said to have bought them eagerly, then worn them with delight after cutting two holes in front to make themselves more comfortable.[24] A third tale speaks of two Yapese schoolteachers from Gagil who were compensated for their work in a local village school with stone money. The two, "dolled up to a fare-thee-well, with bright new purple and white banana gee-strings, hibiscus blossoms in their hair and ears," tried unsuccessfully to use the stone money to purchase trade goods at the ITC store on Yap. The story went on to narrate how "when the storekeeper remonstrated through his translator, the customers first became dissatisfied and then irate. They pulled up the stone disk, slammed it back on the counter . . . waved their arms, slapped their bronzed, coconut-oiled chests and filled the air with shouts and betel juice."[25] They calmed down and left the premises after learning that traditional Yapese stone money was not acceptable currency for trade store purchases. Similarly, a narrative from Palau speaks of a local chief whose expectations of trade were markedly different from modern economic understandings: the chief is said to have berated the ITC store manager in Palau for failing to supply a husband for his daughter.[26]

What Nicholas Thomas has called the idea of "savage commerce" clearly evidences itself in these navy stories.[27] The desire for Western goods, especially cigarettes, is depicted as obsessive. The proverbial "walk a mile for a camel" was nothing compared to the distances Micronesians were said to travel by outrigger canoe to procure cigarettes when the supply at their local trade stores became exhausted. A story from the Mortlocks underscores the point.[28] Desperate for a smoke and with no cigarettes available on their home atoll of Etal, seven men set out in a canoe for the Chuuk Lagoon area to procure cigarettes. During their journey, the group was blown off course by a storm. They drifted for sixty days and across seven hundred miles of ocean. Of the seven, only two survived to reach the island of Sorol, where their craft was blown ashore. The moral of the story for those who told it concerned the potential for tragedy that lurked beneath the desires of mindless savages.

Stories could underscore too the problems that Micronesians supposedly had in comprehending the most basic of modern concepts and practices. Dr. Nathaniel R. Kidder, an anthropologist with the Coordinated Investigation of Micronesian Anthropology (CIMA) project that operated in the Trust Territory during the navy's administration, recounted in a speech before the American Sociological Society on 28 December 1949 how a Yapese chief described himself in a census interview as being forty-four years old.[29] The statement did not coincide with other information about the individual in question. When pressed, the chief showed Kidder an identification card given him by an officer of the occupation forces some four years earlier in 1944. On that card, he was listed as forty-four years of age; it was the chief's understanding, according to Kidder, that his age would be forty-four for the rest of his life.

Naval administrators and ITC personnel looked with bemusement on the way island peoples paged carefully and with amazement through mail-order catalogues. Their amusement turned to nervous trepidation, however, when Micronesians actually began to order items from the catalogues of the Sears Roebuck, Spiegel, and Montgomery Ward companies. When fears arose that catalogue sales might seriously undermine the position of the ITC trading stores in the islands and the economic lessons and values they sought to inculcate among the people,[30] there were calls for the government to intervene in behalf of the ITC and market education. In a peculiar, revealing twist of colonial logic that underscored at once the self-defining and sometimes contradictory posture of American colonialism, the Trust Territory administration decided that restrictions on consumer preferences were undemocratic. Such restrictions, noted Deputy High Commissioner Wright in a letter dated 2 April 1948, would result in widespread popular dissatisfaction. Wright, therefore, directed that the "final decision as to how an individual shall spend his money shall be left to him and not to another person."[31]

With the government refusing to interfere with consumer preferences, catalogue sales grew dramatically in the Trust Territory; the companies did more than $300,000 worth of business in 1948. In Palau, the value of catalogue orders averaged $7,000 a month. The infusion of new and different kinds of material goods was not the only consequence of the mail-order business. One education official in Palau conceded that being able to order by catalogue provided a strong incentive for the learning of mathematics; eighth-grade pupils at the Koror Intermediate School in Palau became proficient in preparing money orders for their families, clans, and villages. More distressing to American administrators was the "aesthetic" value of otherwise unusable or impractical items ordered by catalogue. One Marshallese bought an expensive record player, which for lack of electricity in his home he could never hear; the mere sight of his acquisition, however, was said to give him untold satisfaction. Another islander ordered a leather traveling bag. Rather than use it when traveling, he suspended it from the rafters of his thatched hut, content simply to stare at it for long stretches of time each day.[32]

It is difficult to know the basis in fact, if any, for these stories and the deeper, more culturally rooted values affecting what naval personnel chose to dismiss as instances of silly, primitive consumerism. The value of these stories, I think, lies in how they reflected or even fed the prejudices of government administrators. Indeed, so powerful was the general indictment of Micronesian abilities as evidenced in these stories that naval officials assumed more direct or overt instances of protest to be the like product of primitive phantasy and ignorance. In Yap, there was outright resistance to the imposition of taxes designed to provide revenue for recently established municipal governments.[33] The taxes were to come due on 1 July 1947. According to the civil administrator's report, the people of Yap could see no reason for such taxes. The principal opposition to the tax came from the chiefs, who questioned the right of the United States to impose upon their people what they understood to be tribute obligations. In his response to the report, Deputy High Commissioner Wright noted that it was completely unrealistic to think that the United States would leave the chiefs of Yap completely alone as they wished. Moreover, according to Wright, there were convincing indications that the people of Yap genuinely appreciated and benefited from the programs of the administration. Wright thought it unfair to the American taxpayer to be burdened with the entire costs of administrative and social services in Yap. A different social and economic system on Yap could not be used to justify that island group's unwillingness to help defray the costs of government there. Becoming citizens in the modern world required that a people pay at least part of their way. Missing from the admiral's calculations, of course, were more distinctly Yapese concerns about power, authority, and the relationship between chiefs and people.[34]

Countering Development: The Case of Angaur

To this point, I have written largely of colonial prescriptions for economic development as a discursive strategy designed to promote the transformation or remaking of a people under that alien, indiscriminate, and totalizing term, "Micronesia." Other stories can be told about the first years of American administration, stories that begin to suggest the ways in which different peoples within the region encountered and responded to the forces that sought to control and remake them. The navy accounts speak sparsely, often pejoratively, of the peoples the navy sought to change through the developing of them. The most modest of crosscultural studies would suggest that the negotiations between indigenous systems of exchange and capitalist notions of trade and economy are layered, complex, fraught with misunderstandings and problems, but also offer possibilities for indigenous peoples. I am not able to write a history that could begin to do justice to the diversity of responses that marked islands' encounters with the proposition called "economic development." Accounts drawn from local, ethnographic, and historical texts, however, suggest something of the encounter with the forces of development from the other side of the beach. The histories that I represent here concern the long, troubled history of phosphate mining on Angaur in the Palau group of the Western Carolines, and the somewhat more playful engagement between the people of the Chuuk Lagoon area and capitalist practices involving savings and cooperatives.

Before the American nuclear testing that began on Bikini in 1946, no island in the Caroline or Marshall groups had suffered a deeper, more prolonged colonial disturbance than Angaur. As in the Marshalls, however, development proved not a discourse of false promises but a belated, inadequate package of compensation designed to mollify a people for the wounds caused to their land and society. Begun in February 1909, the mining of phosphate and the environmental havoc it wreaked had quickly turned Angaur into the "hottest place in the Pacific."[35] The construction of a railroad, drying plant, sawmill, loading dock, warehouses, thirty-two European residences, and eleven workers' dormitories further blighted a landscape already ravaged by the open-pit technique used to extract phosphate. German overseers and mechanics drank excessively, fought

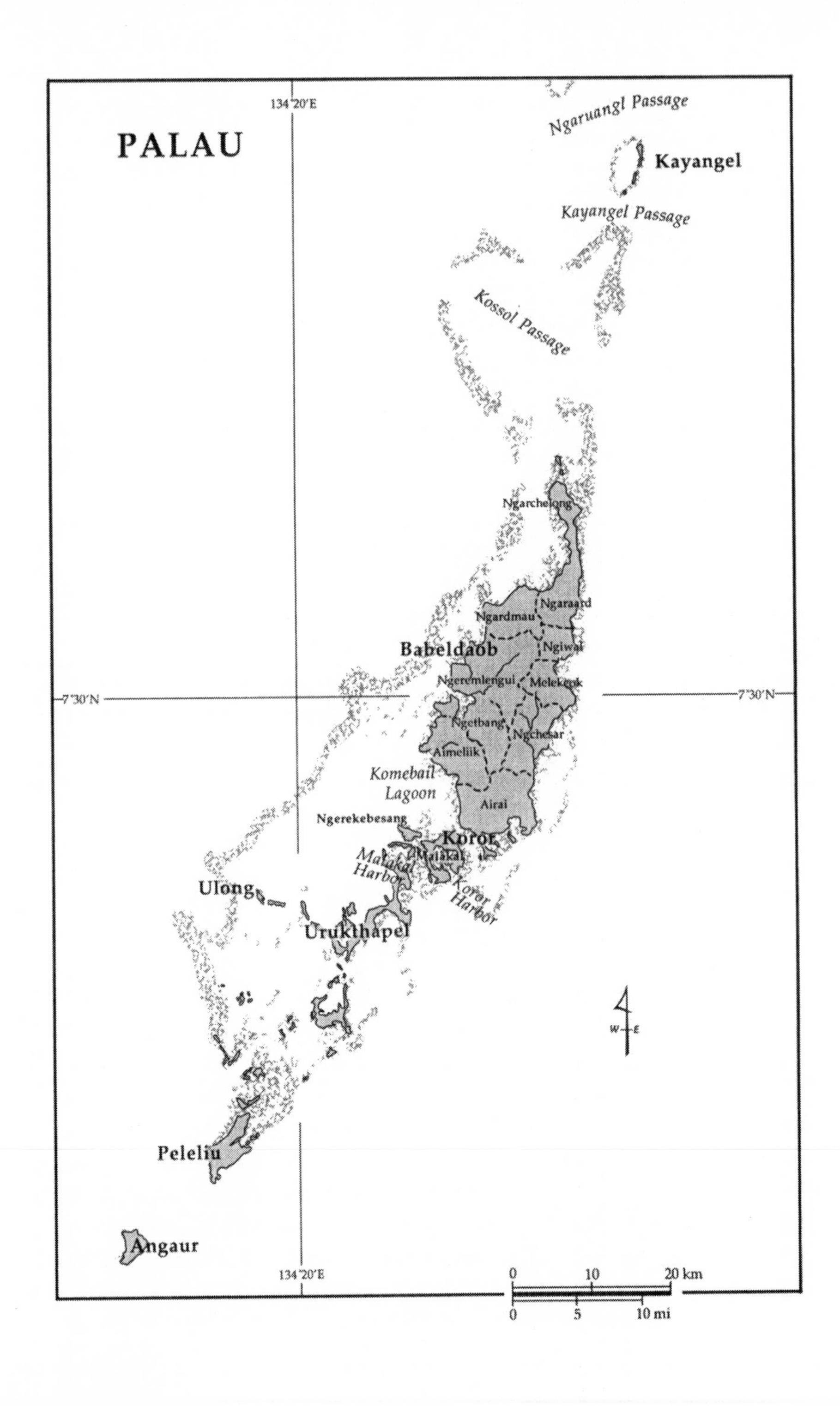
PALAU
134°20'E
Ngaruangl Passage
Kayangel
Kayangel Passage
Kossol Passage
Ngarchelong
Ngaraard
Ngardmau
Babeldaob
Ngiwal
Ngeremlengui
Melekeok
7°30'N
7°30'N
Ngetbang
Ngchesar
Aimeliik
Komebail
Lagoon
Airai
Ngerekebesang
Koror
Malakal
Malakal
Harbor
Koror
Harbor
Ulong
Urukthapel
W
E
Peleliu
Angaur
134°20'E
0
10
20 km
0
5
10 mi

each other, and openly defied their company supervisors. The abuse of Carolinian and Chinese laborers brought to mine the island's phosphate included low wages, frequent payment in the form of near worthless coupons rather than currency, forced purchases with these devalued coupons of overpriced goods in the mining company's store, physical punishment, poor housing, and extended working hours. By 1911, the situation had deteriorated so badly that German colonial officials elsewhere in the Carolines were refusing to assist in the recruitment of islander labor for Angaur.[36]

American naval officials had little interest in this or any history of the islands. For them, World War II created a zero point from which history was to begin. The memory of the past on Angaur, however, was not so shallow or selective. According to a history of phosphate mining recorded in 1941 by Ucherbalau, the paramount chief of Angaur, representatives of the Deutsche Südsee-Phosphat-Aktien-Gesellschaft (DSPAG), a consortium of German banks and other firms, reached the island in 1907 and immediately refused to negotiate with the ranking chief of the island "because she was a woman."[37] The Germans chose, instead, to negotiate with five clan heads whom they took to Koror; there, the group was offered 500 marks and several pieces of traditional shell money for the rights to all phosphate on the island. When the five declined the offer saying they possessed no authority to make such a deal, the Germans forced them at gun point to sign the agreement and accept the money. An investigation in response to a complaint to German colonial representatives in the Western Carolines by the island female chief resulted in an investigation that led to payment of an additional 700 marks, but with no provisions for any royalties and with no requirement that a proper agreement be negotiated with the people of Angaur for the mining of their phosphate. According to Ucherbalau's history, the Germans then deposed the chief, exiled her to Yap, installed her son, and partitioned the island into thirds for purposes of phosphate mining.

Written accounts such as those provided by historian Mark Peattie tend to sustain and complement Ucherbalau's history of the continuation of phosphate mining during Japanese colonial times.[38] Japan seized Angaur and the rest of Micronesia from Germany in 1914; a settlement eventually agreed to in 1922 gave Germany the equivalent of $1,739,960 for all land and mining rights on Angaur.[39] With the coming of the Japanese, the South Seas Construction Company or Nan'yō Keiei Kumiai proved no less exploitative or abusive than the DSPAG. In October 1915, the Japanese naval government, responding to widespread and persistent complaints about Nan'yō Keiei Kumiai, canceled the company's license and assumed responsibility for the mining of phosphate on the island.[40] In Ucherbalau's history, the request of the people of Angaur for royalties and for formal recognition of their ownership of the island received a threatening rebuttal. A Japanese official identified as Lieutenant Ogino replied, "We have conquered the land from the Germans, therefore it belongs to the Japanese. And if you are going to keep bothering us or making trouble we will shoot you all or put you in jail."[41]

Japan's later civilian colonial government assumed supervision of all phosphate mining on Angaur in 1927 and relied upon labor from the Marianas, Palau, Chuuk, and Yap. These island laborers were recruited by village chiefs or headmen who received a small bonus or fee as compensation for the loss of manpower from traditional activities. Most of these laborers, it seems, were drafted against their will for a year of "totally exhausting work."[42] In 1936, the South Seas government transferred mining rights on Angaur to the South Seas Colonization Company, Nan'yō Takushoku Kaisha or Nantaku as it was more commonly known. The company's intensified mining of the island forced the higher-ranking clans living in the phosphate-rich northern areas to migrate south, where they established themselves on agricultural lands belonging to the southern clans. This displacement of northern peoples from their phosphate-rich lands into the territory of the southern clans led to friction, jealousy, and hostility between the two groups that lingered long after the departure of the Japanese.[43]

With the outbreak of war, Angaur's phosphate became important not only as fertilizer but as an additive to explosives. The intensified need for Angaur's phosphate led to the forced transfer of the island's population to Babeldaob, where wartime conditions and the hostility of local communities toward the people of Angaur made for considerable suffering and hardship. The Germans had mined more than 156,000 metric tons of phosphate during their tenure.[44] U.S. naval estimates of the total tonnage of phosphate mined by the Japanese on Angaur amounted to just under 3 million metric tons.[45] By the end of hostilities, thirty-six years of phosphate mining had left more than half of Angaur's total area of 3.14 square miles unusable for any human purposes or activities.

Immediately following the war, the people were allowed to return to their home island and replant their gardens. They hoped that the end of hostilities would allow them to reassert traditional title and organization over their island as well as end any further encroachment on their already damaged, sorely pressed taro lands.[46] Circumstances elsewhere would conspire against these hopes. A particularly disastrous crop year for occupied Japan in 1945 led the supreme commander of the allied powers (SCAP) there to request permission to import 340,00 metric tons of phosphate.[47] An investigator sent earlier to Angaur by SCAP had reported nearly 250,000 metric tons of phosphate stockpiled and available for ready shipment; the investigator further estimated the amount of unmined phosphate reserves on Angaur to be 1,000,000 metric tons. After some internal bickering and negotiating between the Navy and War Departments, a contract was awarded to J. H. Pomeroy Company, a private contractor, for the shipment to Japan of all existing stockpiles of phosphate on Angaur.

Work began in June 1946, with a labor force that consisted of 150 American military personnel, 170 Japanese contract laborers allowed back into Micronesia under special permission from the military government, and 35 men from Angaur itself. Hostilities developed among the people of Angaur over the recruitment of local labor. A former American soldier who had married and settled on the island shortly before the resumption of phosphate mining was approached by Pomeroy Company's labor relations manager to assist in the recruitment of local workers. The ex-soldier's preference for members of his wife's clan brought charges of favoritism from other Angaurese. One of the more vocal protesters was an individual of chiefly standing who had himself been involved in the local labor recruiting and who saw his authority and status being undermined by the involvement of the ex-soldier. When the chief made reference to what company officials understood to be the threat of a strike, he was told that troublemakers of the "John L. Lewis" type would not be tolerated.[48]

Unfavorable weather conditions and equipment problems delayed the final shipment of phosphate reserves until 30 June 1947. Royalties accruing from a severance fee of $0.25 per dry ton of phosphate shipped were paid to the commander of the Marianas area who, in turn, placed them in a trust fund for the people of Angaur.[49] The distribution of these trust fund revenues, modest though they were, was complicated by the fact that different clans had varying claims to the money. Of the eighteen clans resident on Angaur at the end of the war, eight clans, representing a total of thirty-three households and 168 people, controlled land in the areas from which the stockpiles of phosphate had come; of these eight, four clans had particularly extensive claims. Ten clans, representing a total of thirty-seven households and approximately 189 people, did not have any claims to land in the areas from which the stockpiled phosphate had been mined.

Far more devastating for the people of Angaur than the shipment of wartime stockpiles was the decision by the United States Department of War to renew full mining operations on the island and to extend the mining to remaining valuable agricultural lands in the north then being used for taro planting. The American decision to renew phosphate mining on Angaur had to do with its occupation of Japan, where, not unlike Micronesia, an alien land and its people were being remade into allies by a conscious process of rehabilitation and development. Phosphate as fertilizer was needed in Japan to ensure an adequate harvest which, in turn, bore directly on the stability of the nation and the compliance of its people with the American occupation. Not impressed by the strategic importance of Angaur's phosphate, Ucherbalau wrote of the situation, "We, the Angaur people, are disturbed about these things, and our heart weeps to think of them. We are most disturbed over the problem of what will become of our people when this little island that belongs to us has all been mined."[50]

The long, sad history of phosphate mining on Angaur disturbed even some Americans. Lt. H. E. Wohl, an assistant economics officer with the military government, wrote that the Angaurese were very much aware of the value of their phosphate deposits; however, they had not been consulted on this or any previous agreements.[51] Complicating the situation was the crucial importance of land to the people of Angaur. Land provided not only sustenance but social rank and political power. Francis B. Mahoney, the district anthropologist who served in Palau during the navy's administration of the Trust Territory, noted that land and social status were so inextricably interwoven "that it is impossible (and purely academic) to try to determine whether the high-ranking family lines have their present social position because they have more or choicer lands, particularly taro paddies, or whether they acquired those ownership rights because of their high status."[52] Taro patches, in particular, were extremely important; these prized pieces of land belonged to the different clans and were distributed among the different members of the lineage by the male and female lineage heads. Although the right to farm or use a particular taro patch was passed on to heirs in the matrilineal line, the title itself remained with the lineage as a whole. Each taro paddy had a name and a history. Land was so prized as to be almost inalienable for a particular clan, although in very special cases the ownership of a taro patch could be transferred to surviving male children as compensation for the untimely or unexpected death of a parent.

Amidst strong local objections, full-scale mining resumed on Angaur on 1 July 1947. From his office on Guam, Rear Adm. and Deputy High Commissioner Carleton Wright notified navy command of the opposition on Angaur. Wright added that, in his opinion, the mining was detrimental to the economy of Angaur because it was leading to the rapid depletion of a valuable resource, undermining the subsistence economy through the destruction of arable land, and endangering the hydrologic balance of the island. Wright also believed that the Trust Territory government lost valuable revenues by the terms of the contract with Pomeroy and that the territory as a whole suffered from the export of fertilizer badly needed for local agriculture. Wright recommended that the agreement to resume mining on the island be canceled and that Japanese laborers be repatriated at once. The deputy high commissioner further urged that any future mining be carried out only under conditions satisfactory to the people of Angaur, and with just compensation for the sale of their resource and the damages its mining caused to their lands.[53] The chief of naval operations, through then high commissioner, Adm. Louis E. Denfield, responded to Wright's recommendations by halting the mining in the northern agricultural lands and calling for a conference of all concerned parties to discuss the situation.

The conference to address the crisis on Angaur convened on Guam in October 1949; it would prove to be one of several. At this first October conference, the conferees as a group agreed to an immediate increase in the severance fee to $0.60 per dry ton and to a hydrological survey of Angaur by the Pacific Science Board.[54] The decision did not appease the eighteen chiefly representatives from Angaur, who wanted all mining on their island ceased. At a second meeting on Guam the following month, the Angaurese did agree to reconsider their opposition if the hydrological survey showed that the land and the groundwater would not be permanently destroyed by the continued mining of phosphate.

Despite the fervor and skill with which Angaur's representatives approached the negotiations, a number of American officials expressed openly the belief that the people of the island had adjusted too comfortably to a moneyed economy to return to life on the land. They noted that income earned by the people of Angaur from the sale of vegetables, fruits, and fresh and salted fish to miners and company personnel amounted to $10,339.96 for the period from 1 July 1946 to 30 September 1949. Total benefits from the mining presence were placed at $140,000 since 1946 and included medical and dental services, the construction of a water supply system, the provision of electricity for the local church and police station, and the maintenance of roads. American representatives to the conference seemed to believe that if decades of extensive contact with the larger world had not yet transformed the Angaurese into modern economic people, the tangible benefits of industrial mining now being provided them soon would secure their acquiescence.[55] They thought, did American officials, that it was simply a matter of money.

In a sense, it was about money, but money as the Angaurese understood it. To the people of Angaur and larger Palau, traditional shell money was a source and symbol of good. The anthropologist Mahoney wrote,

> To a degree even greater than in the more familiar doctrine of material self-interest that "money makes all things possible," money for Palauans is a "restorer of peace," a justification for clan solidarity, a source of personal honor. To acquire it is therefore considered not merely sensible but actually the foremost service an individual owes his family and the larger kin group.[56]

Mahoney went on to note that these localized or indigenous attitudes had been partially extended to currency of any kind, including the American dollar. To the Angaurese, then, money was not about individual gain or reward but about identity, social relationships, and the very cohesiveness of society itself.[57] The pursuit of compensation and redress by the people of Angaur centered on the acquisition of money to be used to restore solidarity, peace, and honor on Angaur.

Such ethnographic distinctions did nothing to blunt the cynical calculations of some of the American representatives to the conferences on Guam. Nonetheless, Angaur's representatives remained firm in their determination to seek redress for the damage done their island and their society. During the second of the conferences, the Angaurese insisted that the income from the trust fund was nowhere near adequate or just, and that, unless proven otherwise, the threat to their land and water appeared too great to justify further risk. Tulop, the magistrate for Angaur and senior member of the Ngerbuuch clan, proclaimed publicly toward the end of the conference, "If the people have no money but can grow and make everything they need, they have a good condition to live on their island. That latter is the best living I can think of."[58]

The Angaurese position found support from American officials such as Mr. Ernest G. Holt, staff conservationist for the Trust Territory, who conceded that if he were Angaurese and wanted to continue occupying his land indefinitely, he would oppose the continued mining of the island.[59]

Time, it seems, was also an issue at the gatherings. At a later conference on Angaur in October 1951, Mr. Donald Heron, the Trust Territory director of internal affairs, acknowledged that "Americans always like to do things fast."[60] Exploited for nearly half a century, the Angaurese, it seemed to him, saw no need to be bullied hurriedly into signing a death warrant for their island and themselves. Forced to submit abjectly to the dictates of past colonizers, the people of Angaur now seemed to be evidencing an uncanny, patient ability to manipulate through negotiations the liberal ethos of their newest colonial overlord.

Mining on the island, excluding the northern agricultural lands designated as "Area C" on the working maps used by negotiators, continued while the hydrological survey agreed to at the first October conference was carried out.[61] The hydrological survey, conducted during the second week of December 1949, indicated extensive damage to the island's water table caused by the forty-plus years of phosphate mining on the island. The survey found that the extension of the mining into the contested and valuable agricultural areas in the north, where the largest phosphate reserves lay, would result in irreparable harm to the environment. The surveyors believed, however, that the backfilling of lakes created by past and on-going mining operations could restore much of the already used land to a relatively productive state. On the basis of these findings, the representatives from Angaur agreed to a compromise that came to be officially titled the "Angaur Mining Agreement." Under the terms of the compromise, on-going mining would be allowed to continue provided that the lakes created by past and present mining operations were filled and the affected land restored to productivity; at the same time, the severance fee for phosphate mining was increased to $2 per ton. In addition, SCAP in Japan agreed to pay the Trust Territory government a processing tax of 15 percent on the value of all phosphate ore processed.

At the request of the high commissioner, the people of Angaur worked out a system for the distribution of mining income between the 168 people who owned phosphate lands and the 189 who did not. This arrangement, which covered royalties, severance fees, interest, and other related monies earned from the extraction of phosphate, was formalized in the document titled the "Angaur Mining Trust Agreement."[62] The trust principal was to be managed and invested as a single unit; part of the interest earned from the investment of the principal was to be divided into accessible accounts designed to provide money to the people of Angaur for a variety of more immediate needs and purposes. Provisions were also made for the distribution of investment income after the cessation of all phosphate mining on the island, an event that occurred in 1955. With the completion of the agreement, Angaur's trust fund grew quickly. On 30 June 1947, the amount in the fund had registered at $36,312.75; four years later, the total stood at $370,588.17. The processing tax that was part of the Angaur Mining Agreement proved a valuable source of revenue for the Trust Territory. As of 30 June 1951, it stood at $59,150.81 and was allotted directly to the Trust Territory government's Conservation Fund.

The agreement worked well, though officials of the mining company persisted in their efforts to gain access to the valuable, unmined lands in the north. A conference called to press for the extension of mining operations in these areas met on Angaur between 25 October and 7 November 1951.[63] Again, the people of Angaur, through their representatives, refused to agree to any extension of the mining area. In addition, they complained strongly against the American administration's unwillingness to recognize formally their ownership of the island. The departure of the navy from governance of the islands did not bring an end to the problems caused by phosphate mining on Angaur. Over the next twenty years, issues arose among the people of Angaur themselves that ranged from questions of land ownership and compensation for crop damage to matters concerning the distribution of, access to, and investment of phosphate royalties.

Although the exploitative nature of colonialism on Angaur showed itself clearly and strongly, the postwar issues involving phosphate mining on Angaur defy any simplistic Manichean narration. The navy's decision to resume phosphate mining on Angaur in late 1946 exacerbated the divisions within Angaur society between the northern and southern clans, divisions that were themselves the product of deeper colonial and precolonial histories. The recruitment of labor pitted company officials against local chiefs and clan against clan. Although the uniformity of military command generally worked to limit public dissent and disagreement, officers within the interim military government and later civil administrators of the navy's trusteeship took positions in support of the people of Angaur and their grievances. The people of the island, through their representatives, demonstrated skill and adroitness in their negotiations with Americans at the Guam conferences. Although the northern lands remained protected despite the persistence of Pomeroy Company officials, new disputes arose among the Angaurese over the structure and use of the trust fund. If nothing else, the postwar controversy over continued phosphate mining on Angaur demonstrated how messy and entangled development, whether in the form of discourse or as a belated, inadequate package of compensation, could become for both the colonizer and the colonized. This pattern would show itself more and more consistently as Americans and Micronesians encountered and engaged one another over the transformative proposition that was economic development.

Savings as First Fruits in Chuuk

Encounters with development in the Chuuk Lagoon area during the last year of the navy's administration of the islands differed from those on Angaur. On Chuuk, a series of playful confrontations took place between local cultural practices and the establishment of a cooperative savings system. In the narration of this encounter, I draw on the published account of Frank J. Mahony, the government anthropologist assigned to Chuuk. The savings system in question was initiated in 1951 on the island of Weno. According to Mahony, the force behind the establishment of this savings system was Chief Petrus Mailo, an accomplished, versatile, powerful man who headed the most senior of the island's matrilineal clans.[64] Chief Petrus had become concerned about his people's attitudes toward money; they were not concerned about "wasting" it. Initially he had encouraged his people to purchase additional shares in the Truk Trading Company (TTC). Not coincidentally, Chief Petrus held 10 percent of the TTC's total stock and served as the elected president of the company at the time of the inauguration of the savings system on Weno.

Established in January 1948, the TTC stood as the earliest and most successful of the local private trading companies chartered by the Island Trading Company. Known as "10 percent" companies because of the set return of 10 percent on individual shares costing $25 each, these companies traded primarily in the sale of retail goods. Profits earned from the sale of these goods, along with the capital generated by the purchase of shares, were used to make loans to individuals or for larger commercial projects. By the end of its first month of operation, the TTC had sold $14,627 worth of goods at a profit of $1,345. As of December 1949, the TTC recorded total sales of $456,120 and showed a net profit of $22,142. At the formal end of the period of naval administration on 30 June 1951, the company possessed operating capital of $138,431.[65]

The response to Petrus Mailo's call to have people increase their savings through the purchase of additional shares in the Truk Trading Company was disappointing; the set annual return of 10 percent on shares proved not enough incentive, it seems. Chief Petrus then decided to pro-

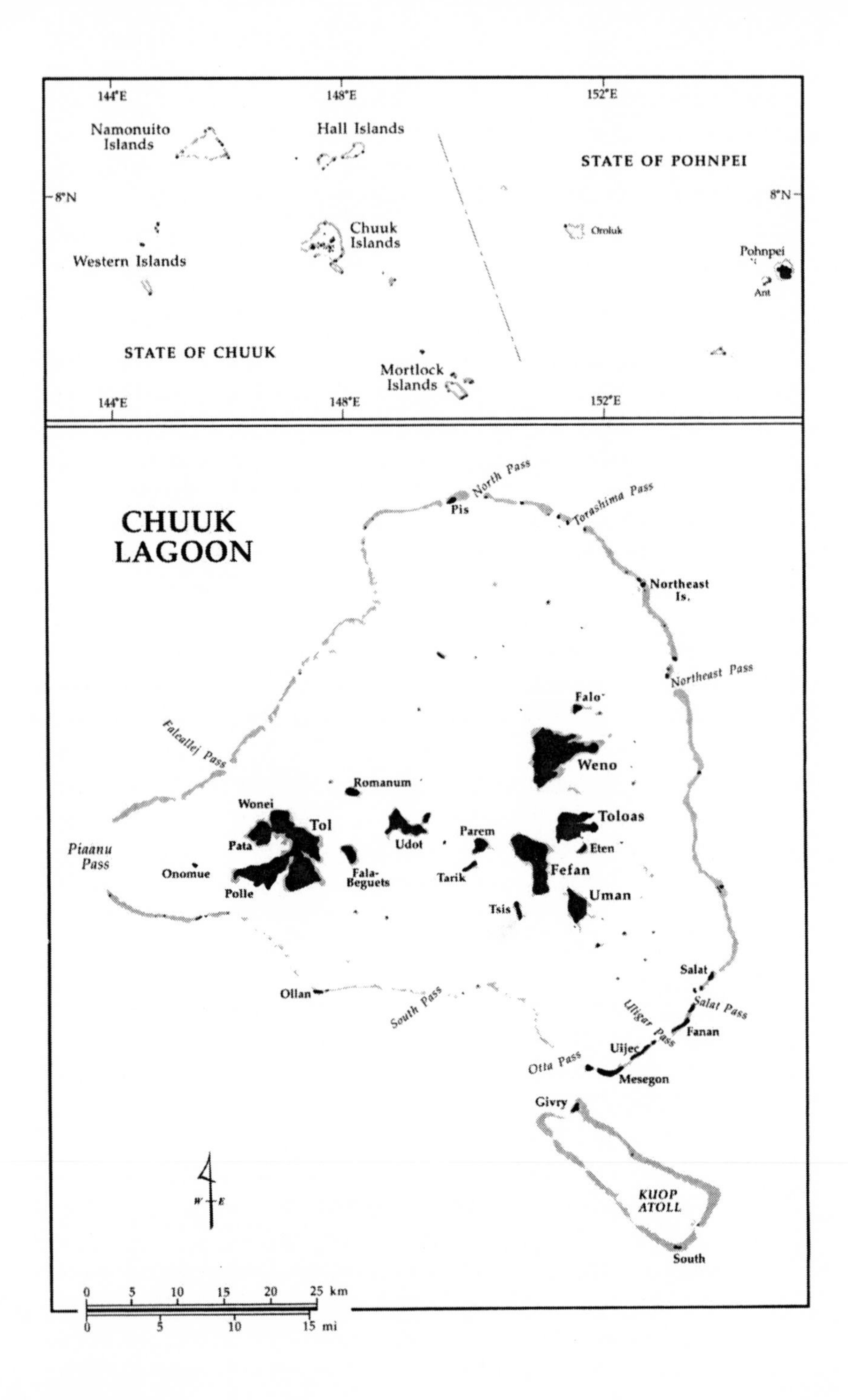
144°E
148°E
152°E
Namonuito Islands
Hall Islands
STATE OF POHNPEI
8°N
8°N
Chuuk Islands
Oroluk
Western Islands
Pohnpei
Ant
STATE OF CHUUK
Mortlock Islands
144°E
148°E
152°E
CHUUK LAGOON
North Pass
Pis
Torashima Pass
Northeast Is.
Northeast Pass
Falo
Falealtej Pass
Weno
Romanum
Wonei
Tol
Udot
Parem
Toloas
Eten
Piaanu Pass
Pata
Onomue
Polle
Fala-Beguets
Tarik
Fefan
Uman
Tsis
Salat
Salat Pass
Ollan
South Pass
Uligar Pass
Fanan
Uijec
Otta Pass
Mesegon
Givry
W
E
KUOP ATOLL
South
0 5 10 15 20 25 km
0 5 10 15 mi

mote a competitive islandwide system of savings organized around surviving cultural boundaries and borders, and playing upon Chuukese obligations toward family and kin. To these cultural structures were added borrowings from a number of Western economic institutions, the most notable being cooperatives and credit unions that promoted the generation of small-scale capital through the pooling of members' investments and dividends.

Petrus Mailo inaugurated this system of savings in his own village of Mwän. Funds were to be collected, held, and administered by the Truk Trading company. With officials from other parts of the island in attendance, Petrus Mailo introduced his "experiment" with speeches followed by songs of welcome and introduction. Following the songs, individuals were asked to stand up, step forward, and place a small contribution, usually a few pennies, on a central table. At the conclusion of the meeting, Mailo had the contributions counted; the effort proved a success. One area of the ritual, however, required adjustment. Mailo, according to Mahony, noticed that most people seemed embarrassed about standing up to make public contributions. He therefore decided to adjust his system in such a way that a bowl or plate would be carried by select individuals to people in their seats. Contributions thus became less a source of public display and consequent anxiety. With this adjustment made, Chief Petrus Mailo decided to try out his culturally nuanced strategy of savings in other districts of Weno.

The island of Weno had been reconstituted into a municipality by naval officials of the Trust Territory government; as a municipality, Weno, then known as Moen, was governed by an elective official, called a magistrate, who was in turn assisted by a secretary, a treasurer, an advisory council, and several clerical workers. The fifteen villages on Weno were divided into five districts, with an average of three villages constituting a district. This division into districts, a carry-over from Japanese times, had little functional importance after 1945, but it did prove vital to Petrus Mailo's plan to prime his savings scheme from established lines of competition within Chuukese society.

Over time, the district savings meetings or competitions incorporated elements of Christian church services as well. Both Catholic and Protestant hymns were sung, and the Bible was a main source of themes and inspirations for the different speeches given. A typical meeting began with a song and a prayer; then one of the island leaders would explain the purpose of the meeting. These speeches were followed by more formal oratorical addresses or *afanafan* that urged the people to be good.[66] Each of these subsequent speeches would be interspersed with songs by the assembled district crowd. The songs welcomed the visiting government officials and dignitaries from other villages, exhorted the assembled to be generous, and gently prodded or poked fun at particular groups whose commitment to or participation in the communal effort was deemed less than satisfactory. This alternating system of songs and speeches often lasted until noon, at which time there would be a break for food.

Following the noon break, women were selected from each village of the district to carry about a plate on which people placed their offerings or contributions. The contributions themselves were called *löchap,* a long-standing, established term referring to some act of daring that involved extraordinary feats of prowess. The use of the term *löchap* to designate the money contributions heightened the people's interest and added an aura of competitive drama to the proceedings. After the collections, the money would be counted and a concluding speech of appreciation and gratitude made by Chief Petrus himself. Word of the size of the collection would eventually spread to other districts and set the target for the later savings meetings.

Savings competitions initially operated at two levels; beneath the interdistrict competition, individual villages vied with each other for distinction. Later, Chief Petrus refined the system of contributions even further by focusing on clans and even lineages within clans as competing units. To underscore the change, Chief Petrus now referred to these gatherings as *mwichen einang,* a term that indicated the clans and clan lineages as the organizational focus. The switch to clans made the competition more personal; it also intensified the stakes considerably by bringing named groups of people into public competition. Identity, reputation, and social standing came into play, and in very serious ways. Individuals now gave money to their respective lineages; this money was added to the contributions from other lineages within the clan. It was then placed in an envelope with the clan's name clearly marked upon it. The money or contributions were called the *masowen futo* or "contents of the envelope." After the formal presentation of the envelope and its contents, there would come a time in the savings meetings when individuals would be encouraged to add *chouchoun futo* or weight to the envelope. The analogous local practice here, writes Mahony, involved the traditional offerings or *rasanap* made at food competitions between different clans or lineages within a given clan.

As the ritual of the meetings developed, the term "daring competitions" or *löchap* came to refer only to contributions made by individuals to clans other than their own. Additional changes followed. Women were no longer used to solicit contributions; instead, two tables were set up at the front of the meeting room where people could place their contributions as they filed past. One of the tables was reserved for all the "contents of the envelope" and "daring contributions"; the other received contributions to weigh down the envelope. To ensure the success of meetings, Chief Petrus arranged to have shareholders' dividends in the Truk Trading Company distributed to a given district just before that district's savings meeting.

Beginning in the summer of 1952, a third table was placed at the head of the gathering room or hall; this table received money for the purpose of "hiring songs" or *satan kön*. A song could usually be bought or "hired" for fifty cents. The idea of daring contributions was also extended to the hiring of songs by different village choirs. Competition now took place at yet another level as village choirs competed against one another in a song contest with nonmonetary prizes being offered to the winners.

Over time, the savings system took on the characteristics of a first-fruits offering. The contributions or offerings were now gathered by lineages and brought to district officials who came to serve in symbolic fashion as the "chiefs" of the savings meetings. The incorporation of cultural patterns, practices, and values into the savings meetings enhanced their popularity and effectiveness. The use of clan and lineage as the organizing units of the gatherings played upon the strong and continuing loyalty individuals had toward these groups in Chuukese society. The effects of these cultural adjustments could be clearly seen in a comparison of the amounts of money gathered by the earlier district rivalries and the later clan- and lineage-oriented competitions. The total collected from the first district meetings amounted to little more than $1,000; the subsequent ten meetings with the clan and lineage as the competing core earned $27,116.75 with one meeting alone bringing in $4,500. These figures become even more startling given the fact that the per capita annual income on Weno at the time was estimated by Trust Territory officials to be $50.

As time passed, modifications in the savings meetings continued to be made. The practice sessions for the meetings themselves became occasions of giving; government officials promoted this practice as a way to limit the length of the formal festivities. Indeed, all of the collections strategies used in the formal sessions came to be employed in the practice sessions. Another innovation concerned the use of the sister's brother to enhance any contribution. By right of Chuukese custom, a man could command his sister's husband to provide food, clothing or money in support of some project or function. This practice, referred to as *ökkunöw,* now showed itself in the savings meeting, heightening even further the level and intensity of the competition. Each time an adult male made a contribution to his own clan, his sister's husband could be called upon to match it.

Foreign influences also exerted themselves in this colonial mix of cultural styles, relationships, and values. American movies being shown on Weno during this time had a decided effect. Borrowing from John Wayne–type Westerns, certain clan and government officials would arrange to have themselves "shot." In accordance with a previously reached agreement, an individual would stand up during a gathering, raise a pointed finger, aim it at the designated individual, and shout "pow." The "wounded" official then rose and called out the names of groups that were expected to make deposits in support of his recovery. Later, at less structured meetings, individuals would wander about indiscriminately "shooting" each other; anyone "shot" was required to make a contribution.

The savings system soon spread to other islands in Chuuk Lagoon, and with varying and distinctive adjustments. On Uman, for example, a lottery was introduced to the proceedings as were love songs sung to the accompaniment of guitars; these songs sometimes took the place of the group singing. Collections on Uman tended to be made by hearths or homesteads rather than by a particular clan or lineage. In the municipality of Pwene on Tol Island, meetings were sponsored by individual villages rather than districts. Uman's and Tol's adoption of the savings system was a signal to other islands; Fefan, Udot, and Eten in the lagoon area, the Namonuitos to the northwest, and Nama and Losap in the Upper Mortlocks all established savings systems on the model created by Chief Petrus Mailo on Weno. The savings system later spread throughout the Mortlocks and was particularly strong on Lukunor. By mid-1955, savings meetings had been held in twelve of the fifteen municipalities of the Chuuk Lagoon area and in ten of the eleven municipalities in the Mortlocks.

The savings system meeting proved extremely popular for several years. People busied themselves composing and practicing songs. The meetings were occasions to dress up and have a good time. For the young unmarried people, there was the opportunity to see, be seen, and flirt with members of the opposite sex. The festivity of the gatherings, however, obscured the harder economic facts. Mahony reports that the people of Weno originally expected the savings system to increase dramatically their income and material well-being. Nonetheless, the intensified competition of the savings system that now involved clan, lineage, village, and district consumed almost all of the available money on Weno. Moreover, individuals lost money on their contributions because the social pressures brought to bear by the increased level of competition forced them to borrow from the savings system fund and at relatively high interest rates of about 10 percent per month. Any dividends people earned on their savings were thus nullified by the interest they were forced to pay on their loans. The Truk Trading Company managers of the savings system found it increasingly difficult to collect either the principal or the interest on loans advanced. Economic factors alone, however, do not explain the demise of the savings meetings. In Pata, one of the municipalities of Tol Island, opposition to the savings meetings developed because they highlighted, even exacerbated, inequalities regarding access to property and income.

Other events intervened to erode the popularity of the savings system. The gradual emergence of the Truk District Congress as a new site of political influence meant another set of dignitaries whose presence at savings meetings both added to the competition and increased the costs of the host community. The realignment of municipal boundaries, a development that accompanied the creation of the district congress, disturbed considerably the geo-cultural map on which Chief Petrus originally had plotted his savings system. After 1957, Mahony notes that savings meetings declined in occurrence and popularity. Their initial effects, however, had been both tangible and beneficial. Acting much like a cross between a cooperative and a credit union, the savings system had provided a source of capital that funded various small-scale commercial projects and that made possible through more private loans the purchase of jeeps, skiffs, outboard motors, sewing machines, cement, lumber, and other building materials.

Exploring the deeper cultural significance of the savings fund experiment, Mahony argues that Chuukese attitudes toward money were much like those toward food. To most of the people of Chuuk, money was a consumable that needed to be used before it went bad. To defer the immediate consumption of money, Chief Petrus Mailo devised a system of savings that played upon the responsibilities and obligations toward family, clan, village, and district. His standing as the leader of Weno's most senior clan added legitimacy, authority, and impetus to the experiment. Its success as a piece of cultural blending and improvisation was real, if limited in time. As an effort at crosscultural translation between very different economic systems, the savings system exhibited a people's appropriation of a foreign practice in ways that were indigenously defined and directed.

The Role of Cooperatives in the Colonization of Micronesia

A more ominous feature lurked within this system of competitive savings with which the people of Chuuk Lagoon played. The remaking of Micronesia involved the linkage of Western economic practices with political purposes in a larger transformative project that was essentially cultural. This process showed itself in the promotion of cooperatives in the Trust Territory. A sense of history informed this promotion. Early reports on the establishment of cooperatives in the Trust Territory made explicit the relationship between democracy and cooperative economic practices. Jim Clark, the cooperatives advisor for the Marshalls District, saw the future of the islands in the history of the international cooperative movement.

Clark wrote of the Industrial Revolution of the nineteenth century as the origins of that movement. The revolution had brought urbanization, low wages, high prices, poverty, and hardship to England's workers. In an instance of defiant but constructive protest on 21 December 1844, a group of weavers in the northern English town of Rochdale formed a cooperative to provide quality goods at lower prices. Each contributed two pence per week to a general fund. Though the weekly contributions seemed small, they eventually created a capital fund of £252 or $84, half of which went to rent a "gloomy little room" that provided business space on Rochdale's equivalent of Toad Lane. The remainder of the capital went to the bulk purchase of butter, flour, sugar, and oatmeal. From that modest beginning, the Rochdale cooperative grew by the middle of the twentieth century to have a membership of fifty thousand and share capital in excess of $1.5 million.[67]

According to Clark, the ultimate legacy of the Rochdale Experiment lay in the establishment of a set of principles that eventually formed the basis for the international cooperative movement. Those guiding principles included democratic control through the one man–one vote rule, open membership, limited and fixed rates of interest on all loans advanced from group funds, and fair, equitable dividends to all shareholders from the profits generated by the sale of the cooperative's goods. Secondary principles advanced by the cooperative movement included cash-only trade, political and religious neutrality, and the education of its members in basic matters involving economics and democracy. The cooperative experience, argued its advocates, not only taught financial responsibility, but also provided important education in matters regarding self-help, thrift, and mutual aid.[68]

A strong political consciousness informed the cooperative movement. The formation of cooperatives offered a vehicle whereby the poor could maximize their financial resources, secure through communal structures the advantages of capital, and gain some degree of power by the formation of an effective association that represented the common interests of its membership. Political stability was also furthered because cooperatives were seen as easing the natural friction between capital and labor by increasing the number of small capitalists with a stake in the country.

Advocates of cooperatives held their advantages to be universally relevant and applicable.[69] In truth, however, these highly Eurocentric institutions infused with the values of capitalist culture served as instruments in the discourse of development that sought to change more local ways of being and knowing. In Micronesia, Trust Territory administrators like Jim Clark argued that cooperatives offered Micronesians the experience necessary to deal with rapid economic, social, and political changes. To add weight to their words, these officials cited the works of global development specialist C. F. Strickland, who wrote of the political as well as economic advantages learned from democratically run organizations such as cooperatives. Strickland felt that the cause of self-government in "backward countries" was too rushed; ill-prepared, largely untrained men confronted the complexities of constitutional government and electoral democracy, and with disastrous results.[70] Too often, the consequence was totalitarian rule. A more intermediary and instructional approach was called for. Employing a decidedly paternalist tone, Strickland wrote that

> we of the West are pledged to lead our wards or our partners from a regime, in which custom predominates over law, towards a state of life in which law prevails over custom, and the transition must not be too sudden or too violent. It is for this reason that I regard cooperatives as indispensable.[71]

The assumed inevitability of change, so recurrent a theme in policy statements and ethnographic studies of the navy period, also fueled the arguments for the establishment of cooperatives in the islands. Micronesians, it was argued, would benefit from the establishment of cooperatives because "modern ways, economically, socially and politically have come to the Pacific and the Micronesian people have no choice but to adjust themselves to the white man's world."[72] While some viewed the communal features of Micronesian society as a foundation on which the cooperative movement might build, others held them to be serious impediments. Indigenous practices of cooperation, although attractive and admirable, were constrained in their enterprising potential by social relationships and kinship obligations. Homer Barnett, an American anthropologist working in Palau, argued that formally organized and managed cooperatives offered Micronesians an escape from the network of kinship obligations that inhibited and undermined all efforts at individual economic enterprise.[73]

The numbers reported by the Trust Territory government on cooperatives suggest that, on the surface at least, considerable progress was being made in transforming the political economy of the islands and atolls. Chartered in 1956 through legislation that gave the high commissioner

Purchasing shares in the Puluwat Cooperative Store. (Trust Territory Archives, Pacific Collection, University of Hawai'i Library)

strong powers of supervision and control, cooperatives grew quickly in terms of membership and assets. By the end of calendar year 1968, there were forty cooperatives with a membership of 7,931 in the six major island districts of the Trust Territory. Dividends paid to members in that year amounted to $130,764; total assets were valued at $2,082,404.[74] Over the next decade, that growth would continue; in 1978, total credit union assets in the Trust Territory reached $7,403,586.[75] The dynamics of the saving system in Chuuk Lagoon, along with other instances of Micronesian expenditure and consumption to be examined in subsequent chapters, suggest, however, that cooperatives in the Trust Territory did not function quite as intended in advancing the larger transformative scheme of which they were a part.

"Our Work in Your Islands": The End of the Naval Administration

The intensive battles fought by different government agencies over initial administrative jurisdiction for the Trust Territory and the general criticism of naval government that surfaced during the debates led early on to the decision that the navy's tenure in the islands would be brief. In addition, the increasing Cold War climate between the United States and the Soviet Union dictated that the navy allocate more of its attention and resources toward the containment of world communism. In the very executive order issued on 18 July 1947 that designated the navy as the initial administering agency for the Trust Territory, President Harry S. Truman added that "it is my intent, however, to effect the transfer of this responsibility from the Navy Department to a civilian agency at the earliest possible date."[76] That transfer came about on 1 July 1951, when the navy relinquished its administrative responsibility to the United States Department of the Interior.

Shortly before the formal end of the naval administration of the Trust Territory, Deputy High Commissioner Rear Adm. Fiske sent his farewell message to the people of the islands. Written in English, the text, went largely unheard; in all likelihood, it did not get beyond the administrative offices of the six district centers of Majuro, Pohnpei, Chuuk, Yap, Palau, and Saipan. To those who did happen to hear or read it, there was Fiske's assurance that the years of naval administration had been guided by the desire to contribute to the well-being of the island peoples as they "progressed toward a better way of life."[77] The deputy high commissioner expressed the hope that the inhabitants of the Trust Territory would come soon to enjoy a greater degree of health, prosperity, and enjoyment of life and a proper place among the self-governing peoples of the world. In closing his message of farewell, Fiske tellingly thanked the people of Micronesia for "your unfailing cooperation and understanding in helping us to carry out our work in your islands." It was a phrase that spoke volumes to the larger intent and purposes behind America's presence in the islands.

In other venues, Fiske voiced not sentiments of gratitude and farewell but of frustration. Speaking before the Trusteeship Council, Admiral Fiske called the Trust Territory a land of anomalies and incongruities.[78] The admiral's exasperation was mirrored in the apology that served as the conclusion to Dorothy Richard's three-volume history of the navy's presence in the islands. Richard wrote that the very nature of the area—its expanse of ocean, limited land area, scattered islands, and general poverty—all posed severe problems for the administration. Before it could begin to formulate a policy, the navy found itself forced to cope with the exigencies of relief, rehabilitation, and repatriation during the occupation and immediate postwar period. The need to incorporate the islands within the naval command system of the Pacific Ocean areas had only complicated matters. The confusion created by the rapid demobilization of American troops in the islands and the intense internecine debates within the American government over the future political disposition of the islands had prevented the navy from concentrating more of its efforts on the advancement of life in the islands.

Turning specifically to the issue of economic development, Richard wrote that experience had forced the navy to qualify its commitment to economic independence. The promotion if not actual achievement of economic self-sufficiency became the navy's objective in its administration of the trusteeship. But even this adjusted goal looked overly ambitious. The historian noted that people who knew the area possessed little hope that economic self-sufficiency could ever be attained. The problem, as Richard saw it, was not the people per se. She described them as "kind, gentle, eager for assistance, willing to learn" and possessed of a sustaining sense of humor that had seen them through three separate colonial regimes in the last half century.[79] No, the problem, as Richard discerned it, was not the people but their culture.

For Richard and others who would follow her in trying to make sense of development in the islands, the word "culture" served as a generic, indiscriminate, catch-all term used to identify the principal impediment to change in the islands. Richard warned of certain ethnic forces that seemed diametrically opposed to capitalistic practices and the competitive principles of commerce. The desire to accumulate could be defeated by the right of clan or family to appropriate the earnings of young members of the group. Political systems that granted status and privilege to a few and that allowed for the appropriation of resources or goods on the basis of this status also constituted impediments to development.[80] Because of "culture," notions of price, profit, credit, savings, and investment remained unintelligible, unworkable concepts for Micronesians. Culture prevented people from engaging successfully in long-term commercial projects; it kept them from expending the time, effort, energy, and creativity necessary to succeed in modern economic undertakings.

In a perverse sort of way, Richard was right. Her assessment of the economic future of the islands indicated just how deeply, fundamentally cultural was the transformative process called development. To satisfy Richard and the navy, the different peoples who inhabited the area called Micronesia would have had to become significantly other than what they were. Summing up the navy's efforts, Richard wrote, "The results, like the resources, were meager and not comparable to the effort put forth. Micronesians had long before recognized and accepted their economic impotence but Americans could not conceive of a non-productive environment."[81] The recognition of the impossibility of economic development in the Trust Territory, however, would not deter the substantive efforts of the next three decades. If Micronesians could not be made to be economically independent or self-reliant as others understood those terms, perhaps they could nonetheless be made into reliable workers and responsible consumers in service to the strategic needs of the world's foremost bastion of capitalism.

Despite the pessimism that haunted the assessment of Richard and others, the rites of closure called for the expression of upbeat, positive sentiments. Richard wrote of the confidence Micronesians had gained in themselves and of their realization that their islands would never again be isolated entities. As an acknowledgment of the awareness of the debt owed the navy, there were the joint words of Mr. Elias Sablan and Mr. Ignacio Benevente, who spoke of their faith in Americans and American principles and of the glorious day of the American invasion of Saipan. The two went on to extol the navy's gifts of food and freedom: "Besides having been fed gratuitously and richly for 3½ years, it is guaranteed to us freedom of speech, of the press and of assembly."[82] Sablan and Benevente closed their speech by stating that the joy of the navy's presence was tempered only by the sadness engendered by their leaving. Things, then, had come full circle; Tomeing's greetings in the just-liberated Marshalls in 1944 were now matched by the equally enthusiastic farewells of grateful Micronesians on Saipan, or so the navy wanted it believed. The 1951 transfer of administrative responsibilities from the U.S. Navy to the Department of the Interior would affect little the tone and tenure of American colonial rule. John Griffin, an editorial-page writer for the *Honolulu Advertiser,* offered a summary of the first ten years of civilian rule in American Micronesia. Griffin wrote of proposals for economic rehabilitation that gathered dust on forgotten shelves while the Trust Territory limped along with a caretaker budget of less than $7 million dollars annually and under the direction of a staff made up of aging holdovers from the navy government, tired veterans of Interior's Bureau of Indian Affairs, and dedicated young recruits who soon became jaded or who left in frustration.[83] The future looked to have the feel of the past about it. In the minds of some, what was needed was a better plan.

Chapter 4

"Planning Micronesia's Future"

Development planning, writes Arturo Escobar, is not a neutral process. It acts as a highly ideological, deeply Eurocentric force that in a seemingly caring but actually insidious way works to chart the procedures by which people can be made docile, productive members of a world capitalist order. Escobar locates the beginnings of development planning within the Enlightenment's advocacy of modernity.[1] The Industrial Revolution disturbed this vision with the general dislocation it inflicted upon European society. Concerns arose about the poverty, disease, and lawlessness resulting from the large influx of migrants into Europe's industrializing cities of the early nineteenth century.

The application of science to these social problems provided the illusion of solutions through the objectification of society as a category of analysis accessible to remedial initiatives. With capitalism's rise to dominance as both an economy and culture by the mid-nineteenth century, planning's locus moved from the social to the economic. Land and labor became commodified, and in the process, older economic systems centered on subsistence, reciprocity, and kinship were increasingly marginalized. The process of planning now advanced strategies for normalizing productive human behavior and regulating it through the application of capitalist economic criteria.

Applied beyond Europe, planning in the post–World War II period served as an indispensable part of the development process that sought to transform the colonized world into national entities with viable economies that mirrored, or at least mimicked, the Euro-American capitalist order. Grounded in the logic and rationality of Western capitalism and the history that made it, development mapped the ways in which non-Western people might become modern. In so doing, planning endeavored first to identify the irrational impediments said to infuse the cultures of others. Terms such as "backward," "primitive," "savage," and "traditional" were employed to sweep away the values, lifestyles, epistemologies, and histories of others. "Underdeveloped" emerged as a vengeful adjective, an indicting synonym for all that existed apart from Western capitalist society. Planning, with its institutions and their professional staffs of experts, constituted an intricate component to the project of development that strove to make over difference, indifference, and resistance in the colonized world. It extended an offer of help that masked the more subtle conveyance of threat and intimidation.[2]

The islands called Micronesia were to prove no exception. There, the practice of planning was employed to give direction, or at least the semblance of direction, to a program of social transformation that had been poorly served by the inexact, conflicting, and distracted ways in which the navy and its immediate civilian successors had practiced economic development. This chapter examines development planning in the 1960s and 1970s and closes with glimpses of alternative understandings of history, economy, cosmology, and power that contested or disturbed the best-laid plans of the Trust Territory government and its corps of contracted experts.

The First Plan

Those familiar with the extant body of literature on Micronesia will recognize the title of this chapter as borrowed from Douglas Oliver's published summary of the first development plan for Micronesia. The history of this first plan begins soon after the cessation of formal hostilities in the Pacific between Japan and the United States. On 1 October 1945, the navy, after establishing its interim military government, commissioned the United States Commercial Company to carry out an economic survey of the islands. The survey was to include recommendations for viable, appropriate, and sustainable initiatives in support of the effort to provide the "highest possible degree of economic security and self-support for the native island populations in the subject area."[3]

The USCC was a subsidiary of the Reconstruction Finance Corporation, a government agency that engaged in the wartime disruption of national economies hostile to U.S. interests and then to their reconstruction or rehabilitation in the postwar period.[4] If Micronesians were not the enemy, they were nonetheless viewed as having been affected by Japan's thirty-year presence. The commission to the USCC also played upon the catastrophic disruption wreaked upon certain island societies by battles, bombardments, and other war-related activities. In carrying out their mission, the survey's investigators were to give particular attention to the development of natural resources, the improvement and promotion of native handicraft manufactures, and the revitalization of copra and other major export crops whose production and profits had been obliterated by the war.

The project, carried out from the Honolulu offices of the USCC, brought to bear the considerable resources and interests of various federal agencies including the Departments of State, Commerce, Agriculture, Interior, and the Navy. Survey personnel concerned themselves first with identifying and collecting all sources of recorded information about Micronesia. Michel Foucault would have a comment here about the archaeology of knowledge and the ways in which an invented Micronesia was now being totalized to serve the purposes of the American state. The excavation of this knowledge included the inventory, location, acquisition, and translation of existing foreign-language materials on Micronesia and the redrawing of existing maps using aerial photographs and other resources and techniques developed during the war. A list of research topics was then drawn up that, in effect, realigned Micronesian life in terms of the priorities, objectives, and analytical categories of an alien social order. Topics of inquiry included geography, population, labor, agriculture, forestry, marine resources, mineral exploitation, finance, transportation, education, trade, land use and tenure, nutrition, and commerce.

With this background work completed, professionally trained personnel were then recruited to conduct on-site surveys of the islands and their resources. Teams of "economists" traveled to "culture areas" to record cultural practices and gather statistics on human demography. The coordinator of the survey and aforementioned author of the project summary, Prof. Douglas L. Oliver of Harvard University, himself placed these terms in quotation marks, suggesting an understanding of the forced structure of the study.[5] The use of economists, in actuality men trained in anthropology and other social sciences, was deemed essential because of the lack of any uniform or consistent pattern in the economic modes and institutions of the people of the islands.[6] To compensate for this immense variability, each economist was to provide a descriptive background against which the findings of other specialists could be projected. Economists spent a minimum of ten weeks in their assigned culture areas; specialists in botany, agriculture, geology, entomology, and marine life spent less time in a given locality but visited a greater number of places overall. The end product was a twenty-volume report and accompanying summary that offered a body of both new and reworked information from which Micronesia could be more effectively remade. Although the authors of the individual volumes provided considerable ethnographic detail on individual islands or island groups, the variety of cultural practices and expressions was subsumed by the need to essentialize the area for purposes of economic development and the larger strategic interests that development promoted.

The summary report certainly did recognize the alien nature of the political construction that was Micronesia and of the previous colonial regimes that had attempted, in different ways, to give Micronesia a cohesive identity that it really did not possess. There was the admission that "Micronesian culture," defined as "social organization, technology, language, values, material possessions, and so forth," might differ from island to island and that "a tool or an industry or a regulation devised for one island" might not be applicable to another. Complementing this sensitivity was an awareness of the power equation that resonated through and indeed dictated the effort. The editor described as a sobering thought the prescription of a totally new way of life for a people who had no effective voice in deciding their future. The summary report distanced itself, in writing at least, from any complacency in promoting the commercial exploitation of Micronesia for the economic benefit of the United States or in helping to identify and mobilize Micronesian economic resources in support of American military bases. There were also cautions against the inappropriate application of American aesthetic standards to island practices and against the judgment that "castoff dungarees, a smattering of English, and a mission handshake" were evidence of Americanization.[7]

Its more liberal sensibilities notwithstanding, the summary report also evidenced a curious mix of contradictions and inconsistencies. It identified the general objective of the overall survey as being the recovery of Micronesia's prewar economic status but failed to note that this prewar status was one of domination under a more efficient, effective, and self-serving colonial power that offered no liberal rhetoric to clothe or obscure its self-interests in the area.[8] Micronesian proclivities toward excessive deference and self-deprecation were described as "unfortunate habits" that had to be eradicated to allow for the full play of talents and ambitions needed to bring about viable economic enterprise.[9] The ultimate irony of course was that the economic plan for Micronesia's future threatened the very stability of local island societies with its endorsement of an alien, disruptive system of productive activity that would make over the natural and cultural environments of the area.

The implementation of the USCC's recommendations proved much more modest than the agenda envisioned. The U.S. Navy's overall administration of the islands, including the program for economic development, suffered from a serious confusion over the strategies and issues involved in administering a program of massive change. Despite an initial commitment to economic development, even independence, for the islands, the navy ultimately opted for a far more modest program that focused on small-scale development projects and the use of trade stores to inculcate necessary market values and practices. Although the navy chose to set aside the recommendations of the USCC survey, this first plan did show the dimensions of the development agenda that would be advanced by later planners, specialists, and civilian administrators.

The "Wisdom" of Solomon and Nathan, Too

A 1961 United Nations Visiting Mission to the Trust Territory of the Pacific Islands concluded in its trip report that the United States must end its neglect and undertake greater efforts to prepare Micronesia for self-government. Economic development was used as a yardstick to evaluate the American administration of the area. The report complained that the economy had been "allowed to remain static for too long" because there had never been a coordinated push for economic development.[10] The report, the emergence of a more strident anticolonial rhetoric at the United Nations, and a series of natural disasters in the islands all combined to bring about the drafting of National Security Action Memorandum number 145.[11]

NSAM 145 created an interagency task force from the Departments of Interior, State, Defense, and Health, Education and Welfare to review the American administration of Micronesia. More specifically, the task force was charged with the development of a coordinated program to raise the living standards of Micronesians and to promote self-government in the area under an American framework. The memorandum also endorsed the commissioning of a survey team to visit Micronesia and to come up with concrete policy recommendations to speed the movement of the territory toward permanent political affiliation with the United States. Anthony Solomon, then professor of business administration at Harvard University and later assistant secretary of state for economic affairs, headed the survey mission. Other members of the team were drawn from the Council of Economic Advisers, the Peace Corps, the Bureau of the Budget, the U.S. Navy, the Agency for International Development, and the academic world. Between July and August 1963, the survey team visited all six districts of the Trust Territory. The survey team's final report reached the White House about six weeks before John F. Kennedy's assassination in November 1963.

Officially titled *The Report by the United States Survey Mission to the Trust Territory of the Pacific Islands,* the Solomon Report, as it is more commonly known, began, as did the USCC's economic survey, with the recognition of the artificiality of the term "Micronesia." The islands were identified as a "series of individual communities rather than a unified nation."[12] The report's introduction affirmed the desirability of economic development, but through a descriptive process that denigrated the peoples of the area called Micronesia. The people of the atolls and islands were said to be largely illiterate and inadequately prepared to participate in political and commercial activities beyond a rudimentary nature. Micronesian attitudes toward work were termed erratic, with the near exclusive focus of all effort being the satisfaction of immediate needs. The report made reference to loafing, the problems involved with Micronesians' supervision of other Micronesians, and the populace's general indifference toward wage employment. The redeeming feature of the Micronesian temperament, according to the report, rested in a good native intelligence, a dignity of person, and high standards of civil behavior "even among those living in small villages, under thatched roofs, without water or electricity or toilets, and only half-dressed by American standards." The report went on to add, however, that, in economic terms, what looked to be Micronesian folly could well turn out to be a viable economy "based on American residents and tourists."[13]

The report recognized the years of neglect, the lethargy of the American administration, and the suspicion of Micronesian elites toward this latest foreign presence. Acknowledged too were the problems of size and distance, confusion over land tenure regimes, inadequate transportation and communication systems, the absence of local industry, a dearth of skilled workers, and a basic misunderstanding among the peoples of the islands regarding the very nature and purpose of economic development. The report criticized Americans for marking time in "self-conscious uneasiness" while watching the deterioration of roads, schools, hospitals, and other public works and the continued stagnation of the local economy. The authors of the Solomon Report worried that while the American administration risked becoming simply custodial, increasingly assertive anticolonial forces within a less malleable United Nations were attempting to promote the development of an independent Micronesia.[14]

The Solomon Report posited the movement of Micronesians into a permanent political relationship with the United States as the ultimate objective of all American effort and initiative in the Trust Territory. Operating on the assumption that such a relationship would require ratification through a plebiscite, the survey team sought to align its prescriptions for economic development to ensure the success of a such a vote. The report projected 1968 as the year of the plebiscite; five years were believed sufficient to overturn the lessons, experiences, and ways of centuries.

With this timetable in mind, the report endorsed a major capital improvements program, the consequent expansion of general employment opportunities, and the implementation of a social security system. Elementary and secondary schools were identified as being at the vanguard of a deliberate, managed process of change. The report called for a standardized educational system, the use of Peace Corps volunteers to promote the American character of this school system, and an increase in the number of scholarships for the brightest, most promising students. Migration of the young to the district centers of the major islands was seen as a way to create a greater concentration of skilled labor, promote higher productivity, and reduce the wide differentials in population densities within Micronesia. With migration contributing to a more effective, efficient labor pool, traditional patterns of behavior that inhibited rising living standards would break down. The persistence of what was called "parochial attitudes" would be reduced and in their place would arise a common culture based on modern economic ways and the use of the English language.[15] Although the report did attempt to pay some attention to the individual differences among the different island groups, the distinctions were seen as inconsequential against the promotion of what was believed to be a better, more comfortable and rewarding way of life compatible with American security interests in the area. Aware that its recommendations meant the disturbance, if not destruction, of patterns of life that had served the peoples of the islands for centuries, the authors of the Solomon Report urged a careful treading on the part of policy makers and administrators.[16]

Serious protests greeted the later publication of parts of the Solomon Report by the Micronesian Independence Advocates, a group of Micronesian students at the University of Hawai'i, in the March 1971 issue of its newsletter, *The Young Micronesian.* Academic analysts, newspaper reporters, and critics of American foreign policy in the world all basically damned the published excerpts from the Solomon team's report as a ruthless plan to systematically Americanize Micronesia in clear and conscious defiance of its trusteeship obligations. Much of the debate focused on whether or not the Solomon Report actually served as the basis for American policy in Micronesia. An editorial in the *Honolulu Star Bulletin* of 26 July 1971 more accurately described the Solomon Report as a historical artifact that showed much of the thinking and ultimate intent, if not policy, behind American strategic colonialism in the Pacific Islands. The Solomon Report revealed then the deep, encompassing character of the development agenda in Micronesia. Much of what was targeted for development could be construed as economic in character but, in truth, the rhetoric of economic development targeted almost every aspect or facet of life in the islands.

If the USCC and Solomon reports made gestures toward keeping Micronesians at the center of economic development efforts, the plan prepared by Robert R. Nathan and Associates of Washington, D.C., held larger purposes, other interests, and third parties to be more critical. Commissioned in 1966 at the urging of the United Nations Trusteeship Council, the Nathan Plan made little pretence about the involvement of Micronesians in any development schemes. Beginning in the summer of 1965, the four-man survey team, composed of academic consultants and professional staffers from Nathan and Associates' Washington offices, spent more than seven months traveling throughout Micronesia. The end product was a four-part, three-volume, 736-page document, which was submitted to the high commissioner's office on 1 December 1966.

To read only the table of contents for the Nathan Plan is to realize how extensive was the effort envisioned and how major would be the implications for every facet of life in Micronesia. Development was not only about generating increased income and revenues through commercial activity; it involved creating a way of life that covered educational, governmental, political, religious, and social considerations as well. Everything from medical services to school facilities, from public services to tax programs, from land holdings to labor-force requirements, from property rights to personal freedoms was to be touched in tremendous ways. The Nathan Plan revealed its understanding of these dimensions in its call for the "strength and courage" needed to effect an entirely new attitude toward economic development in the Trust Territory.[17]

In the compilation of its development plan, the team endeavored to "stand outside" the daily activities of government and administration. Its distance, in an unintended way, gave testament to the alien character of the enterprise it was promoting in the islands. There was little illusion about the role of local choice. The plan identified its ultimate objective as the design of activities, programs, and supplementary measures "for the immediate and long-range which will provide the residents of Micronesia expanded opportunities to participate more fully in modern economic life—as employers and employees, as farmers and consumers, as investors and owners, as contributors and beneficiaries." Throughout its report, the Nathan team showed itself aware of the serious impediments to economic development, if not of the ironies, contradictions, and bad history of the whole process. Geography and history, to the authors of the report, seemed to have conspired against economic development in Micronesia. The small land areas, great distances, poor soil, and lack of accessible resources severely constrained the possibilities of development.[18]

Equally problematic was the nature of Micronesian society which, in the minds of the Nathan specialists, loomed as the most serious impediment to economic progress. The plan noted disparagingly the communal nature of the "primitive" system of economy that had severely constrained interaction with the larger world. Local island economies were characterized as little more than elaborate systems of gift giving. Nowhere did the Nathan team find discernible evidence of any accumulation of material wealth from which a nascent capitalist economy might emerge. Micronesians' cultural attitudes toward work were deemed to be inconsistent with the discipline required for most modern economic undertakings. While providing stability and the satisfaction of basic wants, Micronesian society gave little encouragement to individual freedoms or personal initiative.[19]

The structural deficiencies of Micronesian society further complicated the process of economic development by leaving Micronesians unable to comprehend the larger world, its people, and the meaning and purpose of modern productive economic activities. Micronesians, wrote the authors of the Nathan study, viewed foreigners, more specifically Americans, as people with unlimited access to vast quantities of goods; moreover, the people of the islands had no comprehension of the planning and work that had produced that wealth. In the eyes of the Nathan team specialists, more than a century of contact with the outside world had led the islanders to depend on outsiders to organize and plan their economic activities. The great lesson taught by Micronesian history was that Micronesians enjoyed the most progress when the self-serving interests of some outside group led to the establishment of productive economic activity in the area that produced local benefits as well as foreign profits. Never held responsible, Micronesians now needed to learn to become more reliant upon their own capabilities. The Nathan team concluded that open doors, free markets, and unregulated competition of the kind first defined by Adam Smith his 1776 tract, *An Inquiry into the Nature and Causes of the Wealth of Nations,* would best serve Micronesians.[20]

Emphasizing its external orientation, the Nathan Plan saw the Trust Territory government as both the cause and solution to the problems that hindered effective economic development in the area. The government had done nothing to advance the possibilities of economic self-reliance for the area. The sum total of more than twenty years of American military and civilian government had been a contrived sheltering of Micronesians from the realities and hard choices involved in the process of economic development.[21] Local hiring practices that placed poorly trained, incompetent, less-than-hard-working Micronesians under a few beleaguered Americans had further exacerbated the dilemma. The report concluded that, given the tremendous impediments to government and development in the Trust Territory, what was surprising was that a few American administrators and their Micronesian underlings had managed somehow to "make do."

Despite the overall failures of the Trust Territory government, the Nathan team placed the responsibility for the development of Micronesia squarely with the American administration. The administering authority was charged with remaking Micronesians into a "strong, capable, productive, responsible, and self-reliant people who are developing their abilities and exercising their rights to expanded economic opportunities and freedoms." Meaningful economic development was considered possible only if the government took the lead in drafting and implementing well-conceived, efficient development programs. Noting that a government job was considered the easiest, most secure, and hence most desirable form of employment, the Nathan Plan estimated that the government absorbed 80–90 percent of the best educated, most highly skilled Micronesians available. This, however, was at best a manpower force in training. American managers and foreign labor would most effectively and most immediately spur on economic development. To this end, the Nathan team encouraged doubling the number of American employees of the Trust Territory government and recruiting foreign laborers with the hard technical skills needed to get an economy going. American personnel, in particular, were to have complete freedom of entry and exit, property rights, and prompt and favorable responses to all requests for business permits and licenses.[22]

The Nathan Plan identified the particular sectors of economic activity that seemed to hold the greatest prospects for success. Small business, industrial and commercial activities, travel industry development, commercial agriculture, copra production, and commercial fisheries were all to receive special emphasis.[23] To supplement these efforts, the development and expansion of capital improvements were urged; airports, warehouses, and freezers were to be built or installed. There could and should be histories written about the effects of modern infrastructure development on local island communities—their ritual practices, belief systems, and patterns of interaction. In the Nathan Plan, however, the recommendations for infrastructure development amounted to little more than a line item or, at most, a quick, callous paragraph. Questions of human concern received little attention in a plan so convinced of economic development as necessary and desirable.

Land was viewed as the most pressing of ingredients for development. In examining the issue of land in Micronesia, the Nathan team saw a mix of "lingering anachronisms" involving traditional land tenure systems, confusion over the title and transfer of certain private lands, and the holding of large tracts of land by succeeding colonial governments as combining to create an inaccessible, confounding system of land holdings. The Nathan Plan, ignoring any consideration of what land tenure systems might mean to the different peoples of Micronesia other than as a "lingering anachronism," called a land management program essential to the economic development of the Trust Territory. Ironically, Micronesia's landmass, which had been presented elsewhere in this report and in previous studies as a serious impediment to general development because it was so small, was now described as too large for local populations to develop effectively and profitably.[24] But then, alien prescriptions for indigenous peoples often engendered such contradictions in their efforts to identify as mutual and complementary the needs and interests of colonizer and colonized.

A formal review of the Nathan Plan ordered by the American high commissioner, William R. Norwood, showed general agreement with the document's more than 280 separate recommendations concerning economic development.[25] Peter Wilson, a fisheries officer with the Trust Territory government, endorsed the plan's position on the importation of foreign labor, especially in the development of the local fisheries and boatbuilding industries.[26] Wilson wrote that the lack of skilled labor seriously hindered development in these two areas. Moreover, Micronesians, wrote Wilson, needed to be shown "what it means to put in a full day's labor." Wilson felt that Micronesian laborers loafed on the job, used their potential and their ethnic identity as excuses, and were secure in the knowledge that it would be almost impossible to replace them. Real economic development, argued Wilson, would depend on Micronesians' ability to compete effectively against Japanese, Okinawan, and Taiwanese fishermen. Dr. Luke A. Howe, the assistant director of public health, thought that the Trust Territory would become like an Indian reservation "if we keep it only for Micronesians. Is that our goal?" G. P. Daniels, acting head of the Land Management Office of the Trust Territory at the time of the Nathan team's visit, applauded the abandonment of a protectionist attitude, especially in situations that allowed more-advantaged Micronesians to exploit the less-educated and less-privileged.

Not all colonial administrators thought alike, however. Some in American Micronesia in the late 1960s realized the dimensions of disruption being sketched by the Nathan Plan; their consciousness of the issues at stake also found expression in the high commissioner's review. Strong reservations were expressed about the report's recommendations in the areas of land, the importation of foreign labor, and the disturbance of cultural beliefs and practices. Peter Hill, an educational specialist with the Trust Territory, had few illusions about the extent of the change being proposed by the Nathan Plan. He called the plan's objectives "comprehensive, manipulated revolution. It must be thoroughly considered by the public involved, if there is to be hope of anything but catastrophe." Hill saw the sum effects of the Nathan Plan's recommendations, if implemented, as limiting Micronesian involvement to hewing wood and hauling water. Distinguishing between the invention of Micronesia as political entity and the peoples who actually inhabited the area, Hill concluded that the Nathan Plan seemed "to be preoccupied with a region, Micronesia, without suitable concern for the population of Micronesians whose country it is. What's good for Micronesia is not necessarily good for Micronesians—who may be more speedily disinherited."

The Nathan Plan's recommendation for the relocation of atoll populations to district centers and the policies designed to effect that relocation struck a number of reviewers as particularly ominous. The authors of the plan believed that such relocation would promote the development of a larger, more concentrated, better-trained workforce. To promote this migration to the district centers of the major islands, the report called for the elimination or reduction of health, social, and educational services to outlying atoll and island populations.[27] W. A. Forest thought the relocation plan ignored the vital role that land played in Micronesian cultures; it smacked, he wrote, of a "BIA [Bureau of Indian Affairs] reservation philosophy." Peter Coleman, then district administrator for the Mariana Islands and a Samoan by birth, worried about the disruption that such relocation would wreak on the islands' social systems. Coleman went on to argue for the adaptability of Micronesian traditional systems to accommodate new ways and methods. Communal land tenure systems were not necessarily impediments to development; the solution, thought Coleman, lay in finding ways to ensure rather than deprive group owners of the profits earned from their land. Francis B. Mahoney, the director of community development for the Trust Territory, criticized what he saw as the "people be damned" philosophy behind the Nathan Plan. Despite the gravity of these real concerns, the Nathan Plan seemed to have the look of the future about it, or so thought those charged with developing Micronesia.

Modernization Theory as Bourgeois Realism

Although neither the Solomon Report nor the Nathan Plan made explicit its theoretical underpinning, both drew heavily on the modernization theory that dominated development planning in the 1960s. Influenced heavily by the functionalist theories of Talcott Parsons, writers such as Marion Levy, S. M. Lipset, David McClelland, Walt Rostow, and Neil Smelser set the modernization approach within a decidedly capitalist perspective.[28] To these proponents of what came to be the classical school, modernization involved a phased, homogenizing, irreversible, and lengthy process based on European notions of progress and history. The ways in which "traditional societies" of the non-Western world might become modern proved a particular focus of the modernization school. "Traditional societies" were said to solve the basic problems of labor, production, distribution, and want by procedures devised in the distant past, rigidified by a long process of historic trial and error, and maintained by heavy sanctions of law, custom, and belief. To economists of the modernization school, tradition provided a stabilizing, impelling force that ensured a repetitive cycle of society whereby work would be carried out each day very much as it had been done for centuries. The division of labor was fixed; scarcity in nature was closely managed and in ways that allowed for a considerable degree of economic independence from the outside world.

The cost of this kind of economic tradition, however, was progress. Through time and in the West, there evolved the market system whereby individuals sold their labor, rented their land, and invested their capital with little interference from the totalitarian constraints of tradition. With the monetization of labor, land, and capital, economic transactions became standardized. Over time, procedures were devised to govern commerce, manufacture and the consequent passage from agricultural to market-focused societies. A marked proclivity to increase productivity through a finer division of labor was evidenced in the growth of market societies; increased productivity, in turn, intensified the desire for betterment and profits. Competition—individuals struggling against one another for advantage and gain—was said to provide the natural but invisible instrument of regulation for capitalist societies.

Underlying the development of a market economy were assumptions about the rationality of human beings as economic actors, what Marshall Sahlins has called "bourgeois realism."[29] Given the desire for betterment and increased income that lay at the heart of all market activity, modernization theorists assumed that human beings would consider all available options of procurement and choose the least costly. The picture of humans as rational maximizers was not an altogether flattering one as it suggested more self-interested calculation than philanthropy. Although other economic systems within their own particular rationalities were acknowledged, their survival was seen as anachronistic. In the classical modernization scheme of things, economic development then carried with it a regrettable cultural struggle that involved the nonetheless necessary, inevitable replacement of one tradition with the modern economic practices of another.

More pointedly, most early modernization theorists operated on the assumption that economic advance through the nineteenth century was largely a phenomenon of the West. According to one standard textbook, "there was no economic progress in the rest of the world" through the end of the nineteenth century.[30] The long sweep of Western economic advance had left behind four out of five people on the planet and created what came to be known in development parlance as the "underdeveloped world." By the mid-1970s, a billion human beings in the "underdeveloped world" were described as having an annual per capita income of less than $100, while another billion people earned less in a year than the average American family spent in a month. Imperialism, overpopulation, poverty, and the "customs of backwardness" all were identified simply and dispassionately as causes of underdevelopment.

One of the principal objectives of the classical modernization school, then, was to assist citizens of underdeveloped nations to advance toward a more productive, comfortable, and satisfying life. Writing in 1969, Elbert V. Bowden, a former member of the Nathan team, thought Micronesia best approximated Rostow's "five-stages-of-growth" model.[31] He described half of the people as living under the "preconditions of take off," Rostow's second stage, while the other half, having skipped steps three and four, hovered at the threshold of the "age of high mass consumption," a condition made possible not by their own productive capabilities but by American congressional largesse. Better analysis and planning constituted Bowden's solution to the uneven, irregular patterns of the modernization process in Micronesia. There would be other prescriptions as well.

Other Plans, Other Planners

The Solomon and Nathan plans were but the first in a long line of development studies prepared for the Trust Territory government by a host of outside agencies and organizations. Indeed, development planning from the late 1960s through the 1970s assumed the proportions of a growth industry of sorts. Every conceivable resource was scrutinized for its development or income-generating potential; plans examined the feasibility of establishing rice plantations, piggeries, fishing fleets, poultry farms, feed mills, sawmills, mosquito coil factories, boatyards, a distillery and bottling business, handicraft centers, produce markets, hotels, and small canneries. Other studies, many of them carried out locally by the Trust Territory government's Department of Economic Resources and Development, considered the commercial potential of reef fish, pepper, cacao, local fruits, coir fiber, mangrove wood, palm oil, local plant extracts, and the bark of certain trees. The legacy of these efforts amounted to an extensive collection of bound or stapled reports that were quickly shelved and that, if nothing else, earned income for their authors while sustaining the discourse of development.

These other plans, like the Solomon and Nathan reports, expressed historically contexted, culturally specific ideas about life, labor, and profit. They could also be highly idiosyncratic. Of all the development proposals submitted by various organizations and agencies, none was more peculiar than that presented by the Institute of Cultural Affairs (ICA) in September 1974. Based in Chicago, Illinois, and headed by a Dr. Joseph Matthews, the Institute of Cultural Affairs emphasized an approach to development that focused explicitly on the total transformation of community.[32] The institute concentrated its efforts in Micronesia on the Marshall Islands. Given the islands' centuries of exposure to colonialism, the ICA recommended in reverse imperial fashion that development begin with the renaming of the Marshalls as "Lolwelaplap." As outlined in the document "The Marshall Islands Human Development Program," the reformulation of community required a massive training that went to the heart of identity and social cohesiveness. A combination of American popular psychology and "new age" theories of personal growth applied to whole societies, the ICA's program proposed eighty-eight specific training programs grouped under twenty-two social categories of activity that, in turn, were classified according to the five broader spheres said to constitute the nexus of any healthy, modern community. Total costs for the three-year program were projected at $5,301,405, with the Trust Territory government, the Marshallese legislature or Nitijela, the United States Congress, and a number of private foundations expected to provide the funding required. The anticipated success of this effort at social engineering would mean a "New Tomorrow" for the Marshalls; in addition, the emergence of a new spirit in the Marshalls or Lolwelaplap, wrote the project's directors, would serve as a beacon of hope for other areas of the world seeking to get out from under the yoke of colonialism. Although the ICA's proposal garnered some support within the Marshalls and at Trust Territory government headquarters on Saipan, the "actuation" of the Marshalls Human Development Program never occurred. A review of the ICA's proposal by Stanley S. Carpenter, director of territorial affairs for the United States Department of the Interior, dated 23 December 1974, concluded that the program was too broad, too unrealistic, and too costly.[33]

No less peculiar was Wayne C. Thiessen's proposal to transform the Trust Territory into the mobile nation of "Pacifica" whose economy was to be derived from remittances and tax revenues earned by the employment of five thousand young Micronesians as seamen aboard the ships, barges, and tankers that traversed the world's oceans.[34] Another plan, entitled "Micronesia: An Alternative Description," called for the creation of a Micronesian common market as a first step toward the establishment of a self-sufficient economy for the islands.[35] Development as a contracted service necessitated the assurance of economic privileges and incentives for those private corporations willing to take on the task. Western Islands Development Enterprises (WIDE), based in Houston, Texas, offered to manage the development of the islands in accord with the recommendations of the Nathan Plan.[36] In support of its efforts, the company required a graduated thirty-year tax exemption on all its commercial undertakings. WIDE also insisted that the infrastructure be improved, that gambling be legalized, and that it be granted liquor licenses and other concessions in support of its projected tourist, entertainment, and recreational businesses. In return, the corporation promised a healthy degree of economic development, with a high level of participation by Micronesians.

Frustrated by a decade of inertia and by the irrelevance of more recent prescriptions, the Congress of Micronesia, a representative body created by the Trust Territory government in 1965 to enhance the participation of Micronesians in the political process and the subject of the following chapter, passed Public Law 6-56, which required the formulation of a comprehensive development policy for Micronesia. Another of the forces giving impetus to the formulation of an indicative development plan was the projected termination of the Trusteeship Agreement in 1981,[37] which would not eventuate until 1986 for the Marshalls and most of the Caroline Islands and not until 1994 for Palau. The plan covered the five-year period beginning October 1976, and extending through to October 1981. The law authorizing the plan required a draft document to be submitted to the Congress of Micronesia for review by 31 December 1975. To assist in the formulation of this draft, the Congress of Micronesia contracted the services of the United Nations Development Programme.[38]

A fairly lengthy, extensive document, the indicative development plan began with the characterization of the general Micronesian economy as one of underdeveloped resources, inordinate reliance on the government sector for employment, and consumption levels far in excess of indigenous productive capacities and made possible only by the infusion of American money. To break this crippling dependency, the plan sought an increased standard of living through the creation of a restructured, balanced, and self-supporting Micronesian economy and the maintenance of minimum essential government services. Agriculture, marine resources, and tourism were identified as the productive sectors with the most potential for creating employment and generating revenues to help Micronesia become self-supporting economically. In its language, categories, logic, purpose, and representational strategies, the UNDP-assisted document proved to be very much genealogically linked to its predecessors, the Solomon and Nathan plans.

In support of the Trust Territory–wide plan, each of the island districts except the Marianas, which had already made clear its intention to establish a political relationship with the United States apart from any future Micronesian government, was required to produce its own development plan; these district plans were intended to articulate the conditions, needs, resources, and aspirations of particular locales and their people. The necessity of conforming to the style of the territory-wide indicative development plan, however, created a curious set of documents that differed only slightly from one another. The plans for Palau, Yap, Chuuk, Pohnpei, and the Marshalls varied little in their tables of contents and in the actual substance of the plans that followed. Cursory descriptions of the people, their islands, and their past prefaced more extensive though equally misleading narratives involving population, employment, and income statistics. Summaries of transportation systems, commerce and banking facilities, and the condition of existing infrastructure introduced the analysis of local agriculture, marine resources, tourism, and small industries. The individual district plans then closed with an assessment of on-going economic projects, a statement of goals and objectives, and a commitment to the hallowed but ultimately colonizing principles of self-sufficiency and culturally compatible development. As such, these plans evidenced at a micro level the discursive strategy and normalization process that economic development in Micronesia was intended to be.

This uniformity resulted in part, not from any lack of critical response, but from distant editorial interventions that tended to silence local voices seeking to give these district plans a different character. A separate study produced by the Palau District Planning Office in September 1975 noted that districtwide planning, directed from Trust Territory headquarters on Saipan, could not ignore the variety of regional and sectional interests within Palau itself. This report saw local government as stymied by territorial restrictions and thus unable to respond to the specific requests of locales within Palau.[39] A cover letter that accompanied the submission of a revised development plan for Yap district noted the confusion, uncertainty, and suspicion with which most Yapese regarded the "monetary and knowledge system" of the outside world.[40] An earlier draft introduction to that same plan had identified Yap's land tenure system as a critical part of the island-state's sociocultural system, but not compatible with economic development. The statement elicited a large, pronounced question mark in the margins of the draft document from an anonymous reviewer at Trust Territory headquarters on Saipan.[41] The same reviewer wrote "not feasible—culture discourages work" next to the draft plan's intent to provide jobs for all Yapese who desired them. The final submitted version of the Yap Indicative Development Plan contained no reference to any incompatibility between development and the island's land tenure system and no mention of any commitment to full employment on the island.

To facilitate the implementation of the territorial and local plans, the Congress of Micronesia hired several UNDP economists as consultants. This group produced a total of fifty-six reports between April 1976 and July 1980; the focus of their investigations ranged from specific sectoral development strategies in the different districts to national taxation policies, job training, youth programs, health care planning, education, and historic preservation.[42] Their ideas and approaches to development did not provide any counterbalance to an entrenched American colonial bureaucracy's views on development. Rather, the UNDP specialists would reveal their own very institutionalized, highly standardized view of what economic development should be for the Trust Territory of the Pacific Islands.

Commitments to respect the dignity of local peoples and their ways of living filled the prefaces of UNDP reports. This cultural sensitivity often disappeared in the bodies of these reports, where the UNDP's ultimately standardized treatment of development issues showed itself. Indeed, the UNDP's *Policies and Procedures Manual* included a section entitled "The Project Document" that specified the format for all UNDP reports.[43] The manual prescribed in precise terms the topics of inquiry to be addressed, the methods of analysis to be employed, the exact placement of conclusions and recommendations in the body of the report, and even the language of presentation itself. In effect, this standardization reduced Micronesia to but another indistinguishable area of the underdeveloped world. The UNDP's vision of development, then, endorsed a reigning global economic order that had no place and little tolerance for other ways of being in the world. In a 1989 publication, Graham Hancock criticized international aid bureaucrats as "lords of poverty."[44] It is a phrase that, without much adjustment, could be easily applied to many UNDP personnel and other developmental specialists working in Micronesia during the mid to late 1970s.

The disparity between the UNDP's rhetoric and praxis did not go unnoticed within the islands. Dan Perin, the economic advisor to the Micronesian Commission on Future Political Status and Transition, questioned the data used by UNDP planners.[45] He believed it to be incomplete, misleading in its terms of analysis, and useful only at the most aggregate of levels. Moreover, this flawed database had begun to take on a life of its own as it was cited often and uncritically by other and later planners. The result of this statistical hocus pocus, warned Perin, was a masking of the reality of conditions in the Trust Territory. Perin also criticized plans for a UNDP workshop for Micronesian statisticians on the grounds that it served the conveniences of the sponsor while not at all addressing the needs of local governmental institutions.[46]

The ways in which UNDP reports rendered the islands unrecognizable to Micronesians also elicited strong criticism. In a letter to Dr. Nahum Benzeevi, the project manager for all UNDP development planning in Micronesia, Margie Falanruw, the director of the Yap Institute of Natural Science, criticized what she saw as the irrelevance, error, and cultural insensitivity of a UNDP agricultural survey in Yap. She wrote,

> It appeared that the survey is more suited to a large area with a monocultural cropping system than the highly diversified small holding system of agriculture on Yap. I cannot see how this field

> data could match the precision of the mathematical analysis described, and fear that this may result in an impressive, but probably inaccurate project. Further, I feel that such a detailed island-wide survey would be an invasion of the privacy of Yapese households, especially the work of women. The cultural matters associated with agriculture on Yap must not be known to those who designed the survey.[47]

Not all UNDP personnel were oblivious to the distortion created by their standardized approach to development. An inkling of self-awareness emerged in the evaluation of a UNDP development planning workshop held in Palau from 13 to 16 December 1976.[48] The workshop brought together fourteen UNDP officials assigned to various projects within the Trust Territory or from regional offices in the larger Asia-Pacific region. They were to consider a variety of issues related to the implementation of Palau's five-year indicative development plan. Three local government officials and a Palauan priest later joined the fourteen in a private evaluation of the workshop. A member of the UNDP delegation, Christopher Goss, wrote a somewhat negative assessment of the workshop based on the comments that emerged from the evaluation session.

According to Goss' report, the workshop followed too closely upon local reviews of the plan. Palauans had not had sufficient opportunity to fully grasp and respond to the complexities of the document. The organization of the workshop itself also caused problems. The UNDP experts had wanted to break up into subcommittees to focus on specific topics. Their Palauan hosts, however, insisted on remaining in a general plenary session where everyone could hear everything said. In evaluating the performance of UNDP workshop participants, the assessor remarked that they had not been sufficiently catalytic. There were too many of them; they tended to dominate discussions and to make their points in ways not easily understood by Palauans. And discussants repeated one another's comments. Noting the indicative economic development plan's commitment to reduced government expenditure and to efficiency and self-reliance, Goss concluded that the use of UN money for such a relatively extravagant, ineffective workshop was "not exactly the way" to reinforce the plan's message.

Goss' report also noted what appeared to be a low level of Palauan participation in the workshop; the silence was attributed to cultural constraints within Palau that prohibited people from standing up and speaking their minds. Commenting on the silence from the Palauan audience, one of the four local evaluators said, "We hear each other talking all the time and we want to hear what you have to say." A stronger Palauan voice did emerge during the evaluation session. One Palauan complained that the workshop lacked clarity and focus. Another noted a certain "degree of aimlessness" to the proceedings. The chairman of the workshop was criticized for failing to exert more control over the discussion. In a sense, then, the flawed workshop held to discuss the Palau District Indicative Development Plan served as a metaphor for the process of economic development in the Trust Territory of the Pacific Islands. There was not enough time; the general silence of the people most affected was frustrating, even unsettling; what local responses there were went largely ignored or unnoticed; the experts were too many, too foreign, and possessing of a body of knowledge that was alien, not totally comprehensible, and foreboding in the dimensions of change that it outlined.

The Peace Corps in Paradise

Professional planners understood the need to advertise the idea of development. The Palauan workshop had demonstrated yet again the chasm between those who brought change and those they sought to change. Some intermediary organization that might bridge or at least help to close the development divide in the Trust Territory seemed necessary. What might be employed to soften the harsher aspects of development? Who could be used to show the energy, vitality, potential, and exuberance that economic development might unleash in Micronesia and among Micronesians? Some thought the Peace Corps was just the institution to put a young, energetic, happy face on the American presence and the objectives that underlay it. The Peace Corps, of course, defined itself in less political, more humanitarian terms. The gap between self-definition and the process of Americanization in which it was enlisted to serve forms part of the complex, sometimes troubled history of the Peace Corps in Micronesia.

The Solomon Report had recommended the use of Peace Corps volunteers as a way to strengthen the educational system, maximize contact between Micronesians and Americans, and promote, through a favorable plebiscite vote, the islands' permanent affiliation with the United States. Hesitancy greeted the first proposals to put the Peace Corps in the Trust Territory. Though not an explicit instrument of American foreign policy according to its founders, the Peace Corps worked exclusively in developing countries. Micronesia, however, occupied a liminal space in terms of political geography. The 1947 Trusteeship Agreement blurred the islands' status as foreign; the presence of an American administration gave the area a near-domestic quality in the minds of many. Initially, then, Micronesia as an American territory was not foreign enough for the Peace Corps. The situation changed, however.

The real impetus for the placement of the Peace Corps in Micronesia came from a series of international criticisms of the American administration. The previously cited report of a 1961 United Nations Visiting Mission had criticized the failure of the United States to meet its obligations under the Trusteeship Agreement.[49] A 1965 study by the World Health Organization deplored the poor services and lack of trained personnel that severely hampered the health care system in the Trust Territory. Sensitive to the increasing volume of criticism in a United Nations becoming more and more strident on the issue of decolonization, United States Ambassador to the UN Arthur Goldberg is said to have taken the initiative in urging the Peace Corps be sent to the Trust Territory. Goldberg secured the support of the Johnson administration, including Secretary of the Interior Stewart L. Udall, whose department had administrative responsibility for the islands. The decision to send the Peace Corps into Micronesia was announced in May 1966, during the Trusteeship Council meetings.

Within days of Goldberg's announcement, the Peace Corps launched its most intensive and publicized recruitment campaign ever.[50] Posters were hastily printed and distributed on college campuses across the nation just before the spring semester's end. "The Peace Corps Goes to Paradise" was the title of a recruiting brochure to enlist prospective volunteers for service in the Trust Territory. The cover of the brochure pictured an idyllic stretch of white sand beach, a row of low-lying atolls on the horizon, and, in the foreground, a canoe paddled by two young boys. The text mentioned tropical islands, enchanted evenings, swaying palm trees, and sun-kissed maidens. But there was also trouble in Paradise. The islands, proclaimed the brochure's text, suffered from understaffed schools, bad roads, inefficient medical facilities, an excess of imported food, and inadequate water and sanitation systems.

The brochure and the larger campaign of which it was a part achieved the intended effect. Within a few weeks, three thousand applications had been received; these numbers were aided by a special abbreviated application form and an exemption from the standardized placement tests usually required for entry into the Peace Corps. In addition, applicants were promised an answer by telephone within fifteen days of the receipt of their application. The first contingent of volunteers received twelve weeks of culture and language training on an abandoned movie set in Key West, Florida, where *PT-109*, a movie about the wartime heroics of John F. Kennedy, had been filmed. Preparations for the arrival of the volunteers in the islands involved extensive consultations between Peace Corps representatives and Trust Territory government officials on matters ranging from housing and medical care to job placement and supervision. In addition, the Trust Territory government undertook an extensive public relations campaign to prepare host communities for the influx of hundreds of young Americans. Radio announcements, newspaper stories, and public seminars were all used to educate and prepare the public. Optimism, and naivete, abounded. Ross Pritchard, the director of the Peace Corps' Far Eastern Region, which supervised operations in Micronesia, proclaimed, "The Peace Corps intends to alter substantially in a relatively short period of time, say three to five years, the twenty year record of neglect and dismal achievement."[51] Such a statement suggested little real deviation from the established discourse of development in the Trust Territory; the Peace Corps simply promised to work harder and better for change.

By December 1966, the first 323 volunteers had arrived in the Trust Territory. Many in this first group were originally slated to work in public health, but a lack of technical skills coupled with a dearth of positions and programs at the local Micronesian level led to the reassignment of these volunteers as teachers in elementary school classrooms. Indeed, the first Peace Corps volunteers, most of whom held a recently awarded bachelor's degree in the humanities, worked most often in elementary education. The number of Peace Corps volunteers soon increased dramatically; by the summer of 1967, there were more than 452 in Micronesia.[52] In 1968, some 940 volunteers were serving in the Trust Territory, creating a ratio of one volunteer for every hundred Micronesians—by far the highest in the Peace Corps world.[53] Unlike Trust Territory personnel, who concentrated in the district centers, volunteers lived in remote villages, on outer islands, and with Micronesians. Relations between volunteers and expatriate government workers became strained in the first years because of the often critical posture of volunteers toward the Trust Territory government and their expressed sympathy for Micronesians.[54]

The political effect of the Peace Corps during its first years proved a concern to some. A June 1972 editorial in Guam's *Pacific Daily News* noted that the Peace Corps' presence and the activities of its volunteers had not always been conducive to the objectives of American policy in Micronesia. The editorial went on to blame the Peace Corps for instilling the troublesome concept of independence in the minds of Micronesians. The Micronesian Legal Services Program, created and initially staffed by Peace Corps lawyers, proved particularly nettlesome to Trust Territory officials in its advocacy of the legal rights of Micronesians. Referring to the political posturing of volunteers in the first years, John Carver, assistant secretary of interior during the Kennedy administration, thought Micronesia marked "the most unworthy page in Peace Corps history."[55] Others held that the Peace Corps, though a more liberal, accessible, even manipulable presence for Micronesians, constituted but a minor variation in the larger American effort. Perhaps, an insight into the relativity of things proved for many volunteers the at once most subversive and redeeming feature of their experience. One volunteer wrote that the Yapese were a careful, thoughtful, highly selective, and ultimately contented people; as a result, they saw little value in change.[56] Another expressed the opinion that Yapese villagers, with their very deliberate pace of life, were at least as well off as harried American commuters who worked hard and saved money all their lives to visit places in the Pacific like Yap.[57] In any event, the recruitment of older volunteers with more technical backgrounds soon would give the Peace Corps in the islands a very different look.

Within a decade of the Peace Corps' arrival in Micronesia, greater emphasis began being placed on specific skills that could contribute more immediately and directly to economic development in the islands. By 1978, individuals were being recruited and placed as accountants, small business consultants, credit union specialists, urban planners, construction engineers, heavy equipment operators, and fisheries advisors. In the job descriptions for these more technically skilled positions lay clearer specifications for the ways in which Peace Corps volunteers would contribute to the development of the islands. These carefully detailed job descriptions spelled out the problems to be addressed by the volunteers, whose prime responsibility now lay not with language learning or cultural adjustment, but with their job assignment.[58] For those volunteers working in development, the impediments to progress remained the same: lack of hard data, inadequate infrastructure, faulty or nonexistent technology, and unreliable market conditions. Volunteers were cautioned to expect Micronesians' "lack of interest on a sustained basis" in most things and an extended family structure that discouraged individual initiative through its insistence upon sharing. No matter what the particulars of their individual job descriptions, all volunteers were told to expect living and work situations that would be demanding, frustrating, and difficult. The lack of conveniences, the generally slower pace of life, and the very different sense of time were identified as some of the more frustrating aspects of their job assignments.

In a speech given at Columbia College on 14 February 1968, Jack Hood

Vaughn, head of the Peace Corps, had talked of the Peace Corps' mission to oppose the "shrinking man" syndrome described in the writings of Marshall McLuhan. Peace Corps volunteers, argued Vaughn, were breaking beyond structures set by bureaucrats and social engineers to a deeper realization of the possibilities of human development and the potential of the human spirit.[59] By 1978, however, Jack Vaughn's Renaissance volunteer had faded; it seemed as if McLuhan's controlled, bureaucratized "shrinking man" had returned, all in the name of cost efficiency, behavioral objectives, and appropriate development planning.

More Than a Living

Fisheries, agriculture, and tourism constituted the three areas around which development planners and Trust Territory officials believed a more self-sufficient if not totally self-reliant economy might be built. A long, thick, tedious history on the order of Dorothy Richard's three-volume study of the naval administration of the islands would be needed to record all the efforts in these three areas of anticipated economic growth. Rather than attempt such an inventory, I choose instead to characterize these areas in their more general patterns and to complement this admittedly sweeping approach by examining more recent ethnographic texts that indicate the dimensions of transformation involved in these development undertakings and the histories, epistemologies, and hierarchies that informed local responses to them. Development, as we shall see, did not go as planned by the USCC or the Solomon and Nathan reports.

The Trust Territory government and later the Congress of Micronesia expended considerable time, effort, and money on development of marine resources. The 1960s witnessed efforts to develop refrigeration and cold-storage facilities on the major islands. Micronesians traveled to Hawai'i and later Taiwan and Singapore to receive training in fishing skills, technology, and industry management, while an extended, ultimately successful initiative was begun to eradicate the crown-of-thorns starfish that threatened the islands' coral reefs. The 1964 opening of a tuna-processing plant in Palau by Van Camp Seafood Company appeared to mark a major advance in the commercial possibilities of fishing in Micronesia. In the 1970s, efforts intensified. The establishment of the Micronesian Maritime Demonstration Center in Palau in 1973 evidenced a strong commitment, at least initially, to the fields of both fresh- and saltwater mariculture. There followed local boat-building projects, more infrastructure development, and a plethora of surveys and workshops run by a host of not entirely altruistic international aid agencies such as the Japan International Cooperation Agency, the South Pacific Commission, and the United Nations Fish and Agriculture Organization. Japan used the 1974 gift of seven fishing vessels to deflect criticism of its failure to redress Micronesian war claims. Corporate-sponsored organizations such as the American tuna industry's Pacific Tuna Development Corporation offered assistance to local tuna fishermen as a way ultimately to promote access to Micronesian waters for wide-ranging American tuna boat operators.

All of these efforts seemed not to make a great deal of difference. Although the reported total value of marine exports increased from $27,000 in 1963 to roughly $3 million by 1976, commercial fisheries in Micronesia never generated the kind of revenues required to make fishing a viable, major contributor to the territory's economy; indeed, total exports, earned primarily through copra, fisheries, and tourism, never exceeded more than 14 percent of annual cash flows into the territory between 1963 and 1979.[60] Only with the establishment of the Micronesian Maritime Authority in 1978 and the subsequent licensing of foreign fishing vessels within the territorial waters of the three self-governing entities to emerge from the Trust Territory would commercial fishing provide any consistent form of revenue.

Micronesians topped the list of the many causes cited to explain the failure to develop marine resources. Planners, consultants, and specialists all despaired of making the islanders commercial fishermen. Ronald Powell, however, had better sense than most of what was entailed in making fishing a business in Micronesia. In a November 1971 report on fishing in Chuuk, Powell, a Trust Territory fishing gear and methods specialist, noted that the best results occurred when local fishermen worked in familiar areas, during times they preferred to fish, and with gear they had chosen. Teams led by people of stature and respect in the community fished well; their catches proved consistently high.[61] Teams composed of fishermen from different areas and with no clear leader fished poorly and, according to Powell, proved difficult to manage. Powell reported too that different areas of Chuuk's Lagoon seemed to be the preserve of certain groups or clans; he recommended that the ownership of the reefs be carefully considered when strategies to improve or extend fisheries development were developed.

Powell conceded that much about the life of indigenous people might seem anomalous or confusing to strangers to the Pacific islands; yet subsistence fishing possessed a logic and a practice that worked effectively in meeting the needs and priorities of communal groups. The division of the catch, for example, reflected values or concerns that were more social than economic.[62] Matters affecting seniority, rank, and extended family obligations defeated any simple distribution of the catch along lines that Americans saw as equitable or fair. Powell concluded,

> In any closely knit community where births, marriages, deathes [*sic*], feasts, epidemics, public holidays and mechanical breakdowns are everyday events, this factor will not improve until a great change comes from improved communications, skilled mechanics, stocks of engine parts, pressure from social changes and eventually the motivation that is so necessary to a full monetary economy to operate. These are all cultural changes which no amount of wishful thinking will change quickly.[63]

Powell's report hints at fishing as a deep, encompassing social practice not easily or quickly made into a business. Michael D. Lieber's recent ethnography, *More Than a Living: Fishing and the Social Order on a Polynesian Atoll,* underscores that point dramatically. Writing about the Polynesian outlier of Kapingamarangi in the Eastern Caroline group, Lieber describes a people once possessed of eighty-four different kinds of fishing activities ordered through seven distinct techniques ranging from netting, poling, and trolling to the use of weirs; moreover, they could name more than 260 separate species of fish that moved through the waters about their atoll. More important, fishing for the people of the atoll once held deep cosmological significance with the Kapinga word for fishing translating as "surfacing the sacred," a phrase indicative of the formerly intense relationship between the Kapinga and their gods.[64]

As Lieber notes, the survival of the people of Kapinga was dependent upon their relationship with their deities. Political authority rested in the organization of the priesthood which, in precolonial times, was the institution that held the community together. The high priest or *di aligi hagamadego* controlled the resources of the island, determined the timing of their use, and oversaw their allocation among the community.[65] With regard to "surfacing the sacred," this meant that the high priest effectively decided upon the number of canoes to be built, conducted the rituals associated with fishing, set the actual timing of the expeditions, and directed the distribution of the catch. The men's clubhouses, led by the headman or *tomono,* served as an intermediary institution between the head priest and the larger Kapinga community.

Like most other activities on the island, fishing required the cooperation of the high priest and the *tomono.* Acting together, these men determined the ownership of the canoes and the composition of the crews who

Men fishing or surfacing the sacred on Kapingamarangi, 1950. (Kenneth P. Emory, Bishop Museum)

worked them. A fisherman's knowledge of the reef derived from his actual experience of it which, in turn, depended upon the cordiality of his relations with the high priest and *tomono.* The symbolically rich, dense practice of fishing also provided the measure of men on Kapingamarangi: to be a good fisherman was to be a good man. A fisherman's career paralleled his journey through life and could be construed as a series of concentric, expanding circles that radiated from the island toward the horizon. A man's ability to move from one circle to the next marked his increasing social status as well as his skills as a fisherman.

If fishing brought people close to the sacred, it also approached a science in the mechanics of its practice. Kapinga named, remembered, mentally mapped, and thus knew the reefs, shallows, and open ocean areas of their environment.[66] Seasonal and climatic variations were observed, studied, and noted. The gods proved as variable a category of environmental influence as the wind, currents, tides, and stages of the moon. Men trained their sons to observe the regularity in the habitats and habits of different ocean creatures so that they might recognize the intervention of the gods in the deviations and departures from those observed patterns.

Given the centrality of fishing to Kapinga society, it is not surprising that historical changes in fishing technologies, methods, and larger cosmological beliefs disturbed life on the island.[67] Conversion to Christianity and the imposition of colonial rule worked to transform fishing from a symbol of social order to a metaphor evoking the disruption brought by foreign influences. Lieber writes that initial contacts with Europeans in 1877 introduced sailcloth, metal hooks, flies, and pliers. These first foreign influences had little initial effect; Kapinga preferred their own strategies, techniques, and technologies. The arrival of Europeans, however, did present Kapinga with alternative sources of wealth and power independent of the atoll's gods and the priests who were their agents. The consequent decline in this cosmological order was exacerbated significantly by the establishment of Japanese colonial rule over Micronesia in 1914. A series of natural disasters, compounded by the arrival of an aggressive, demanding, and militarily backed Japanese trader bent upon reorganizing the nature and purposes of economic activity on the atoll, disturbed life on Kapingamarangi in profound ways.

The cult house was abandoned, Christianity adopted, and a Kapinga colony established on the island of Pohnpei, the closest center of Japanese administrative authority in the area. These developments broke the link between the secular and the sacred in Kapinga society, created a new form of government around a king chosen by popular consensus, and allowed for a fairly consistent flow of people, goods, and ideas between Kapingamarangi and a now much larger, not so easily ordered or understood world. Men's houses also declined as the Protestant Congregationalist church became more central to life on the island. By 1919, the entire hierarchy of constraints emanating from the presence of the gods, along with the gods themselves, had been eliminated.

This cosmological collapse secularized fishing and gave the Kapinga greater access to native and nonnative technology. The most dramatic change came in canoe ownership. The demise of the priesthood left landowners free to control their own trees; this, in turn, made it possible for more individuals to make more canoes. Individual and small group fishing became increasingly common by the late 1930s, and at the expense of more communal efforts that had once characterized the organization and practice of fishing on the island. Later, during the American administration of the area, the introduction of imported fishing equipment, most notably the spear gun and outboard motor, would individualize fishing even further on Kapingamarangi.

Lieber's ethnography contains within in it a cultural history of fishing that examines the disturbance wrought by colonialism on a practice inextricably linked to notions of identity and community on the atoll. The practice of fishing, believes Lieber, is thus intimately linked with and deeply reflective of the Kapinga's view of themselves. Although colonialism and market forces have brought major changes to Kapingamarangi, fishing continues as an essentially social activity in support of the Kapinga community. The Kapinga's ability to cope with an expanding, strange, sometimes hostile world is mirrored in the changes that have taken place in their practice of fishing. The centrality of fishing on Kapingamarangi proved just how much was at stake in the effort to commercialize what had once been a deep, sacred activity and one that, despite the formidable forces of modern colonialism, remains closely liked to the notion of community. Development planners had no consciousness of such a history in their dealing with a sphere of activity that had once been more than a living—and remained, though in reduced form, much more than a business.

Losing Big

The history of agricultural development in the Trust Territory during the 1960s and 1970s parallels that of marine resources.[68] All of the consultant reports, experimental programs, overseas training, pest eradication projects, international assistance, and foreign corporate dabbling would not make agriculture a viable sector of the Trust Territory economy. Only copra production generated any kind of consistent income during the 1960s and 1970s, averaging just over $2 million per year in total earnings during the two decades.[69]

The exasperation of agricultural specialists was compounded by their unmitigated conviction that major economic change was inevitable. A survey of agriculture conducted by the United States Department of Agriculture in 1975 made the point assertively. An appendix to that report entitled "The People" began with a three-sentence history on the simple needs, subsistence economy, and communal exchange system that characterized Micronesian societies in precolonial times and that persisted into the contemporary period. The authors of the report conceded the basic conflicts inherent in the imposition of a money-based economy on a subsistence lifestyle. To more liberal-minded individuals who might ask why these people could not be left alone, the response was, "They will be drawn into a money-based economy no matter what kind of government they have in the future. They will be forced to accept, at least to a degree, the concept of commercial agricultural production."[70]

To the dismay of planners, agriculturists, and other officials, the commercial activity for which the people of the islands exhibited the most enthusiasm was the establishment of small retail stores. As early as July 1947, there were 112 Micronesian-owned businesses.[71] In that same year, the navy received 129 applications for licenses from Palau and another 47 from Kosrae. The interest did not subside over the years; by July 1974, there were 450 Micronesian-owned businesses licensed and operating in the Trust Territory, the vast majority of which were small family retail stores.[72] Development specialists tended to view these retail stores as economically inconsequential and as indicative of people's blind, senseless attraction to Western consumer goods and to their modest, misguided understandings of investment, expenditure, and business in general. The eventual failure or closure of many of these small retail stores only served to indicate how flawed was Micronesians' business sense. This assessment reflected the widely held assumption that when capitalist practices were introduced into non-Western cultures, local systems of economy disintegrated and the logic that informed them was perversely transferred to modern economic practices.[73]

Glenn Petersen provides a cultural explanation for the large number of small business failures on Pohnpei that suggests a very different sense of economy bound up with prestige-enhancing strategies designed to advance the rank and status of the bankrupt store owner.[74] Petersen writes of a deep, historical pattern whereby foreign goods and resources are incorporated into the island's political economy to serve decidedly local goals. Much of this traditional economy focuses on a system of intense, competitive feasting whereby groups or individuals vie for merit, distinction, and increased status.[75] In these competitive feasts, emphasis falls on size, quantity, and expense. Pohnpeians' use of the English language phrase "go for broke" marks the intensity of the effort and its costs. Those who produce the biggest yams, kava plants, or pigs, or who contribute the largest amounts of material goods ranging from bags of rice, canned food, and bolts of cloth to pick-up trucks earn the greatest acclaim, often signified by the awarding of a high title. In something resembling the potlatch, these feasts speak ultimately to the very meaning of being Pohnpeian.

Culturally informed, prestige-enhancing strategies manifest themselves in other, seemingly more modern areas of life on the island. Focusing on the community of Awak in the northeastern section of the island, Petersen writes of stores that have a commercial life span of four to five years.[76] These stores open with a flourish, prosper for a while, and eventually fade into decline and bankruptcy. The process begins with a loan or the sale of a small piece of land, which provides the initial capital forma-

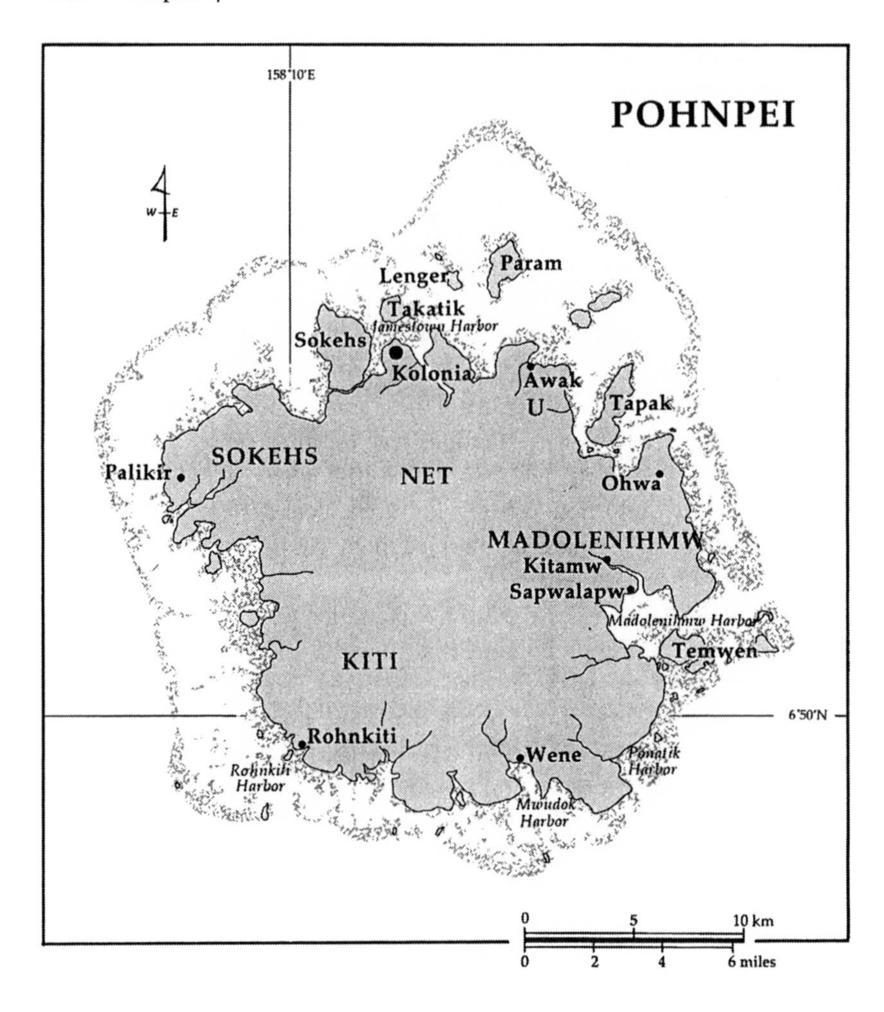

tion for the opening of the store. The store owner, usually but not always a male, then establishes accounts with wholesalers on the island. Initially, only family members receive credit; other members of the community are expected to pay cash for goods purchased. Over time, however, credit is extended to more people, with the result that the store owner's debt begins to increase significantly. Although the benefactors of this extended credit do make payments on their debt, these payments do not keep up with the liabilities of the store owner. Wholesalers eventually cut off the store owner's accounts, and the business has to close. In strict economic terms, the store's demise results from the overextension of credit. The regularity of this pattern has frustrated business advisors who see the

Feasting at Nan U on Pohnpei, 1973. (Trust Territory Archives, Pacific Collection, University of Hawai'i Library)

cure of better fiscal management as obvious, if ignored. Petersen, however, sees larger cultural dynamics at work. He writes,

> Individuals seek ways of demonstrating prowess and generosity over a long period of time, and it turns out that a store is an excellent way of doing so. It allows one to lose—while the community benefits—slowly and publicly. It converts an accumulation of cash into stock and a business that is visible for years. The loss itself, then, is the investment; it is converted into social gain.[77]

Luhs loud or "losing big" is the phrase Pohnpeians use to refer to the commercial collapse that advances the store owner's standing in the community. Petersen concludes that the people of Pohnpei diffuse the pressure to develop by diverting foreign dollars and goods through the channels of their political economy. In terms of the island's economy, production, possession, and distribution are a part of a larger process that cannot be easily or neatly separated into capitalistic schemes. With goods moving so quickly through the system, there is no time for accumulation; to produce, writes Petersen, is to distribute.[78] Like Sahlins, then, Petersen sees a process concerned not with capitalist notions of economy but with the development or elaboration of local culture. Petersen ultimately reminds his readers of the cultural persistence on Pohnpei that seeks to control the forces of development through the enhancement of local systems of economy.

The Battle of Map

The planning literature from the 1960s and 1970s cited tourism as the third major area of economic activity through which Micronesia might achieve a viable, self-sufficient economy. Roland Force, an anthropologist who had worked in Palau, later stated a highly idealized, almost romantic argument for tourism in a UNDP-commissioned study he conducted. Force wrote,

> To note with appreciation someone's prized possession is to compliment him. What greater compliment can be paid anyone than to appreciate his or her heritage. In the final analysis, tourism is a matter of personal relations, of contact between people who are brought together on the home territory of one of them. The more the guest understands about his host, the more successful will be their relationship and ultimately the visit.[79]

Great irony pervaded the argument for the development of tourism in Micronesia, however: cultural practices, regarded as the foremost impediment to general commercial development, needed to be enhanced to emphasize the exotic and make profitable the different if tourism was to flourish.

An indication of just how extensive were the adjustments required for the expansion of tourism comes from a document prepared for a planning conference held in June 1973 on Saipan.[80] At the district level, the document called for the establishment of tourist commissions and of educational programs for businessmen, government officials, and other directly affected parties and for impact studies, guidebooks, and training programs in hotel and restaurant skills. Needed also were tax incentives, high-priority loans for tourist-related businesses, government financial assistance to district tourist commissions, the enhancement of local handicraft manufacture, the promotion of cultural and artistic activities believed to be of interest to tourists, the maintenance of law and order, and the establishment of currency exchanges. Responsibilities at the territory-wide level included the establishment of a tourist board or commission, an extensive marketing and advertising campaign, production and distribution of general promotional materials, the development of effective record keeping, the creation of land use and zoning regulations, the setting of architectural and construction standards, and the passage of legislation designed to regulate a host of tourism-related issues ranging from the environment to pricing to artifact and site preservation.

Statistics from the early 1970s seemed encouraging. With direct government assistance beginning in 1968, the average annual increase in visitor entries between 1968 and 1974 was 35 percent.[81] A total of 66,017 visitors entered the Trust Territory in 1975, spending $4,951,275; this dollar amount made tourism the most profitable sector of the local economy for that year.[82] These figures proved misleading, however, as the Marianas by itself accounted for more than three-quarters of all tourists, most of them from Japan. With the withdrawal of the Marianas in that same year to become a commonwealth of the United States, tourist numbers and dollars for the rest of the Trust Territory dropped by almost half for the rest of the decade.

In a 1974 public address on the future of tourism in the islands, Chief of Tourism for the Trust Territory Mike Ashman tried to survey the social dimensions of the industry. Ashman could detect no real problems—bad service yes, but no negative trends. Misunderstandings could of course arise and did. Tourists' desire for fresh fruits and native foods conflicted with many Micronesians' perceptions of papaya as pig feed and bananas as low-status food for the poor and impoverished.[83] The accommodations available often proved disappointing; most tourists aspired to stay in thatched cottages along pristine beaches only to discover cement block hotels with hot tin roofs situated along heavily trafficked roads in the middle of noisy district towns.

Micronesian attitudes toward tourism varied, and in surprising ways. In his address, Ashman told of a chance encounter with a group of Micronesian political leaders in front of the Ala Moana Hotel in Honolulu. An advocate of controlled tourism, Ashman asked the members of the delegation if they would like to see something as mammoth as the Ala Moana Hotel built in Micronesia. The answer came back "yes"; the big hotel seemed an impressive structure, the kind that could provide a substantial number of jobs for Micronesians. Ashman then baited the group by asking if they would like to see their sons and daughters working as bellboys and waitresses in such an establishment. The reply was again affirmative; "The only people in that hotel that are smiling are the bellboys and waitresses. They look happier than the tourists do and probably have more money in the bank, too." The politicians' endorsement notwithstanding,

Ashman understood the kinds of objections raised by others who likened tourism to cultural prostitution and who bemoaned the disturbance to the meanings and purposes of traditional activities performed before audiences of tourists. Ashman himself took a more practical approach toward the issue, emphasizing the employment and income benefits and the chance for young Micronesians no longer interested in the old ways to interact with the larger world. To him, Micronesian culture was strong and resilient and had been coping with change for centuries. Ashman doubted that tourism would "wipe out things which are Micronesian."[84]

Local reservations over tourism proved deeper, more extensive, and more entangled than Ashman's address suggested. They also demonstrated the confluence of sometimes conflicting interests that defied simple categorization or analysis. On Pohnpei, there was stiff opposition to a proposal to build a Continental-Travel Lodge Hotel in the district in 1971.[85] The proposal called for the construction of a fifty-unit, Western-style complex using imported materials and at a cost of approximately $30,000 to $50,000 per unit. Writing to the high commissioner in behalf of an interim committee created by the then Ponape District Legislature to investigate the issue, Santiago Joab, the chairman, cited the project's disruption to the island's culture and, along more utilitarian and political arguments, its failure to involve local people and local resources. The committee believed strongly that the materials and expertise needed to build the hotel already existed on the island; moreover, there were a number of locally owned and operated tourist facilities currently under construction and being funded with loans from the district legislature. Joab and the other members of the interim committee concluded that the Continental-Travel Lodge Hotel, being such a foreign enterprise in conception, construction, and operation, would have a negative cultural and economic effect. "We assume," concluded Joab, "that neither the Trust Territory government nor Continental would wish to build a hotel in a district that strongly opposes it, and therefore ask that you make the necessary arrangements to prevent the hotel from being built." A resolution passed by the Ponape District Legislature on 4 October 1971 supported the findings of the interim committee as relayed to the high commissioner by its chairman, Santiago Joab.[86]

No district of the Trust Territory, however, was more reluctant to engage in tourism development than Yap. Through the 1960s and 1970s, Yap consistently registered the lowest visitor counts among the districts of the Trust Territory, and not by accident. In 1968, the Yap District Legislature passed a resolution that Trust Territory officials regarded as

YAP
138°10'E
RUMUNG
MAP
FANIF
Tageren Canal
GAGIL
TOMIL
Gachpar
WELOY
Tomil Harbor
Nimar
Colonia
DALIPEBINAW
9°30'N
9°30'N
RULL
KANIFAY
GILIMAN
Guror
W
E
0
2
4
6 km
0
2
4 mi
138°10'E

expressive of an antitourism sentiment. William C. Rhyne, the director of economic development, commenting on the resolution in a memo to the high commissioner, stated that the Yapese would not be troubled by foreign entrepreneurs since "private enterprise is not likely to seek to push itself into areas where it is not wanted—particularly when there are innumerable claimants for attention in the vast underdeveloped areas."[87] Rhyne noted, however, that other areas of economic development were limited on Yap and that the people were apparently not content with subsistence living and a barter economy. Rhyne went on to add that if the Yapese were unwilling to accept the social and cultural risks that would accompany the advent of tourism, he saw no practical method of handling a growing population that sought meaningful work, except through migration to areas more inclined toward "progress."

A serious confrontation developed between the chiefs of the district of Map on Yap proper and the Yap Nature Life Garden, Inc., a resort complex funded by the Transpacific Development Corporation of Tokyo.[88] The confrontation involved land, power, and the role of chiefs in Yapese society. On 3 January 1973, the chiefs of Map had drafted and translated into English a petition, "To Whatever Legal, Governmental and Other Authorities or Persons It May Concern Within and Beyond the District of Yap in the Trust Territory of the Pacific Islands and to All Who Love Justice." The presence of the Yap Nature Life Garden was regarded as an "unwelcome invasion" that had taken advantage of the people's hospitality, goodwill, and inexperience to establish itself unlawfully on land belonging to the villagers of Cho'ol and Wachalab in Map. The petitioners, 168 of the 241 adults residing in Map, accused the project of usurping lands, displaying dictatorial manners in the area, intentionally obscuring the nature and extent of its ambitions, and causing inevitable and irreversible injury to the pride and customs of the people. The petitioners pledged to take every legal step to bring about the early and complete removal of the Yap Nature Life Garden from Map, including "all its existing pretensions, presumptions, foreign personnel and effects."

The signers of the petition denied any intent to keep Map and larger Yap in a perpetual state of economic stagnation. The welfare of the people most definitely required that there be economic improvement, but it had to be an improvement locally controlled and free of foreign exploitation. Copies of the petition were sent to the high commissioner, the Trust Territory economic development officer, the members of the Yapese delegation to the Congress of Micronesia, district officials within Yap itself, and the directors of the Yap Nature Life Garden, Inc., and its Japanese parent company.

Bound up in this initiative against tourism was a larger attempt by the chiefs of Map to reassert control over their lands and against modern bureaucratic systems of colonial government. At the same meeting that drafted the petition, the leaders of Map gathered together as *pilung* and *langanpagel*, or as high chiefs and elected officers, to affirm their unity of purpose in defending the land they had inherited in trust from their fathers. The group constituted itself as the Council of Map and under a charter that specified its purpose and procedures. The Preamble to the Council of Map Charter read,

> This council is brought together to speak for all of the people of Map, so that our will may be made clear; to preserve such things that we love, so that we do not forget our centuries; to defend us from the piracy of those who covet our land, so that it may be lovely still for our children; to nurture us and make us strong, so that we may never have to depend upon either the charity or the bondage of others, or be forced by weakness to adopt ways that will pit us against each other and make us ill at ease; and to work together and in trust with our neighbors of the other islands and with our friends from afar to make a nation for us in this sweet place, where at last we may be free.

Under its charter, the council was to be convened by the chief magistrate of Map or at the request of any of its members. Its decisions were to be binding in custom and effective as municipal law when approved by two-thirds of a quorum which, in turn, was defined as three-fourths of the council's membership. The charter authorized the creation of special committees to deal with specific issues and acknowledged the need to secure the approval of the district and Trust Territory governments for its actions. The charter closed by pledging to face with resolve the unfamiliar contingencies of this age and the ages to come "so that our home may not be vulnerable to the casual invasions of those who do not know our hearts or the disloyal speculations of those who do." Among the most privileged in a highly stratified, acutely rank-conscious society organized around castes, the chiefs of Map, in their self-proclaimed "Battle of Map," had struggled against "the sensible predictions of those who do not love us enough."[89] The Yap Nature Life Garden was eventually required by the Trust Territory government to abandon its project and "remove all evidence of its intrusion."

Tourism and the larger agenda of economic development were sensible predictions, necessary and needed developments to those who advocated them. The Council of Map, expressing itself through the language

A Men's House on Yap. (Johannes Ngiraibuuch, Trust Territory Archives, Pacific Collection, University of Hawai'i Library)

and idioms of those who ruled over them, offered alternative, equally sensible predictions that sought to counter the forces of development. The words "to combat the sensible predictions of those who do not love us enough" have a haunting quality to them. There is perhaps no clearer, more poetic counterhegemonic statement made publicly and in English about local understandings of the discourse of economic development. Other and like statements would be pronounced in Yap and elsewhere in the Trust Territory. From the Congress of Micronesia, an institution created to promote American-style democracy, would emanate criticism of development not anticipated or appreciated by the colonial government that had created it. The role of the Congress of Micronesia in the history of economic development constitutes the subject of the following chapter.

Chapter 5

Congressing over Development

The complex cultural system of which fishing was an integral part on Kapingamarangi; the long-standing political economy of Pohnpei, which incorporated both local and foreign forms of production into a competitive feasting complex concerned with rank, honor, and status; and the deeply embedded relationship of chiefly power, social class, and land tenure on Yap provide glimpses of the local histories and cultural environments that confronted foreign notions of development. I cite these examples to underscore the already established, preexisting systems of economy that held different, varying notions of productive activities and their purposes. To ask the Kapinga to fish commercially, Pohnpeians to farm for profit, or the Yapese to accept complacently the presence of a tourist enterprise on their land was to challenge in serious, disruptive ways the cultural order of these islands and the histories that had informed them. The result of such challenge certainly could involve overt resistance; more often than not, however, local engagements with capitalist initiatives were more subtle and complex in their opposition. Domination sought through an externally imposed discourse of development also led to entangled encounters in which each side attempted, if unequally, to appropriate the presence of the other. As in Yap, the struggle with colonial forces that sought extensive change certainly could prove internally divisive or exacerbate existing tensions within local societies.

Micronesians would face the colonizing discourse of development in other theaters as well. The Congress of Micronesia stood as the most public and prominent of these sites. This chapter examines the varied, contentious, imperfect, conflicting, and sometimes contradictory ways in which this brought-together body of island representatives, between the years 1965 and 1978,[1] engaged American democracy through structures, procedures, and processes of government employed to hasten the remaking of Micronesians into near-Americans. Considered also is a more locally situated form of congressing that took place in the late 1970s over the prohibition of alcohol in Chuuk. Here the discourses around development came to include the voices of women who successfully sought to counter a serious source of disruption to Chuukese society. Despite the patterns of established gender relations on Chuuk and the patriarchal biases of a colonial economy, groups of local women took for themselves a more prominent, effective role in the construction of public policy. In so doing, they demonstrated the ways in which the forces of modernization and development might be countered effectively and from a curious blending of local and foreign practices.

Gramsci and Guha in Micronesia

In his explanation of the exercise of power, the twentieth-century Italian Marxist Antonio Gramsci argues that domination can occur symbolically as well as materially.[2] Control over the natural resources of production is often replicated at the level of ideas and through cultural, religious, educational, and social forms in which the ideology of the dominant lies deeply enmeshed. From this multidimensional imposition emerges hegemony, a domination so total that it affects the fundamental worldview and social practices of subjugated peoples. The notion of class constituted the locus of Gramsci's analysis; hegemony showed itself most clearly in the class structure of a European society that delineated the few with power from the many without. According to Gramsci, the ability of a privileged class to dominate rested not so much in the use of force or coercion, but in the assent of subordinated classes to the circumstances of their subjugation; "co-conspirators in their own victimization" is the way James C. Scott, borrowing from Gramsci's theory of hegemony and domination, has described the acquiescence of subordinate classes to their domination.[3]

It has proved a quick, relatively easy application of Gramsci's theory of ideological hegemony to colonial situations. Those who colonize can be understood as seeking a domination of subjugated peoples that is so sweeping as to be ultimately ideological.[4] Certainly, Micronesia's different colonizers attempted a remaking of the islands that was near total in its aspirations, if not its effects. Such a neat extension of the Gramscian argument overlooks, however, the ways in which colonial programs were met and responded to locally.[5] In so doing, it ignores the consciousness of the colonized to the conditions of their domination and thus misses the subtle, complex, varied, and culturally and historically informed ways in which subjugated people engage colonialism.

It requires no great extrapolation of Gramscian analysis to view the creation of the Congress of Micronesia as an instrument of hegemony designed to effect the organization of government in ways that, in their mimicry of the principles and procedures of democratic government, served America's agenda of domination in the islands. Things proved more complicated than this, however. Ranajit Guha, in various publications that have resulted from his subaltern studies project, has written of the ways in which ideological tools and constructs of domination can be used by subordinate or subaltern peoples for counterhegemonic purposes.[6] The point is instructive in helping us to understand how efforts at hegemony could be deflected through such a seemingly artificial, colonially self-serving creation as the Congress of Micronesia.

Colonialism needs to be understood as something less than a totally efficient, all-consuming process. It can be possessed of contradictions, tensions, and conflicts within itself that dilute its force or make it vulnerable to local machinations. In short, we might advance Guha's point a bit by arguing that those who seek to dominate can become encumbered by the very strategies through which they try to make palatable their presence. Though secure in its total control of the islands, the United States found itself confronted by trusteeship obligations, international criticism, and its own ideology of democratic government for all people. This confluence of circumstances eventually resulted in the creation of the Congress of Micronesia in 1965.[7] On the surface of things, the Congress of Micronesia seemed but another vehicle to facilitate the Americanization of the islands. A closer look reveals that counterhegemonic discourses resonated at times from this body and that they evidenced a very shrewd assessment of what development, more particularly economic development, was really about.

The Beginnings of the Congress of Micronesia

The delay with which the United States moved in the area of political development resulted in part from local reluctance, even resistance on occasion, to the adoption of foreign forms of government.[8] In 1947, the United States Navy created municipal governments, along established regional or sectional divisions, within the different island groups or districts. These bodies were to be governed by charters and composed of chief magistrates and councilmen. The establishment of these municipal councils met with considerable suspicion especially from local chiefs who wondered about the effects of secret ballots and public debate on their own powers. The navy found itself in these first efforts at elected government forced to accommodate the powers of custom. Under revised procedures, magistrates could be chosen through election, approved simply by right of their publicly acknowledged standing as paramount or high-ranking chiefs, or selected after consultations involving naval officials and local leaders. This earliest selection process tended to confirm the authority of chiefs, though the requirements of local government as set by the navy ultimately led to the resignation or withdrawal of many chiefs from practices of governing too alien and at odds with indigenous systems of rank and power. In 1949, the navy sought to advance the process of local government by creating district congresses on each of the islands, though with limited powers and responsibilities.[9]

While individual islands struggled with the organization of local government, the navy and later the Department of Interior sponsored leadership conferences with representatives from each of the six districts of the Trust Territory. From these first territory-wide gatherings of island leaders, there developed the Inter-District Advisory Committee, which met once each year to advise the high commissioner on issues of policy. In 1961 this committee reconstituted itself into the Council of Micronesia. Taking themselves more seriously than the Trust Territory administration intended, the members of the Council of Micronesia envisioned creating a legislative body for the islands that would actually possess the power to govern. In the promotion of this event, members of the council considered drafting a Bill of Rights, queried the high commissioner about lifting the existing ban on foreign investment in the islands, and challenged the two-tiered salary schedule in the Trust Territory, which favored expatriate workers over Micronesian employees.[10] Pressures to create a Congress of Micronesia thus had their genesis within as well as beyond the islands.

Chartered by Secretarial Order number 2882 issued on 28 September 1964 by U.S. Secretary of the Interior Stewart L. Udall, the Congress of Micronesia was modeled after the bicameral structure of the United States Congress with proportional representation in a General Assembly and with each of the six districts electing two members to a House of Delegates.[11] The term of office for members of the House of Delegates was set at four years; members of the General Assembly sat for two years. The names of these two legislative bodies were later changed to the Senate and the House of Representatives, respectively. As initially constituted, the Congress was to serve as a body of advice and consent with only a small portion of the territory's funding to allocate and little or no effective governing power. Any legislation passed by the Congress of Micronesia was subject to final veto by the high commissioner. Limits on congressional powers were compounded by the requirements to work under the 745-page law code of the Trust Territory and to abide by legislative regulations governing quorums, conferences, resolutions, votes, committee reports, protocols of address, the introduction of bills, the rules of debate, and budget authorizations and appropriations.

To all appearances, the Congress of Micronesia seemed severely constrained by the conditions placed upon its activities and jurisdiction. Created by and designed to serve the interests of the United States, the Congress of Micronesia might easily be construed as a body of "mimic-men" in V. S. Naipaul's sense of the word. Their language, procedures, methods, and purpose all seemed to support and reflect the larger agenda of a Micronesia being remade yet again by its latest colonial overlord. It is, however, a more accurate assessment to view the Congress of Micronesia as a body attempting to co-opt the language and institutions of colonial domination for more local purposes and objectives. Mimicry there certainly was, but mimicry that Homi Bhabha describes as unsettling to colonial authorities in its "almost the same but not quite" features.[12]

Although modeled closely after the United States Congress, the Congress of Micronesia could be deceptive, even subversive in its hybridity. The localized cultures and histories that informed its operation created critical distinctions and crucial differences that made it exasperating for those who expected an exact duplication, a mirror image, an eminently manageable mock legislative body that would serve the dominant interests of the larger political system that had created it. To be sure, the members of the first Congress of Micronesia came to their elected positions privileged by varying circumstances that included chiefly rank or support, relatively high levels of education, an advanced and distinguishing competency in the English language, success in commercial endeavors, and previous work experience provided through positions of standing within the Trust Territory government. Many of these men would become prominent in the local governments that replaced the Trust Territory administration after 1986. Amata Kabua and Tosiwo Nakayama served as the first presidents of the Republic of the Marshall Islands and the Federated States of Micronesia, respectively. John Mangefel of Yap and Sasauo Haruo of Chuuk, who later changed his last name to Gouland, were elected governors of their island states. Dwight Heine of the Marshalls and Roman Tmetuchl of Palau proved themselves to be adroit politicians and skillful negotiators in their island republics. Although some might describe them, and correctly, as an emerging elite, their efforts also need to be understood as affected by a host of personal relationships, kinship obligations, ethnic loyalties, private ambitions, and localized politics and rivalries. Micronesia's representatives knew there was no Micronesia. They also understood that they would have to deal with each other and with the administering authority through a colonial structure, especially in areas involving power and money. Their willingness to engage each other as Micronesians and largely through the language of the colonizer evidenced what Pierre Bourdieu would call a practical encounter with the social and economic conditions of their predicament.[13] In Micronesia, the weapons of the weak would come, in part, from the arsenal of the strong.

Planning First

There are ethnographies of power, style, negotiation, and language that need to be written around the different forms of government, colonial and indigenous, in Micronesia. In the absence of such needed ethnographies, I concern myself with the more modest but still insightful consideration of the Congress' public engagement with the discourse of development. Indeed, economic development and the politics surrounding it proved a major focus of the criticism emanating from the Congress of Micronesia during its fourteen-year existence. A major point of leverage for the Congress resulted from its willingness to consider seriously what for the American administration had become largely a matter of self-justifying rhetoric. Understanding the social dimensions involved in general development projects, the Congress of Micronesia sought to create structures that provided local input into the development planning being carried out in the islands. The effort began modestly enough but soon developed an assertiveness about it.

The members of the Congress of Micronesia initially acquiesced to the logic that development planning could best be accomplished by outside specialists, but they were insistent upon their right to comment and advise. Trust Territory government officials touted the 1966 plan prepared by Nathan and Associates as something ultimately necessary, appropriate, and desirable for Micronesia's future. Members of the Congress responded by asking for the specifics of implementing this plan. Speaking in vague, somewhat evasive terms, High Commissioner William Norwood, in an address to the third regular session of the Second Congress of Micronesia on 12 July 1967, said that the Nathan Plan had made policy recommendations and set guidelines: "But if it is to become more than just another expensive, dust-gathering study, we must use it."[14] It was not a perfect plan, conceded Norwood; he doubted the advisability of allowing non-Micronesians to own land or permitting the large-scale importation of low-cost foreign labor. Norwood called for a broad, tolerant understanding of what economic development entailed and the promise that it held for the future of the islands. By 1969, however, patience with the planning process had begun to wear thin. Rep. Sasauo Haruo of Chuuk, during the second regular session of the Third Congress, expressed the sentiment that there should be development and not simply development planning. John Mangefel of Yap noted that there were all kinds of plans, but none were being implemented. Chutomu Nimwes of Chuuk asked if Micronesians were really satisfied with the plans offered, and Ekpap Silk of the Marshalls thought Micronesians, not foreign experts unfamiliar with the islands and atolls, should do their own planning.[15]

A further indication of the growing disillusionment with the Trust Territory government's efforts in development planning was evidenced in early 1971 with the introduction of House Joint Resolution 14 requesting the high commissioner to explore the possibilities of involving the World Bank, its affiliated agencies, and the United Nations in the economic development of Micronesia.[16] House Joint Resolution 75, introduced by Rep. Charles Domnick of the Marshalls in January 1972, specifically invited the United Nations Development Programme into the planning process.[17] In explaining his resolution, Domnick noted that large sums of money from a limited budget had been appropriated for various economic studies and with little result to date. Domnick believed the UNDP could assist the planning process with considerably more efficiency and at less cost than those hired or commissioned by the Trust Territory government. Congress' desire for greater control over the planning process informed these efforts to recruit more neutral development agencies whose immediate loyalties and obligations would lie with the body that contracted their services.

The Congress' search for expertise outside the Trust Territory and beyond the direct influence of the United States continued over the next several years. House Resolution 15, introduced in 1974 during the first special session of the Fifth Congress of Micronesia, requested the high commissioner to seek UNDP assistance in establishing indicative planning figures for the Trust Territory.[18] Reflecting a growing consensus within both houses of Congress, a special committee report filed the next year cited the lack of local planning as the most serious obstacle to economic development in the Trust Territory.[19] In 1975, the Congress of Micronesia passed Public Law 6-56, which mandated the submission of a five-year indicative development plan to be drafted with the assistance of the United Nations Development Programme and submitted for congressional review and approval.[20] The motivation for turning to the UNDP could be heard in a 1977 speech given by Rep. Ataji Balos. The representative from the Marshalls called the record of the U.S. Department of the Interior in the area of economic development "dismal." Balos believed that part of the problem lay with those who had been recruited to direct economic development, both in Washington and at Trust Territory headquarters.

> Under the keepership of the Department of the Interior, Micronesia has for decades continued to suffer so-called advisers, consultants, and experts whether we want them or not. Many have good intentions. However, in most cases, they are inept and useless. Others have actually done great harm to the present and future course of Micronesian development. These are the theorists, the intellectuals, the Ph.D. biologists, and anthropologists who do nothing but make feasibility studies and produce nothing but reports. . . . We do not need theories, research or needless studies. We require solid business fundamentals. We require development planning, funding, and financing of and for business.[21]

Despite the general interest within the Congress for soliciting international expertise, not everyone in the Congress was convinced that the UNDP offered real and meaningful assistance. John Mangefel doubted that the involvement of foreign development agencies would advance the economy of the islands or even give Micronesians a greater voice in the process. As early as 1971, Mangefel saw UNDP involvement in the Trust Territory as but another duplication of effort, another resort to bureaucratic layering.[22] Rep. Roman Tmetuchl of Palau wondered about the relevancy of so many development plans and proposals when basic skills, it seemed to him, were needed most. The Solomon Report, the increasing number of Peace Corps volunteers in the islands, and an American educational system all suggested to Tmetuchl that the real process afoot was not economic development but Americanization.[23] Amata Kabua, president of the Senate, offered a more pessimistic assessment of the situation in his remarks at the opening of the second regular session of the Fourth Congress of Micronesia in January 1972. Kabua noted that the number of studies on economic development was exceeded only by the number of speeches on economic development.[24]

The adoption of a five-year indicative development plan and the host of sectoral studies commissioned in support of it appeared to make little difference. Despite the promise of more independent assistance, the UNDP specialists showed themselves no more adept or skilled than the planners who had preceded them. In early 1978, Rep. Chuji Chutaro of the Marshalls expressed concern that none of the plans or reports produced by the UNDP had yet been implemented. In fact, a number of the plans had caused friction between the education and public health departments within his home district. Dwight Heine seconded Chutaro's reservations, expressing doubts about the UNDP's ability to solve development problems or issues in the Marshalls.[25] Heine also thought the UNDP had enough money of its own and really did not need funding from the Congress of Micronesia to carry out its mission. Kasuo Isisaki added his concerns about the continuing use of specialist and experts in the development process. The congressman from Kosrae publicly urged the high commissioner to be more discriminating in evaluating the qualifications, even the necessity, of development experts including those with the United Nations.[26] Isisaki concluded by saying there were too many experts, too few developments, and too much confusion.

Consciousness and Criticism in the Congress of Micronesia

The gradual disillusionment with planning reflected a larger and earlier critique of economic development that emanated from the Congress of Micronesia. Taking the need for development seriously and at face value, Amata Kabua criticized the handling of Micronesia's economy in a speech given at the closing of the Second Congress on 6 August 1968. Kabua complained of the islands' subjugation to a "succession of unskilled, unqualified, inept and disinterested administrative personnel" who were patronizing to an offensive degree.[27] Despite more than two decades of American administration, economic development in the Trust Territory amounted to nil. American complaints about Micronesian laziness and apathy were nothing but excuses contradicted by the talents, skills, and courage that had been used to discover, settle, and survive in the islands. Looking eastward, Kabua found no comfort in continental American history where native Americans had been removed from their lands and confined to squalid reservations. American Blacks, in Kabua's mind, had been emancipated from forced labor only to be enslaved anew in urban ghettos. In the Pacific, Kabua looked to avoid the fate of Native Hawaiians who, to his way of thinking, had been reduced to the status of professional entertainers in their homeland. In light of America's failures, Kabua later offered his own hard prescription for economic development that included tax laws, a revised salary schedule for Micronesian workers, merit incentives for government employees, more funding for fisheries and agricultural development, a plan to stimulate foreign investment, guidelines for improved health and environmental programs, and a proposal for the return of public lands to Micronesians.[28]

Kabua's criticisms were echoed by other members of the Congress in subsequent sessions. On 25 August 1970, Sasauo Haruo, during the Third Congress' third regular session, denounced the poor economic development planning that had done nothing to prevent the exploitation of Micronesia's vital marine resources by foreigners. Haruo, as he would throughout his congressional career, pointed to the burdens of administrative costs, an incompetent bureaucracy, and the Trust Territory government's near-total control over budget matters as the causes of the dismal state of economic development in the islands. Heinrich Iriarte of Pohnpei and Hans Williander of Chuuk spoke the following day and from a perspective that underscored the political dimensions to the issue of development. Iriarte advocated independence as the most appropriate status to secure freedom, pride, and self-respect; he, like Haruo, saw the salaries paid to American expatriate workers as a severe drain on the precious monies available for development in Micronesia. Noting the bleak history of exploitation and domination that formal colonialism had brought to Micronesia, Hans Williander argued for a small-scale form of development more appropriate to an island area such as Micronesia.[29]

Representatives from the poorest, most heavily populated district within the Trust Territory, Williander and Haruo continued their criticism of what they saw as the deep political agenda behind economic development. America, stated Williander in August 1972, came to Micronesia not as developer, but as conqueror, exploiter, and oppressor. The experiences of people in Puerto Rico, Hawaii, Guam, and American Samoa were testament enough to this.[30] Haruo likened the Trust Territory administration's program for economic development to an inflated puffer fish: large, ugly, thorny, and dangerous.[31] He went on to describe the economy as in a jumbled, confused, and bleak state, suffering from a lack of continuity, direction, and commitment; all this was compounded by bureaucratic lethargy, a plethora of inappropriate programs, and a general disregard for quality and consequences. Haruo added that Micronesians, despite the artificiality of their nation, belonged far more to each other than to the United States.

Tosiwo Nakayama of Chuuk, Kabua's successor as president of the Senate, possessed a vision of Micronesia's economic future that stood in marked contrast to prescriptions of development planners and consultants. Addressing a gathering of island leaders from the Upper Mortlocks on 13 July 1973, Nakayama remarked on the ways in which Micronesians had been led by outsiders to believe they had little to develop. Nakayama called these outside experts liars who were trying to hide the true worth and potential of Micronesia's resources from its people: "They tell us we have nothing to gain from the land, and practically nothing to gain from the sea. These people are a bunch of liars. They lie; they fool us. . . . In Japan, they bottle and sell Fujiyama air. Things will change. Air will become very precious. Sunshine might become like medicine."[32] Bottled air and sunshine—here was a very distinctive sense of economic resources that flew in the face of conventional expertise and the limitations that expertise attempted to impose on Micronesian peoples, their imagination, and their futures.

For Nakayama, the impediments to development lay within as well as beyond the islands. In an address to the Senate earlier in 1973, the Chuukese leader spoke of a cultural intimidation so deep that Micronesians were made to feel ashamed of their laws, customs, traditions, and cultures.[33] Micronesians, argued Nakayama, were in danger of losing the ability to do things for themselves. Nakayama also pointed to the involvement of "ignorant men" who thought their ways were better than those of Micronesians. It was time, said Nakayama, for Micronesians to work, stop complaining, lay the foundations for a strong government and economy, and cooperate with other Micronesians. Although there were contradictions within Nakayama's position, his attitude evidenced a decidedly different view of economic development, a view of development as a way in which Micronesians might prove their worth to dominant groups of foreigners in ways that those foreigners would understand and at the same time restore to themselves their independence and self-respect as a people.

Bureaucracy, the most immediate instrument of American colonial control and domination for most of the islands, bothered others in the Congress. Rep. Timothy Olkeriil of Palau complained about the bureaucracy that crippled more local and immediate efforts to address development concerns. In an address before the House of Representatives on 8 February 1973, Olkeriil noted that the Economic Development Loan Fund, established by the Trust Territory government in 1963 to provide funding for local projects, had become hampered in its operations and effectiveness by too much red tape at the top; "It appears to me a sign of the times: progress, rules, regulations, requirements, and paperwork." Six days later, Olkeriil spoke about the United States' deliberate refusal to honor its obligation to develop Micronesia economically in favor of a more deliberate promotion of consumerism that made Micronesians increasingly dependent upon the United States. Sasauo Haruo seconded Olkeriil's assessment in a speech given on the House floor on 26 February 1973. Haruo noted that thirteen years of steadily increasing appropriations from Washington had served only to fatten the bureaucracy.[34] Despite this increased funding, money for economic development remained insufficient and inappropriately allocated. The Department of Resources and Development lacked imagination; too much time, effort, and money were being spent on experimental programs in agriculture and marine fisheries. Efforts to circumvent bureaucratic requirements could actually create additional bureaucracy. Congress' attempts to appropriate money directly to the district governments for local fisheries projects were hampered by a six-month delay during which Trust Territory government officials drafted regulations governing the management of the projects and the reporting of expenditures. Infrastructure languished, while a continuing Trust Territory government prohibition on foreign investment denied the islands the capital vitally needed to develop and progress.

As negotiations over the future political status of Micronesia intensified, so too did criticisms of the Trust Territory administration from members of the Congress of Micronesia. On 1 July 1975, Haruo again delivered a highly critical assessment of economic development in Micronesia. Haruo thought that America's strategic colonialism explained the lack of progress in this area.[35] He asked why it had taken so long for the Micronesian Development Bank, created by congressional legislation more than a year earlier, to begin operation. Why had legislation petitioning for membership in the Asian Development Bank hit a snag? Why was the United States so resistant to calls for local taxes on American military personnel and installations in the Trust Territory? Why had there been no assistance from the United States in the Law of the Sea negotiations? Why had it taken thirty years to finally open Micronesia to foreign investment? The answers to all of these questions, believed Haruo, had to do with the primacy of American military interests in the islands.

Dreaming the Future

The issues at stake in the discourse of economic development could find expression in novel ways. On 21 August 1970, Rep. Charles Domnick of the Marshalls addressed the third regular session of the Third Congress of Micronesia about a dream he had had concerning the islands' future.[36] In his dream, Domnick beheld a vigorous economy driven by American money, protected by American laws and bureaucratic regulations, and beyond Micronesians' control. Every home had a television set on which families could watch news reports of riots in Micronesian schools. Debates among family members over which channel to watch led to the purchase of second sets. Individual family members could now move between the different rooms of their large, comfortable houses, depending upon their viewing preference. But these were the privileged few, the elite of a Micronesian society who had somehow managed to find comfortable niches for themselves in a more general process of displacement. Most Micronesian lived in shanty towns easily identified by their squalid appearance.

In Domnick's dream, these shanty towns or Micronesian ghettos had a transient quality; they could be torn down or moved quickly depending upon the overriding American security interests in the different Micronesian islands. Television commercials showing well-dressed Americans had dramatically changed Micronesian tastes and introduced in powerful, irresistible ways the idea and practice of material consumption. The whole of Micronesian life had become commoditized. Rents for land and housing had skyrocketed beyond the means of average or ordinary Micronesians.

Micronesia had become like Hawai'i or, more accurately, like the images of Hawai'i and larger Polynesia promoted by an American-dominated tourist industry. The only feasts now celebrated in Micronesia were carried out at tourist hotels for the amusement of foreign visitors who, in addition to viewing the bastardized spectacle, ate Polynesian food, drank exotic tropical drinks, and listened to Hawaiian tunes strummed on ukuleles. The forests on the larger islands had been cleared to make room for rice and sugar plantations run by businesses operating out of Hawai'i. Temporary workers were brought in to work on the plantations because foreign entrepreneurs and businessmen held Micronesians to be lazy and indifferent toward the hard economic values of thrift, productivity, and efficiency. The better-educated, bureaucratic elite among Micronesians held cocktail parties, talked about appliances, worried over the troublesome, rebellious behavior of their younger children, and wondered why their older, college-aged children seemed so reluctant to return home upon completing their degrees. For those youth less academically inclined, there were only servile, demeaning jobs in a tourist industry that had come to dominate Micronesians and to drastically alter Micronesian identity or, at least, outsider understandings of that identity.

Charles Domnick dreamed of his son as a baggage handler and tour guide at one of the major tourist hotels. In his dream, he visited the hotel where his son worked and was quickly approached by the doorman, who directed him to the service entrance at the rear of the hotel where all Micronesian workers entered and exited the premises. "I guess he mistook me for one of the workers," said Domnick, "because not very many Micronesians went to the hotels except to work." Domnick's dream, then, was one of development and dispossession—legally justified, bureaucratically regulated, and commercially driven by foreign, essentially inaccessible and hence uncontrollable forces. Agreements of free association had given way to territorial commonwealths and ultimately to total absorption by the United States. What made this view of Micronesia's future so horrific was a memory within Domnick's dream, a memory of earlier, once-considered alternatives to development that had promised greater self-determination and independence.

Four years later, Timothy Olkeriil described a nightmare and a daydream to colleagues meeting during the first special session of the Fifth Congress of Micronesia in August 1974.[37] Olkeriil's nightmare was one of political disunity and the consequent vulnerability it brought to the different island groups of Micronesia. In his nightmare, Olkeriil saw the Marianas and the Marshalls as incorporated territories of Guam, while the islands of Pohnpei, Chuuk, and Yap formed a loose association with no real central government. The resources and general economy of this loose federation deteriorated, thus leaving the people to subsist as best they could. Micronesia as a distinct entity had disappeared. Huge foreign banking and commercial interests had a stranglehold over all the districts, while the United States military ruled its preserves. Third-country nationals replaced Americans as technical and administrative personnel; unpopular but needed, they built their own small economic empires at the expense of local Micronesian peoples. Well-trained, capable Micronesians left their islands to be absorbed into the economic mainstream of the United States; the almighty dollar and the almighty yen had induced Micronesians to sell almost all their available land to foreigners. In Olkeriil's nightmarish vision, Micronesians joined their Hawaiian brothers and sisters as exploited, oppressed, and diminished people.

Olkeriil's other dream, his daydream, involved a strong, united Micronesian nation comprising the six major districts. It was a model Pacific nation, a neutral state with an initial protective treaty with the United States to provide for its security and defense. At the conclusion of the thirty-year period of that treaty, Olkeriil dreamed, the treaty or compact was terminated, and the various military leases over Micronesian land

and water were not renewed. This new Micronesia was no longer dependent on U.S. government monies, but had a viable, self-sufficient economy based on marine and coconut products, ocean mining, and controlled tourism. The nation's duty-free status helped it to become a major financial center of the Pacific, with a progressive economy directed by Micronesians themselves.

What emerges from both Domnick's and Olkeriil's dreams is a series of associations that suggest the totality of the process called economic development and the stakes involved. The more ethnographically inclined among us might be led to examine the role of dreaming as a source of knowledge and power in different Micronesian societies. In these two cases, we might remember as well the writings of Homi Bhabha and Ranajit Guha and the ways in which mimicry and the co-opting of foreign ideas and practices make possible expressions of resistance.

Differing over Development

Throughout its fourteen-year history, the Congress of Micronesia sought to assert control over the process of economic development through a series of legislative initiatives. There resulted joint resolutions that criticized the ineptness of the Trust Territory government's Department of Resources and Development; that asked for the removal of protective tariffs on marine products and other Micronesian goods imported into the United States; and that sought formal association with regional agencies and bodies concerned with common approaches to economic development. Such efforts did have some success. Pressure from the Congress of Micronesia in the form of resolutions, press releases and public speeches contributed to the removal of the prohibition on foreign investment in the islands as announced by Secretary of the Interior Rogers Morton in 1974.

Other measures established economic planning and development authorities at the district level, expanded the power of district economic development boards, and endeavored to expedite the development of infrastructure and transportation facilities. The Congress of Micronesia passed legislation that created district fisheries offices; that funded a host of development projects in agriculture, tourism, marine fisheries, and vocational education; and that gave responsibility for the collection and marketing of copra to district governments, thus increasing revenues to local producers by eliminating the fees charged by private firms. Tax exemptions were granted certain Micronesian businesses, while other bills provided tax relief for local harvesters of copra and trochus shell. A

Micronesian Development Bank was authorized to manage locally and more effectively the funds appropriated by the United States Congress to the Economic Development Loan Fund. The Congress of Micronesia also established foreign investment boards in each of the districts and levied taxes on nonessential items as a way to limit consumption, promote import substitution, and generate local revenues. One of the Congress' more notable accomplishments was the passage of a 1977 law that provided for the establishment of a 200-mile economic zone and the regulation of all commercially exploitable marine resources within it.[38]

The Congress' general willingness to engage critically the question of economic development did not diminish the massive dimensions of social transformation that development entailed. Serious reservations about the social costs of development did exist within the Congress. What, then, of the distinctive and varied ways in which some Micronesian elected leaders expressed their doubts about an alien order of living in the world intricately tied up with capitalist notions of productivity and measurement? What were the cultural metaphors that expressed their consciousness, their ideologies if you will, of the tremendous social change that economic development threatened? An examination of the public record of the Congress of Micronesia affords a number of crucial glimpses.

On 31 July 1967, Sen. Francis Nuuan of Yap spoke before the third regular session of the Congress of Micronesia on Senate Bill 49, a measure requiring persons subject to income taxes, fees, or other legal charges to maintain accurate records of their transactions.[39] Nuuan argued that a lot of people in Micronesia couldn't sign their names, let alone keep accurate and current business records. Nuuan thought it was too early in Micronesia's development for a bill such as this. He felt several more years would be required before affected citizens of the islands could satisfy the requirements of this law. The objection might seem a petty one against the larger concerns of political autonomy and economic self-sufficiency, but it nonetheless indicated the very different skills, behaviors, values, and attitudes that Micronesians were being asked to accept and adopt.

The issue of definition was a real and troubling one for Rep. Polycarp Basilius of Palau. Basilius asked his fellow congressmen in 1977 about the meaning and relevance of such terms as "self-reliance," "self-sufficiency," and "dependence."[40] Basilius also expressed concern about the very particular historical origins of development models being applied in Micronesia and about the appropriateness of the criteria against which economic progress was being evaluated. Basilius' concerns reflected the kinds of larger epistemological doubts that had been raised earlier and repeatedly by John Mangefel. Back in 1972, Mangefel had spoken publicly of his frustration in translating concepts such as "fiscal year" into Yapese.[41] In a telling phrase that summed up the issues at hand, Mangefel noted that Micronesia was a young nation made up of old peoples who had inhabited the islands for centuries, if not millennia. Three years later, in February 1975, Mangefel spoke against a bill to establish a mortgage law for the Trust Territory.[42] The Yapese representative expressed strong reservations about the effects of mortgages and foreclosure proceedings on a communal land tenure system such as existed among his home islands.

Throughout his career in the Congress of Micronesia, Mangefel showed himself to be the most adept and adroit commentator on the clash of cultural systems and practices that resulted from the proposition that was economic development in American Micronesia. Mangefel's most humorous and effective critiques of the American administration were delivered through a series of public letters to and from his mythical cousin Ngabchai; more often than not, these letters were given their first public exposure during sessions of the Congress of Micronesia. Mangefel read the first in this extended series of letters on 26 February 1976.[43] The now senator from Yap introduced Ngabchai as a young Yapese man in his early twenties who was majoring in anthropology and psychology at a university "somewhere between the east and west coasts of the continental United States." He explained his cousin's decision of a major as motivated by the recognition of the need for an indigenous anthropologist to explain some of the strange, often unnatural habits and behaviors of Americans. A strong, poignant counterethnography thus wove its way through Mangefel's humorous, seemingly benign narrative.[44]

Ngabchai, or Mangefel, wrote of the Americans as ingenious people who had developed a new category of weather condition called "smog." Though not pleasant, it seemed to be popular, as almost all American cities now experienced it. Ngabchai, however, recommended against Yap's adoption of smog as a new weather pattern because it was extremely expensive to create and maintain. Ngabchai commented that Americans seemed to have an unhealthy interest in sex and violence, treated their enemies better than their allies, and, as evidenced by the Watergate scandal, had a penchant for secret activities that ran counter to their claims to be an open, democratic society.

Ngabchai also noted problems that Americans had in understanding non-Western peoples and in determining what was and was not primitive. In one of Ngabchai's anthropology courses, a professor called the Yapese "primitive" and then proceeded over the next three classes to

An older John Mangefel at his inauguration as governor of Yap on 8 January 1979. (*Micronesian Reporter*, 26, 4 [1978]; Trust Territory Archives, Pacific Collection, University of Hawai'i Library)

come to grips with the land tenure system in Yap. The professor never did come to an explanation of the complexities of the system which, to Ngabchai, was just as well "since we don't want non-Yapese to really understand it anyway." Ngabchai thought that Americans had a very distorted view of Yapese based on the 1952 film *His Majesty O'Keefe*, which starred Burt Lancaster "as the Great White Father of Stone Money, and a cast of hundreds of dark-skinned Hollywood extras running up and down a sandy beach (probably somewhere in Malibu), dressed in outlandish and very un-Yapese costumes, yelling 'uga, uga.'" Writing in 1976, the year of the American bicentennial, Ngabchai commented that it seemed quite odd to him that among the indigenous people who had greeted the Pilgrims nearly four hundred years ago, there was no celebration of America's two-hundredth birthday as a nation; the young Yapese anthropologist concluded that there must be a lesson for the people of Yap in this fact.

There is in Mangefel's prose a purposeful distancing that worked to shield Yap and things Yapese from the reach of an alien, aggressive, self-serving cultural order. In many ways, the Congress of Micronesia can be seen as a theater in which men endeavored to mimic the ways of those who governed and controlled them. In these performances lay less than complete or satisfying reassurances for Americans that the people they called Micronesians were changing in ways they were supposed to. In these performances could often be found varying subplots designed to diffuse, subvert or manipulate hegemonic structures and practices for more locally appropriate and meaningful ends that involved cultural identity and survival. We must be careful, though, about making a trope of heroic resistance among those called Micronesians in their encounters with powerful and alien systems of knowing, being, producing, and controlling. The responses to the agenda of economic development in the Caroline, Mariana, and Marshall Islands were layered, deep, and complex. Colonialism had made Micronesia and had brought together different peoples as Micronesians. There could and did exist tension among the colonized as well as between colonizer and colonized. Micronesians could and did struggle with each other as well as with those who purported to rule over them.

John Mangefel, for example, wondered why members chose to wear neckties on the floor. What kind of choke hold did American patterns of dress have on the bodies and minds of Micronesia's representatives? Before the second regular session of the Sixth Congress in early 1976, Mangefel marveled at the way members of the Congress could be at once busy and unproductive. The problem, thought Mangefel, lay in the definition of the word "busy." Reading, laughing, talking, joking, debating, making speeches, and chewing betel nut constituted activities that could be construed as busy, mused Mangefel. The real question was whether or not Micronesia's representatives considered being productive to have a place in their applied definition of busy. Mangefel noted ruefully that as of the thirtieth day of that session, the Congress had passed and sent to the high commissioner only five bills. By comparison, the second regular session of the Fourth Congress of Micronesia, which had convened in January 1972, had by the thirtieth day of its session approved and sent to the high commissioner a total of sixteen bills.[45]

Mangefel thought that Micronesians believed too much in the efficacy of imitation. Looking around the floor in July 1976, the Yapese congressman noticed the beads of perspiration trickling down the faces and backs of his colleagues as they sat in layers of clothes designed "to keep men warm in South Dakota—not in the South Pacific."[46] Attempting to explain this phenomenon, Mangefel thought back to the coming of the first Europeans and Americans to Micronesia. Reaching the Pacific,

Europeans and Americans had not possessed enough good sense to change their style of dress. Micronesians, reasoned Mangefel, showed even less sense. They came to regard foreign dress as a way to foreign wealth and thus dressed as uncomfortably and as inappropriately as the strangers in their land.

Moreover, Mangefel believed that clothing was not the only item of Western culture alien to and problematic for Micronesians. Mangefel thought the workday should be reduced from eight to six hours; such a change would bring about a 25 percent reduction in salaries and would help reduce absenteeism, especially on the Friday afternoons and Monday mornings that bordered pay-day weekends. The senator from Yap also thought the reduction in workweek hours would give people more time to spend with their families and more time to pursue individual fishing and gardening which, in turn, would help to promote a more self-sufficient, locally appropriate form of development.[47]

Resistance to the Trust Territory government on Saipan led some Micronesian representatives deeper into the very heart of the American empire. Earlier on in his career, Mangefel had cautioned his colleagues about the "shining illusions" behind such words as "independence," "self-determination," and "self-reliance." In August 1972, he had told the second special session of the Fourth Congress that Micronesia was still very much in need of help and would have to depend on continued American assistance and the formalization of some long-term political association with the United States to achieve any real and meaningful economic development.[48] While Mangefel had gone on to alter his views considerably, other congressmen continued to look to the United States as the ultimate source of funding for economic development in Micronesia.

During the life of the Congress of Micronesia, criticism of the Trust Territory government's failure in economic development was more than equaled by resolutions and requests for increased assistance from the United States Congress. It seemed to many observers that Micronesians were playing the more distant capital of American power and wealth in the world against its local offices and agencies on Saipan and in the districts. Mangefel again had words of caution, this time for those Micronesians who confused economic development with something akin to Christmas. In a letter to Ngabchai read before the Senate on 4 February 1977, Mangefel stated that Micronesians could not expect the "great white Santa" to keep bringing gifts forever.[49] He hoped that Christmas a year hence would find Micronesians still possessed of a sense of direction, purpose, and roots.

There was then great irony, almost contradiction in the Congress' request to higher levels of the American federal bureaucracy to provide funds to promote autonomy and self-government. It may be true, at one level, that Micronesians' desire for autonomy and self-government led them deeper and deeper into the recesses of the American federal bureaucracy and, in effect, enhanced rather than overcame dependency. But things are often turned upside down and inside out in colonial situations where indigenous interest groups are seeking to both counter and use the hegemonic instruments of their domination. Things could and did get messy.

An indication of this entangling can be heard in remarks made by Rep. Kiku Apis of Pohnpei before the House of Representatives on 6 February 1978.[50] Apis attempted to give order to a confused, distracted world gone a little crazy. The congressman from Pohnpei noted that there were indicative development plans for all the districts, but that these plans were useless unless implemented. The Trust Territory administration, said Apis, had demonstrated through three decades that it did not consider economic development and Micronesian self-sufficiency to be priorities. Members of Congress, said Apis, found their attention and energies diverted by political negotiations with the United States over a future political status, the question of unity, and concerns for their own reelection. Local government, in general, was too often aloof from its citizens, while the people themselves had come to see the United States government as the giver of gifts to which they were entitled. The Congress of Micronesia could perhaps have done more to promote economic development, but the real impediments to national economic advancement lay in the Trust Territory system. What the future might bring Apis could not say.

Differences of opinion within the Congress of Micronesia involved matters of ethnicity as well as politics, policy and priorities. Indeed, the Congress of Micronesia as a body representing peoples bound together by the forces of American colonialism struggled continually with the consequent tensions and divisions within its ranks. Rep. Julio M. Akapito of Chuuk sensed an incipient anti-Chuukese bias in some of the criticisms made of the Congress regarding economic development. Speaking to the House of Representatives on 27 February 1978, Akapito took exception to those who implied that the Chuukese delegation and its staff were only looking out for themselves in the appropriation of development funds and the authorization of projects. "We act," said Akapito, "on belief and convictions and what is best for the Congress and people of Micronesia."[51]

Tosiwo Nakayama acknowledged the fears of Chuukese dominance that worked against efforts to forge a new autonomous federated states of

Micronesia out of the tired colonial structure that was the United States Trust Territory of the Pacific Islands. At a meeting with local Pohnpeian officials on 16 July 1973, Nakayama called overpopulation in Chuuk a myth. Endeavoring to allay fears of the pressures that would be brought to bear in relatively land-rich Pohnpei district by an influx of Chuukese people under the open migration provisions of a national constitution, Nakayama declared there was and would always be enough land in Chuuk district itself.[52] The Chuukese were not the only group regarded unflatteringly. At different times and under varying circumstances and changing coalitions, the Yapese might be described by other Micronesians as intransigent, the Saipanese as haughty, the Marshallese as aloof, the Pohnpeians as particularly opportunistic, and the Palauans as especially assertive.

The diverse, often conflicting interests of different groups of people brought together, identified, and administered as Micronesians showed itself clearly in the debate over the location of local tax revenues. Put succinctly, those districts of the Trust Territory that generated the largest tax dollars wanted those revenues used for local purposes and projects rather than as subsidy for the more impoverished districts. Local control over tax revenues had been one of the issues that had led the Northern Marianas to abandon any prospect of involvement in a future, autonomous Micronesian government in favor of becoming a commonwealth of the United States. The same issue would now be seized upon by representatives from the Marshalls and would serve as preface to their own political separation from the rest of Micronesia. In 1972, Charles Domnick of the Marshalls had introduced legislation requiring half of all tax revenues to be returned to the districts from which they had come. Contributing more than half of the internal revenues over which the Congress of Micronesia had control, the Marshalls stood to gain the most from any reapportionment of tax monies, and at the expense of the less advantaged districts within the Trust Territory. Not surprisingly, the Congress as a whole refused to act favorably on Domnick's bill. At the second regular session of the Fifth Congress in 1973, the Marshallese delegation reintroduced the revenue-sharing bill, and with the warning that the Congress' failure to pass it would induce the Marshalls to begin separate political status negotiations with the United States. When the bill was defeated, the Marshallese members of Congress staged a temporary walkout. Said Amata Kabua, "Our fear is now greater with respect to other Micronesians than with the United States."[53] As in the Marshalls and the Northern Marianas, the people of Palau considered options and possibilities that suggested a future apart from the rest of the islands. The Congress of Micronesia, however, was certainly not the only forum in which Micronesians debated foreigners or each other over economic development. Differences over development could also bring men and women into conflict with each other, and in ways that both manifested and advanced changes taking place in gender relations. I turn from the elite, almost exclusively male forum that was the Congress of Micronesia to more local debates over development in which were heard the voices of women.

Silent Voices Heard in Chuuk

Women both affected and were affected by the agenda of development in Micronesia, but in ways we are only beginning to understand.[54] Recent feminist anthropology has added new and critical perspectives on the ways in which women encountered development's progenitors, colonialism and capitalism. Whereas earlier ethnographies, including Marxist and feminist-oriented studies, often presumed colonialism's devaluation of women's labor, productivity and consequent status, more contemporary gender studies by Marilyn Strathern, Jocelyn Linnekin, Annette Weiner, and Maria Lepowsky indicate persisting if somewhat altered and varied patterns of agency, efficacy, power, and even equality in areas that involve or affect economic production and social relationships.[55]

Within the Micronesian geographical area, Palau and Pohnpei have proved the most prominent sites for the practice of a more decidedly and much needed feminist ethnography. In their different but equally effective ways, DeVerne Reed Smith and Lynn Wilson demonstrate how women have remained central to *siukang,* the persisting, complex system of exchange involving food, money, and social relationships that binds Palauan society together. In their roles as mothers, sisters, and wives, women continue to serve as prime mediators of wealth in Palauan society.[56] Their marriages and the children of those marriages unite society and establish lines of obligation and reciprocity through which land, goods, and resources move. According to one Palauan woman, "A man who has no sisters is unlucky."[57] Through the satisfactory performance of obligations and responsibilities, women earn place, voice, and power in their clans. Indeed, the women of the clan choose the clan chief; without their support and the material resources they are able to call upon, no man could lead. Women's continuing and central role in feasting and exchange activities has sustained their considerable economic power and political influence on Pohnpei as well. In a situation somewhat analogous to that in Palau, Pohnpeian women's material production, public performances, and access to property by right of clan or kinship ties earn them crucial roles in both the reproduction and transformation of Pohnpeian society.[58]

Women's power can also show itself at times in larger and more public political arenas. In 1987, a group of female elders or *machas* filed a lawsuit against the Palau District Legislature's unilateral efforts to change the requirements for amending the Palauan constitution from a 75 percent popular vote to a simple majority.[59] The legislature's move was part of the effort to facilitate the approval of the draft Compact of Free Association with the United States, which had been slowed by the antinuclear provisions in Palau's constitution. The United States government found the constitution's prohibitions against the use, storage, transfer, and transshipment of nuclear materials within Palauan territory incompatible with its strategic interests in the western Pacific. Violence, including the murder of a prominent male elder or *rubak* opposed to any circumvention of the Palauan constitution, caused the women to withdraw their suit, but only temporarily. Reinstated a year later, the women's suit sought to protect the integrity of the constitutional process in Palau.

In the Marshalls, women voiced some of the loudest, most passionate, and most effective criticisms of nuclear testing and its effects upon lives, land, and society there.[60] In this section, I focus on the role of women as effective critics of another form of social and communal disruption resulting from efforts to develop the islands economically and to promote consumerism among their populations; I refer here to the sale and consumption of alcoholic beverages, the problems that resulted, and the efforts of women in Chuuk to control them.

On 15 January 1978, the Truk District Legislature passed a law banning the sale of alcoholic beverages on the island of Weno or Moen.[61] Pressure for the law came from Chuukese women who felt compelled to constrain a male drinking culture on the island that had become increasingly hostile and aggressive, publicly disruptive, and that more and more involved forms of physical violence including assault, spousal abuse, murder, and suicide. An understanding of Chuukese women's efforts to prohibit the sale and consumption of alcohol requires first a historical and cultural contextualization of the issues.

That drinking should become a serious social issue on Weno was not surprising; as Chuuk district's governmental seat, commercial center, principal port, and major communications and contact point with the larger world, the island showed dramatically the effects of the material transformation wrought by efforts at modernization. Concrete-block houses, tin shanties, jet planes, pickup trucks, motor boats, electric fans, freezers, refrigerators, and frozen chickens replaced the thatched dwellings, wood fires, sailing canoes, and fresh fish that had been the material markings of an earlier way of life. Given its political, commercial, and material prominence, Weno attracted considerable migration from the other islands of the Chuuk group as well as from the Hall, Mortlock, Namonuito, and Western Islands. A September 1980 census recorded Weno's population at 10,351 with the median age being 17.7 years and with 46 percent of that population identified as under 16.[62] With a land area of only 7.3 square miles, Weno was by far the most congested, overcrowded island within the Carolines and had many of the social problems associated with congestion and overcrowding.

A more than century-long, troubled, and sometimes violent history prefaced the crisis of the late 1970s.[63] This history included the Japanese and early American administrations' ban on the use of alcoholic beverages by Chuukese and other Micronesian people. After the Trust Territory government rescinded that ban in 1958, the consumption of foreign alcoholic beverages resumed, and with dramatic increase. Despite the social disruption that followed, elected officials and other local government leaders showed themselves reluctant to place any limits or controls on the distribution and use of alcohol. Money from taxes and licensing fees around the retail sale and individual purchase of beer and hard liquor accounted for 41 percent of the estimated local revenues available to the legislature, then called the Truk District Congress, in 1960.[64] The economics of alcohol in Chuuk, coupled with the existence of a prominent male drinking culture, helps explain why Chuuk's leaders were reluctant to act when public drunkenness began to become a serious problem in the late 1960s. By the mid-1970s, the situation had worsened considerably.

Drawing upon an extensive set of field interviews, Mac and Leslie Marshall write of Chuukese women's reaction to this latest period of intensified alcohol abuse:

> They associated it with criminal activities, with violent assaults and homicides, with general community disruption, with domestic violence such as wife-beating, with the destruction of property, with arguments among family groups that sometimes led young men to commit suicide, and with the waste of money that could have been used otherwise to benefit the entire family. Women were opposed to the public violence that increasingly was the order of the day in their communities. Women were

> opposed to having their husbands come home dirty after drinking, without money to run the household until the next paycheck, or to having them gone several nights while on a drinking binge. Women were tired of being berated or beaten by their husbands after the men had been out drinking. Women were categorically opposed to the deaths resulting directly or indirectly from drinking via homicide, suicide, car accidents, drownings, and alcohol-related illnesses (including ethanol overdose). Women were unwilling to see their children abused by their drunken fathers.[65]

Women, by all accounts, had not been involved in any of the early public or legislative debate about the control of alcoholic beverages in Chuuk. This situation changed markedly in 1976 when Chuukese women and their male supporters worked to have two bills introduced into the district legislature: one would have banned drinking throughout the district; the other would have eliminated the importation of foreign alcohol but allowed for the production, sale, and consumption of local brews. Debate over the bills brought startling public information to light.[66] In testimony in behalf of the first bill, it was noted that one-third of all suicides and 51 percent of all homicides involved alcohol and that forty percent of the patients in the district hospital were there for sicknesses resulting from the consumption of alcohol. Witnesses testified that the physical costs resulting from abuse of alcohol were many and great; business losses, insurance claims, property damage, and lost productivity were threatening to undermine the local economy. Although neither bill passed, their introduction heralded the arrival of a more visible and assertive posture for women in Weno.

The intervention of Chuukese women in public, male-dominated areas and against such an exclusively male activity as the drinking of foreign liquor might have surprised some. The general ethnographic literature describes the women of Chuuk as quiet and modest, adept at household management and domestic chores, submissive to male kin and spouse, and never very far from home.[67] Such descriptions, however, do not suggest that women in Chuukese society were without power or influence. Women in precolonial times had a significant voice in collective decisions though they seldom occupied positions of authority over the entire society; their access and influence tended to be private.[68] In contemporary times, women's groups, more particularly the Protestant church's Fin Anisi and the Catholic mission's Mwichen Maria, served as vehicles through which women exercised influence. These two church groups, especially Fin Anisi, would prove quite effective in the battle for prohibition on Weno.

Colonial policies addressed, at a general level, the role of women in Chuukese and other Micronesian societies. Since navy times, the American colonial administration had proclaimed the right of women to vote, to receive equal pay for equal work, and to have equal access to educational and occupational opportunities at an official level. Women's rights to own property, bring suit in a court of law, control earnings, act as legal guardians, and engage in business were all guaranteed under the Trust Territory Code. The formation of women's groups or associations was also encouraged and supported by the American administration. While avowing the equality of women in all matters, however, the Trust Territory government denied any intent to intervene in the local determination of appropriate gender roles.

Statistics on the education and employment of women evidenced the considerable gap between government policy and practice.[69] In 1951, only 9 of 106 students enrolled at the Pacific Islands Teacher Training School in Chuuk were female. Before 1958, fewer than 10 girls attended Truk Intermediate School in any given year. Before 1965, just over 200 Chuukese had completed high school, and only 13 percent of them were female. The discrepancy in the representation of the sexes induced the 1964 United Nations Visiting Mission to urge the American administration to encourage the education of girls beyond elementary school. Although the numbers of high school graduates rose sharply for Chuuk in the early to mid-1970s, women remained significantly underrepresented. To be sure, long-standing cultural and parental resistance to the education and travel of daughters contributed significantly to colonial patriarchy. One female student summed up the prevailing attitudes in Chuuk with these words: "Men have wings, women only have feet."[70] By the late 1970s and 1980s, however, increased education provided women with more and better employment opportunities and hence greater power, influence, and access to the public sphere. By 1979, female students in Chuuk made up almost 50 percent of the total elementary school enrollment and accounted for roughly 42 percent of the secondary school population; in that same year, women, employed primarily as bookkeepers, teachers, clerical assistants, nurses, and domestic workers, constituted 25 percent of the total paid labor force in Chuuk.[71] *Raa feffeyittá* or "Women are coming up" was the statement Chuukese women employed to characterize their changing circumstances in the latter decades of the Trust Territory administration.[72]

Women now stepped forward in the late 1970s to address the public crisis caused by the abuse of alcohol in Chuuk. This assertiveness challenged both colonial and indigenous restrictions on women's activity while at the same time calling upon foreign resources and locally established precedents and practices. The latest and most serious set of disturbances involved a near war between young men from Weno and those of nearby Wonei Island that began with a drunken brawl in early 1977. In response to the danger, women from Fin Anisi attended a special emergency meeting called by the district administrator. At that meeting, the women urged a petition drive to ask voters to decide the question of prohibition. The strategy was inspired by a 1976 conference on alcohol abuse attended by members of Fin Anisi; the gathering, held in Honolulu, Hawai'i, was sponsored by the United Church of Christ's Women's Board of Missions for the Pacific Islands and was attended by delegates from Micronesia and the larger Pacific region.

Provisions in the existing district code allowed for individual municipalities to decide upon the sale and consumption of alcohol within their territorial boundaries. To be successful, a petition requesting a special referendum required the signatures of two-thirds of all registered voters in a given municipality. The law mandated the holding of a special election within ninety days of the submission of the petition and its verification by the municipal clerk. If a majority of voters approved the referendum, the municipal council was required to prepare and adopt an ordinance in accord with the public vote.

Leaders of the two women's religious groups, Fin Anisi and Mwichen Maria, along with sympathizers from the Weno or Moen Municipal Council, circulated petitions during the late spring of 1977. On 2 July 1977, the referendum was held. Voters of Weno were asked, "Should the sale or consumption of intoxicating beverages in Moen Municipality be prohibited? Yes or No?" Of 2,163 votes cast, 2,014 (93 percent) favored prohibition. Given the overwhelming vote, the council had no choice but to draft Municipal Ordinance 5-77 banning the sale and consumption of alcoholic beverages on Weno. Because Weno was the port of entry for the entire Chuuk district, provision was made in the ordinance for licensed importers to legally store alcoholic beverages for transhipment to wet municipalities elsewhere in the district.

One of the immediate effects of the prohibition measure was to undermine the district legislature's principal source of local revenue, namely, the taxes earned from the licensing and sale of alcohol. Revenues dropped from $441,605 in fiscal year 1977 to $403 for the first full fiscal year following the implementation of prohibition. Given this serious decline in revenues, the legislature announced plans to override the Weno ordinance on grounds that the district or state government had ultimate jurisdiction over such matters. In response to the legislature's plan, members of Fin Anisi and Mwichen Maria organized women throughout Chuuk in an effort to establish prohibition in all 39 municipalities. Petitions were drafted and circulated. On 28 March 1979, the district legislature, now referred to as the state legislature because of Chuuk's place in the newly formed government of the Federated States of Micronesia, established a Special Committee on Alcoholic Beverage Control to review the alcohol issue and to make recommendations to the full legislature by May 1979. The creation of the special committee struck many as more than a little suspicious. One Weno woman wrote in a letter dated 20 April 1979 to the editor of the *Truk Chronicle*,

> I know the Truk legislature is going to make drinking legal again and I don't like it. Last year, they asked my people from Moen if we want drinking and we voted that we don't want it. Now it seems like they don't care what we want, they only care about getting money for their pay. I hope they won't bring back drinking because I don't want any more fighting and drunk people around my house.

In addition to their statewide petition drive, the women solicited and received the support of the mayor of Weno and the governor and lieutenant governor of Chuuk State. Efforts to meet with members of the legislature over the issue were rebuffed, however. When it became clear that the legislature planned to proceed with its efforts to override the Weno prohibition ordinance, the Protestant and Catholic women's groups called for a public demonstration of protest. The appeal attracted 200 participants who marched on the legislature with signs that called attention to the social devastation alcohol was wreaking upon families and communities in Weno. With the protestors surrounding the building, the lone female member of the legislature requested her male colleagues to recess so that they could all read the signs carried by the marchers.

For the next week, the women occupied the grounds and waited patiently for a meeting with the very reluctant speaker of the legislature. When the speaker finally relented, the women presented him with their petitions and spoke of their deeply felt reason for wanting to keep Weno dry. One woman later stated, "We were carrying out the wishes of the people and encouraging the senators to give the people peace and not destruction." The legislature's general response to the women's challenge was to conduct business behind closed doors. Their efforts to ignore the women's protest proved futile, however, as the state court upheld the jurisdiction of municipalities over local-option liquor laws. The ruling, combined with the women's march, convinced the legislature to back off from efforts to abolish Weno's prohibition law.

There would be two other attempts to repeal prohibition on Weno. In late 1979, the municipal council met to consider repealing the prohibition law on the ground that it was unenforceable and that it had inadvertently given rise to a black-market trade in liquor that was making very wealthy men out of those who ran that trade. In 1983, the council again tried to repeal the prohibition law. In both these latter instances, women mounted effective public protests that stymied the repeal efforts. Women's intervention against alcohol abuse on Weno did not end abuse, crime, violence, or even drinking in the state. These continued, of course, but at reduced levels. The percentage of alcohol-related arrests dropped from 84 percent of the total in the last quarter of 1980 to 57 percent for 1981. For the following four years, alcohol-related arrests averaged 63 percent of total yearly arrests. More importantly, female voices, which had perhaps never been as completely silent as the extant ethnography would suggest, asserted themselves in ways that borrowed both from indigenous channels of influence and from outside practices. From this mix of styles and strategies, came the empowerment of women and the alleviation of serious social problems stemming from the excessive consumption of alcoholic beverages. Such can be the unintended but nonetheless real developments that occur in colonized settings from a curious blend of the local and the foreign. There would be other debates of a more general but equally critical nature, debates, for example, about the dependency ultimately engendered by the efforts at development in the islands. It is to the variety of culturally informed understandings of that dependency that I now turn.

Chapter 6

Dependency? It Depends

The specter of the impending termination of the United Nations Trusteeship Agreement both haunted and compelled the Congress of Micronesia's deliberations over the issue of economic development. The Carter administration's intention, announced in early 1977, to terminate the trusteeship by 1981 heightened the anxiety of a Congress struggling with internal divisions as well as outside pressures. Working within the constraints imposed by the nation-state construct, members of the Congress considered what a more autonomous, self-governing, perhaps independent federated grouping of islands might look like and the ways in which such a governmental entity might sustain itself economically.

What confounded movement toward a more autonomous form of government was, among other things, the lack of anything even remotely resembling a viable, self-supporting economy. In the estimate of most contemporary observers, three decades of American colonial rule, and with it nearly one billion dollars in financial aid, had left the islands hopelessly dependent. Members of the Congress of Micronesia certainly acknowledged the problem. In 1976, the future president of the Republic of Palau, Lazarus Salii, reflecting on his earlier experiences in the Senate wrote, "We were witnessing the birth of an economy that would soon be—and today now is—thoroughly dependent on imported goods, contracted skills, and annual outside aid."[1] There was blame to go around, of course, but as in most colonial settings, the majority of that blame fell on the colonized. Federal officials, Trust Territory government personnel, academic experts, and travel writers all held the indigenous citizens of Micronesia ultimately responsible for the dependency that seemed to have infected their islands so fatally.

Consider, for example, the words of David Nevin, an American writer of popular nonfiction who visited the United States Trust Territory of the Pacific Islands in the mid-1970s:

> The issue is that Micronesians have been offered a world that bears no relationship to their own capacities. . . . They lack the wherewithal. The most striking physical thing about the islands aside from their physical beauty is the lack of economic infrastructure that people in advanced countries take for granted. With the lack of infrastructure goes an even greater lack of understanding of the nature of commerce, of capital accumulation, of how credit works, and why schedules are important.[2]

"Commerce," "capital," "credit," "infrastructure," "schedules"—the indictment of Micronesians in Nevin's text locates itself around the peoples' alleged inability to master these concepts and the larger process of economic development of which they are an integral part. In *The American Touch in Micronesia,* Nevin goes on to draft a scathing indictment of the United States for creating a welfare state in Micronesia and of Micronesians for accepting it without question. His account reads almost as apocalyptic prophecy against the judgments of a more recent literary visitor to the islands. Paul Frederick Kluge, a former Peace Corps volunteer now novelist who wrote the preamble to what became the constitution of the Federated States of Micronesia, describes the islands in his 1991 book, *The Edge of Paradise,* as hopelessly dependent, totally demoralized, and completely corrupted by American colonialism.[3] I will return to this book and its assessment of contemporary Micronesia in a later chapter.

Professional writers are by no means the only ones to comment on dependency as the first fact of life among the different political entities that have emerged from the superstructure of American colonialism. Citing a well-established litany of impediments, economists such as John Connell have written of the isolation, remoteness, lack of infrastructure, and paucity of natural resources that place prohibitive restrictions on the development of viable economies in island microstates such as those found in the former Trust Territory. John Cameron, in his assessment of economic development options in the Federated States of Micronesia, views as nearly terminal the legacy of dependency engendered during the American trusteeship period. One of the most serious casualties of American largesse, according to the development specialist from the United Kingdom, has been the people's will to work. Cameron forecasts a bleak future for the FSM marked by national bankruptcy, political disintegration, and the extensive migration of local peoples to the United States and its territories as provided for under the terms of the Compact of Free Association.[4]

The assessments of these popular writers and academic analysts constitute but a portion of an extensive body of literature that has attempted to explain the failure and folly of economic development in the Caroline, Mariana, and Marshall Islands. Much of this writing reflects implicitly, though dispassionately, the basic premises of classical dependency theory. Arising out of Latin America in the early 1960s, early dependency theorists such as the young Andre Gunder Frank focused their analyses not on the primitive, traditional, or feudal features of local economies, but on the havoc and distortion wreaked by the experience of colonialism on the non-Western world.[5] Frank wrote of the "development of underdevelopment" as not a natural condition but the product of a long, lingering legacy of colonial domination in the Third World. He went on to detail the ways in which metropolitan nations, through the patterns of economic domination originally established by colonialism, continued to exploit the resources of their colonies-turned-satellites on the periphery of the global capitalist system.

Developing further the actual processes of dependency that resulted from the legacy of imperial control, Theotonio Dos Santos explained how the economies of once colonized, now underdeveloped countries remained dependent on the financial, industrial, and technological resources of metropolitan nations. Dos Santos argued that Western monopolistic control of capital, finance, and technology, not local failures or inadequacies, kept the Third World essentially marginalized and with the consequent problems of backwardness, misery, and poverty. In short, theorists of the classical school such as Frank, Dos Santos, and also Paul Baran and Martin Landsberg posited dependency as a general condition of all Third World economies. Under this line of analysis, the islands called Micronesia qualified as one of the most dependent of dependencies, their only natural resource said to be their strategic geography as determined by the global security interests of the United States. Most critics of the American presence in Micronesia point to the long-standing primacy of strategic interests in the area and the consequent need to bind the islands closely to the United States through some long-term political arrangement.[6] Given this line of argument, economic development amounted to little more than a cover or charade for more-political machinations. There is, however, another way to read the general situation of dependency in American Micronesia.

In this chapter, I look in particular at the debate that developed over the use of American domestic welfare programs and monies and their effects upon Micronesian societies in the mid-to-late 1970s. Many scholars argue that the failure of initial efforts at substantive economic development led to an eventual abandonment of the effort and a resort instead to a massive infusion of federal grants and domestic services that had the effect of remaking the islands into little pockets of America in the western Pacific (table 1). There is a fair amount of substance to this summary argument. I endeavor, though, to avoid simple schemes of binary opposition involving American and Micronesian, strategic politics and economic development, change and custom. A consideration of the complex swirl of issues in and around the debate over dependency underscores, I think, (1) the massive cultural redefinition ultimately required by the developmental agenda; (2) the changing, often conflicting variety of colonial plans and policies used to promote that agenda; and (3) the diversity and polyvocality of local Micronesian responses that worked to challenge the very meanings of development and dependency. As preface to a consideration of the crosscultural dimensions of the debate over increased federal monies and the application of American domestic welfare programs into Micronesia, I consider first a larger history.

Money for the West, Kinship to the "Rest"

The consensual observations on Micronesian dependency that riddle the popular and academic literature reflect something more than coincidence.[7] This shared assessment is reflective of historical processes deeper than the colonialism, war, containment policy, and global security concerns of the twentieth century addressed earlier in this study. I refer here to historical processes that involved the emergence in the West of capitalism as not just an economic system but a culture. The rise to dominance of capitalism in the West entailed a new definition of society with economic values at its core. This new centrality of economic values in European society meant the devaluing of all other and earlier forms of social organization. The Mexican scholar Gustavo Esteva writes that the communal and cooperative aspects of sociality declined as the forces of the market transformed "commons into resources, men and women into commodifed labor, tradition into burden, wisdom into ignorance, and autonomy into dependency."[8] The individual, now helpless and cut off in this new economically centered construction of society, faced scarcity, that most central of economic problems. The concept of scarcity, argues Esteva, assumed that human wants were great, potentially infinite, though the means to satisfy them were limited and unequally shared. Thus, competition exacerbated the anxiety that surrounded the recognition of scarcity.

Table 1 Export Earnings and Total U.S. Assistance: 1947–1982
(in U.S. $millions)

Year	Value of exports	Total U.S. assistance	Exports as percentage of total money inflows
1947	–	1.0	–
1948	2.4	1.0	70.6%
1949	2.1	1.1	65.6%
1950	1.6	0.8	66.7%
1951	2.2	1.0	68.8%
1952	1.8	4.3	29.5%
1953	1.2	5.2	18.8%
1954	3.3	4.3	43.4%
1955	4.3	5.0	46.2%
1956	1.7	5.0	46.2%
1957	1.6	4.8	25.0%
1958	1.7	6.2	21.5%
1959	1.2	4.9	19.7%
1960	1.9	5.2	26.8%
1961	2.1	5.9	26.3%
1962	2.1	6.1	25.6%
1963	2.2	17.0	11.5%
1964	2.7	18.0	13.0%
1965	3.2	21.5	13.0%
1966	3.6	21.9	14.1%
1967	2.3	25.2	8.4%
1968	3.0	26.3	10.2%
1969	2.9	36.2	7.4%
1970	4.2	54.6	7.1%
1971	3.0	67.3	4.3%
1972	2.6	68.1	3.7%
1973	1.9	69.4	2.7%
1974	8.0	69.5	10.3%
1975	6.8	81.7	7.7%
1976	4.8	100.9	4.5%
1977	10.3	114.2	8.3%
1978	–	132.6	–
1979	16.5	138.7	10.6%
1980	15.6	124.5	11.1%
1981	–	120.0	–
1982	8.1	119.9	6.3%

Source: Francis X. Hezel, S. J., "A Brief Economic History of Micronesia," in *Past Achievements and Future Possibilities, A Conference on Economic Development in Micronesia,* Ponape May 22–25, 1984 (Majuro, Marshall Islands: Micronesian Seminar, July, 1984), p. 36.

Addressing the issue of scarcity, men calling themselves economists devised laws and codified practices whereby individuals, working in accordance with the dictates of the market, might satisfy their immediate needs and help ensure their long-term survival. Productive, economic activity thus came to be seen as the central and necessary object of all human effort.[9] The effect of capitalist market practices on social perceptions was so powerful that common sense soon came to be intricately bound up with economic practices. Although purported to be the truths that governed human society, the economic laws derived by David Ricardo and the classical economists constituted but deductive constructions derived from the observation of social behavior under market conditions.[10] The "discovery" of these economic laws through the observation of commercial practices constituted a new construction of reality. Capitalist economics, then, became more than a sphere of human endeavor; its redefinition of the purposes, prime activities, key values, and governing laws of life gave it the force of culture.

Christopher Herbert advances the argument of Western culture as fundamentally economic in his recent work, *Culture and Anomie: Ethnographic Imagination in the Nineteenth Century*. Employing a more expansive approach that focuses on the similarities rather than distinctions in early economic theory, Herbert argues that the writings of the earliest political economists, individuals such as Adam Smith, David Ricardo, Thomas Malthus, and John Stuart Mill, were essentially about the development of a concept of culture that sought to prescribe productive economic activities for human energy displaced by the intensified enclosure movement of late-eighteenth-century England. Adam Smith, for example, described a society as an integral, self-sustaining, self-regulating system whose dynamic, most fundamental characteristic was manifested through the process of material manufacture. Thomas Malthus, in his *Essay on Population*, concerned himself with the idea of human desire as a social construct that inscribes value, thus giving meaning to natural materials and creating a metanational system of capitalism that constitutes human beings' habitat or culture.[11]

The ascendancy of capitalism to the status of culture proved not a gentle transformation, but a violent, wrenching, destructive alteration in the European past. E. P. Thompson writes of enclosure movements and industrial revolutions that disrupted communities, transforming both agrarian tillers and town artisans into an industrial working class. The development of the factory system demanded transformation in the patterns of human behavior; the independence of the artisan or field worker had to be adapted to the discipline of the machine. The first step in this process of transformation, wrote Thompson, was the realization that an individual's chief happiness lay not in the present but in a future state.[12] There was an act of faith here that required the support of organized religion; with its emphasis on restraint, frugality, sacrifice, and deferred pleasures, Methodism had cultivated that fragile faith in early-eighteenth-century England. Religious faith, however, could not obliterate a consciousness of the inequalities and injustices that surrounded the industrialization of English life.

Thompson cites a written document, "The Journeyman Cotton Spinner," as indicative of this consciousness.[13] Produced in Manchester, England, during an 1818 strike of textile workers there, this address to the larger, affected public sought to define the features of exploitation that had led to the strike. The document spoke of the rise of a new class of masters without deeply rooted authority or obligations, the increasing distance between master and worker, and the all-too-painful exploitation that made possible the wealth and power of the new masters. In addition the loss of independence for the worker, the crippling dependency upon the master's technology of production, and the partiality of the law ultimately reduced the employee to the status of instrument. The document lamented the passing of the social economy of preindustrial England and its replacement by the regimen, discipline, monotony, long hours, and generally poor work conditions of the factory. Despite the separation in terms of time, place, and culture, the industrialization of England and the development of Micronesia might be seen as parts of a larger story or history. It would not be too irresponsible an extrapolation, I believe, to regard the discourse of economic development in Micronesia as similar in the violent, disruptive transformation of life it proposed; as a process that, if implemented as prescribed, would work to shatter links with the past and undermine satisfaction in the present by promoting the idea of a better, more comfortable, and more secure future earned by regulated wage labor.

The course of events would also disturb economic theory, though not nearly as severely as it disturbed people who came to form England's working class. Arturo Escobar describes how neoclassical economists' focus on capital accumulation, economic growth, and the idea of labor as the basis of all value gave way to a more general theory of equilibrium whereby the free play of supply and demand came to regulate a closed, circular, harmonious culture of economy. This idea of an economy regulated by pure market forces was upset, in turn, by events in the twentieth century that forced governments to assume a more interventionist posture. World wars and the rise of fascism and communism resulted in more direct supervision of national economies by Western governments. The rise of new world powers and new forms of institutional organization accompanied this great change in the management of economies.[14] In the United States, the center of the capitalist system after World War II, there developed corporate forms of organization that linked the political and the economic and that refashioned the relationship between the public and the private.

The rise of corporations had major and traumatic effects on the conduct of American life. Dating back to the late nineteenth century, worries over the growth of corporate power aroused new sources of anxiety in America. To older historical dualisms of rich and poor, damned and saved were added new dichotomies involving bigness and smallness, hierarchy and independence, homogeneity and diversity.[15] By the middle of the twentieth century, the corporate reorganization of American society had become a fait accompli. The question was no longer whether or not new corporate strategies would reshape America, but rather how individuals would cope with life in a corporate setting heavy with bureaucratic structures and capitalist values. For C. Wright Mills, the corporatization of American life meant the loss of those most prized social attributes, individual autonomy and independence.[16] The American playwright Arthur Miller expressed that same sentiment in more dramatic form. Biff, Willy Lohman's eldest son in Miller's *Death of a Salesman,* gave simple but eloquent expression to the oppressive nature of modern business culture when he said,

> It's a measly manner of existence. To get on that subway in the hot mornings in summer. To devote your whole life to keeping stock, or making phone calls, or selling and buying. To suffer fifty weeks of the year for the sake of a two-week vacation, when all you really desire is to be outdoors with your shirt off.[17]

Taking a little metaphoric license with Arthur Miller's words, it strikes me that economic development in Micronesia, in its most general dimensions, directed Micronesians to put on their shirts, get on the subway, and go indoors.

Most Marxist critiques posit the general primacy of economic activity, or the relations of production, in human society. Although Marxian analysis has had a limited influence on the study of American society, there is a school of Marxist-influenced thought within American historiography that posits the primacy of economic institutions and values as lying at the heart of American society and history. The most noted work of this school is Charles Beard's *An Economic Interpretation of the Constitution of the*

United States. In a second but related volume, *The Idea of National Interest,* Beard argued that United States foreign policy, despite the ideological covering that cloaked it, stood not upon abstract principles, but upon the pursuit of national interests as defined by the realities of political economy.[18] While acknowledging the complex mix of capitalism, socialism, and liberalism in the making of American society, later revisionists such as William Appleman Williams, Gabriel Kolko, and Martin J. Sklar continued to focus on the economic forces that affected both the domestic and foreign policy of the United States. Sklar, in particular, describes the United States as a "market" or "economic" society whose essence resides in its modes of production, its system of exchange, and its concerns for property.

> In U.S. history, market development has correlated strongly with societal development. The history of the United States has centered upon the stages of development of a market society, or of market societies codeveloping and interacting within the framework of one governmental system.[19]

From Federalism to Jacksonian Democracy through the Civil War, Open Door, the New Deal, and the Great Society, Sklar views the United States as itself a developing nation concerned to a large and essential degree with adjusting its modes of production to the changing historical circumstances affecting market economics.[20]

Marshall Sahlins translates this emphasis on the primacy of economics into more fundamentally anthropological terms. In *Culture and Practical Reason,* Sahlins endeavors to reveal the fundamental economic values that infuse American society's priorities, concerns, and definitions of achievement and satisfaction. Conceding the durability of the concept of utility from neoclassical principles of economy, he writes of people in American society as measured in terms of their usefulness or utility; the value of work an individual does determines not only that person's level of compensation and consumption, but his or her place in society and relationship with other people and institutions. Where, to paraphrase Sahlins, people were once the object of production, the object of human activity in the modern economic world now becomes production.[21] Rather than kin or kith, individuals follow an assumed utilitarian rationality that identifies consumer goods as desirable ends made accessible through intense, dehumanizing, and highly regulated patterns of economic behavior. I would extend Sahlins' argument back in time a bit to assert that this refocusing of human energies away from social groups or communities toward private, individual consumption resulted from the aforementioned historical processes that displaced peoples from their land, separated them from each other, and linked their welfare, indeed their survival, with the work they did for others.

Anthropologists working in the Pacific remind us of the complex, intricate, inseparable ways in which economic, political, social, and religious spheres of belief and practice are bound together for indigenous societies of the region. We who come from European and American shores deceive ourselves a little with the belief that, in Western societies, such spheres of activity are easily distinguished, separated, and isolated for study by those with appropriate training and credentials. Given the writings of Esteva, Escobar, Herbert, Thompson, Sklar, and Sahlins, and the global and national histories to which they refer, it seems possible to view the emergence of modern economic society as an essentially cultural phenomenon in which concerns for labor, production, consumption, profit, and capital came to infuse heavily the very character of daily life and activity. Enclosure movements, industrial revolutions, the emergence of nation-states, imperialism and colonialism, the rise of corporate structures, and the bureaucratization of government are all, I believe, a part of the history that the United States brought to its colonization of the Caroline, Mariana, and Marshall Islands.

"Money for Nothing and Your Frozen Chickens for Free"

A cliometric measure of the intent to remake Micronesia lies in the amount of American monies provided the Trust Territory.[22] Between 1951 and 1962, total congressional appropriations amounted to $56.9 million, a very modest sum by most calculations. Levels of funding and program activity would change dramatically, however, beginning in 1963. Prompted in part by the international criticism that followed the 1961 UN Visiting Mission's report on America's misadministration of the islands, the United States Congress moved quickly to increase appropriations to the Trust Territory. From $6.1 million in fiscal 1962, appropriations jumped to $15 million in 1963; by fiscal 1976, steady increases in appropriations brought direct American assistance to $75.1 million (table 2). With this rise in congressional appropriations, exports as a percentage of total cash inflow dropped dramatically. In 1948, the value of Micronesian exports had equaled 70.6 percent of total money inflows; in 1979, the value of exports out of the Trust Territory dropped to 10.6 percent of all revenues and monies received.[23]

Economists tell us that the declining role of exports in the Trust Territory's increasingly subsidized economy resulted from a change in development strategies. New monies went not into direct development

Table 2 U.S. Assistance by Category, 1947–1982
(in U.S. $millions)

Year	CIP[a]	Federal programs	DOI and Other[b]	Total
1947	0.0	0.0	1.0	1.0
1948	0.0	0.0	1.0	1.0
1949	0.0	0.0	1.1	1.1
1950	0.0	0.0	0.8	0.8
1951	0.0	0.0	1.0	1.0
1952	0.0	0.0	4.3	4.3
1953	0.0	0.0	5.2	5.2
1954	0.0	0.0	4.3	4.3
1955	0.0	0.0	5.0	5.0
1956	0.0	0.0	5.0	5.0
1957	0.0	0.0	4.8	4.8
1958	0.0	0.0	6.2	6.2
1959	0.0	0.0	4.9	4.9
1960	0.0	0.0	5.2	5.2
1961	0.0	0.0	5.9	5.9
1962	0.0	0.0	6.1	6.1
1963	0.0	2.0	15.0	17.0
1964	0.0	3.0	15.0	18.0
1965	0.0	4.0	17.5	21.5
1966	0.0	4.5	17.4	21.9
1967	0.0	6.0	19.2	25.2
1968	0.0	6.1	20.2	26.3
1969	7.6	6.2	22.4	36.2
1970	20.6	6.5	27.5	54.6
1971	25.3	7.4	34.6	67.3
1972	20.7	8.1	39.3	68.1
1973	16.3	9.4	43.7	69.4
1974	10.2	11.1	48.2	69.5
1975	14.8	11.9	55.0	81.7
1976	14.3[c]	11.5	75.1	100.9
1977	14.4[c]	25.1	74.7	114.2
1978	30.7	31.0	70.9	132.6
1979	54.3	24.1	60.3	138.7
1980	41.9	25.5	57.1	124.5
1981	20.7	25.5	73.8	120.0
1982	2.0	21.3	96.6	119.9

[a] Capital Improvement Projects

[b] United States Congress through United States Department of the Interior

[c] Figures incomplete

Source: Francis X. Hezel, S.J., "A Brief Economic History of Micronesia," in *Past Achievements and Future Possibilities, A Conference on Economic Development in Micronesia;* Ponape, 22–25 May 1984 (Majuro, Marshall Islands: Micronesian Seminar, July, 1984), p. 40.

projects, but into administrative and social services. Despite the recommendations of the various development plans and studies, the Trust Territory government identified the more effective functioning of government and the health and education of the population as necessary prerequisites for long-range economic development. To outside observers and specialists, this revised agenda for development had its flaws. For fiscal 1975, more than $21 million dollars, or 40 percent of the Trust Territory's total budget, was allocated to health and education; of this allocation, 70 percent or approximately $15 million went to pay the wages and salaries of employees in these two areas.[24]

Congressional appropriations were not the only avenue of federal assistance for the Trust Territory. Funding for capital improvement projects proved a second and separate column of American aid. From $7.6 million in fiscal 1969, money for capital improvement projects rose to $25.3 million in 1971, declined to $10.2 million for 1974, and then increased sharply to $54.3 million in fiscal 1979.[25] The publicly expressed purpose of these capital improvement funds was the development of a viable infrastructure that would facilitate economic development and make possible greater political autonomy and self-government.

American federal programs, concerned primarily with the provision of essential social welfare services to poor and low-income families within the United States, accounted for a third and significant source of funding for the Trust Territory. The strange history of American domestic welfare programs in Micronesia begins with President Lyndon B. Johnson and a speech he gave at the University of Michigan at Ann Arbor on 22 May 1964. In that speech, an insecure but ambitious Johnson sought to get beyond the legacy of his predecessor, the slain John F. Kennedy. At Ann Arbor, Johnson outlined a program that, in the words of his biographer Doris Kearns, was intended as a gift to America and a monument to himself.[26] The president sought to eliminate poverty and by so doing, create a "Great Society" for all Americans,

> where leisure is a welcome choice to build and reflect, not a feared cause of boredom and restlessness . . . where the city of man serves not only the needs of the body and the demands of commerce, but the desire for beauty and the hunger for community . . . where men are more concerned with the quality of their goals than the quantity of their goods . . . where the demands of morality, and the needs of the spirit, can be realized in the life of the nation."[27]

Johnson spoke of three billion people in the rest of the world who had never known pleasure, prosperity, and freedom; they were waiting, he said, with hope and anticipation for their own societies to become great. Micronesians, however, would not have to wait.

Congressional legislation passed earlier in 1963 had made the Trust Territory eligible to apply for domestic assistance programs administered through federal agencies in Washington, D.C., and their regional offices throughout the country. Johnson's program for a Great Society sought to revitalize a declining nation and, in its extension to the Trust Territory of the Pacific Islands, offered Micronesians the status of an American minority group. Little thought was given to the matter of whether or not the people called Micronesians wanted to become members of Johnson's Great Society. It was simply assumed that they did.

The Reach of U.S. Federal Programs in American Micronesia

There is a need here, I reluctantly concede, to pay some attention to the econometrics of federal programs in Micronesia. The Trust Territory government received about $120 million in welfare assistance funds between fiscal years 1974 and 1979, an average of approximately $20 million a year for that period.[28] Most of the federal assistance programs through which this money was administered supplemented efforts in health and education, the two budget categories receiving almost half the total annual congressional appropriations in this same period. In fiscal 1977, a total of fourteen federal agencies provided $28,514,444 to the Trust Territory, a dollar amount that represented 25 percent of total U.S. assistance to the islands.[29] The U.S. Department of Health, Education and Welfare accounted for more than half of these federal funds; the U.S. Department of Labor, primarily through programs established by Congress under the Community Education and Training Program (CETA), extended another $5,253,003. The Departments of Agriculture, Commerce, and Energy, along with the Action Agency, which now had administrative responsibility for the Peace Corps program, also proved to be major sources of domestic assistance funds for the Trust Territory.

These figures did not begin to approach the potential scope for American domestic welfare programs in Micronesia. A 1978 report by the Department of the Interior discovered that the Trust Territory was participating in only 166 of the 482 programs for which it was eligible.[30] The findings presented in the report had a quick, dramatic, and visible effect. By March 1979, 90 federal offices were operating within the islands and under the organizational framework of the Trust Territory government;

in addition to these ninety, another eight federal agencies, including the U.S. Weather Service, Post Office, and Coast Guard, were active in Micronesia but worked outside the Trust Territory government's administrative structure.[31]

Federal programs in education focused on teacher training and the development of special English language programs. Later programs provided funding for work in special education, curriculum development, and vocational training.[32] In its extension to the Trust Territory, CETA sought to provide job training and temporary work opportunities for economically disadvantaged, unemployed, and underemployed persons—distinctions imposed crudely and that rested awkwardly against the nature and purposes of work in different Micronesian societies.[33] Social welfare proved a major focus of many of the federal programs extended to the islands. The passage of the Economic Opportunity Act of 1964 allowed for the establishment of community action agencies, a Micronesian legal services office, and economic opportunity offices in each of the then six districts of the Trust Territory. The local community action agencies were charged with surveying and analyzing the causes of poverty, designing strategies and mobilizing private and public resources to alleviate those causes, developing innovative solutions to problems of public organization, and coordinating activities with appropriate agencies.[34] The Head Start program for preschool-aged children, the Neighborhood Youth Corps, the Job Corps program, and special programs for the elderly were all funded through and administered by the district community action agencies. The agencies programs were seen as assisting the general goal of economic development, which was said to include promoting the acceleration of economic growth compatible with orderly social, cultural, and political change.[35]

Whereas larger U.S. interests were overwhelmingly strategic, the nature of the American colonial presence for most of the islands, the Marshalls excepted, was primarily bureaucratic. Federal programs added to this bureaucratic layering as the laws under which they were authorized required the establishment of advisory councils, liaison officers, and local offices with salaried staffs. The positions created through these legal requirements, coupled with the temporary employment training positions supported by CETA money, accounted for a third of the 8,600 Trust Territory government jobs in fiscal 1978.[36]

Federal programs designed to respond to American domestic needs and situations could become inanely distorted crossing Micronesian beaches. According to the definition of poverty drafted by the Office of

Economic Opportunity, one of the principal administrative vehicles of Johnson's Great Society, almost all indigenous residents of the Trust Territory qualified as members of poor and low-income families and were thus eligible for benefits from a variety of assistance programs. Many Micronesians discovered that they were not only poor but old, or at least older than they thought. Title III of the Older Americans Act was extended to Micronesia on 26 May 1970 and led to the establishment of the Territorial Office of Aging under the Community Development Division of the Trust Territory Public Affairs Department.[37] The criterion for identifying the elderly in Micronesia was a liberal, expansive one. The harsh conditions of life caused by "particularly subsistence levels of existence" led the Territorial Office of Aging to consider those as young as forty-five to be potential members of a category called the "premature elderly" and thus entitled to enrollment in special programs for senior citizens in employment, education, transportation, housing, and health care.

Equally ironic was the Historic Preservation Program administered through the U.S. Department of Interior's National Parks Service. The program sought to protect important historic properties in the Trust Territory by requiring formal identification, survey, and review procedures for any capital improvement or construction project using federal money.[38] Sites of particular importance were eligible for inclusion on the United States Register of Historic Properties, an option that seemed as much about possession as it did preservation. What often went unchallenged was that the threats to historic properties in Micronesia often came from construction or development projects made possible by other federally funded programs. The definition of what constituted a "historic" property and the criteria by which the preservation requirements of a designated historic property were evaluated constituted yet another set of ironies in the administration of the program.

By the end of the 1970s, "welfare state" and "economic basket case" were the phrases being employed to describe the economy of the Trust Territory. The figures to support these descriptions seemed incontrovertible. In fiscal 1970, total American funding from congressional appropriations, capital improvement projects, and domestic federal assistance programs amounted to $54.6 million; by 1979, total federal assistance had skyrocketed to $138.7 million with federal programs and capital improvement projects accounting for nearly 60 percent of that figure, or more than $70 million. In this same ten-year period, the value of exports as a percentage of total cash inflows ranged between 7.7 percent and 10.6 percent, while the value of imported goods was nearly six times that of export earnings.[39] Even more shocking to some was the character of these imports. Rice, alcohol, and tobacco products constituted the three largest categories of imported goods; their prominence in the Trust Territory's import structure suggested to some consumption of a most irresponsible sort.[40]

The physical appearance of the islands had changed, especially in the district centers, and for the worse in the minds of most development specialists. Where there had once been only one motor vehicle on Majuro as late as 1960, there were 200 by 1965, all traversing the thirty-mile stretch of road that connected the islets that made up the Majuro Atoll complex.[41] By 1972, the number of vehicles owned by Marshallese had reached 510, with the total number of indigenously owned vehicles for the entire Trust Territory registering at 2,929.[42] The increase in American funding meant more jobs and higher wages which, in turn, drew greater numbers of people to the district towns or centers. Island entrepreneurs built pool halls, bars, movie theaters, car shops, and numerous retail stores to serve this increased population. The haphazard mix of new concrete buildings, dilapidated quonset huts from navy times, simple plywood structures with corrugated tin roofs, and lean-tos made out of available scrap material led one observer to call the urban centers of the islands "the most beautiful scrap heap in the world."[43]

The variety of goods appearing in Micronesian stores and the increasing size of those stores struck some as markedly at odds with popular conceptions of life on Pacific islands. On Majuro, Robert Reimer, a local Marshallese businessman, opened an air-conditioned supermarket advertised as the largest, most complete of its kind in the entire Trust Territory. The inventory of goods offered for sale from aisles upon aisles of open shelves included

> New York–made bell bottom trousers, a bottle of Philippine beer, an assortment of hose and pine fittings made in Michigan, English tea biscuits, French perfume, Swiss cheese, New Zealand leg of lamb, Hongkong toys, Japanese tape recorders, Australian butter, Danish luncheon meat, California dates, Argentine corned beef, Taiwan artificial flowers, German tools, Italian olive oil, Hawaiian jellies, and a custard cone whipped up while you wait at the store's snack shop.[44]

The seeming lack of order, direction, and sense to all of the construction and consumption made possible by increased American funding scandalized those sent to help develop the islands economically. Reports from specialists in the field were despairing. An economic development officer with the Trust Territory government on Yap told a *New York Times* reporter in 1977,

> Yap is a living refutation that there is no such thing as a free lunch. Here, it's a smorgasbord . . . a post-industrial leisure society with a guaranteed annual income. They just skipped the industrial part. Fortunately, they have a good growth-sector, federal funds.[45]

A United Nations development economist on the same island added, "We told them [the Yapese] you can't have both welfare and development; they clearly prefer welfare."[46]

The Politics of Feeding

No federal assistance program extended to Micronesia generated more controversy, however, than the Needy Family Feeding Program. Indeed, the word "feeding" strongly suggests colonial hierarchies of power as revealed by the identities of those who feed and those who are fed. In American Micronesia of the mid-1970s, students were the first fed. In November 1975, the United States Congress passed Public Law 94-105 authorizing the implementation of the National School Lunch and Breakfast Program. In that same month, a food services officer from the U.S. Department of Agriculture (USDA) arrived on Saipan "to begin quelling this last frontier in Child Nutrition."[47] By 1979, 275 out of a total of 311 schools in Micronesia, including the Commonwealth of the Northern Marianas, were participating in the school feeding program; only 2,682 students out of a total territory-wide enrollment of 38,447 remained beyond the reach of the project.[48] In addition to feeding almost every student in the Trust Territory, the program included funds for special summer school programs, nutrition education workshops, and the purchase of utensils, dishes, pots, pans, and even building materials for cookhouses. Total expenses for the program in fiscal 1979 came to $8,855,534.[49]

In late 1978, the Trust Territory food services officer, George Bussell, announced plans to extend the school feeding program to all needy families in the islands. Given the definition of poverty provided by the Office of Economic Opportunity, Bussell's announcement meant that, in effect, the United States Department of Agriculture would undertake to feed every woman, man, and child identifying themselves as Micronesians. Projections called for the feeding of 86,000 people at an estimated additional annual cost of $39,695,940.[50] Every Micronesian was to receive twenty pounds of rice, ten cans of evaporated milk, and a specified mix of other food items and canned goods designed to provide a balanced diet; these supplies were to be distributed every sixty days and were regarded as sufficient to provide three meals a day per person over the two-month allotment period.

Reaction to the Needy Family Feeding Program was immediate and diverse within and beyond the Trust Territory. Enthusiasm for the federal feeding program was most pronounced in Chuuk. In a speech before the Congress of Micronesia, Senator Nick Bossy declared emphatically that there was a need and desire for the Needy Family Feeding Program in Chuuk and that the United States "did not ram the feeding program down the throats of the people of Truk."[51] Chuuk district's large population and its scarcity of land and other natural resources made the program necessary. Bossy took strong exception to criticisms that asserted the irreversibility of dependency if Micronesia continued to accept federal assistance programs on such a massive scale. Quite the contrary, insisted Bossy; food assistance would allow the people time to raise more local

Boxes of USDA food on a beach in the Marshalls. (Trust Territory Archives, Pacific Collection, University of Hawai'i Library)

crops. The people of Chuuk would not permit themselves to become dependent on USDA surplus food; they desired to be self-reliant "just as any people anywhere." In an 8 November 1978 letter to Resio Moses, the chief administrator of the Trust Territory government's Community Services Department, Simeon Innocenti, a member of the Chuuk State Legislature, described external food supplements as of vital importance "until such time [as] locally produced food stuffs are enough to substitute for the frightening volume of imported food whose prices are so murderous to the needy people."[52]

Voices of opposition to the feeding program were heard loudest in areas immediately to the east and west of Chuuk. Representative Kiku Apis of Pohnpei expressed his deep reservations in a speech delivered from the floor of the House of Representatives on 10 November 1978.[53] Apis decried the lack of economic development in Micronesia. The congressman complained that an extravagantly paid army of American civil servants and expatriate contract employees had turned Micronesia's islands into "graveyards of their poorly planned and impractical projects." Given the identity of the planners, Apis wondered if there was an element of intent in the deplorable mess that economic development had become in the islands. Apis then turned specifically to the subject of federal programs that, he said, subverted Micronesian efforts at self-reliance. Commenting in particular on the Needy Family Feeding Program, Apis worried that within a few months Micronesians would lose all capability of feeding themselves, becoming, in essence, slum dwellers in a land controlled and inhabited by increasing numbers of non-Micronesians. "Believe me," declared Apis, "colonialism is not dead and we are not free."

Though ethnically Pingelapese, Apis echoed the concerns of many Pohnpeians among his constituents over culturally prescribed notions of personal responsibility and autonomy. *Ohl sohte kin kamwenge ohl*—"Men do not feed men"—is a Pohnpeian proverb that regards as shameful and unacceptable the dependence on another for one's livelihood and sustenance. Not everyone in Apis' congressional district felt this way, though. Although a plurality of his multiethnic constituency were, like him, from the island of Pingelap, some two hundred miles southeast of Pohnpei proper, these Pingelapese held decidedly different notions of dependency drawn from the experiences of their past and their present. The limited land area and environmental inventory of their home island, coupled with the extremely crowded urban conditions of their large community on Pohnpei, made the Pingelapese more wary of dependence on Pohnpeians than on Americans. For the Pingelapese, then, reliance on the wealth of distant colonizers was preferable to dependence on their more physically proximate, considerably less wealthy, and oftentimes less hospitable Pohnpeian hosts. Apis' opposition to the Needy Family Feeding Program cost him his congressional seat in the next election.

John Mangefel, one of the two senators now representing Yap in the Congress of Micronesia, resorted to humor and satire to convey his concerns over the extension of American domestic feeding programs in Micronesia.[54] A graduate of the University of Hawai'i with a degree in English literature and a privileged, high-caste member of Yapese society, Mangefel took a position that reflected the sentiments of a still powerful, deeply entrenched, subtly resistant council of paramount chiefs wary of the

A "Needy" Micronesian family. The caption to this photograph, which accompanied an article, "Nutrition: A Social Problem," by World Health Organization nutritionist Moises Behar, reads "Low income groups inevitably consist of uneducated people with low social status. Many of the children die at an early age from disease and malnutrition, resulting in the need to compensate by bearing a larger number of children." (*Micronesian Reporter,* 24, 2 (1976); Trust Territory Archives, Pacific Collection, University of Hawai'i Library)

threat posed to their rank and status by the structures and policies of American colonialism. Unlike Apis, Mangefel would pay no political price for his dissent. In one of a series of public letters to his imaginary cousin Ngabchai, the Yapese senator remarked that Micronesia had joined Russia and China as recipients of American farm surplus. Observing that the two Communist nations were considered enemies of the United States, Mangefel wondered about the implications of Micronesia's receipt of such aid. Had the United States declared a food war on Micronesia too? More than a little suspicious of the statistics and criteria used to ascertain Micronesian eligibility for welfare assistance programs, Mangefel marveled, for example, at how 41,000 Chuukese had been declared eligible for the feeding program when working figures in Micronesia indicated a population for Chuuk of 35,000. "How they managed to feed six-thousand (6,000) who do not exist is beyond me," Mangefel mused.

Mangefel suspected that there were many Americans who probably needed the food far more than most Micronesians, and he expressed belief that many in the islands would end up feeding the food allotments to their pigs and chickens. All in all, Mangefel thought the gift horse of American domestic programs might be a Trojan horse; he offered the opinion that American largesse in Micronesia altered the adage "Never look a gift horse in the mouth," to read "Always look a gift horse in the mouth and the stomach too." Another congressman, Julio M. Akapito of Chuuk, challenged the culturally arrogant, racially biased, and politically self-serving assumptions and definitions that underlay the extension of American domestic welfare programs into Micronesia. Akapito saw no need whatsoever for the family feeding program in Chuuk: "I have lived in Truk for the past thirty years and I have never gone 'hungry.'"[55]

American officials working in the Trust Territory were quick to respond to criticisms of the Needy Family Feeding Program by members of the Congress of Micronesia. George Bussell accused Micronesian congressional critics of perpetuating an old tribal system of control by keeping people ignorant of modern-day options and opportunities.[56] N. Neiman Craley, a special assistant to High Commissioner Adrian Winkel, scoffed at the suggestion of potential conspiracy behind the infusion of federal program money into Micronesia. Reflecting on the situation in a letter to former high commissioner William R. Norwood dated 11 February 1980, Craley wrote, "In no way do I regard it as a clumsy attempt by the United States to disrupt native cultural patterns and force islanders to increase their dependence on our life style and standards. This they are prepared to do without any encouragement by United States officials."[57]

Micronesian officials of the Trust Territory government such as Resio Moses, the chief administrator of the Department of Community Services, and Lazarus Salii, the director of the Department of Social Services, took a far more conciliatory approach that exposed their own personal, professional, and cross-cultural dilemmas. In a gentle letter to Mangefel, Moses noted that the people of the Marshalls, Pohnpei, Chuuk, and two atolls in the Yap group, through their elected leaders, had all clearly requested federal program assistance. Moses also could have mentioned in his letter a request for food assistance from the chiefs of the villages of Utwe, Tafunsak, Malem, and Lelu on Kosrae.[58] Moses reminded Mangefel that neither the Trust Territory nor American governments were attempting to force federal programs on the people of Micronesia. The programs were being made available to the people of Micronesia: "It is," wrote Moses, "our people's decision to accept or not accept such a program." In a separate letter to Akapito, Moses admitted that he shared many of the congressman's doubts about the actual existence of hunger and poverty in greater Micronesia but nonetheless felt bound to facilitate the implementation of federal assistance programs as requested by the peoples of Micronesia. In response to a request from the high commissioner, Lazarus Salii wrote a sixteen-point, three-page memorandum detailing his office's on-going review of federal programs, their effects, and applicability to Micronesia. Salii's report, inconclusive and ambivalent in its analysis, left open the question about future involvement and levels of funding.[59]

The debate over the Needy Family Feeding Program and the more general issue of dependency it raised extended beyond the islands. John Mangefel's speculation on the actual uses to which Micronesians might put free American food proved prophetic. In mid-1979, a Columbia Broadcasting Company film crew shooting footage for the television news program *60 Minutes* came across—or perhaps had staged—a young Chuukese male on Weno feeding a can of clearly labeled USDA meat to a pig. The inclusion of the footage in a segment highly critical of the American administration of the Trust Territory caused a minor outcry in the United States. The *National Enquirer*, a highly sensationalist tabloid with a large national readership, alerted its readers to a situation in Paradise where unemployment was twice the American national average, where beer cans littered the beaches, and where federal programs paid for by American taxpayers' money provided each resident of the islands with an annual average assistance of $797.[60] An audit of federal grants carried out by the U.S. Comptroller for Guam and the Trust Territory in December 1978 concluded that, by and large, feeding programs created a debilitating preference for foreign goods over locally grown foods, undermined the strong work ethic needed for economic development, diminished the possibilities of self-reliance, and, in short, promoted dependency.[61]

Official responses to the controversy were cautious at first. In a series of letters to High Commissioner Winkel, Ruth Van Cleve, the director of the Department of the Interior's Office of Territorial Affairs in Washington, D.C., reacted to the criticisms with mildly skeptical queries about the need for and appropriateness of American domestic welfare assistance in Micronesia. Responding to the pressures and passions of the debate, Winkel, on 31 October 1978, ordered a containment of all federal programs at the levels of funding and program activity then existing.[62] In addition, the high commissioner mandated the aforementioned review by Lazarus Salii's office with the intention of identifying programs for immediate elimination or general phase-out because of their inappropriateness or marginal utility. The high commissioner's directive, made with the concurrence of the Department of Interior officials in Washington, curtailed the expansion of American domestic welfare programs in the Trust Territory. From $25.5 million in fiscal 1980, the dollar amounts of federal programs would drop to $25.3 million and $25 million dollars, respectively, over the next two years.[63] After 1979, the matter of federal programs would become a critical element in the negotiations over future political status between the United States and the different Micronesian political entities that were emerging from the old colonial structure known as the U.S. Trust Territory of the Pacific Islands.

There were other takes on the assumed correlation between increased federal programs and greater dependency. A review conducted by Urban Systems Research and Engineering of Cambridge, Massachusetts, and published in 1982 under the title *Grant Consolidation for the U.S. Territories* regarded the problem of federal programs in Micronesia as more structural than political or economic.[64] The study concluded that the administration of individual or categorical grant programs imposed particular burdens and created additional barriers for American territories already disadvantaged by their small size, geographical remoteness, cultural and linguistic diversity, less-developed economies, and limited managerial resources. The authors of the report recommended consolidating categorical grant programs under a bloc arrangement as a way to eliminate the duplication, inappropriateness, mismanagement, and bureaucratic complications of many federal programs. Under grant consolidation, the different Micronesian governments would be offered a lump-sum dollar amount that they could then apply to the funding of specific federal programs they themselves chose. Not coincidentally, the recommendations of the report mirrored the American negotiating team's position on the future role of federal programs in the Federated States of Micronesia, the Republic of the Marshalls, and the Republic of Palau.[65]

The issues involved in the debate over American welfare programs in Micronesia were considered by local groups in venues outside the power centers of Washington, D.C., and Saipan. A conference sponsored by the Micronesian Seminar, a Catholic Mission organization then situated on the island of Weno in Chuuk Lagoon, brought together missionaries, academic specialists, Micronesian elected officials and government employees, and representatives from American federal agencies. The focus of the conference was an assessment of the overall effect of federal programs on Micronesian societies, and the drafting of an effective set of guidelines for determining the relevance and appropriateness of a given federal program before its acceptance and implementation. The overall tone of the conference reflected the conveners' deep concerns over the negative effect of the programs on the ability of the people to develop an effective, self-reliant economy that would help ensure the autonomy of their governments. The conference's Jesuit sponsors also sought to address the moral and ethical dilemmas they saw posed by the extension of American domestic welfare programs into Micronesia. Having listened to a number of presentations on the dimensions and devastating effects of federal programs in the Trust Territory, many participants readily agreed that there was much to be concerned about. The dependency of Native Americans on federal assistance and the general character of life on government-run reservations were noted for their disturbing parallels with the situation in Micronesia.[66]

During the course of the seminar, however, other voices emerged that suggested different understandings of the issues raised by the influx of American federal programs into Micronesia. Micronesian employees of the Trust Territory administration acknowledged the mismanagement and inappropriateness of some of the programs but considered the majority of them to be helpful. Andon Amarich of Chuuk, the chairman of the Federated States of Micronesia's Commission on Future Political Status and Transition, described the financial resources provided by federal programs as necessary and vital to the survival of his fledgling government and its people. Anthropologist Mark Borthwick from Duke University reminded the gathering of the problematic and various meanings of the word "dependency." Borthwick contrasted the complex, dependent, and ultimately nourishing social relationships that gave order and cohesion to Micronesian societies with the dependence of national economies on contributing domestic sectors and larger global systems. Still other comments made during the course of the gathering hinted at more local, deeply rooted ways of living and being in the world. At the conclusion of the conference, one participant wondered tellingly whether dependence was an American or a Micronesian fear.[67]

The question suggested something of the fundamentally different views that informed the whole issue of federal programs and economic development in Micronesia and of local efforts to invert the debate and to redefine the reigning notions of dependency and responsibility. Sasauo Haruo, in a speech before the House of Representatives on 10 November 1978, noted that he had never opposed federal programs in Micronesia because they were so relatively modest in size and scope compared to the needs of the people. Haruo also pointed to the need to consider more fully and carefully America's obligations by international agreement to provide for the welfare and development of Micronesia. Playing on the word "welfare," Haruo noted that the Needy Family Feeding Program was indeed about welfare—people's welfare. Haruo went on to add a cultural dimension to the issue. The congressman noted that in larger Micronesia it was customary not to refuse a gift. A gift represented a sign of goodwill and friendship and was often expressive of social relationships and the obligations that those relationships entailed. Haruo said that, given these cultural circumstances, many Micronesians in his district found it difficult to understand the debate over food assistance and other federal programs.[68]

Haruo's comments hinted at the ways in which goods, and the norms and values embedded in them, become changed, their meanings altered, in crossing cultural boundaries. The insight does not belong to Haruo alone. Nicholas Thomas has reminded us about the culturally and historically contexted entanglement of objects exchanged between Pacific and Euro-American peoples. So have ethnographers James Peoples, Glenn Petersen, and DeVerne Reed Smith. Peoples, specifically addressing the relevance of dependency theory to late-twentieth-century Kosrae, concludes that the interplay of endogenous and exogenous forces on the island is too complex and locally affected to speak about the triumph of imperialism or even the ascendancy of the forces of global capitalism. Lingering memories of a precolonial past, the prominence of an appropriated Congregational Church, persisting patterns of subsistence production and land use, the continuing strength of kinship ties, and the frequency of a variety of ceremonial occasions and celebrations all work to sustain a unique, locally focused society. On Pohnpei, Petersen has written of people not at all reluctant to take advantage of most material goods and technologies brought to their island from foreign shores, but who remain essentially unwilling to transform themselves into productive, thrifty, cost-conscious capitalists. In her study of Palauan social structure, Smith calls our attention to the still active, integral role of women and matrilineages in the determination of value, the obligations of exchange, and the distribution of land and important cultural goods.[69]

Other expressions of developmental dilemmas by Micronesians distinguished themselves significantly in tone and character from either politicians' speeches or ethnographers' analyses. A report produced by the governor's office in Chuuk—*Sudden Impact: Social and Economic Consequences of U.S. Federal Program Withdrawal*—made it clear how necessary federal programs had become to the local economy and how disruptive would be their elimination.[70] Noting Roosevelt's New Deal as establishing precedent for Americans' rights to certain social entitlements, the local authors of *Sudden Impact* argued that federal programs in Chuuk had become fundamental; bureaucratic concerns over whether or not federal grants would supplant rather than supplement local resources made no sense and were irrelevant. The report spoke of the obligations of the United States toward Chuuk. Inverting traditional liberal concerns over self-reliance and social welfare, the report went on,

> Much has been said, especially by Americans, about how good it would be for Micronesians to have federal grant programs withdrawn form the area. This "stop the welfare" mentality is as shallow as the Truk reef. It presumes that the nature of U.S. grants has been to give a "free ride" to money-hungry and lazy populations. The same ideas have been expressed domestically in the United States, about Latinos and Native Americans—and, of course, the entire black population. Whenever a people has been systematically denied access to rapid, improved quality of life, compensatory programs from those holding power have been assailed by racists, reactionaries, and liberal know-nothings as "destructive of the work ethic," or "damaging to culture" or "leading to increased expectations." Such notions are integral to the historically impossible task of keeping the native population down.[71]

The report concluded that, history aside, the effects of reducing federal programs in Chuuk would be social and economic chaos, labor unrest, massive layoffs, and increased crime and violence.

Having Their "Cake of Custom" and Eating It Too?

What sense to make of these discourses? What I think emerges first and foremost is the polyvocality of comments. Distinct groups of colonizers spoke to the issues differently. Development experts expressed frustration and exasperation at the pace of economic development and at the undermining counterforce to development that federal programs seemed to pose. Federal bureaucrats acted from the charters and regulations that governed their lives and professional responsibilities, while Trust Territory officials reacted cautiously to pressures from within and beyond the islands. Missionaries insisted on more attention to what they perceived as the moral and ethical dilemmas of development and to the social disruption brought on by major changes in patterns of living, working, and interacting as a community. Academic observers and liberal commentators expressed a mix of criticism that often indicted the American government for its exploitation of the area and blamed Micronesians for submitting so uncritically to that exploitation. All of these varying responses, however, lay subsumed under a larger American ethos that held economic development to be an essentially necessary, desirable, and inevitable process. There were different ideas about how Micronesia was to be remade and for what purposes, but all agreed it would be remade.

Walter Bagehot, the political economist of the late nineteenth century, wrote of the "cake of custom" in primitive societies that repressed liberty, originality, and social development.[72] Bagehot argued that freedom of thought and the spirit of invention, the prerequisites of progress, could only occur after the "cake of custom" had been cracked. It would be, I think, reductionism of a gross sort to characterize Micronesians in their responses to the dependency debate as trying to have their "cake of custom" and eat it too. Responses from island societies varied widely. Some elected officials, speaking in English and in ways that might sound alarmingly familiar to postmodernist sensitivities, seemed to concur in the perception of the threat that American domestic welfare programs posed to local efforts at self-sufficiency and self-reliance. Some spoke of immediate, seriously felt physical needs alleviated significantly, if only temporarily, by special American assistance. Others expressed a consciousness of the issue of dependency that hinted at more localized, culturally contexted understandings of power, responsibility, obligation, and gift. And there was that document from the governor's office on Chuuk, *Sudden Impact,* which challenged liberal American criticisms of development and colonialism in Micronesia as constituting an essentially racist, inaccurate, privileged perspective that refuted or suppressed more indigenous conceptions of the dependency issue.

We are, I believe, only at the beginning of understanding what economic development really is and what it might mean to others who are the objects or subjects of its agenda. Much remains to be considered. Race, gender, and class are fundamental categories of analysis in any consideration of economic development. In American Micronesia, these issues haunt the crosscultural politics of development in deep and troubling ways. It would be a short, partial, but not necessarily inaccurate history that wrote of economic development as the business of men, white men, who, in their efforts to remake Micronesia and Micronesians, sought to recruit and educate a few good local mimic-men in the replication of an economic culture heavily infused with notions of patriarchy and class, if not race.

And there is the undeniable link between economic development and domination in American Micronesia, a link that I believe shows itself elsewhere in other continuing colonial arrangements in the Pacific and the world. Maurice Godelier writes that "the power of domination consists of two indissoluble elements whose combination constitutes its strength: violence and consent." The disruption to established, localized patterns of human organization wrought by efforts at economic development is most certainly violent. I prefer, however, the word "assent" rather than "consent" to characterize the variety of local Micronesian responses to the forces of domination. As Inga Clendinnen has shown in her study of Maya and Spaniard in the Yucatan, the use of the word "assent" admits to the possibility of local, alternative processes employed to blunt and transform the instruments of hegemony and control. In American Micronesia, understanding dependency depends, I think, on taking up Raymond Williams' call to unlearn the "inherent dominative mode" through which ultimately self-serving knowledge about ourselves and others is derived and reified.[73] The discourse in favor of American-style development worked to block alternative understandings of the meaning and nature of dependence and the hegemonic history around it. Advertisements for development as necessary, desirable, and progressive could do little, however, to cloak the horrors of nuclear testing in the Marshalls. Here, the exercise of American power was raw, naked, and not much concerned with explaining itself or assuming responsibility, at least initially, for the destruction, disruption, and divisions it caused within Marshallese society. It is to the history of American nuclear testing in the Marshalls that I now turn.

Chapter 7

Dumping on Ebeye

In much of American Micronesia, efforts at cultural transformation through what has been called economic development proved a slow, confused, erratic, incomplete, even contradictory process at times. Not so in the Marshall Islands, however; more particularly on those atolls and islands disturbed directly and deeply by America's nuclear testing program. Here, strategic imperatives allowed little or no time for a program of planned transformation. Understanding the dominant discourse of economic development in Micronesia, then, entails recognizing the consequences of its initial absence. For many Marshallese, there would be no discursive rhetoric with which to contend, but rather an immediate, direct, unsettling confrontation with the hard, cold face of American military power. Proposals for economic development would follow as an almost begrudging, compensatory afterthought on how to redress the environmental and social devastation caused within the Marshalls.

The story of American nuclear testing in the Marshall Islands is a tragic, continuing one that begins on 1 July 1946 with the detonation of a nuclear device, code named Able, on Bikini Atoll. The story includes 68 separate nuclear tests between 1946 and 1958; the forced displacement of the peoples of Bikini and Enewetak atolls, their sufferings in search of new homes; the disease and death caused by nuclear fallout on the inhabitants of the nearby atolls of Rongelap, Rongerik, and Utirik; the prolonged efforts on the part of all of these people to seek redress and compensation from the United States government; the failed efforts to rehabilitate a too severely contaminated Bikini Atoll; and, in the case of Enewetak, a return to an atoll once again inhabitable but forever changed by the nuclear explosions that took place on it.[1] The histories here are not of induced transformation, but of violent, immediate, near-total disruption. They are histories that have been recorded by others, histories that need to be confronted.

In this chapter, I focus on the effects of nuclear missile testing in the

Kwajalein Atoll complex, more particularly on the island of Ebeye within that complex. Missile testing in Kwajalein brought disturbance and disruption of a particular character; as in those areas of the Marshalls affected by nuclear detonations, the strategic logic that compelled missile testing in the Kwajalein Atoll complex forced the abandonment of any discourse on development. Ebeye, often likened to a small urban ghetto by the early 1960s, served as a convenient site for the placement of all of the unexpected, barely imaginable, and little-cared-about problems that testing in Kwajalein caused, all of the problems that America's military and later civilian administrations had no time to confront or resolve. Conditions on Ebeye deteriorated so rapidly that, by 1979, American officials began speaking of the need for "redevelopment." Jane Dibblin writes of the "dumping" that resulted on Ebeye from postwar rehabilitation schemes, nuclear testing, and the establishment of the Pacific Missile Range on the island of Kwajalein itself.[2] A cruel metaphor, dumping offers a thematic approach with which to examine the "mess" created on Ebeye by American strategic needs, the culturally contexted ways in which different groups of Americans and Marshallese attempted to understand that mess, and the further entanglements resulting from imposed solutions sometimes as oppressive and demeaning as the problems they sought to address.

Metaphor as a Way of Getting to Ebeye

Greg Dening has stated that metaphor is a strategic tool for manipulating masses of material; it allows for the identification and repetition of a simple, central point and for the dramatization of time and chronological sequence.[3] A metaphor, writes the University of Melbourne scholar, is also a claim, albeit imperfect, for authenticity and for "being there." Metaphor, then, provides access to Ebeye, a place many of us have never heard of let alone visited, but a place whose past deeply affects the global present. The use of metaphor to talk about developments on Ebeye invites risk, but risk which, I think, pales against the larger issues of history, culture, and power that are manifest there.

I choose the unpleasant metaphor of dumping with which to approach a reflection on the social conditions of American missile testing in Kwajalein Atoll because it so effectively reveals the ways in which different groups of colonizers and colonized struggled to make a place for themselves in America's most strategic of Pacific possessions. Ebeye, in particular, became a dumping ground for all of the problems resulting from American nuclear testing in the Pacific. The struggle around Ebeye revealed, exacerbated, and at other times created divisions within both the colonizing and colonized cultures. In short, the history of Ebeye defies the neat analysis, simple categorizations, and extreme oppositions that academic specialists have applied to their studies.

Dumping and other related and employed metaphors such as "slum," "ghetto," "reservation," "cesspool," and "festering sore" are not only cruel, but sometimes dangerous. Rooted in colonial perceptions and values, such metaphors, even when used by sympathetic observers to call attention to the abuses of American policy in the Marshalls, can denigrate inadvertently the subjects of their concern. Critiques of the "Ebeye problem," produced in and enabled by the colonizing culture, can themselves be problematic. The risk in writing about dumping on Ebeye is that it can invite further dumping on Ebeye. The issue of dumping on Ebeye also reminds us of how matters of race and place can be intimately linked in colonized spaces, a topic, I think, barely acknowledged in the body of ethnographic, historical, and social science research in the area called Micronesia. Robert Bullard, in *Dumping in Dixie,* writes of how the economic and political vulnerability of out-of-the-way Black communities on the American mainland encouraged the placement of noxious, environmentally hazardous facilities in those communities.[4] It is no accident that atmospheric nuclear testing took place in an area remote from the North American continent and among people who were not white.

Dumping, of course, is not just a historical metaphor, a way to examine the horrors of a fading colonial past; it is also an all-too-real activity that disturbs and threatens contemporary times. The Republic of the Marshall Islands, a more autonomous local government now in free association with and funded largely by the United States, has entertained at times plans to accept contaminated soil as landfill and to use some of its more remote atolls and their lagoons as dumping sites for nuclear wastes from Japan and the United States. Indeed, a consideration of Ebeye's history from 1944 to the present blurs, even subverts the distinction between colonial and postcolonial periods and shows just how complex, on-going and multifaceted is the process of decolonization.

Beyond Metaphor

Nicholas Dirks has written that colonialism gave impetus to the rise of anthropology and its core concept of culture; in turn, ethnographic findings facilitated the agenda of colonial domination.[5] Put another way, the anthropological concept of culture might never have been invented without the colonial projects of rule that required its existence. Though some might hold such an indictment to be a little too sweeping and indiscriminate in its dimensions, Dirks' attention to the relationship between culture and colonialism is an important one; it serves to remind us of the subtle, invidious ways that colonialism can affect, create, or even take over a body of knowledge. On the Kwajalein Atoll complex, however, colonialism had free rein.[6] No extant ethnography or anthropological study described and, in its description, justified the need for change and transformation. The earliest American ethnographers into Micronesia bypassed Kwajalein, concentrating instead on other islands and atolls in the Marshalls that were more accessible and that seemed more politically and culturally significant. Middle- to late-twentieth-century anthropological inquiries into Kwajalein Atoll often begin with mention of the 1941 seizure of the island by Japanese forces, the subsequent establishment of an air base there, the capture of that base by American forces in 1944 and include generalizations on cultural practices drawn from other, more-studied areas of the Marshalls.

Edward Said has argued that in the culture of empire can often be found a magisterial denial of the fact of empire.[7] Such was certainly not the case in the Marshall Islands, where the dictates of American strategic interests were bold and immense and could be intensely seen, heard, and felt in the terrible light, heat, flashes, mushroom clouds, and rolling thunder from nuclear testing. In the Marshall Islands, more particularly the Kwajalein Atoll complex, American colonialism showed itself raw and naked, and with little concern for liberal platitudes designed to mask or cover its force. Kwajalein was a stage for empire revealed.

Poststructural sensibilities need not disturb too quickly, I think, the received facts about the nuclear history of the Kwajalein Atoll complex; those facts are disturbing enough. Made up of 93 separate islands and islets in the Ralik or western chain of the Marshall Islands, Kwajalein Atoll possesses a total land area of 6 square miles; its lagoon, the largest in the world, covers 839 square miles. Of the islands and islets that make up the Kwajalein Atoll complex, the island of Kwajalein is itself the largest; its enormous lagoon and deep anchorages attracted the attention of the United States military, first as a naval base, then as a support facility for nuclear testing on Bikini and Enewetak, and later as a missile testing range.

The land, air, and sea battles of World War II would create the first real mess on the atoll complex. The 1944 destruction of the Japanese air station on Kwajalein proper necessitated an intense cleaning and clearing of the island before it could be used as a support facility for American

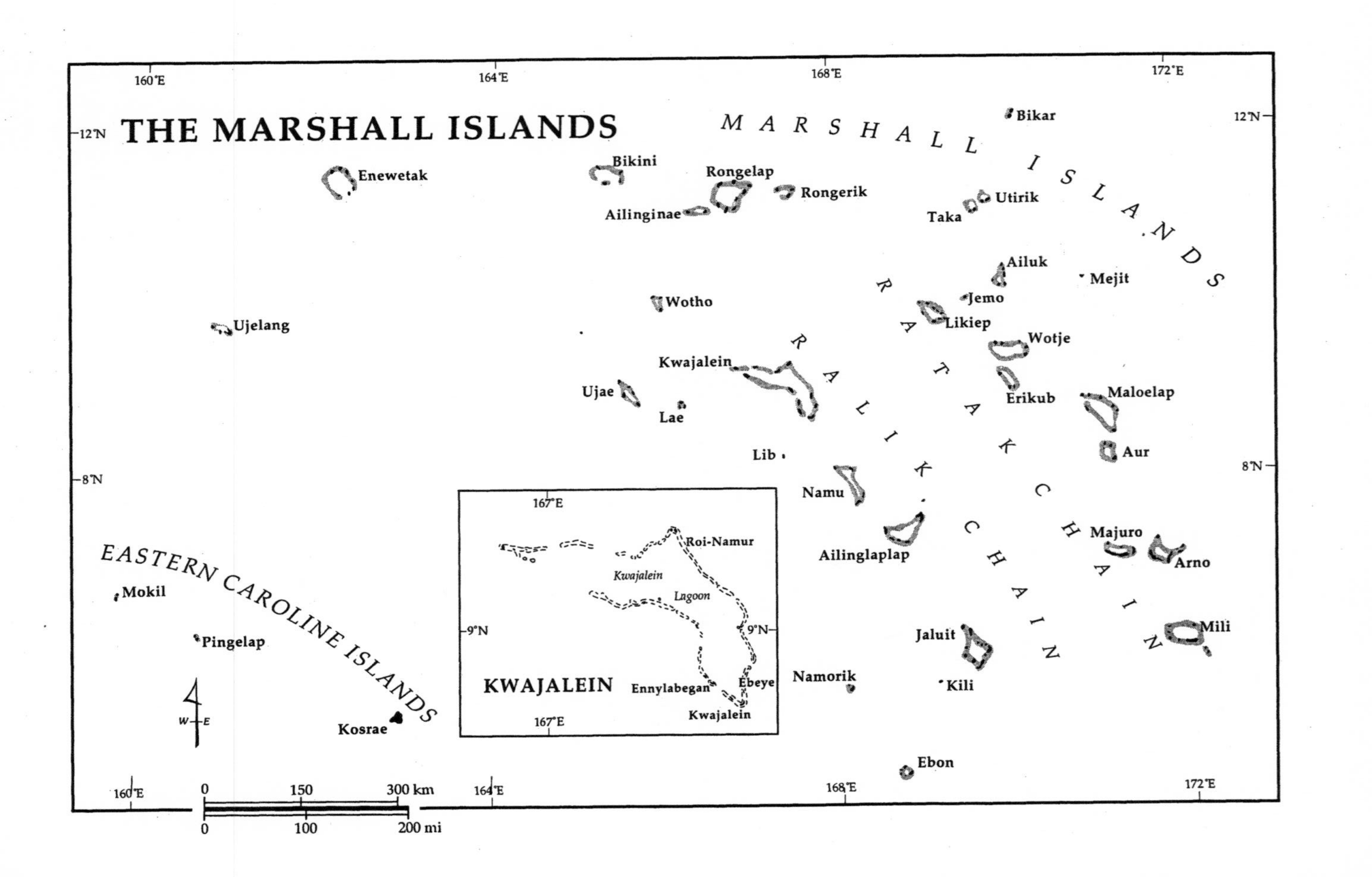
THE MARSHALL ISLANDS
MARSHALL ISLANDS
RATAK CHAIN
RALIK CHAIN
EASTERN CAROLINE ISLANDS
Bikar
Enewetak
Bikini
Rongelap
Rongerik
Ailinginae
Utirik
Taka
Ailuk
Mejit
Jemo
Likiep
Wotje
Erikub
Maloelap
Aur
Wotho
Ujelang
Kwajalein
Ujae
Lae
Lib
Namu
Ailinglaplap
Majuro
Arno
Mili
Jaluit
Kili
Namorik
Ebon
Mokil
Pingelap
Kosrae
KWAJALEIN
Roi-Namur
Kwajalein
Lagoon
Ennylabegan
Ebeye
Kwajalein
167°E
9°N
160°E
164°E
168°E
172°E
12°N
8°N
0
150
300 km
100
200 mi
W
E

military actions elsewhere in Micronesia and the western Pacific.[8] This first development project led the navy to move most of the surviving indigenous population of Kwajalein Island to nearby Ebeye. Before 1946, fewer than 20 people lived on Ebeye, a 78.5-acre island in the southeastern corner of the greater Kwajalein Atoll complex some three miles north of Kwajalein Island. The relocation of the Kwajalein people to Ebeye increased the latter's population to 300. Freed of its resident population, Kwajalein became a labor camp in which islanders from other parts of Micronesia as well as other areas of the Marshalls were brought to work. With the debris of war strewn along it shores and over its interior, Kwajalein came to resemble "not an outpost of the Navy, not a crossroads of the Pacific, but a back alley, a junk pile"; one American naval officer called it the "ugliest acquisition since the Gadsden Purchase."[9] Built hurriedly and poorly, the military barracks, storehouses, and roads deteriorated rapidly under tropical conditions, thus adding to the sense of desolation that, for Americans, seemed to enshroud the island. Eventually, the Kwajalein labor camp was itself moved to Ebeye, increasing that island's population by another 560 people. At the same time, other Marshallese people began moving to Ebeye, attracted, it was said, by the lure of employment, wages, material goods, and the general excitement of its urbanlike lifestyle.

The transfer of administrative responsibility for the larger Trust Territory from the navy to the Department of the Interior did not affect the military's landholdings on Ebeye. The U.S. Navy retained rights over the northern half of Ebeye for a transmitter; the Coast Guard operated a station of its own on 10.73 acres at the southern end of Ebeye. A small island thus was made even smaller by a military presence that took up almost two-thirds of its total land area. By 1951, some 1,200 Marshallese laborers and their dependents were crammed into an area of less than twenty-seven acres.[10] This figure did not include a considerable number of visitors who arrived via small boats from other areas in the atoll complex or the larger Marshalls Islands group, stayed for a period ranging from days to months, and then departed to return to their homes. With an average of approximately 46 people per acre, Ebeye had already reached its maximum sustainable population density. In 1955, the navy, pressured by the Trust Territory government to help redress the overcrowding, agreed to limit the recruitment of laborers for Kwajalein Island to residents of the atoll; this reduced the number of what were euphemistically referred to as "visitors," but only somewhat. To further ease conditions, the navy, in 1959, agreed to return the 39 acres it controlled in the northern half of Ebeye.

The relief provided by this release of military land was quickly offset by the relocation of more people to Ebeye. This essentially forced migration of people resulted from the increasing safety and security requirements of more sophisticated missile testing. In 1960, the navy, responsible for the operation of what was then the Pacific Missile Range, removed the people of Roi-Namur, the northernmost islands of the Kwajalein Atoll complex, as a precautionary measure in connection with the testing of the Nike-Zeus weapons system; the following year, the 100 people of Lib, an island fifty miles southwest of Kwajalein Atoll, were also relocated to Ebeye.[11] The navy insisted that the residents of these islands would have to remain on Ebeye for the duration of the Nike-Zeus tests, a period it estimated to be about five years.

The congestion was aggravated even more by the U.S. Army's assumption in 1964 of control over Kwajalein Island and the subsequent testing of the Nike-X missile system there. The testing of the Nike-X missile system, and later the tracking and the retrieval of intercontinental ballistic missiles (ICBMs) and submarine-launched ballistic missiles (SLBMs) from the Kwajalein lagoon, necessitated the exclusive use of the central two-thirds area of the atoll complex, including the islands of Meck, Lagan, and Ningi.[12] The use of this area, termed the "Mid-Corridor" in missile-testing parlance, necessitated the relocation of its 372 residents to Ebeye. Most of the owners of land on these Mid-Corridor islands were already resident and working on Ebeye, but they had been using their home islands as a supplemental source of food.

Concerned to legitimate its use of land in the greater Kwajalein Atoll complex through legal contract, the United States initially sought an indefinite use agreement and offered a lump sum payment of $300,000, presented in bundles of one dollar bills, to elicit Marshallese acceptance. Resentment over both the approach and the terms eventually led representatives of the United States government in 1964 to offer the landowners $750,000 for a 99-year lease.[13] With annual payments to each landowner averaging less than $10 per acre, the lease agreement was little more than a gesture; it did, however, contain a provision calling for review and possible renegotiation of existing terms at regular five-year intervals, a provision that some Marshallese would come to exploit.[14] In addition to this more general agreement, a monthly allowance of $25 was provided each person displaced from the Mid-Corridor islands. As we shall soon see, these arrangements proved totally unsatisfactory for the people of the Mid-Corridor islands, the other affected landowners in the Kwajalein Atoll complex, and the native people of Ebeye as well.

Ebeye's intimate relationship with American missile testing on Kwajalein gave it a look and style different from every other island in the Trust Territory. In a memorandum of 23 June 1967 to High Commissioner William R. Norwood, William V. Vitarelli, the district administrator's representative on Ebeye, identified those factors that made Ebeye unique among the islands of the United States Trust Territory of the Pacific. Vitarelli noted that Ebeye was the only island community in Micronesia that depended solely on a money economy. Ebeye had the highest number of skilled Micronesian workers, the highest per capita income, the highest retail prices, and the highest concentration of population per acre of any island or atoll environment in the Trust Territory. Another observer characterized Ebeye as the "largest and wealthiest slum" in Micronesia. A third termed it an "island of affluent paupers." To many, including Vitarelli, Ebeye existed as it did because of its immediate, deep, and inextricable link to the now Kwajalein Missile Range.[15]

International organizations and other local constituencies drew attention to American exploitation of the Kwajalein Atoll area. As we have seen, the 1961 UN Visiting Mission had accused the United States of subordinating the welfare of the natives people in the Marshalls to the military exigencies of the United States, thereby violating the United States' responsibilities under the 1947 United Nations Trusteeship Agreement. Others called Ebeye a "disaster waiting to happen." That disaster occurred in 1963 when a polio epidemic hit the island; the incidence of affliction reached 91.3 per 1,000 and caused eleven deaths and 212 recorded cases of full or partial paralysis. The epidemics of gastroenteritis and influenza that soon followed proved especially virulent among the infant and elderly segments of the population. Studies done on each of these three incidents of epidemic disease implicated the extreme overcrowding and unsanitary conditions. By 1966, Ebeye had come to be described as "the most congested, unhealthful and socially demoralized community in Micronesia" with its population of more than 4,500 people crammed into an area a little more than a tenth of a square mile.[16]

The Trust Territory government, already strained and exasperated by the social consequences of extended missile testing on Kwajalein Island, insisted that the U.S. Department of Defense fund a major renovation and development project for Ebeye. In 1966, the U.S. Department of Defense reluctantly and belatedly agreed to the construction of a "model community" on Ebeye at a cost of $7 million; it included 77 four-unit, two-bedroom apartments, a freshwater distribution system, an electric power plant, and a sewage disposal facility that used saltwater.[17] This Ebeye

Improvement Program stated as its goal the creation of a healthful, modern community on the island equipped with necessary utilities and services to adequately care for its resident population. A corollary objective of the project was the development of a self-reliant community willing and able to initiate and maintain activities designed to achieve social, cultural and economic betterment. A press release on the program quoted High Commissioner William R. Norwood as saying that the rehabilitation of Ebeye would be one of his highest priorities and that he was confident, along with Kwajalein Test Site Commander Col. Frank Healy, that Ebeye would emerge as the most modern, prosperous, and well-organized community in the Trust Territory.[18]

Prepared for the Department of Defense by Hawaii Architects and Engineers, the plan called for limitations on street space; restrictions on motor vehicles; a centralization of commercial facilities; development of an integrated civic center; construction of seven nursery, elementary, and secondary schools; creation of adequate recreational facilities including beaches; and planting of trees and shrubs.[19] In its concept, design, and sketches, the plan envisioned Ebeye as something akin to a Southern California suburb. The plan also claimed to be in accord with the larger goals of the Trust Territory government, which included accommodating American strategic interests, fostering unity in greater Micronesia, and promoting the understanding and adoption of democratic governmental processes. In its making over of Ebeye, the plan embodied the totality of the colonial agenda, including all the contradictions and paradoxes that riddled America's possession of Kwajalein Atoll and indeed all of Micronesia.

Despite the seeming totality of its view, the plan suffered from serious flaws in both its conception and attempted implementation. The improvement program, initially predicated on an existing population of 2,500 people, had become woefully outdated by 1966, when continued hiring and unrestricted migration swelled Ebeye's population to 4,500. Land proved an exceptionally critical and highly troublesome issue on an island so overly populated as Ebeye. Despite the navy's cavalier decision regarding relocation, Ebeye was not a free or deculturated zone. All of the land there was privately owned and divided into ten *weto* or land parcels; ownership rights were shared among a paramount chief or *iroij*, 4 lineage chiefs called *alab*, and approximately seven hundred lineage members, many of whom lived elsewhere in the greater Kwajalein Atoll area.[20]

Not at all concerned with the complexities of the land tenure system on the island, the United States Department of Defense stipulated that none of its funding for the Ebeye Improvement Project could be used to build structures and utilities on private land directly under the control of the Marshallese people.[21] To satisfy the Department of Defense, the Trust Territory government was required to acquire control over all land on the island; this was accomplished through long-term lease agreements exacted under the threat of government confiscation by declaration of eminent domain. The Trust Territory government was further required to demolish all existing structures on the newly leased land, but with no compensation to landowners for the destruction of those structures. People inhabiting those structures were moved to temporary quarters in already overcrowded areas of the island. Moreover, in an ironic twist to an already perverse, badly distorted situation, landowners on Ebeye were required to pay rent for using or inhabiting any new structures built on their land after the implementation of the new lease arrangements. The agreements, insisted upon by the Department of Defense and executed by representatives of the Trust Territory government, angered the major landowners and the many others who, by dint of Marshallese custom, held land use rights on Ebeye. Although all but one of the major landowners agreed to lease their land rather than face confiscation through eminent domain, there were bitter complaints about the low rental payments and the length of the lease.

Equally complicated and potentially destabilizing was the continuing dissatisfaction of the Mid-Corridor population that had been moved to Ebeye. Unlike the Ebeye landowners, the Mid-Corridor residents relocated to Ebeye received a monthly stipend and paid no rent for the housing built specifically for them by the government. Despite this relative "privilege," the Mid-Corridor people were far from content with their situation. Persistent complaints, registered mainly through the Congress of Micronesia, led the United States to increase their individual monthly stipends from $25 to $40 per month. This increase failed to address the more crucial issue of just compensation for long-term land use, however. In 1969, the Mid-Corridor islanders left Ebeye to reoccupy their home islands in the strategic impact zone. This temporary reoccupation resulted in the cancellation of two scheduled missile tests and induced the United States government to offer total adjusted compensation that now amounted to a yearly sum of $420,000. All of this unsettled the Ebeye landowners, who now felt considerably more disadvantaged and discriminated against than their uninvited guests.[22]

Ebeye, 1978

The problems already plaguing Ebeye by 1954 continued and intensified over the next two decades. By 1978, Ebeye's population had grown to more than 8,000. Mary M. Kearney, an American attorney working in behalf of the greater Kwajalein Atoll landowners, placed the issues of population and population density in a perspective that American nationals might better understand. She wrote, "If the population of the entire United States—about 224 million—were moved to Connecticut the popula-

An aerial view of Ebeye with Kwajalein Island in the background. (Gliff Johnson)

Children on the beach at Ebeye. (Giff Johnson)

tion density would be considerably less than that of Ebeye."[23] Special Representative William Vitarelli defined congestion as something that involved more than numbers or ratios:

> It is too many people crouched in a room where the sound and smell of each man's breath becomes as one and where to turn in one's sleep means a concession on the part of all. It means thanking God for the cool rain that fills the drum outside but at the same time damning the devil for the leaky roof. Congestion means lack of privacy and learning to time one's regularity to meet the secret dusk of night or the tide or the privilege of the benjo. It means learning to suffer thirst, to wash clothes in brackish water or to go without a bath because there is no water. Congestion . . . is the unnatural accumulation of people in one place caused by a disregard for space and a disregard for the planning of space to accommodate human beings. It is insensitivity to man's need and a lack of concern for the natural resources that are required to serve man's needs. Congestion is noise, soggy air and cockroaches.[24]

Vitarelli's sense of space may have differed considerably from that of the Marshallese. By any cultural standards, however, Ebeye was an overcrowded, unpleasant, difficult place to live.

Problems identified as serious in 1954 had become critical by 1978. With slightly over 50 percent of the population under fourteen years of age in 1978, reports out of Ebeye pointed to problems involving gangs, juvenile delinquency, drug and alcohol abuse, venereal disease, and unwanted pregnancies. Education offered little relief or recourse to the problems facing Ebeye's youth. A dilapidated, poorly equipped elementary school, staffed by thirty teachers, offered education in split sessions to 1,107 students. Journalist and author Paul Jacob visited Ebeye in 1977 and wrote of children with nothing to do after school "except hang around. . . . Juvenile delinquency keeps growing, along with alcoholism. I've seen 10-year old kids so drunk they cannot walk."[25]

New housing, identified as inadequate and substandard to begin with, deteriorated rapidly. In some instances, up to 54 people occupied a single dwelling, with the average occupancy at 13.6 people in a housing unit or apartment designed for a family of four.[26] The physical infrastructure and public utilities available to the people of Ebeye proved no less scandalous. Water storage facilities on Ebeye, which included catchment systems, large tanks, and drums of imported water brought by barge, could carry only a third of the island's water needs at any one time. Numerous unscheduled outages made electric power on the island unpredictable. The lack of a consistent reliable source of power, in turn, played havoc at times with the provision of vital social and medical services.

Sanitation facilities on Ebeye were described as particularly appalling. Rubbish collection for the population of 8,000-plus was handled by nineteen trucks that dumped untreated garbage at the northern end of the island, a place called "dumptown."[27] Over-the-water outhouses meant the deposit of raw sewage directly into the lagoon. The bacteria count from that lagoon at times reached levels 25,000 times higher than those identified as safe by the United States Health Service and the World Health Organization. A 1978 study noted that the shortage of water and the poor state of sanitation combined to cause an extremely high rate of sickness on the island. That report noted that "foul odors and visible water pollution are part of the normal environment in which people must live and work, and the children must play."[28]

Another equally dangerous but less publicly discussed source of pollution was the uranium 238 that had been used as ballast to stabilize the warhead portion of test missiles during reentry and splashdown in the Kwajalein lagoon.[29] The dumping in this instance came literally from the skies. Since 1961, the missiles had been shot from Vandenberg Air Force Base in California and monitored in flight by an elaborate global tracking system. The Pentagon downplayed the amount of depleted uranium leaked into the lagoon, saying that it posed no significant radiation hazard. As late as 1982, the commander of the Kwajalein Missile Range denied any leakage of uranium into the waters of the lagoon. A spokesman for the Kwajalein range stationed at a support facility in Huntsville, Alabama, conceded, however, that a problem did indeed exist; this individual admitted that despite intense salvage efforts, quantities of depleted uranium were left at the bottom of the lagoon.

The sorry state of medical facilities and services on the island received widespread comment and condemnation. Two physicians and thirty nurses, technicians, and support personnel staffed a poorly built, four-year-old, twenty-seven-bed hospital that averaged 123 admissions, 1,993 out-patient visits, and 26 live births monthly. Professional observers blamed the 1963 outbreak of polio on the island in part on the American administration's failure to immunize the population of Ebeye against the disease despite the existence of an approved, available, and cost-efficient vaccine developed some eight years earlier.[30] In 1977, the hepatitis rate on Ebeye was three times higher than that recorded for any other island in Micronesia.[31] A 1978 measles epidemic afflicted 329 people and resulted in two deaths.[32] Erratic supplies, inadequate storage and refrigeration facilities, and a general lack of space complicated the already precarious and fraught endeavor that was public health care on Ebeye. Greg Dever, the author of the 1978 study *Ebeye, Marshall Islands: A Public Health Hazard,* called the public health situation on the island "a direct result of the relocation of the people of the Kwajalein Lagoon to create the Kwajalein Missile Range and the indifference of the KMR to the problems of the people of Ebeye."[33]

Home, Home on the Kwajalein Missile Range

What made the situation on Ebeye especially deplorable was the very different kind of life being enjoyed by American military personnel and expatriates who worked for the Kwajalein Missile Range (KMR), formerly called the Pacific Missile Range, on Kwajalein Island.[34] Situated three miles south of Ebeye, and possessing a land area of 900 acres, Kwajalein showed itself to be the source not only of Ebeye's existence but of all of its problems as well. To most of the residents of Ebeye, Kwajalein represented first and foremost the principal source of employment for their island. In 1978, some 700 Marshallese who lived on Ebeye worked on Kwajalein; this figure accounted for about 60.6 percent of the actual labor force on Ebeye.[35] On Kwajalein, Marshallese worked largely in low-paid, unskilled, and semiskilled jobs as gardeners, cooks, warehouse workers, and maintenance personnel—jobs necessary to maintain the base for its 1,200 American civilian residents and a military staff of about 22.[36] Some worked as secretaries, mechanics, and heavy-equipment operators. Most earned from $2.10 to $2.40 per hour, with those women who worked as maids for American families receiving $5 to $6 a day, plus lunch money. Although significantly higher than the wages paid to indigenous employees throughout the rest of the Trust Territory, the earnings of Marshallese on Ebeye were dramatically below the compensation American expatriates received on Kwajalein and elsewhere in Micronesia.

A feature article in the Long Island, New York, newspaper *Newsday* examined in detail the social consequences of the missile-testing industry in the Marshalls; it cited Marshallese workers who pointed to racism as the prime reason for the disparity in wages, the low-level jobs given them, and the unlikelihood of promotion or advancement in those positions.[37] Security checks reinforced the general sense of discrimination experienced by Marshallese workers on Kwajalein. Ebeye workers were ferried to Kwajalein in the morning and returned home that evening. To get on and off the boat, they were required to show a guard their special yellow or "D" passes; upon both their arrival and departure, workers from Ebeye were subject to arbitrary searches at the army checkpoint through which they passed. In response to a 1981 suit against this practice brought by a Marshallese landowner, a U.S. judge ruled that the army was within its right to carry out such searches because the KMR base commander held the inherent authority to protect the integrity and security of the facility. As local journalist Giff Johnson has noted, the irony of the situation was that the KMR searches, unlike most security checks, were intended not to detect dangerous weapons, but to prevent any food, soda, cigarettes, or general consumer goods from getting out of Kwajalein to Ebeye and beyond.[38]

Adding to the situation was the prohibition against the Marshallese use of American facilities on Kwajalein.[39] No Marshallese worker was allowed to shop in the well-stocked stores of Kwajalein, eat in the restaurants there, attend movies, swim in the swimming pools, play tennis, or use the library. Medical and dental facilities were made available only in times of emergency. Moreover, no Marshallese child was allowed to attend school on Kwajalein. To enforce these rules, there were the Kwajalein police employed by Global Associates of Oakland, California, the main civilian contractor for support services at the missile range. The perverse rationale given to justify the prohibition on Micronesian patronage of Kwajalein shops was that businesses on Ebeye would suffer severely because of the markedly lower price of goods on Kwajalein. United States Congressman John Seiberling summed up the chasm that separated the two islands during a congressional hearing in 1984:

> In January, 1982, I personally visited both Kwajalein Island and Ebeye Island. The contrast couldn't be greater or more dramatic. Kwajalein is like Fort Lauderdale or one of our Miami Resort areas, with palm tree-lined beaches, swimming pools, a golf course, people bicycling everywhere, a first-class hospital and a school; and Ebeye, on the other hand, is an island slum, overpopulated, treeless filthy lagoon, littered beaches, a dilapidated hospital, and contaminated water supply, and so forth.[40]

"Apartheid, U.S. Style" is another, more pointed description used by one on-site journalist in the Marshalls to characterize the contrast between Kwajalein and Ebeye.[41]

Colonial Perceptions and Prescriptions

The situation on Ebeye reveals the diverse, sometimes conflicting interests and agenda of different groups within the colonizing nation.[42] The diversity within the colonial gaze showed itself not only in the identification of problems but also in the proposed solutions to those problems, solutions derived from culturally determined and explicit notions of what was deemed appropriate and possible, and within the necessary and accepted paramountcy of American strategic interests. One of the most ironic, perhaps racist episodes in the nuclear history of Kwajalein Atoll centers on Operation Exodus. This 1967 program, sponsored and directed by the Trust Territory administration, sought to reduce the population on Ebeye through the forced repatriation of "unnecessary" people to their home atolls and islands. Advertised as necessary to ensure the health and welfare of all concerned, Operation Exodus had as its goal the removal of roughly 25 percent of Ebeye's population, which then stood at 6,500.

The program was inaugurated officially through the high commissioner's issuance of Executive Order 101.[43] Taking effect on 8 November 1967, the order forbade further migration to Ebeye from areas outside Kwajalein Atoll, though there were provisions for temporary visitations. Operation Exodus was to be implemented in two phases. Phase one consisted of open meetings designed to elicit public acceptance for the plan; these meetings closed with a call for volunteers and a promise that the government would provide boat passage, clear new house sites on the returnees' home islands without costs, purchase necessary building materials, and cover the shipment of household goods. Predicated on the assumption that such inducement would not be sufficient to reduce the island's population by 25 percent, phase two called for the forcible eviction of those people either not employed or unable to pay for utilities or rental housing on Ebeye. Though 1,500 people were temporarily removed from Ebeye, Operation Exodus proved ultimately unsuccessful. Protests from the Marshalls district government to the high commissioner, coupled with the logistical impossibility of identifying, registering, and removing unauthorized residents who left only to return soon after, defeated the Trust Territory government's Operation Exodus. Later efforts at social redress evidenced seemingly more humanitarian but nonetheless colonizing concerns with their emphasis on the betterment of Ebeye as defined by American understandings of "better" and "appropriate."

A 4 September 1979 report from the high commissioner to the director of the United States Department of the Interior's Office of Territorial Affairs characterized Ebeye as in need not of development but redevelopment.[44] Despite the fast colonial clock that had transformed Ebeye from an island into a ghetto in less than twenty years, Elbert V. Bowden viewed the "Ebeye problem" as essentially economic. In Micronesia with Robert Nathan and Associates to draft an economic development plan for the Trust Territory, Bowden visited Ebeye and offered his prescription for problems that he saw as essentially economic; his recommendations had more the character of social engineering than economy to them, however. Acknowledging the acute problem of overcrowding on Ebeye, Bowden called for rigid residency requirements to be established and enforced as well as the implementation of a comprehensive land use program. He also urged greater cooperation and consultation between the military on Kwajalein and the Trust Territory government, noting that problems between the two were only adding to the difficulties on Ebeye.

As an economist, Bowden paid particular attention to the issue of wage compensation; he expressed strong reaction against any application to Kwajalein of the Fair Labor Standards Act, legislation passed by the United States Congress in 1966 that required equal pay for equal work under set job classifications. Bowden believed that paying islander laborers the same salaries as American expatriates for equivalent work, while seemingly just and desirable in principle, would have a devastating effect on Marshallese employment at Kwajalein.[45] He noted that Global Associates would not be able to afford such a law. Bowden estimated that the more skilled and technically expert workers would be laid off, while the unskilled and semiskilled workers would retain their jobs at minimal wage. The perverse logic of strategic colonialism thus dictated discrimination as being in the best interests of those discriminated against, or so Bowden's recommendations seemed to suggest.

Emmett Rice, then acting director of the Department of the Interior's Office of Territorial Affairs, took a trip to Ebeye in December 1976. His understanding of things was at once global and generic. In the written report on his visit, Rice called Ebeye a ghetto like any of the countless others that had developed near American military installations throughout the world. He noted the plethora of studies on the Ebeye problem that had accomplished nothing.[46] He called Operation Exodus impractical and wrote that people were there to stay. The Washington bureaucrat saw the Congress of Micronesia as not being able to contribute significantly to the solution and placed responsibility for the problems on Ebeye with the Departments of the Interior and the Army. Rice believed that calls to give the Marshallese general access to commissary privileges on Kwajalein would undermine local businessmen on Ebeye almost overnight. An unending, unnatural dependence on the army would result, and the motivation of the Marshallese to do anything for themselves would be destroyed. All things considered, Rice looked to Global Associates to provide Ebeye with the expertise and efficiency it possessed.

Rice envisioned Global Associates as creating the kind of totally planned community on Ebeye that it had arranged on Kwajalein. A Marshallese corporation, under Global Associates' direction, would be established as the sole wholesaler for Ebeye; the costs of imports would be reduced further by seeking the army's permission to use its military vehicles to transport all consumer goods to Ebeye. The savings earned from this arrangement would be funneled into community services on Ebeye. Rice also called for Global Associates to contract with the district administration to manage the public works facilities, the school, and the hospital on Ebeye.

This more private form of enterprise would bring additional savings in a more effective, streamlined method of administration. If the plan succeeded, argued Rice, Ebeye would end up being more efficiently managed and with lower retail prices in its stores. Community services would be upgraded and new sources of employment generated; congestion and overcrowding would be alleviated, and a decent, more sanitary lifestyle would be created for the inhabitants of Ebeye. In more intangible areas, Rice envisioned such a plan as injecting new enthusiasm into the area and helping to develop a spirit of self-sufficiency, while promoting the spirit of private enterprise among local merchants and without doing violence to the traditional system and culture.

The army, which had assumed responsibility for the Kwajalein Missile Range in 1964, held its own vision of how to correct conditions on Ebeye, but for reasons that had far more to do with strategic and military concerns than with local development. In 1977, an investigative team from the Department of the Army produced the *Report of Fact-Finding Team on Kwajalein-Ebeye.* Not surprisingly, the army's concerns were about politics, public image, and national security. The report began with the admission that the disparity in the quality of life between the two islands might jeopardize the continued use of Kwajalein as a national missile range. The preface of the report also noted that more than a hundred newspaper articles had appeared recently on the Kwajalein situation. These accounts were "not a spontaneous outpouring, but were part of a carefully orchestrated effort to secure a separate political status for the Marshall Islands in negotiations of Micronesian status."[47] The report saw the Marshall Islands Political Status Commission as being behind the separatist movement in the Marshalls and, by implication, the media campaign. This institutionally self-serving understanding of public criticism as politically motivated did two things: it worked to downplay the severity of conditions on Ebeye and thus to minimize the army's responsibility for those conditions.

In identifying solutions to the problem, the army report contained recommendations for the Trust Territory government that included a more aggressive approach to solving sanitation and health and public works problems; greater encouragement of copra production in light of the then growing market for copra; and, ironically, an emphasis on the value of traditional life. In essence, the report showed that the army ultimately believed the problems on Ebeye to come under the jurisdiction of the Trust Territory government. This 1977 report reflected the longstanding tension between the Trust Territory government and the Department of the Army over responsibility for Ebeye. As late as 1982, a high-ranking Pentagon official stated, "We have no authority or responsibility for the island of Ebeye, or for any locally inhabited island, village or community."[48]

The differences between military and bureaucratic officials over the responsibility for conditions on Ebeye hints at the larger issue of just how problems were perceived and solutions or remedies prescribed. Debates among Americans, however, diminished against the shared belief in Marshallese culpability for the circumstances on Ebeye. A sense of what we might call "savage consumerism" shows itself at work.[49] Popular, academic, and official accounts all consistently commented on what their authors assumed to be an intense attraction for imported goods among the Marshallese. Most Americans, whether employees of the army or the Trust Territory government, contended that the people on Ebeye were there by choice. An editorial in the *Pacific Daily News* of 16 August 1976 noted that nobody was forced to live on Ebeye: "Most of its people left their clean, peaceful coconut-and-fish outer islands long ago to come to Ebeye because of the high wages paid by the Americans on Kwajalein."[50] The image of savage consumerism touched even the most sympathetic observations of the Marshallese plight on Ebeye. William Vitarelli credited Ebeye's population explosion between 1944 and 1969 to the "attraction of wealth and what it can provide in the way of consumer goods, education, entertainment and a 'better life.'"[51] Colonial observers also cited the lack of true community on Ebeye in their litany of social ills. An attachment to a memorandum of 25 February 1977 called the population of Ebeye extremely mixed in terms of both national citizenship and ethnic background. Cultural differences, varying levels of education, and disparities in wage earnings all made it difficult to find a common denominator "except for the unhappiness shared by many people."[52] All of this ignored, of course, the need for Marshallese labor on Kwajalein and the history of forced migrations resulting from safety and security measures associated with missile testing on the island. Calling the Marshallese the ultimate makers of their own problems helped to obfuscate the more direct and immediate causes of the situation in the Kwajalein Atoll complex.

Other voices struggled to be heard amidst the bureaucratic mess and tangle—voices that expressed important, insightful, more locally focused understandings, but voices that were also affected, even restrained, by the colonial contexts in which they spoke. A July 1972 report, issued through the office of Oscar DeBrum, the district administrator for the Marshalls, attempted to explain why Marshallese chose to stay on Ebeye.[53] The report had somewhat of an ethnographic as well as political sensibility about it that acknowledged social relationships and human aspirations as well as simple material attraction. The report noted that employment on Ebeye was preferable to making copra or living at a bare subsistence level. Many chose to work for wages on Ebeye so they could afford to send their children to school on Majuro, Pohnpei, Palau, Guam, or the North American mainland. Others, wrote the author of the report, worked to accumulate capital and savings to build homes or establish businesses. As badly flawed as the health care system was on Ebeye, it still afforded better medical treatment than was available on the other nearby and surrounding islands. Access to a usually stable and steady supply of imported and expensive canned foods was also an attraction. While conceding the lure of bright lights and new forms of entertainment, the report concluded that since 1964 people had been coming to Ebeye to be with their children, their family, and their relatives. Perhaps one of the more succinct assessments of the entangled mess on Ebeye came from Harold Jackson of the *Manchester Guardian*, who summarized the divergence in American and Marshallese views as follows: "In American eyes, the base is the honey pot around which the Ebeyeans swarm. The contrasting Marshallese view is that the largest and most inhabitable island in their atoll has been taken from them. Recognizing that they are not likely to get it back, they want to continue declaring their rights and to seek proper compensation."[54]

Distance distorted perceptions of Ebeye, but with considerable consequence when those perceptions came from people in positions of power. Ambassador Peter Rosenblatt, the president's personal representative to the Micronesian political status negotiations in the late 1970s, understood the situation on Ebeye in terms of Vietnam. Responding to a memo from Ruth Van Cleve, the director of the Department of the Interior's Office of Territorial Affairs, Rosenblatt voiced his opposition to plans for a government-funded reconstruction of Ebeye. Rosenblatt felt that such reconstruction would not only fail to address the deep-seated problems of the Ebeye community, but would substantially impair the social and economic viability of all the Marshall Islands and hence the prospect of a stable, long-term relationship between the United States and the Republic of the Marshalls. In his 2 November 1978 response, Rosenblatt wrote that building "turn-key" towns for displaced people in Vietnam hadn't worked; he saw no reason to expect better success in the Marshalls. Oblivious to the struggles being waged by the landowners of the Kwajalein Atoll area, Rosenblatt said that Vietnam had imparted the lesson that the people themselves must be involved in the rehabilitation of their community and that "they must sacrifice and labor in the creation of their new facilities if the rehabilitation is to take hold and if progress achieved is to be maintained."[55] In Rosenblatt's estimation, the expansion of employment opportunities on both Kwajalein and Ebeye, the improvement of training facilities and programs, and the generation of local businesses were paramount and the surest way to improve things in the Kwajalein Atoll area.

Rosenblatt did not prove as blind or as hardheaded as his successor, Fred Zeder. Whereas Rosenblatt wrote of the morally uplifting values of free enterprise and the capitalist ethic, Zeder invoked a more paternalist vocabulary that exalted American beneficence and underscored Micronesian dependence. In a 14 October 1982 letter to Rep. Henry J. Nowak, Zeder stated,

> [On Ebeye] there are schools, a hospital, commercial enterprises and other amenities. . . . It should be noted that the U.S. government provides all Micronesians free hospitalization and education as well as job opportunities that pay well in excess of the local wage level. . . . I can think of nowhere in the United States or, for that matter, the world where any government so provides for its citizens or, indeed, for individuals outside its domain.[56]

Local and Conflicting Agencies

How did different groups of Marshallese respond to the devastation and disruption inflicted upon their lives? For those of us determined to locate islander voices in the parts of the past we study, there is no problem with hearing Marshallese voices. They resound loudly through the literature, but not always in unison or unanimity and not, at times, without their own sense of conflict, doubt, uncertainty, and ambiguity. Ataji Balos, Kwajalein Atoll's representative to the Congress of Micronesia, spoke clearly enough. Testifying on Ebeye in 1976 before members of the visiting U.S. House of Representatives Subcommittee on Territorial and Insular Affairs, Balos accused the United States of violating the terms of the Trusteeship Agreement and that this violation had made possible the deplorable conditions on Ebeye. He recounted a sad history of exploitation that could only be corrected by a future in which the people of the Marshall Islands stood up and exercised their rights as a sovereign and independent people. He noted that the Fourth of July, American Independence Day, had been celebrated in 1976 on Kwajalein with a prefatory order that had closed the island to all Marshallese on that day: "So American independence was celebrated at Kwajalein Atoll by enforcement of an all-out and total segregation."[57]

Other Marshallese voices made themselves heard earlier on, and in ways that were at once less official and more communal. The people of Lib certainly did not accept their relocation to Ebeye in 1961 passively or understand it to be permanent. They showed themselves to be adept in negotiating the terms of their return to Lib,[58] a return that took place in June 1966 when the impact zone for missile testing shifted exclusively to the Kwajalein lagoon. In their dealings with representatives of the Marshalls District administration, they secured financial commitments for new house designs; for the construction of community structures; for the provision of support facilities including a two-way radio, a medical dispensary, and regular field trip service; and for food supplements in the period immediately following their return to Lib but before they were once again self-sufficient in terms of food production.

Marshallese also had their own political arithmetic with which they calculated loss, compensation, and responsibility. The actual relocation of the Mid-Corridor people to Ebeye in 1964 proved somewhat farcical by American standards. At the time of the announcement to relocate the people, many were already resident and employed on Ebeye. Following the announcement, many of these Mid-Corridor islanders returned to their ancestral homes to qualify for the official tally that made them eligible for the benefits being given to relocated people. A December 1963 count by the army identified approximately 158 people to be moved. A second count in September 1964, just before the evacuation, showed 364 people to be relocated. The actual relocation ended up moving 487 people. In the words of Peter T. Coleman, then the district administrator for the Marshall Islands, "a good number of people moved back to the mid-atoll islands to be moved to Ebeye by us."[59]

More official bodies in the Marshalls and greater Micronesia addressed the problem on Ebeye in ways that were at times fairly forthright and at other times guarded in their sensitivity to political pressures and bureaucratic entanglements involving Saipan and Washington. A special committee of the Congress of Micronesia created to investigate the Mid-Corridor situation reported to Speaker of the House Betwel Henry on 26 August 1969 that the people of that area had received no viable and appropriate compensation for what in effect amounted to the U.S. military's taking of their islands.[60] Moreover, the members of the committee believed the land use agreement for the Mid-Corridor area contravened the obligations of the United States under Article VII of the 1947 Trusteeship Agreement, which committed the administering authority to respect the freedoms of movement and migration of the islands' people. The committee's report went on to point out the inherent contradiction between American security interests and the welfare of the people of the Trust Territory.

Governmental bodies at both the Trust Territory and district levels adopted a less assertive, more cautious posture than the Congress of Micronesia. An ad hoc committee, convened in early January 1976 at the request of the high commissioner, addressed the issue of overcrowding on Ebeye, but in oblique ways.[61] Composed of representatives from Trust Territory headquarters on Saipan, the Kwajalein Missile Range, the Peace Corps, the Marshallese district legislature or Nitijela, and the district government on Majuro as well as traditional leaders and municipal officials from Ebeye, the committee showed the political and cultural entanglements of the Ebeye problem. At the first meeting of the Ebeye Ad Hoc Committee, the group considered the issue of immigration controls and forced relocation. Hermos Jack, the legal counsel for the Nitijela, and Murphy Ownbey, a Trust Territory government representative to the committee, both expressed fears about the possible violation of Micronesian rights caused by the reimposition of measures to restrict immigration to Ebeye. The two men reminded those assembled that the 1947 UN Trusteeship Agreement committed the United States to protect, without discrimination, the rights and fundamental freedoms of the inhabitants of the Trust Territory. Another member of the committee, Harley Earwicker of the Trust Territory government, said that such commitments could be outweighed by the larger right of the legal residents of Ebeye to basic health, sanitation, and fresh water. By the end of the meeting, the group agreed, nominally at least, to immigration controls.

At the request of the high commissioner, the Nitijela passed Resolution 6-16 during its first regular session in 1976. The resolution requested the district administrator of the Marshalls to use his executive powers to implement emergency orders restricting immigration to Ebeye and encouraging those without work, means to pay for housing, or a place to live in the Kwajalein Atoll complex to leave. On 13 April 1976, Oscar DeBrum, district administrator for the Marshalls and a Marshallese himself, issued Emergency District Order 76-1 ordering all visitors on Ebeye to leave the island within forty-eight hours of the issuance of that order.[62] In the order, "visitors" were defined as those "persons who are not bona fide residents of Kwajalein Atoll." A second Operation Exodus was now being undertaken, but this time with the support and supervision of Marshallese officials. The limited effectiveness of these renewed measures to limit migration to Ebeye reflected varying understandings made complex by negotiations across cultures and involving colonial asymmetries of power and force both within and beyond the Marshalls. Later, the policy of forced migration and even immigration controls were declared ineffective. Terms such as "visitor" and "bona fide resident" did not translate easily or clearly among those on Ebeye.

As was noted earlier, Ranajit Guha has written about the ways in which colonized groups often employ for counterhegemonic purposes the ideas, practices, and institutions of those who dominate them. Handel Dribo did just that. On 8 August 1972, the *alab* who owned the *weto* of Mwenen on Ebeye sued the United States Trust Territory government for the return of his land.[63] Dribo claimed that on 13 April 1967 he was wrongly coerced by agents of the Trust Territory government to sign a lease agreement for his land that in essence denied him the benefits of ownership during the life of the lease agreement.

In his suit, Dribo claimed that he was denied due process of law as specified in the Fifth and Fourteenth Amendments to the United States Constitution and endorsed in Title One of Chapter Four of the Trust Territory Code. Dribo further stated that he had found himself forced to capitulate after the government filed a declaration of intent with the Trust Territory High Court to seize his land by right of eminent domain. Though he eventually signed the agreement, he had never recognized its validity. The forced signing cost him not only the use and income from his land, but the loss of his house and business as well as damage to his reputation and standing in the community. As redress, Dribo sought the restoration of his property, compensation for lost income in the sum of $576,000, and punitive damages of another $250,000.

Other forms of resistance, more physical and demonstrative in nature, also showed themselves on Ebeye.[64] In late 1978 came word that the United States government had agreed to pay $9 million a year for the usage rights to the Kwajalein Missile Range and affected areas once the Compact of Free Association with the Republic of the Marshall Islands was ratified and signed. Questioning why they had to await the conclusion of political negotiations for compensation long due them, five hundred landowners in the Kwajalein Atoll complex left Ebeye to reoccupy their home islands in the restricted areas around the missile range. This late 1978 reoccupation had been preceded by sail-ins and temporary occupations in 1969, 1977, and early 1978. This latest protest induced the United States to agree to a one-year interim use agreement for the Kwajalein Missile Range that provided a total of $9 million of which $5 million went directly to the affected landowners; the balance was earmarked for development projects on Ebeye that included the immediate renovation of Ebeye's sewer system and power plant.

A second interim agreement was signed for the 1980 fiscal year. An attempt to renew the agreement for yet a third year met with strong resistance from the Kwajalein landowners who had by now formed the Kwajalein Atoll Corporation (KAC). The corporation sought negotiations with the United States on compensation for the use of the atoll between 1944 and 1979. Calling past use claims a dead issue, Ambassador Fred Zeder, the president's personal representative to the Micronesian status negotiations, refused to negotiate any retroactive land use agreement. Under pressure from Washington, the newly constituted Republic of the Marshall Islands government went ahead and signed a third interim use agreement with the United States for the Kwajalein Missile Range. The Kwajalein Atoll Corporation countered with the call for an atollwide referendum on the continued use of Kwajalein Island as a site for American missile testing.

Relations between the KAC and the Marshalls and American governments worsened with the May 1982 signing of the Compact of Free Association. The compact granted a fifty-year lease on the use of the Kwajalein Missile Range. Members of the KAC thought the terms of the lease too long, worried about the actual distribution of the compact monies, criticized the agreement's omission of capital improvement funds for Ebeye, and were bitterly disappointed that the document did not specify better, more respectful treatment of the Marshallese by the United States Army in its administration of the missile range. Nuclear colonialism and the negotiations over its extension had now come either to divide the Marshallese or to intensity already existing divisions within the larger island group once known as Ralik Ratak. Such would be one of the legacies of American colonialism in a postcolonial order that was really not postcolonial at all.

Frustrated by the situation, the Kwajalein landowners in June 1982 staged Operation Homecoming, in which about a thousand landowners reoccupied their home lands on Kwajalein, Roi-Namur, and the islands of the Mid-Corridor group. In the early stages of the protest, about fifteen people were arrested. These arrests failed to deter the movement, however. More and more people sailed to their home islands to set up camps. With the occupation came the rediscovery of an older way of life. Kotak Loeak, a Kwajalein *alab*, said,

> Our people are happy living as they now are, especially in the islands where there are no military facilities, nor armed guards to keep them in restricted areas. After years on crowded Ebeye island, where we were forced to live by the US, we have discovered the joys of natural living, especially the freedom to move around, fish, plant and build living structures from the surrounding elements. I cannot begin to tell you how good the people feel. . . . For the older people, the return brings tears of joy. For the children, it is an all new experience.[65]

The occupation forced the cancellation of at least one missile test when the people occupying Roi-Namur refused to either evacuate or take cover on 3 August 1982. American efforts to bring about the termination of Operation Homecoming involved economic and social pressures, including an increase in the number and intensity of security searches for workers traveling between Ebeye and Kwajalein, the suspension of all unessential workers employed on Kwajalein Island, the closing of the Bank of America branch there, the shutting off of water to those areas occupied by the protesters, and an embargo on the transshipment of food bound for Ebeye through Kwajalein. A journalist, commenting on the occupation and American responses to it, wrote, "If it were not for the numbing squalor of Ebeye, there would be something almost comic about the uninventive stupidity with which the U.S. military has handled the sit-in. But after a look at Ebeye, nothing seems particularly funny."[66]

The impasse over the four-month occupation was finally ended with the opening of talks between the KAC and the American and Marshalls governments. The talks led to a three-year agreement that included a reduction in the length of the lease for the missile range from fifty to thirty years, a $10-million capital improvements fund for Ebeye, the return to their owners of six islands in the north of the atoll's restricted area, and the granting of access to the Mid-Corridor islands for three six-week periods a year. The negotiations led to the June 1983 signing of a revised Compact of Free Association and a general plebiscite on that compact in September of the same year. Although the compact passed by comfortable margins in most areas of the Marshalls, the people of Kwajalein Atoll rejected it by a three-to-one margin. Their chief source of objection was the thirty-year lease and the intervention of the Republic of the Marshalls in the use and distribution of the lease payments for Kwajalein.

Tensions thus remained high. With the expiration of the three-year agreement between the KAC and the two governments, the landowners declared American lease rights to the Kwajalein Missile Range null and void and again occupied the missile range and other restricted area in the atoll complex. Handel Dribo stated his intention to remain on Kwajalein Island despite the threat of physical violence. "Death for a good cause is life itself," he said.[67] Forced removal of the protesters followed with the commander of the Kwajalein Missile Range ordering military police to shoot to wound if necessary. With the protesters removed, the Republic of the Marshall Islands condemned through eminent domain Kwajalein Island and its surrounding strategic zone and then reaffirmed the integrity of the thirty-year lease with the United States under the 1983 Compact of Free Association and for an annual fee of $9 million. The government later backed down, however, rescinding its condemnation and agreeing that all rental monies would be paid directly and totally to the Kwajalein landowners.[68] In a statement that revealed the infectious legacy of colonialism in local agents, Amata Kabua, then president of the Republic of the Marshall Islands but once an outspoken critic of the United States while a senator in the Congress of Micronesia, defended his government's action: "What can you do? I mean when you grow up with your brother and he is a lot bigger than you and he slaps you, what can you do? It's better to earn some money out of the situation than having nothing."[69]

The Future as a Foreign Country?

And so what sense to make of the history of dumping on Ebeye and the future that it portends?[70] The three interim-use agreements for the strategic areas of the Kwajalein Atoll complex and the Compact of Free Association between the United States and the Republic of the Marshall Islands have provided millions upon millions of dollars in capital improvement and infrastructure development funds. Since 1986, a new power plant and desalination facility has been constructed, the hospital on Ebeye has been renovated, maintenance of all public utilities has been upgraded and regularized, recreational programs and facilities have been expanded, and the physical appearance of the island has been made more attractive through community-wide landscaping and home improvement projects.

The 1989 *Marshalls Islands Guidebook* describes Ebeye as "on its way to becoming the first planned community in the Marshall Islands, and probably all of Micronesia." Antagonism between Kwajalein and Ebeye is said to have been replaced by a new spirit of cooperation between the two islands. The Kwajalein Atoll Development Authority (KADA) has drawn up a long-range plan for redeveloping Ebeye, the centerpiece of which is a causeway to link Ebeye with six islands to the north. Resettlement of the population to these northern islands is expected, with the consequent alleviation of the tremendous overcrowding that still exists on Ebeye. The guidebook closes its section on Ebeye with a comment about "a perceptible feeling of excitement and enthusiasm among Ebeye residents for the change that is taking place on their island. Once forgotten and often neglected, Ebeye is now a center of development activity."[71]

Despite the optimism and happy-face approach, the serious problems that persist on Ebeye and in the greater Marshalls temper optimism and raise questions about the postcolonial environment. Once the prerogative of the colonizer, dumping is now a metaphor become a development project with which the Republic of the Marshalls Islands looks to the future. In recent years, the Republic of the Marshall Islands has indicated repeatedly a willingness to accept barges of municipal garbage and drums of toxic wastes from Japan, Hawai'i, and the east and west coasts of the continental United States. The late first president of the Republic of the Marshall Islands, Amata Kabua, described his government's interest in such projects as a mix of pragmatism and principle. Revenue would be secured while the larger Pacific ocean environment would be freed of unregulated, oftentimes unreported dumping of toxic wastes. One proposal, advanced by the American firm Admiralty Pacific, offered the Marshall Islands government $16 million a year to accept 10 percent of California's garbage; the trash was to be placed on barges and shipped to the Marshalls. The Marshalls, said Admiralty Pacific, would have landfill with which its low-lying atolls could combat the rising ocean levels caused by the greenhouse effect, while California would be cleaner and greener.[72]

There have also been reports of government officials in the Marshalls who want to take one of the nuclear-damaged islands of the chain, say Bikini, and rent it to the world as a site for the dumping of atomic waste.[73] Such plans, reported in tentative, only whispered terms, have been advertised as generating about $50 million a year for twenty years. Alliances have shifted as well around the issue of land use and the politics of compensation. Whereas the tensions between the Kwajalein landowners and the Republic of the Marshalls were once pronounced, new concerns have arisen over the government's designation of the landowners as the sole recipients of lease monies for Kwajalein through the Compact of Free Association. Individuals holding land use rights under these landowners feel this system of distribution ignores the sacrifice and deprivation they have experienced in being kept from their lands by the requirements of missile testing in Kwajalein Atoll. We might ask ourselves what manner of independent postcolonial mentality is manifest in these developments.

I have endeavored to examine the postwar history of Ebeye through the metaphor of dumping, a metaphor that I think underscores the terrible human costs of American nuclear colonialism, a metaphor that subverts the distinction between the colonial and the postcolonial, and a metaphor that offers a critique of colonialism and is yet itself significantly affected by the culture of the colonizer from which it comes. In examining the causes, understandings, critiques and proposed solutions of the "Ebeye problem," I have endeavored to show the diversity, and sometimes divisions, within the cultures of both the colonized and the colonizer. Various groups of Marshallese and Americans understood Ebeye differently against a mix of factors that involved race, class, profession, location, clan and kin obligations, indigenous politics, and the proximity and relationship to sources of colonial power and policy. In the spirit of these postmodern times, I think it is important to appreciate the ironies, polyvocality, contradictions, and paradoxes of writing in and about an allegedly postcolonial situation such as Ebeye. At the same time, we should not lose sight of some things that are more certain. Colonialism did create the multidimensional mess that Ebeye became and is. Hear the simple yet eloquent and moving witness of Johnsay Riklon, who describes life on Ebeye as brutal and like an assault, or Lijon Eknilang who says, "I hate living on Ebeye, it's a terrible life there. . . . I hope to move away one day but right now I don't dare. I'm afraid."[74] In our recognition of complexities and complications, there needs to be an appreciation for clarity as well.

The Continuing Story of Etao

I close this chapter with a story that suggests the ways in which colonialism affects local perceptions of the past, but a story that also reveals the ways in which colonialism can itself become ensnared and thus accessed by its incorporation into local renderings or histories. The story I pass on concerns Etao, the magician and trickster, whose magical travels from west to east across the atolls and islands of the Marshalls left in their wake a variety of geographic features and also a host of cultural practices resulting from his prankish flouting of local chiefly authority.[75] Etao's travels through the Marshalls end on the easternmost island of Mili where, through an act of deadly deception, he stole the attractive daughters of the paramount chief there.

The stories of Etao's journeys within the Marshalls are many, varied and long-standing. More recent versions extend the travels of the trickster into contemporary times. Leaving Mili, Etao and his new wives travel first to Kiribati and then to Fiji. Setting out from Fiji alone, Etao resumes the easterly course that had characterized his earlier travels through the Marshalls and that had been such a prominent, symbolically rich feature of the narratives about those travels. Etao eventfully reaches America, where he himself is tricked. Captured and placed in a bottle, the powerful magician is forced to cooperate with the American government on the development of planes, rockets, missiles, spacecraft, and atomic bombs. In a sense, a powerful force in the Marshallese cosmos is co-opted to serve the military interests of the United States.

The effects of Etao's cooperation are manifest locally through the United States' expulsion of the Japanese from the Marshalls and its later nuclear and missile testing on Bikini, Enewetak, and Kwajalein. Regarded by the Marshallese as the strongest force on earth, America's might, according to the continuing story of Etao, draws from primordial powers within the Marshallese cosmos. In the minds of the Marshallese, World War II, nuclear testing, and the Vietnam War are all part of a single struggle between the United States and its enemies in the Pacific. For the Marshallese, this extended struggle as meant great suffering, displacement, disease, and death. The continuing story of Etao, however, tempers this traumatic past with hopes for a better future by linking the Marshallese genealogically and cosmologically to the great force that is the United States. Etao's contributions to the formation of American power in the Pacific create obligations of reciprocity; congressional appropriations, federal programs, compact funds, and compensation for the human and environmental costs of nuclear testing are all required by the relationship between the United States and the Marshalls as underscored in the continuing story of Etao. This linkage also speaks to the redress of grievances resulting from the abusive privileges of chiefs, a theme that lies at the heart of the earlier Etao stories. The medium or relay for the contemporary travels of Etao and their significance is the anthropologist Laurence Carucci; he concludes,

> Etao's path from west to east retraces the steps of primordial Islanders who first came to the Marshalls. He continues his route, eventually being out-tricked by the stealthy Americans, far to windward. At the same time, Marshallese become figurative ancestors of the Americans (and current Islanders become collateral kin) by weaving part of their substance into the physiological and geographical path travelled by Etao to America. From their Bible mentors, Marshall Islanders learned *A ro etā burueir re naj jolit ene eo* (or *Re naj jolit lōl*), "the meek shall inherit the land" (or "the earth") (Matt. 5.5). With the high chiefs having claimed rights of access to the land, however, by Marshallese reckoning, what better way to secure one's inheritance than through established claims to a primordial place on the path that leads to the source of the force.[76]

In a history that concerns itself with the discourses around economic development in Micronesia, there needs to be a place for such tales that reveal the ways in which even the most horrific of colonial practices become entangled in local histories that give meaning to the present, that provide some hope for the future, and that challenge the very notion of development as Americans have presented it.

Chapter 8

The End of History for the Edge of Paradise?

All of the discourses over economic development in Micronesia anticipated the termination of the 1947 Trusteeship Agreement between the United States and the United Nations. Negotiations over an alternative and future political status for the islands came to center on free association, a curious hybrid concept that sought to sustain American strategic interests through limited concessions to local autonomy. For the Caroline and Marshall Islands, free association seemed to offer a constrained, almost neocolonial future. For the United States, free association presented, in the words of one astute observer, the opportunity of "staying while leaving"[1] and of buying out of direct responsibility for the morass that it had made of development in the islands.

The Compact of Free Association, implemented on 3 November 1986 for the Federated States of Micronesia and the Republic of the Marshall Islands and on 1 November 1994 for the Republic of Palau, looms then as the potentially culminating arrangement in a process designed to secure continued American control of the area under rhetorical pledges to respect the sovereignty of island governments and to contribute to their economic development. Francis Fukuyama would identify this larger process, of which the Compact of Free Association is a part, as the end of history. In this final chapter, I examine the Compact of Free Association between the United States and the three Micronesian governments in light of Fukuyama's thesis. I also offer readers a tour of "compacted Micronesia" through a critical reading of P. F. Kluge's book *The Edge of Paradise.* I conclude with several thoughts on how both the history and future of economic development in "American Micronesia" might be calculated or figured differently from the ways and means advanced by Fukuyama, Kluge, and others who think like them.

Ending History?

"The end of history" comes from Fukuyama's 1992 work *The End of History and the Last Man.*[2] Fukuyama's thesis is that liberal democracy constitutes the endpoint of ideological evolution and the final, most nearly perfect form of human government; as such, the triumph of liberal democracy throughout the globe represents the end of history, or, to put it another way, the obliteration of difference through the transformation of the other into the like or familiar. Fredric Jameson's concerns about colonialism's denial of other people's histories seem realized in Fukuyama's vision of the new world order.

Fukuyama's idea of the end of history draws heavily from the work of the German philosopher G.W.F. Hegel, who understood and wrote about history as a single, coherent, evolutionary process—directed, discernible, and inevitable. Hegel saw human history as working its way from simple tribal societies based on slavery and subsistence agriculture through various theocracies, monarchies, and feudal aristocracies, and ultimately to modern liberal democracy based on technologically driven capitalism. In Fukuyama's analysis, the inevitable triumph of liberal democracy results from the interplay of pragmatic economics, rational science, and a primordial human drive for recognition. From this complex interplay emerges a mature capitalist economy capable of meeting the needs of all. The end of history brings too the appearance of a universal "last man," content, democratic, free, prosperous, productive, and globally conscious.

Marx, as Fukuyama notes, also wrote of the inevitable march of history, but a history whose end was marked by the realization of the ideal socialist state, not the ascendancy of liberal capitalist democracy. To Fukuyama's way of thinking, the events of the late 1980s and early 1990s have proved Hegel right and Marx wrong. The decline of communism in Eastern Europe, the disintegration of the Soviet Union, and the weakening of Castro's Cuba leave the United States as the most perfect example of a liberal capitalist democracy, an example to be embraced and emulated by others. The world, according to Fukuyama, seems in the process of becoming like "US". Not surprisingly, more conservative constituencies within the American political arena have responded enthusiastically to Fukuyama's thesis and to the recent political events in the world that would seem to validate it. Fukuyama's work pays little attention to matters of culture, colonialism, and the politics of development. Colonialism comes under what Fukuyama would describe as history with a small "h"—events in time that are negative, destructive, and seemingly regressive, but that are ultimately overcome by History with a capital "H." Big

History works as a single, progressive movement leading to a universal and homogenous global economic system. Culture for Fukuyama constitutes only a series of obstacles to economic development that include religion; admittedly formidable national, racial, and ethnic loyalties; highly stratified social systems; and rigidly centralized forms of power and government that preclude or severely limit the ability of people to associate freely with one another.[3]

I call attention to Fukuyama's *The End of History and the Last Man* not because I think it represents a particularly salient, valuable treatise on political economy, but because it reflects what some observers believe or, in other instances, fear to be the ultimate resolution of American colonialism in the Caroline, Mariana, and Marshall Islands. Fukuyama presents a vision of a world order that transcends independent national entities in favor of a simple, universal state that makes all one, or all a part of one. The end of history for Micronesia, then, means the absorption or incorporation of these islands by the United States. In the Northern Marianas, that eventuality might already appear accomplished through the 1975 commonwealth agreement that makes those islands an American territory. In the Caroline and Marshall Islands, the political status of free association with the United States looks, in the minds of many both within and beyond the region, to be an intermediate status ultimately leading to a closer, more permanent affiliation with the United States.

Negotiations

Begun in 1969, negotiations over a different political status for the islands presumed the strategic importance the United States attached to the islands' geographical location. The centrality of that strategic geography led one Washington official to remark, "If it weren't for the Defense Department interests, the negotiations would have been over a long time ago."[4] The Nixon Doctrine seemed to underscore the importance of the islands' strategic geography in the negotiations. Articulated on Guam in 1969, the Nixon Doctrine called for the shifting of the American defense perimeter away from contested bases in Japan, Okinawa, and the Philippines toward more secure sites in the American Pacific, most notably Guam and the Trust Territory. Emboldened by this pronouncement, negotiators for the Congress of Micronesia, the sole representative government for the islands at the time, put forth a series of demands in their initial encounter with American representatives in Washington, D.C., during October 1969. At this first round of negotiations, the Micronesians insisted upon the return of all public land held by the Trust Territory government on behalf of the United States, the settlement of all claims resulting from the destruction of life and property in the islands during World War II, unrestricted access to the United States for Micronesian citizens and products, and guaranteed financial assistance from the United States over a mutually-agreed-upon period of time. At the second round of negotiations on Saipan the following year, American representatives countered by extending an offer of commonwealth status with the United States holding full sovereignty over the islands. In a speech before the Congress of Micronesia, Lazarus Salii of Palau, the head of the Micronesian Future Political Status Commission at the time, gave his understanding of what commonwealth status would mean for the islands: "Micronesians would become the newest, the smallest, the remotest non-white minority in the United States political family—as permanent and as American, shall we say, as the American Indian."[5]

Calling the offer of commonwealth status unacceptable, the Congress of Micronesia charged its Future Political Status Commission with investigating the option of independence. Although some members of Congress spoke ardently of the desirability of independence, general sentiment remained in favor of some form of continued association with the United States. Over the next two years, negotiations bogged down over disagreements regarding the levels of American financial assistance, the length of an agreement, and the procedures for any early termination of that agreement. On the American side, the transfer of responsibility for the conduct of negotiations from the Department of the Interior to an interdepartmental task force, titled the Office of Micronesian Status Negotiations and headed by an individual of ambassadorial rank, delayed the negotiations further. Displeasure within the Congress of Micronesia over the United States' insistence upon a termination clause that required the consent or approval of both parties scuttled an initialed agreement of free association between the two negotiating teams in 1972. More serious, however, were the divisions that showed themselves among Micronesians.

By 1975, the Northern Marianas had left the rest of Micronesia to become a commonwealth of the United States.[6] In that same year, representatives of both Palau and the Marshalls made known their desire to negotiate separately with the United States as governments in their own right. Both groups reiterated their intention before the United Nations Trusteeship Council the next year. In 1977, the Carter administration's ambassador to the Micronesian status talks, Peter Rosenblatt, agreed to open separate negotiations with both Palau and the Marshalls. There would follow another five years of negotiations before a draft compact of free association was ready to put before the United Nations Trusteeship Council, the United States Congress, the respective congresses of the three Micronesian governments, and the general citizenry of the islands.

Particularly ominous was the inability of negotiators to reconcile the antinuclear provisions of Palau's constitution with American defense requirements as recognized by the compact and its attendant mutual security pact. A compromise of sorts was reached through the establishment of a referendum that would ask Palauans to vote on the compact and on an amendment to their constitution that would soften its antinuclear provisions, thus making legally possible an acceptance of the compact. Approval of the compact itself required only a majority vote; the endorsement of 75 percent of those voting, however, was needed for passage of the constitutional amendment. With these arrangements agreed upon, general negotiations were concluded in 1982 and plebiscites arranged for the following year in all three areas. Voters in the Federated States of Micronesia and the Republic of the Marshall Islands endorsed the compact by considerable margins, though pockets of resistance showed themselves on Pohnpei and among those islands in the Marshalls most directly affected by nuclear testing. In Palau, voters accepted the compact but failed to provide the 75 percent majority required to amend their constitution. There would be for Palauans another decade of votes, governmental consultations, political infighting, violence, and heavy-handed American pressure.[7]

A lengthy review process in the United States Congress delayed the actual implementation of the compact in the FSM and the Marshalls. Fearing extended scrutiny from an increasingly critical United Nations Trusteeship Council angered by the United States' failure to consult more closely with it over the matter of the Micronesian status negotiations, the Reagan administration simply declared the Compact of Free Association with the FSM and Marshalls governments operational on 3 November 1986.[8] A series of lengthy, complex, and highly controversial maneuverings within Palau eventually lowered the requirements for a constitutional amendment from 75 percent of participating voters to a simple majority; this move made possible the approval of the compact in an eighth plebiscite vote held in Palau in November 1993. By the terms of a preexisting agreement reached between the United States and Palauan governments during the American Congress' general review of the document, the compact took official effect a year after its endorsement by the voters.

The Compact as a "Mechanism" of Continuing Domination

Fukuyama writes of a uniform "mechanism," fueled by the powers of modern natural science, that directs human social organization toward liberal democracy.[9] It would not be too extended an extrapolation of Fukuyama's argument, I think, to view the Compact of Free Association between the United States and the governments of the Federated States of Micronesia, the Republic of the Marshall Islands, and the Republic of Palau as being a part of the "mechanism" that moves the islands toward the end of history. I would like, then, to consider the Compact of Free Association as a "mechanism" or vehicle that seeks to overcome what might be different and distinctive about the people of the area called Micronesia. In short, the compact can be read as preface to the eventual subsumption of the islands into a global economic order dominated by the United States. I would like to indicate here, though, that the Compact of Free Association does not mark the end of history or anything close to it. In the matter of economic development in American Micronesia, an understanding of the compact requires a more careful, cross-culturally nuanced consideration of attempts to transform island peoples into productive workers and responsible consumers, and of local understandings, responses, and resistance to those attempts.

The Compact of Free Association between the United States and the FSM, the Marshalls, and Palau has been characterized by its supporters as satisfying American security interests while recognizing the integrity of Micronesian governments.[10] The compact provides funding to maintain existing governmental operations and to develop self-sustaining national economies for the three Micronesian governments. In outline form, the Compact of Free Association with the three Micronesian governments recognizes their sovereignty, their right to complete control over all domestic and internal matters, and their authority to conduct their own foreign affairs though in consultation with the United States. The United States, assuming responsibility for all defense and security matters, pledges in the compact to defend the freely associated states "as if they were a part of the United States."[11]

For the FSM and the Marshalls, the compact has a fifteen-year life; the agreement with Palau extends over fifty years.[12] The Micronesian governments promise to refrain from any activity that the United States government deems to be incompatible with its commitment to ensure the security of the area and agree, essentially in perpetuity and through accompanying mutual security pacts with the United States, to the closure of their lands and waters to the military forces of other nations unless specifically requested by the United States government. Separate, respective agreements with the Republic of the Marshalls and the Republic of Palau grant the United States military continued operation of the Kwajalein Missile Range and use options to lands on Babeldaob and to parts of Koror's Malakal Harbor. Under the terms of the agreement between the United States and the three Micronesian governments, the compact may be terminated either by mutual agreement between the freely associated state in question and the United States or unilaterally by either the Micronesian or United States governments. Under Title IV of the compact, certain provisions relating to economic assistance and security matters would remain in force in the event of early termination. Finally, the compact provides that on the thirteenth anniversary of the enactment of the compact, representatives of the United States and the freely associated state will commence negotiations to renew, revise, or let lapse the Compact of Free Association.

The financial terms of the Compact of Free Association provide the FSM with an annual block grant of $59.06 million and the Marshalls a yearly allotment that averages $37.06 million.[13] Estimates for the compact with the Republic of Palau project a yearly average assistance level of roughly $24 million from the United States. Forty percent of this block grant money, designated in the compact as the "capital account," is earmarked for economic assistance with projected uses including infrastructure development and revenue-generating projects. The remaining 60 percent of the block grants, defined as the "current account," is allocated for the administrative costs of government and related services. The compact's funding scheme provides for the diminution of United States grant assistance to the FSM and the Marshalls after the fifth and tenth years. Although the terms of the compact with Palau extend over a fifty-year period, most of the financial assistance offered by the United States is "front-loaded" during the first fifteen years of the agreement. The interest and investment income earned from a first-year, lump sum payment of $66 million comprises the principal source of projected U.S. funding for Palau between the sixteenth and fiftieth years of the compact.

The compact also specifies, under section 177 and related provisions in Public Law 99-239 implementing the agreement, a first-year appropriation of $150 million to cover United States liabilities incurred by its nuclear-testing program in the Marshalls. In addition, the people of the irradiated atolls of Bikini, Enewetak, Rongelap, and Utirik are guaranteed a total of $183,750,000 in payments, while another $45.75 million has been set aside to handle any outstanding or additional claims filed before a government-appointed claims tribunal following the implementation of the compact. Other monies are provided for the management and dispersal of these sums. Total compensation for American nuclear testing in the Marshalls as authorized in the compact and related agreements comes to about $420 million.

The compact and its subsidiary agreements also commit the United States to provide at no cost to the FSM, the Marshalls, and Palau an extensive international telecommunications network, airline and airport safety services, a regulatory system for commercial air traffic, natural disaster relief, weather forecasting services, and use of the United States Postal Service's international facilities. Other subsidiary agreements address marine space jurisdiction, military use and operating rights agreements, and legal matters involving extradition, liability, prosecution, and immunity.

During the course of congressional hearings, representatives of other American territories complained about the special tax and trade incentives denied them but granted to the Micronesian governments under the terms of the compact.[14] The complaints led to the dropping of these special incentives from the final version of the compact. As compensation, the Micronesian governments receive access to the domestic assistance programs of a number of federal agencies including the Federal Deposit Corporation, the Small Business Administration, the Economic Development Administration, the Rural Electrification Administration, the Job Partnership Training Act, the Job Corps, and the Department of Commerce's programs in the areas of tourism and marine resources development. Such additional access to United States federal programs supplements significantly the continuing and nonreimbursable technical assistance already committed in the compact from the United States Forest Service, the National Marine Fisheries Service, the United States Coast Guard, and the Department of the Interior's Advisory Council on Historic Preservation. The actual dollar amounts provided for by the compact are difficult to calculate because of provisions for inflation, the contributions of above-mentioned U.S. federal programs whose services are authorized but not specified in dollar amounts, and compensatory adjustments, again unspecified in dollar amounts, in health, education, and environmental impact. Best estimates put the total cost of the compact with the three Micronesian governments at roughly $2.7 billion.[15]

Debating the Terms of Endowment

In Fukuyama's vision of the end of history, national sovereignty and independence ultimately count for little in a process that culminates in a universal, homogenous, triumphant structure of liberal capitalist democracy. Sovereignty and independence, however, proved key concerns in the negotiations between the American and different Micronesian governments over the Compact of Free Association. At the start of those negotiations in October 1969, the Congress of Micronesia, still representing all the island groups that made up the United States Trust Territory of the Pacific Islands, endorsed four fundamental principles to guide any formal deliberations on the termination of the Trusteeship Agreement and the establishment of a future self-governing political status for the islands.[16] The first of these four principles identified the sovereignty of Micronesia as residing in the people of the islands and their duly constituted governments. Principle two asserted that Micronesians possessed the right of self-determination and with it the power to choose between independence and a status of free association with any other nation or organization of nations. Principle three endorsed the right of Micronesians to adopt a constitution and to amend, change, or revoke that constitution at any time, while principle four stipulated that any agreement to associate freely with another nation should be expressed in the form of a revocable compact terminable unilaterally by either party.

The debate over just how effectively these four principles are honored in the Compact of Free Association remains intense. Official representatives of the Micronesian governments all spoke positively and enthusiastically about the Compact of Free Association, at least in public. In 1983, the FSM Congress' Committee on External Affairs had endorsed the compact initialed at Hilo, Hawai'i, on 1 October 1982 as recognizing the Federated States of Micronesia as a "sovereign nation, established under a constitution adopted by its people, with full control over its internal and foreign affairs."[17] Speaking before a subcommittee of the United States House of Representatives Committee on Interior and Insular Affairs, Bailey Olter, then vice-president of the Federated States of Micronesia, described the Compact of Free Association as offering both the United States and the FSM the opportunity to replace the dated and inadequate Trusteeship Agreement with a "healthy and solid relationship designed for the future."[18] Olter went on to affirm that the people of his small island nation understood quite well the terms of the Compact of Free Association and desired deeply the close relationship with the United States made possible by the compact. Before a similar congressional hearing, Oscar DeBrum, chief secretary for the government of the Republic of the Marshall Islands, called the compact a less-than-perfect document of compromises that nonetheless allowed for a fair and equitable relationship between the United States and the Marshall Islands.[19]

Representatives from the United States Congress and from the various offices and agencies of the federal government also spoke in support of the compact. These many commentators agreed that the end of an era was at hand; comments, testimonies, and opening and closing remarks employed words such as "culmination," "conclusion," "termination," and "finalization" in assessing the negotiations over the Compact of Free Association. Those words, I believe, were not limited to the end of protracted negotiations over the dissolution of the Trusteeship but reflected as well a sense that the differences between Micronesians and Americans had been overcome. The compact, along with its subsidiary agreements, sought to make the islands compatible with American notions of life and government; it promised, through provisions for economic assistance, to complete Micronesians' transformation from backward island peoples into productive, responsible, hard-working near-Americans in close association with what some held to be the world's leading capitalist democracy.

Outside, and even sometimes within the arenas of official comment and review of the compact, could be heard dissident voices that had a decidedly different understanding of the compact, its effects and purposes. In quiet, more private moments, men like Andohn Amarich and Lazarus Salii, the chief negotiators for the Federated States of Micronesia and the Republic of Palau respectively, conceded with a decided air of resignation that the Compact of Free Association with the United States was the best deal that could be secured under the circumstances.[20] Dwight Heine, an opponent of the Kabua family with a long and distinguished career in education, government, and politics, offered a more pointed assessment of the compact. From his position as leader of a dissident political organization known as the Voice of the Marshalls, Heine called "free association" nothing more than a term; the approval of the Compact of Free Association, he said, would only increase the Republic of the Marshalls' dependency on the United States: "Who are we kidding? The fact of the matter is that for forty years, U.S. administrations have conditioned us to be dependent on the U.S. mentally, socially and economically. The Marshalls will have no choice but to renew the compact . . . making the region even more dependent on the U.S."[21]

The Pohnpei State Legislature made known its reservations about the compact, especially those sections that specified the overriding paramountcy of American security interests and that allowed for American review of all financial accounts and records at every level of government within Micronesia.[22] The Pohnpeian legislators saw these latter powers as constituting a serious, disruptive incursion on the autonomy and integrity of both the national and state governments of the FSM.

During the course of the United States Congress' review of the document, a host of witnesses from legal, academic, and church communities stepped forward to voice their concern or opposition to the compact. Dr. Mark Roberts of Harvard University described the compact as hundreds of pages long and written by a very clever bunch of American lawyers with a very convoluted, ultimately self-serving system of cross referencing. Roberts described the compact as a difficult document for even a trained professional to comprehend. Roberts' assessment was seconded by Senator Johnson Toribong of the Palau legislature, who characterized the compact as a "masterpiece of cross-referencing . . . difficult to read, written in English by attorneys, full of ambiguities." Prof. Roger Clark of Rutgers University Law School and a consultant to different Micronesian governments during the negotiations over the Compact of Free Association, likened the document to something designed by one of the more unscrupulous insurance companies. Speaking before the United Nations Trusteeship Council on 1 December 1982, Clark pointed out that what is given on the first page may be taken away by the small print in one of the eleven subsidiary agreements attached to the compact. Arnold Leibowitz, in his 1989 book *Defining Status: A Comprehensive Analysis of United States Territorial Relations,* characterized the various subsidiary agreements as often containing provisions too difficult politically to be placed in the text of the compact itself.[23]

This was especially true in matters involving the deployment of nuclear weapons and radioactive materials through Micronesian land, seas, and airspace. With direct reference to section 324 of the Compact of Free Association, Roberts pointed to how the restrictions on the use, testing, storage, or disposal of nuclear, toxic, chemical, gas, or biological weapons by the United States could be circumvented by provisions in the Mutual Security Pacts and Military Use and Operating Rights Agreements.[24] These provisions distinguish in finely legalistic terms between armed and unarmed nuclear weapons; they also designate the United States as the ultimate determiner of crises that necessitate the legal presence of nuclear weapons within Micronesian territory. Roberts concluded that the subsidiary agreements concerning security issues and military operations in the islands ultimately permit the United States to do whatever it wants whenever it wants.

More long-standing critics of the American presence in Micronesia have viewed the Compact of Free Association as doing little more than ensuring the primacy of American defense and security interests in the area. Catherine Lutz, writing in the *Bulletin of Concerned Asian Scholars* in

June 1986, charged that the United States was buying out Micronesia not with the prospects of genuine economic development but with "imported food, tobacco, alcohol, and government payroll checks" that only ensured the continued dependence of the area on the United States. Addressing the plebiscites on the Compact of Free Association that were held in 1983, Lutz likened the "free" choice of Micronesian voters to "those of boat passengers who have been taken far from their shore by a pilot whose interests and itinerary are not their own and who are then given the choice of remaining on the boat or swimming the 200 miles back to shore."[25] An anthropologist with extensive field experience on the atoll of Ifaluk in the central Carolines, Lutz argued that the statements of American congressional and government witnesses in support of the compact evidenced the language of a paternal colonialism: Micronesians were said to have "come of age" under the "guidance and tutelage" of the United States. In Lutz's estimation, the compact ultimately disguised the annexation of Micronesia under the persisting myth of an anticolonial America.

Henry Schwalbenberg, the assistant director of the Micronesian Seminar on Weno in Chuuk, undertook an extensive, thirty-month analysis of the Compact of Free Association between December 1981 and April 1984. Schwalbenberg expressed particular concern about the mutual security pacts between the United States and the Micronesian governments.[26] In agreeing in perpetuity to the principle of strategic denial—the principle that denied other nations access to Micronesian lands, harbors, waters, and airspace without the direct consent of the United States—the Federated States of Micronesia, the Republic of the Marshall Islands, and the Republic of Palau were depriving themselves, in Schwalbenberg's estimation, of their most crucial bargaining chip in any future political negotiations with the United States. All things considered, the Jesuit brother concluded that the compact was "more association than free."[27]

Those concerned about how free the Micronesian governments really were under the Compact of Free Association with the United States would find much to be concerned about in a letter written to three very conservative members of the United States Congress on 4 June 1981 by James L. Buckley, the undersecretary of state for security assistance, science and technology.[28] In that letter, Buckley noted that modernization and development in Micronesia were being imperiled by what he called "traditionalism." Buckley stated his belief that until governing elites could overcome the impediments inherent to their culture, gross social and economic inequities would continue within the Micronesian communities. Buckley added that Micronesian sovereignty was not innate, as the compact seemed to acknowledge, but was rather a matter of United States congressional discretion. The United States' responsibilities toward the area and its people transcended the limitations and concerns of international law; solid proof of local Micronesian governments' ability to ensure the welfare of their citizens was required before absolute sovereignty could be granted. Buckley expressed his own view that free association in Micronesia would lead most likely toward a closer, more permanent relationship with the United States. Buckley envisioned some form of commonwealth status for the FSM, the Marshalls, and Palau or a union with other American Pacific territories that might eventually evolve into statehood.

Buckley's comments on the restrictions and conditions of Micronesian sovereignty seem to be mirrored in those provisions of the Compact of Free Association that permit the United States to intervene in local government. Section 102 of Title I of Public Law 99-239 approving the Compact of Free Association between the United States and the FSM and Marshalls governments stipulates the submission of economic development plans by both Micronesian governments. Section 231 of Article II of the Compact of Free Association with the government of Palau also calls for the submission and review of a national development plan. These national development plans, to be submitted at regular intervals by the three Micronesian governments over the life of their respective agreements with the United States, are to be reviewed by the president, who then reports the findings to Congress within sixty days of receipt of the documents. In making this assessment, the president is required to solicit the views of the secretary of the interior, the administrator of the Agency for International Development, and the heads of such executive departments as he or she deems appropriate and advisable.

In testimony before a House subcommittee, Ambassador Fred Zeder, the president's personal representative to the Micronesian status talks between 1981 and 1986, said that the purpose of this requirement was to ensure the success of a mutually appropriate, desirable set of economic goals and objectives involving the American and Micronesian governments. Zeder characterized this system of monitoring and control as being sufficiently rigorous to assure the prudent allocation of compact funds and sufficiently flexible to be consistent with the self-governing status of the Micronesian governments.[29] Zeder further justified this requirement of the compact by calling it a remedy for the chronic lack of long-term economic planning in the Trust Territory. Thinking it ironic that the world's leading capitalist economy would be insisting upon a national development plan, representatives of the Federated States of Micronesia, during the course of negotiations over the compact, facetiously asked their American counterparts for a copy of the United States' national development plan or, if that were unavailable, a copy of the development plan for New York City.[30] They received neither because neither development plan had ever existed.

If free association is understood to be more about association than sovereignty, the provisions of the compact designed to promote the national economies of the islands might be construed to be more about control than development. Section 233 of Title II of the compact authorizes audits on all monies extended as economic assistance and identified in section 211 of the same Title II. Even more sweeping, however, are the provisions in section 102.c.1 of Public Law 99-239 implementing the compact for the FSM and Marshalls governments. This section provides the comptroller general of the United States and his General Accounting Office with the authority to audit all grants, program assistance, and other forms of aid provided to the Federated States of Micronesia. In pursuing this duty, the comptroller general is given access "to such personnel and to such records, documents, working papers, automated data and files, and other information relevant to such a review."

These extensive, wide-ranging powers are enhanced further by other legal requirements in the legislation approving the Compact of Free Association. Under section 102.c.4, the government of the Federated States of Micronesia is required to provide financial statements that account for the use of all funds provided by the United States under the compact. The submission of such financial statements is required within 180 days after the end of the fiscal year in the United States. Section 103.m.1 of Public Law 99-239 makes similar requirements for audits and the submission of annual financial statements by the Republic of the Marshalls.[31] In addition, supplemental provisions to section 177 of the compact providing money for validated claims against damage, loss, and suffering as a result of the American nuclear testing in the Marshalls require the services of a fund manager to supervise the expenditure and recording of all monies in connection with this authorization. Similar requirements are placed upon the lump-sum payment of $66 million made to the government of Palau during the first year of its compact with the United States; section 211, Article II, of the compact's Title II calls for a separate agreement on the monitoring and review of all investment income earned by this money.

In short, a scrutiny of the Compact of Free Association, particularly those areas dealing with economic assistance and with the management and supervision of that assistance, suggests that economic development remains subordinate and subservient as it always has been in American Micronesia to the dictates of strategic politics.[32] Behind the dollar amounts of the compact are stipulations that allow the rhetoric of development to persist as an essentially discursive strategy of domination. If the history of the islands called Micronesia were only about American colonialism and compacts of free association, the future would look a great deal like the past. There is, however, more to be said about the pasts and futures of the islands than this.

Touring the Edge of Paradise

What of American Micronesia in the years immediately following the implementation of the Compact of Free Association? A more personal account of life in the islands might provide a welcome respite from the legal terminology and technicalities of the Compact of Free Association. P. F. Kluge, in *The Edge of Paradise,* offers a very personal and particular vision of the islands, but a vision that distorts and disturbs in its strong resemblance to other and earlier accounts of American efforts in Micronesia. Kluge's account takes us a bit beyond the temporal limits of this study. I trust this will not disconcert readers too much. Historians find it relatively easy to establish temporal borders for their studies; the relationship between present and past is not so easily fixed, however. Any study of a past time is never very far from the present in which it is produced. Histories always bring a cargo of meanings and lessons for their contemporary audiences. So it is with *The Edge of Paradise.*

Kluge writes of the Caroline, Mariana, and Marshall Islands in 1989, three years after the implementation of the compact in the FSM and the Marshalls and fourteen years after the inauguration of the commonwealth agreement in the Northern Marianas. A former Peace Corps volunteer, author of what ultimately became the preamble to the constitution of the Federated States of Micronesia, and now professor of creative writing at Kenyon College in Ohio, Kluge details a trip he took to Micronesia in search of the meaning behind the suicide of his close friend, former senator in the Congress of Micronesia and second president of the Republic of Palau, Lazarus Salii. Kluge's text is deeply affected by what I take to be grief, angst, a consciousness of aging, a sense of loss, and a feeling of powerlessness. Shattered hopes and failed dreams provide the metaphors that organize Kluge's narrative and shape the meaning he finds in Salii's death.

Kluge had once looked at a younger, more idealistic, charismatic Salii as the one who would take a group of conquered, colonized, misadministered islands and transform them into proud, bustling island communities that stood at the center of the Pacific. For Kluge, the contemporary situation in the islands now mirrors Salii's own personal fate. Kluge sees the islands as possessing the same kind of dilapidated quality that characterized their physical infrastructure in the immediate post–World War II years. Almost fifty years after America's initial occupation, Koror in Palau, like most of Micronesia, still exudes the ambience of a "ruined estate, abandoned by owners and overseers, inherited by local workers, newly liberated and somewhat at a loss." Concrete houses, air conditioners, sewers, paved roads, and shopping malls are all products of the American presence; they do not change, however, the town's essential nature which is "ramshackle and nondescript, a disappointment to visitors who expected thatch roofs, breezy porches, and raffish charm."[33]

Kluge chronicles, and pessimistically, a Micronesia in which the different island groups have settled their fates and made their deals with the Americans. He counts a total population of less than a hundred thousand, speaking nine mutually unintelligible languages and surviving on "a shaky, artificial lopsided economy based on scrap metal, copra, fish and government subsidy in an area . . . so far, so small and located off the edge of the world."[34] The net effect of five decades of American bumbling and mismanagement is the creation of an improbable welfare state that resembles more an urban ghetto or a North American Indian reservation than a Pacific island. Kluge comments that those, like himself, who had once rooted for Micronesians now find themselves confronted with the prospect that island leaders are using their new powers to trash the place and each other.

Based on his island travels, Kluge writes of opportunities turning into opportunism and leaders gone bad; he sees only corruption, nepotism, conflicts of interest, privileges abused, cronyism, carpetbaggers, extravagant finders' fees, and sweetheart deals. Majuro, the atoll capital for the Republic of the Marshall Islands, presents itself to Kluge as a "feast of ironies, a warren of houses and warehouses and shacks that feels like a slovenly picnic in the mid-Pacific, like Central Park after one of those Puerto Rican holidays, all trashed and pissed on." Majuro suffers from a plethora of "Third World" problems that include unplanned urbanization, rising expectations, doubling populations, polluted lagoons, and poisoned reefs. Assaulting the physical senses are "the smell of rotting wood, the sight of rusty roofs, the mid-day heat, the flies and mosquitos, potholes and puddles, ghetto crowding, and bus terminal torpor."[35]

Moving farther west on the Air Micronesia island hopper from Honolulu, Kluge reaches Pohnpei, where he comments on the proclivity toward excessive drinking there and on the "beer tumors" of Micronesian males that give them the look of a life-long pregnancy. Meanwhile, American expatriates sit in local bars and speak of the island in renal, anal, and crude sexual metaphors that underscore their alienation, ignorance, and racism. Chuuk, for Kluge, remains "dreaded Hogoleu" with too many people, so many problems, and not enough land. Moen or Weno Island, the site of Chuuk state's district government, exists as a dusty, crowded dead-end place, all shacks and wash lines, plastic buckets, dying dogs, dead cars, idling people, and monotonous Chuukese music. With the exception of Yap, which is described as small, conservative, careful, prudent, free of major population pressures, and led by an effective collaboration of traditional chiefs and elected local officials, the islands of the Caroline group that constitute the Federated States of Micronesia struggle on as troubled places; they flounder some days, "floating and drifting the rest; less like islands than lifeboats, left behind by a large ship's sinking, paddling in circles, waiting for something to show up on the horizon, a continent they can land on or a rescue vessel that will toss them a line."[36]

Saipan, with the financial windfall resulting from Japanese tourism and the financially lucrative terms of its commonwealth status, is described as looking like an American suburban fantasy-land and as being the most corrupt place on earth. Prosperity has brought complaint as well as wealth to the Chamorros of the island. There is, writes Kluge, considerable fear, distrust, and abuse of alien workers from as far away as Sri Lanka who crowd the garment factories and work in the hotels, and of Chinese and Korean merchants who outwork and undercut local merchants. Having completed his tour through the islands, Kluge reaches Palau, his ultimate destination, and proceeds to indict that island group for its pride, malice, opportunism, and mystery. Kluge cites one expatriate observer's comments that Palauans are "just as fouled up as the other Micronesians are."[37] Government provides the first refuge of employment, the religion and opiate of the people.

Kluge suggests that Palau with its layers of national, state, and local governmental institutions, offices, and departments may be both the most overgoverned and the most ungovernable area of the world. Palauans' penchant for bickering with one another is manifest in their modern-day proclivity to sue and in their use of outside agencies and experts for advantage against local rivals. Even the most promising and carefully planned development projects fall victim to disputes among different groups of Palauans over land use and ownership. Kluge sees the future of the Caroline and Marshall Islands as a source of intense local anxiety. He quotes one long-time expatriate resident of Pohnpei who understands well the intimate, long-standing relationship between global strategic politics and American levels of funding for the islands:

> There's no god damned source of funding to run the fucking place. What source of money is going to take the place of the millions they're getting now? They're supposed to lose four or five federal programs next year, and they're talking like its the end of the world. . . . If Gorbachev winds down the fucking cold war, we're fucked. Anybody who goes to bed here and prays for peace ought to be shot.[38]

For Kluge, Micronesia represents a once gallant, well-intentioned exercise in trusteeship gone tedious and corrupt. Trying to work through his affection, nostalgia, and longing for the islands of his youth, Kluge acknowledges that his great hope was that the islands would remain stable and stationary. Instead, they became something else, he writes, "something . . . loose and drifting, small-feeling places to escape from, not to."[39] With direct reference to the pressures that caused his friend Lazarus Salii to take his own life, Kluge comments that no man is an island and that no island is an island either. If the Compact of Free Association and its accompanying discourse of development have brought the end of history to American Micronesia, it is a bad end, to read Kluge's vision of it.

Beyond Ends and Edges: Recalculating Economic Development

Kluge's *The Edge of Paradise* does not stand alone; it is but the most recent example of an extensive body of both popular and academic literature, cited throughout this study, that addresses the failure of economic development in American Micronesia. In a sense, things have come full circle as Kluge's assessment of the islands' present and future situations would seem to give the force of prophecy to that first official history of the early years of American rule in the islands; I refer specifically to Dorothy Richard's three-volume work, *United States Naval Administration of the Trust Territory of the Pacific Islands.* Richard's despair over the failings of Micronesians and over the impossibility of approximating Western economic development in the islands finds strong echo and clear reflection in Kluge's more contemporary account. The professor's criticism of American policy in the islands is only seemingly more liberal than the lieutenant commander's apology. Denigration of the islands and their people accompany Kluge's condemnation of more than fifty years of American control. The stories passed on by Kluge about Micronesian greed, corruption, and opportunism differ little from the tales of islanders' follies narrated by Richard. Micronesians as "moderns" or "near moderns" provide no more reassurance or satisfaction for American colonizers than Micronesians as "primitives." In trying to make sense of the dominant discourse of development that permeates the American presence in Micronesia and that shows itself in a range of writings from Richard to Kluge, we are left with larger questions about the nature of history, culture, and the power of representation in the islands.

Throughout this book, I have endeavored to examine American efforts at economic development as an ultimately discursive strategy of domination designed to better possess Micronesians by remaking them in an image and likeness, if not substance, that served the interests of an American society at whose cultural core rest the principles of capitalist economics. No history can isolate itself from the patterns and events of deeper, broader pasts. I have attempted to address the ascendancy of capitalism as culture in the West, the rise to power of the United States as the new center of the post–World War II global order, the strategic character of American interests in the islands called "Micronesia," and the contexts of containment and Cold War that fed this strategic obsession. Representations of islands as devastated by war and of islanders as grateful primitives in need of what Rear Adm. Carlton H. Wright termed "mild benevolence" served to explain America's presence and the necessity of development. The United Nations Trusteeship Agreement provided an international imprimatur that worked at once to veil and to justify American colonialism in the islands. A critical assessment of economic development in American Micronesia also necessitated reference to earlier colonial regimes in the region, each with its own distinctive patterns and practices of domination, and to the histories of such paradigmatic concepts as development, modernization, and dependency.

There is the need, I believe, to take the concept of economic development both a little more and a little less seriously. The issues at stake behind economic development cannot be measured simply in terms of gross national products, per capita income, import-export ratios, foreign investment, or even employment statistics. There needs to be a consciousness of economic development as a part of a larger transformative process that aspires to be near total in its reach and effects and that is resisted in subtle, masked, confounding, and even contradictory ways, ways that are informed by local histories and local traditions of economy and that contribute to a sense of community expressed through a contested, competing terrain of practices, beliefs, and relationships we might call "culture." Fishing on Kapingamarangi, feasting on Pohnpei, the battle against tourism on Yap, and the earliest efforts at the establishment of a competitive savings systems in the Chuuk Lagoon area all underscore the importance of this point.

In raising the topic of resistance to economic development, I do not mean to invoke old, tired, worn, and ultimately ethnocentric Manichean or romanticist notions of opposition. More local voices of protest can certainly be heard in speeches from the floor of the Congress of Micronesia or around the debate about dependency, but there exist too divisions and rivalries within given island societies that are sometimes created but more often exacerbated by local competitions over development projects or development-related issues. The struggle among different groups of Palauans over the antinuclear provisions of their constitution, the dispute between the Kwajalein landowners and the Republic of the Marshall Islands government over the lease of lands for American missile testing, and the contest between men and women on Chuuk over the prohibition of alcohol offer three prominent examples. Disconcerting too is that autonomous governments, led and staffed by island peoples, must now engage in the discourse of development to ensure their survival and sustain their power.[40] Hard realities and mean facts haunt the exercise of sovereignty; only a space distinguishes the phrase "in dependence" from the word "independence." The logic of development can become mutated, almost surreal in postcolonial environments; the acceptance of toxic garbage as landfill or the leasing of abandoned islands as dumping sites for the nuclear wastes of foreign countries are rationalized as development projects of a different but plausible sort.

Similarly, I do not intend by focusing on the discursive features of development to deny or dismiss the physical and social change affected in the islands by more than a half-century of formal American influence. The construction of roads, bridges, wharfs, airports, and power plants has touched deeply the way people relate to their environment, interact with each other, and understand themselves and the larger world. The linking of the islands to the larger world through modern systems of communication and transportation has made possible the movement of ideas, peoples, and technologies. In the conclusion to his history of colonialism in Micronesia, *Strangers in Their Own Land,* Francis Hezel writes of survival and cultural persistence amidst an increasingly complex, uncertain and changing world:

> Mormon missionaries, dressed in white shirts and ties, bicycle in pairs, waving to those who pass. "Seabees," members of the US Civic Action Teams, wear other uniforms, military fatigues, as they ride along in their weapons carriers or their distinctive green trucks. Pickup trucks haul Filipino workers to and from their job site, and on the street one may meet Asian or African doctors, Chinese, Korean and Australian businessmen, and American lawyers or accountants.[41]

Young Micronesians journey abroad for college or vocational training, while tourists arrive in greater numbers to see the museums, historic parks, and cultural centers created for their entertainment and their money. Hezel goes on to write that electricity, piped water, telephones, television sets, and video cassette recorders can now be found in even the more remote villages of the islands. There are ethnographies to be written of these encounters with modernity and of the ambiguity, uncertainty, and confusion they engender.

In organizing these concluding thoughts on calculating or figuring economic development differently in American Micronesia, I do not mean to portray American colonialism as a monolithic force—focused, directed, and efficient in its program of rule, administration, and change. Colonialism looms as a deep, penetrating program of change operating on almost all levels of a colonized society; it can also be complex, varied, uneven, and sometimes self-defeating in its workings. It is important, I think, to realize colonialism's particular features in a given locale and time and also to recognize the diverse, conflicting agenda and strategies sometimes employed by different groups of people from a single colonizing nation. In the case of American Micronesia, substantive and critical differences separate international bureaucrats, federal officials, local administrators, development planners, expatriate businessmen and entrepreneurs, missionaries, Peace Corps volunteers, professional researchers, and media people. The messy entanglements that marked efforts at economic development by the mid-1970s resulted in part from Trust Territory government offices, federal bureaucracies, and international aid agencies working at cross-purposes or against one another in institutionally prescribed ways in the development game.

Some Americans did articulate a consciousness of American colonialism's transforming agenda and of the violence it could and did inflict upon island societies. There were naval officers who recognized the discriminatory, destructive character of phosphate mining on Angaur; Trust Territory officials who criticized the grossly mechanistic, totalizing features of development plans; and journalists, doctors, and academic observers who wrote against the horrendous social, environmental, and medical consequences of nuclear testing in the Marshalls. At the same time, there is also the need to recognize the power and pervasiveness behind the very concept of development. Whatever their professional biases, political leanings, and socioeconomic backgrounds, almost all Americans subscribed to a belief in some form of development or betterment that was itself culturally and historically contexted in very pronounced ways. Such is the confounding, almost debilitating paradox that confronts any critique of development from what Laurence Carucci would call the "source of the force."

The Compact of Free Association does not mark the end of history for the Marshalls, Palau, and the Federated States of Micronesia. The people of the area called Micronesia are much more than simple victims of progress; their futures have the look of something more complex and promising than doomsday scenarios.[42] Despite colonialism's efforts to make its history the history of the islands, local voices that speak of different experiences and understandings persist. The islands of the former Trust Territory of the Pacific Islands have not been made over into liberal democracies. The people of Micronesia struggle to be more and other than simply productive workers or responsible consumers in "free association" with one of the world's major capitalist countries. Disputes are more numerous and complex than simply those between colonizer and colonized. The landowners of Kwajalein Atoll wrestle with the government of the Republic of the Marshall Islands over matters of compensation and representation as do the citizens of the irradiated atolls of Bikini, Enewetak, Rongelap, and Utirik.[43] The group known as the Voice of the Marshalls, representing those islands and atolls to the south, continues to resist the dominance of the north and the Kabua family. In the Federated States of Micronesia, individual states and various factions grapple with each other in ways that lead many to expect the eventual dissolution of the entity.[44] Pohnpei contests for advantage with Chuuk, while within Chuuk itself, the Faichuk area persists in its efforts for recognition as a separate and fifth state. Political divisions within Palau, a major contributing factor in the more-than-decade-old battle over the approval of the compact there, have not ceased.

An affirmation of the future for history in the islands is not to deny that money matters and can disrupt. The current threat to local autonomy posed by the activities of foreign investors in Palau is real and increasingly manifest, as are the abusive labor practices inflicted upon foreign workers in the homes and sweatshops of the Northern Marianas. Despite the funds provided, the Compact of Free Association has resulted to date in little demonstrable economic development for the Carolines and Marshalls. Negotiations over the renewal of the compact, set to begin in 1999 for the FSM and the Marshalls, could lead to a drive toward commonwealth status, an option originally shunned by Micronesian negotiators at the beginning of political status talks back in 1969. Cynical observers and hardened experts see the sacrifice of autonomy to commonwealth status as the only viable alternative to economic chaos and political collapse in the islands. Micronesian understandings and appropriations of the term "commonwealth" may prove more complicated than this, however. Guam is currently pursuing this option in an only seemingly ironic effort to escape the more onerous and oppressive features of the Organic Act that has bound it to the United States since 1950. Just what commonwealth status might mean for the Caroline and Marshall Islands and how the attendant issues of dependency and autonomy are to be understood constitute vital issues in reassessing economic development for the area. It may be too that the end of the Cold War and the elimination of the Soviet threat will lead to a considerable decline in the islands' strategic value. The United States government may seek to reduce significantly its financial obligations under any extension or renewal of the Compact of Free Association. Given this scenario, the most important part of the existing compact may prove to be Article IV of Title I, which allows for citizens of the different Micronesian nations to enter, work, and establish residence as nonimmigrants in the United States and its territories. In all likelihood, the future histories of the people of the greater Micronesian area will involve an intensification of current migration to places such as Guam, Hawai'i, and the North American continent.

Those of us who like our development quantifiable and our heroes clearly identifiable, rooted in place and time and engaged in what we perceive to be overt acts of resistance against forces of exploitation and control, may find it difficult to keep up with the movement of people and the changing character of life in Micronesia. We may need to develop a greater sense of nuance and subtlety that admits to both the polyvocality and polylocality of the Micronesian diaspora to other areas of the Pacific and the world. Such a journey for those who undertake it will involve extensive, complicated, intensely personal, and wrenching negotiations over meaning and identity in distant, alien, sometimes hostile settings within the parameters of a global economic order. It may be a world of on, suffering, mimicry, violence, discrimination, and suffering. so prove a world in which there results something creative, resis- l syncretic; something, to paraphrase James Clifford, that is more ambig ous and more historically complex and that requires that we perceive both the fading of certain orders of diversity and distinction and the creation or reformulation of others.[45] The future of the islands and more particularly of economic development may occur in ways and places that we have yet to recognize or anticipate. The purpose of this study has been to provide a more locally focused, culturally nuanced, and historical perspective on island peoples' struggle to persevere against those powers that have sought to dominate them, and through the invocation of often insidious, self-congratulating platitudes such as economic development.

Notes

1: As the Frigate Bird Flies

1 Bernard Smith, *European Vision and the South Pacific,* p. 269. Smith writes of scientific naming and knowing as one of Europe's ways of understanding and controlling the larger world.

2 Norman Meller, *The Congress of Micronesia;* p. 1.

3 The remark was made by the Jesuit priest Fr. Faustino Hernandez and is cited in Francis X. Hezel, S.J., *The First Taint of Civilization,* p. xi.

4 For more on this point, see David Hanlon, "Micronesia: Writing and Rewriting the Histories of a Nonentity," pp. 1–21.

5 Raymond Williams, *Marxism and Literature,* p. 109. Williams' definition of ideology is also employed by Jean Comaroff and John Comaroff in their brilliant piece of historical anthropology, *Of Revelation and Revolution.* See especially the subsection "Culture, Hegemony, Ideology," pp. 19–27, within their general introduction.

6 Thomas G. Paterson, *American Foreign Policy,* p. 346.

7 Thomas Gladwin, "Anthropology and Administration in the Trust Territory of the Pacific Islands," typescript, p. 6, 1954, Trust Territory Archives (TTA), reel no. 0106, frame no. 003, document no. 01687. Complete sets of the 2,169 reels of microfilmed archives are at the Alele Museum in Majuro, Republic of the Marshall Islands; at the College of the Northern Mariana Islands on Saipan; at the Federated States of Micronesia's Office of Administrative Services in Palikir, Pohnpei; at the Palau Ministry of Administration on Koror, Republic of Palau; at the Micronesian Area Research Center on Guam; at the University of Hawai'i's Hamilton Library; with the United States National Archives in Washington, D.C.; and in Canberra at the Menzies Library, Australian National University.

8 Quoted in E. J. Hobsbawm, *Nations and Nationalism since 1780,* p. 12.

9 Charles A. Beard, *An Economic Interpretation of the Constitution of the United States,* p. 16–18; Marshall Sahlins, "Cosmologies of Capitalism," p. 413; idem, *Culture and Practical Reason,* p. 166–67; Stephen Gudeman, *Economics as Culture,* p. viii.

10 Greg Dening, "Review of *Marists and Melanesians,*" p. 82.

11 Leo Migvar and Manny Sproat, "How To Plant Coconuts," Agricultural

Circular 7, published in cooperation with the South Pacific Commission (Sydney: Bridge Printing, 1964), TTA, reel no. 208, frame no. 0185, document no. 3596.

12 Cited in Paul Rabinow, ed., *The Foucault Reader*, p. 16.

13 This explanation of Foucault's thinking is from Arturo Escobar, *Encountering Development*, pp. 60–61.

14 Gustavo Esteva, "Development," pp. 8–10.

15 Ibid., pp. 6–7.

16 Ibid., p. 7.

17 Escobar, *Encountering Development*, pp. 3–4. For a full treatment of the ideas that shape Escobar's approach, see pp. 3–20. James Ferguson's *The "Anti-Politics" Machine* offers another excellent, slightly different critique of the politics of development. Herb Addo and George Aseniero also have written on the Eurocentric character of development and various development theories. See Addo's "Beyond Eurocentricity," pp. 12–47; also Aseniero, "A Reflection on Developmentalism," pp. 48–85.

18 Escobar, *Encountering Development*, pp. 6, 146, 9.

19 Max Weber, *The Protestant Ethic*, p. 2.

20 James C. Scott, *Weapons of the Weak*, p. 307. For an extended, highly sophisticated treatment of the issue of hegemony, see pp. 304–350.

21 Comaroff and Comaroff, *Of Revelation and Revolution*, p. 15.

22 Ibid., pp. 21–22.

23 Marshall Sahlins, "The Economics of Develop-Man in the Pacific," p. 14.

24 Ibid., p. 13.

25 Appadurai makes much the same argument in his excellent introduction to *The Social Life of Things*, pp. 3–63.

26 Stephen Gudeman, "Remodeling the House of Economics," pp. 151–152.

27 Escobar, *Encountering Development*, p. 62.

28 Sahlins, "Cosmologies of Capitalism," p. 416.

29 As an example of this more tragic encounter between global and local systems, Sahlins cites nineteenth-century Hawai'i. See his "The Economics of Develop-Man in the Pacific," pp. 21–23, and "Cosmologies of Capitalism," pp. 429–435.

30 Ranajit Guha, *Elementary Aspects of Peasant Insurgency in Colonial India*, pp. 333–334.

31 Nicholas Thomas, *Colonialism's Culture*, p. 17.

32 Paul Rabinow, "Representations Are Social Facts," p. 241; also Greg Dening, *The Bounty*, p. 112–116.

33 Ester Boserup, *Women's Role in Economic Development.*

34 Francis X. Hezel, S.J., *Strangers in Their Own Land*, p. 251.

35 There is a small but growing body of literature on Micronesian women. On the colonial politics behind the representation of Micronesian women, there is Catherine Lutz and Jane L. Collins, *Reading National Geographic*, pp. 134–144. One of the most insightful and enduring works is DeVerne Reed Smith's study of the centrality of women in Palauan society; see her *Palauan Social Structure.* A recent study of the continuing prominence of Pohnpeian women in their island's economy is Kimberlee

S. Kihleng's "Women in Exchange." A more general study is Penelope Schoeffel's *Women in Development;* Schoeffel, unlike Smith and Kihleng, sees the general decline in traditional economic roles as having marginalized Micronesian women in contemporary times. The more public, overtly political profile being evidenced by some groups of women in Micronesia is the topic of Mac Marshall and Leslie B. Marshall's *Silent Voices Speak.* On the topic of Micronesian women's recent political engagements, see also Zohl dé Ishtar, *Daughters of the Pacific;* and Teresia K. Teaiwa, "bikinis and other s/pacific n/oceans."

36 Following local recommendations for English-language publications, I employ the term "Palau" rather than "Belau"; on this point, see "Is It Belau, Palau or Both?" in the *Palau Gazette,* 19 February 1996.

37 Fredric Jameson, "Third World Literature in the Era of Multinational Corporations," pp. 68–69.

38 Homi Bhabha, "Sly Civility," p. 74.

39 Homi Bhabha, "The Other Question," p. 75.

2: Beginning to Remake Micronesia

1 Roy Harvey Pearce, *Savagism and Civilization.*

2 Ibid., p. XVII.

3 Hezel, *The First Taint of Civilization,* p. 244; see also David Hanlon, *Upon a Stone Altar,* pp. 127–128.

4 Hanlon, *Upon a Stone Altar,* pp. 141, 142.

5 Fletcher Pratt, *The Marines' War,* p. 144. Figures concerning the devastation are cited in Roger Gale, *The Americanization of Micronesia,* pp. 40, 144. Mark Peattie, *Nan'yō,* p. 285. Douglas Oliver, *The Pacific Islands,* p. 371.

6 See Homi Bhabha, *The Location of Culture;* also his edited volume *Nation and Narration* (New York: Routledge, 1990), and his article "The Other Question: Difference, Discrimination and Colonialism," pp. 71–87. Consult too Patrick Brantlinger, *Rule of Darkness;* Anthony Pagden, *European Encounters with the New World;* Mary Louise Pratt, *Imperial Eyes;* and Edward Said, *Orientalism* and *Culture and Imperialism.*

7 Dorothy Richard, *United States Naval Administration of the Trust Territory of the Pacific Islands,* 1:329.

8 On this point, see Suzanne Falgout, "From Passive Pawns to Political Strategists," pp. 117–148; Robert W. Moore, "Our New Military Wards, the Marshalls," pp. 325–352; and John Useem, *Report on Yap and Palau.*

9 Gilbert Bailey, "Freedom on Kwajalein," p. 440; also Hezel, *Strangers in Their Own Land,* p. 244.

10 Richard, *United States Naval Administration,* 2:49–50.

11 Ibid., 1:339, 341.

12 Ibid., 2:54.

13 Interview with Mr. Lino Miquel of Ohlipel, Kiti, Pohnpei, at Ninseitamw, Kolonia, Pohnpei, on 15 May 1983.

14 Quoted in Richard, *United States Naval Administration,* 1:339–340.

15 On this point, see Hezel, *Strangers in Their Own Land,* pp. 249–250.

16 Laurence Marshall Carucci, "The Source of the Force in Marshallese Cosmology," p. 75.
17 Ibid., p. 86.
18 Karen Nero, "Time of Famine, Time of Transformation," pp. 133–134.
19 Hezel, *Strangers in Their Own Land,* p. 246. Nero, "Time of Famine, Time of Transformation," p. 144.
20 Richard, *United States Naval Administration,* 1:380.
21 Ibid., pp. 381, 478.
22 For an overview of the diversity of opinion and debate around the anthropological issue of exchange, see C. A. Gregory, *Gifts and Commodities;* Marcel Mauss, *The Gift;* Marilyn Strathern, *The Gender of the Gift;* and Nicholas Thomas, *Entangled Objects.*
23 John F. Embree, "Field Report on a Trip to Micronesia," p. 64; Embree dates the incident as 25 December 1945. This incident is also narrated in Richard, *United States Naval Administration,* 2:336.
24 Richard, *United States Naval Administration,* 2:405.
25 Ibid., pp. 408, 409, 131–136.
26 Ibid., 1:272.
27 Ibid., pp. 290, 384.
28 Ibid., p. 264.
29 Ibid., 2:29–33.
30 Hezel, *Strangers in Their Own Land,* p. 249.
31 Richard, *United States Naval Administration,* 1:197.
32 Forrestal quoted ibid., p. 212; see also p. 518.
33 The petition in its entirety is found ibid., 3:1076–1079.
34 Quoted ibid., 2:405.
35 For a summary of economic development efforts under the Spanish, German, and Japanese colonial regimes, see David Hanlon, "Patterns of Colonial Rule in Micronesia," pp. 103–110.
36 Peattie, *Nan'yō,* 157–161. For more on population issues, see also Tadao Yanaihara, *Pacific Islands under Japanese Mandate,* pp. 29–49.
37 Peattie, *Nan'yō,* pp. 150–152.
38 Useem, *Report on Yap and Palau,* p. 83.
39 Richard, *United States Naval Administration,* 1:18–20.
40 Ibid., p. 19.
41 Hezel, *Strangers in Their Own Land,* p. 257.
42 Richard, *United States Naval Administration,* 1:vi. The admission comes from Adm. Arthur W. Radford, former high commissioner for the Trust Territory of the Pacific Islands, who specifically acknowledged these two prime objectives of the navy's administration in the preface to Richard's three-volume study.
43 Quoted in Richard, *United States Naval Administration,* 2:406.
44 Ibid., pp. 422 f, 430, 432, 437.
45 Ibid., pp. 473, 474.
46 Ibid., pp. 446–447.
47 Ibid., pp. 453, 455.
48 Ibid., p. 453.

49 Hezel, *Strangers in Their Own Land,* p. 266.
50 Useem, *Report on Yap and Palau,* p. 83.
51 Ibid., p. 410.
52 Excerpts from this document can be found in Richard, *United States Naval Administration,* 2:415–417.
53 Ibid., p. 418.
54 Frederick Cooper, "Colonizing Time," pp. 209–211.
55 Greg Dening, *Islands and Beaches,* p. 264.
56 Walter B. Harris, "South Sea Islanders under Japanese Mandate," p. 693.
57 Richard, *United States Naval Administration,* 2:488, 492.
58 Ibid., pp. 489–491.
59 Ibid., p. 487.
60 Ibid., 3:654–655. For a consideration of the patriarchal, sexist nature of development discourse that fails to take account of women's productive roles, consult as a start Escobar, *Encountering Development,* pp. 171–192; Boserup, *Women's Role in Economic Development;* Annette Fuentes and Barbara Ehrenreich, *Women in the Global Factory;* Nuket Kardam, *Bringing Women In: Women's Issues in International Development Programs;* Maria Mies, *Patriarchy and Accumulation on a World Scale;* and Aihwa Ong, *Spirits of Resistance and Capitalist Discipline.*
61 Richard, *United States Naval Administration,* 2:486.
62 Ibid., p. 483.
63 Ibid., pp. 486, 483. In this and much of her assessment of the skills and abilities of Micronesian labor, Richard draws heavily from J. A. Decker, *Land Problems in the Pacific Mandates.*
64 For an examination of the long-standing, deeply embedded concept of the primitive in Euro-American thought and culture, see Marianna Torgovnik, *Gone Primitive.*
65 Gale, *The Americanization of Micronesia,* p. 53.
66 Earl S. Pomeroy, *Pacific Outpost,* p. 170.
67 Cited in Hezel, *Strangers in Their Own Land,* p. 255, 254.
68 Hoover's position was articulated in a speech given to the graduating class of the United States Naval Academy in 1947; his speech is summarized in Richard, *United States Naval Administration,* 3:17.
69 Quoted ibid., p. 8.
70 Ibid., pp. 18–19; *NYT* editorial and letters quoted ibid., pp. 19, 20.
71 For an account of this compromise, see Rupert Emerson et al., *America's Pacific Dependencies,* p. 121.
72 Rear Adm. Carleton H. Wright, "Let's Not Civilize These Happy People," pp. 23, 149–150.
73 Ibid., p. 23.
74 Hezel, *Strangers in Their Own Land,* p. 259.
75 Quoted in Richard, *United States Naval Administration,* 2:375.
76 Ibid., p. 23.
77 Quoted ibid., 3:961.

3: Strategic Developments

1 The phrase comes from Willard Price, *America's Paradise Lost* p. 98.

2 Quoted from a copy of the *United Nations Trusteeship Agreement: United States Trust Territory of the Pacific Islands* in Sue Rabbitt Roff, *Overreaching in Paradise*, p. 191.

3 Roff, *Overreaching in Paradise*, p. 58.

4 Richard, *United States Naval Administration*, 3:385.

5 Ibid., p. 748. A large portion of this very extensive, highly revealing letter is reproduced ibid., pp. 743–749.

6 A copy of the naval directive establishing the Island Trading Company and its responsibilities is ibid., p. 668.

7 Ibid., p. 686.

8 For an unpublished history of the ITC, see John S. Spivey, "History of the Island Trading Company of Micronesia (1947–1954)," TTA, reel no. 0118, frame no. 0000, document no. 1914.

9 Richard, *United States Naval Administration*, 3:694.

10 Ibid., pp. 783–785, 788.

11 Ibid., p. 752.

12 Ibid., p. 753.

13 Ibid., pp. 754, 763–764, 772. Marshall himself urged the creation of a forestry program in the Trust Territory. He described forestry, along with agriculture, as having the duty "of providing the basic plan for the development of the natural resources of these islands, for procuring a total land use, a plan of efficient terracultura."

14 Ibid., pp. 624–625. The Navy also created a civilian-staffed Conservation Committee for Micronesia, which advised and assisted on environmental matters. Between 1949 and 1951, an atoll research survey, under the project title of the Scientific Investigation of Micronesia (SIM), was conducted for the navy by the Pacific Science Board. The purposes of this survey were in part to aid in the general conservation effort in the islands.

15 Ibid., p. 357. A major clash over the issue of commercial exploitation involved Atkins, Kroll, and Company of Guam and its entry in 1950 into the Trust Territory copra trade. Atkins Kroll's policies placed all risks for the procurement, storage, transfer, and sale of copra on the producer. Moreover, Atkins Kroll would accept copra only in the major district centers of the Trust Territory and would make no payments until the copra had been safely unloaded at Guam. The ITC was left to service the more remote island communities. This tactic led to considerable hardships for both local producers and the government, which lost the processing tax that Atkins Kroll refused to pay on copra that spoiled or was lost during shipment to Guam. The government's dissatisfaction with Atkins Kroll's way of doing business led to the withdrawal of the company's commercial license. For an account of the issue, see ibid., p. 242; also, Admiral Radford's letter to the Chief of Naval Operations in Richard, ibid., 745–747.

16 Wright's comments were made in a speech before the Commonwealth Club of California on 28 October 1947; excerpts are quoted ibid., p. 360.

17 Ibid., pp. 642–645.

18 Ibid., pp. 654–655. The district government in Yap, which had listed no female workers among its 110 employees in December 1948, failed to file statistics for the next three years. There are, thus, no official statistics on the employment of women in Yap from 1947 through the second quarter of 1951.

19 Ibid., pp. 648–649.

20 Ibid., p. 646. There is no indication in Richard whether or not any sexual exploitation had taken place within the households that employed these women.

21 Ibid., p. 643.

22 Ibid., p. 657.

23 I am indebted to Vicente Diaz for pointing out the ways in which tales of cultural demise or indictment can also contain counternarratives of cultural persistence. See his "Simply Chamorro," pp. 29–58.

24 Richard, *United States Naval Administration,* 3:697–698.

25 Ibid., p. 991. Richard's account is credited to a Lt. Cdr. George Taggart, USNR, who recounted it to a P. Drucker; see p. 991, n. 45.

26 Ibid., p. 698.

27 Thomas, *Entangled Objects,* p. 11.

28 Richard, *United States Naval Administration,* 3:698.

29 Ibid., p. 416.

30 Ibid., pp. 699–700.

31 The quote is from a letter by Deputy High Commissioner Carleton R. Wright dated 2 April 1948 and quoted ibid., p. 699.

32 Ibid., pp. 699, 700.

33 Ibid., p. 409.

34 For an in-depth treatment of the complexities of Yap's chiefly polity, see Sherwood Galen Lingenfelter, *Yap: Political Leadership and Cultural Change in an Island Society.*

35 This description of Angaur comes from the German Colonial Office's yearly publication, *Kolonialamt: Die Deutschen Schutzgebiete in Afrika und in der Südsee, 1910/1911* (Berlin, 1911). Relevant portions pertaining to Angaur have been reproduced in Francis X. Hezel, S.J., and Mark L. Berg, eds., *Winds of Change,* pp. 421–423.

36 Ibid., p. 423.

37 Ucherbalau's history of phosphate mining on Angaur is contained in a letter he wrote to the military government officer on Angaur and dated 10 June 1947; the document, along with other relevant historical and anthropological background material, can be found in the TTA on reel no. 4128, frame no. 0137, item no. 38,661.

38 Peattie, *Nan'yō,* pp. 132–133.

39 District Anthropologist Shigeru Kaneshiro to Trust Territory Director of Internal Affairs, "Phosphate Mining on Angaur," 15 November 1951, TTA, reel no. 4128, frame no. 0137, item no. 38,661.

40 Peattie, *Nan'yō,* p. 67.

41 Ucherbalau to Military Government Officer, Angaur, "Mining of

Phosphate in Relation to the People of Angaur," 10 June 1947, TTA, reel no. 4128, frame no. 0137, item no. 38661.

42 Peattie, *Nan'yō*, p. 83.

43 P. Drucker, Head of Social and Scientific Division, to High Commissioner, "Report on Investigation of Angaur Land Situation," 5 November 1949, TTA, reel no. 4130, frame no. 0000, item no. 3876.

44 Hezel and Berg, *Winds of Change*, p. 423. Ucherbalau gives a figure of "300,000 tons" in his history of phosphate mining on Angaur; see TTA, reel no. 4127, frame no. 137, item no. 38661.

45 Richard, *United States Naval Administration*, 2:465.

46 P. Drucker, Head of Social and Scientific Division, to High Commissioner, "Report on Investigation of Land Situation on Angaur," 5 November 1949, TTA, reel no. 4130, frame no. 0000, item no. 3876.

47 Richard, *United States Naval Administration*, 2:465–467.

48 John Useem, "South Sea Island Labor Strike: Labor Management in the Caroline Islands, Micronesia," TTA, reel no. 120, frame no. 0144, document no. 2006. A copy of this work can also be found in the Pacific Collection, Hamilton Library, University of Hawai'i at Manoa; quote, p. 5.

49 Richard, *United States Naval Administration*, 2:469.

50 Ucherbalau to Military Government Officer, Angaur, "Mining of Phosphate in Relation to the People of Angaur," 10 June 1947, TTA, reel no. 4128, reel no. 0137, no. 38661; cited also ibid., p. 3:820.

51 Wohl's assessment of the situation is reported as part of a larger memorandum on the history of phosphate mining on Angaur to Rear Adm. Leon S. Fiske, Deputy High Commissioner, from Cmdr. William R. Lowndes, Economics Officer, and dated 7 November 1949; TTA, reel no. 0638, frame no. 0098, item no. 11386.

52 Contained in P. Drucker, Head of Social and Scientific Division, to High Commissioner, "Report on Investigation of Angaur Land Situation," 5 November 1949; TTA, reel no. 4130, frame no. 0000, item no. 3876.

53 Richard, *United States Naval Administration*, 3:821, 822.

54 Ibid., p. 824.

55 "Minutes of the Angaur Mining Conference," 9 November 1949, pp. 24, 74; TTA, reel no. 4130, frame no. 0000, item no. 3876.

56 District Anthropologist (Francis B. Mahoney) to (Palau) District Administrator, "Report on the Angaur Situation with Relation to Current Mining Negotiations," 26 December 1953, p. 2, TTA, reel no. 0517, frame no. 0216, document no. 8895.

57 Ibid., p. 2.

58 Cited in "Minutes of the Angaur Mining Conference," 9 November 1949, p. 99; TTA, reel no. 4130, frame no. 0000, item no. 3876.

59 "Minutes of the Angaur Mining Conference," 9 November 1949, p. 65; TTA, reel no. 4130, frame no. 0000, item no. 3876. Holt's opinion was shared by other American representatives at the conference including Lt. Cmdr. P. Drucker, Head of the Trust Territory Social and Scientific Division, the Staff Anthropologist, and Mr. Daniel P. Luten, Technical Advisor for the Natural Resources Division of SCAP, Tokyo.

60 "Minutes of the Angaur Mining Conference," Angaur, 25 October 1951; TTA, reel no. 0525, frame no. 0070, item no. 9076.

61 Richard, *United States Naval Administration*, 3:824–828.

62 An account of the Angaur Mining Trust Agreement and its first four years of implementation can be found in ibid., pp. 824–832.

63 For the transcript of these meetings, see "Conference on Phosphate Mining on Angaur, With Related Dispatches and Correspondence, 1951; TTA, reel no. 525, frame no. 0070, item no. 9076.

64 Frank J. Mahony, "The Innovation of a Savings System in Truk," pp. 465–482. For ethnographic background on Chuuk or Truk, see Thomas Gladwin and Seymour B. Sarason, *Truk: Man in Paradise*; and Ward H. Goodenough, *Property, Kin, and Community on Truk*. For a biography on the life of Chief Petrus Mailo, see Thomas Gladwin, "Chief Petrus Mailo," pp. 41–62. Joakim Peter of Etal in the Mortlocks informs me through a personal communication of 11 October 1996 that Petrus Mailo was not actually a member of Weno's most senior clan, Sapun; rather, he hailed from the Western Islands of the larger Chuuk area and was a member of the clan Sor. His affiliation with Sapun resulted from adoption; his rise to leadership of that clan involved a remarkable decision to depart from established criteria in the determination of clan leadership.

65 Richard, *United States Naval Administration*, 3:705–706.

66 I have retained the spellings employed by Mahony in his article "The Innovation of a Savings System in Truk." For a more modern orthographic rendering of Chuukese words, readers may want to consult Ward H. Goodenough and Hiroshi Sugita, *Trukese-English Dictionary/Pwpwuken Tettenin Foos, Chuuk-Ingenes*.

67 Jim Clark, *Cooperative Advisors' Handbook*, n.d., pp. 2, 5, TTA, reel no. 0226, frame no. 0012, document no. 4501.

68 Jose A. Benitez, "Opening Remarks" to a Seminar on Cooperatives in Palau, 21 July 1961, supplemental pp. 2, 3, TTA, reel no. 0406, frame no. 0076, document no. 7112.

69 Clark, "The Role of Cooperatives in Developing Countries," in *Cooperative Advisors' Handbook*, TTA, reel no. 0226, frame no. 0012, document no. 4501.

70 Cited in Harry H. Jackman, *Some Observations and Recommendations on the Development of Credit Unions and Other Cooperatives in the Trust Territory of the Pacific islands*, 1963, p. 2, TTA, reel no. 0574, frame no. 0018, document no. 9989.

71 Ibid., p. 2.

72 Ibid., the opinion here is Jackman's.

73 Cited ibid.

74 William C. Rhyne, "Report on Cooperatives and Credit Unions in the Trust Territory," 25 June 1969, TTA, reel no. 0861, frame no. 0019, document no. 14356.

75 United States Department of State, *Thirty-Second Annual Report to the United Nations on the Administration of the Trust Territory of the Pacific Islands*, (1979) pp. 31–32.

76 Richard, *United States Naval Administration,* 3:48.
77 Ibid., pp. 1109–1110.
78 Ibid., p. 1113.
79 Ibid., p. 1110.
80 Ibid., pp. 837–838.
81 Ibid., p. 640.
82 Ibid., p. 1115.
83 Griffin made his assessment in a preface to the 1971 reissue of Oliver's *Planning Micronesia's Future.* This evaluation of the first ten years of civilian rule in American Micronesia is also cited in Gale, *The Americanization of Micronesia,* p. 82.

4: "Planning Micronesia's Future"

1 Arturo Escobar, "Planning," pp. 140, 132–133.
2 Marianne Gronemeyer's "Helping," p. 53.
3 This quote appears in a letter dated 1 October 1945 from the Commander of the Marianas to the Chief of Naval Operations; it is cited in USCC, *Summary of Findings and Recommendations,* p. 2. The survey was published in 1951 under the authorship of Douglas L. Oliver as *Planning Micronesia's Future,* (reprinted 1971).
4 USCC, *Findings and Recommendations,* p. 2. See also the chapter on the USCC in Richard, *United States Naval Administration,* 2:419–44.
5 USCC, *Findings and Recommendations,* p. 4.
6 On the relationship between anthropology and colonialism in the area, see David Hanlon, "Magellan's Chroniclers?"
7 Oliver, *Planning Micronesia's Future,* pp. 6, vi; quotations on p 6.
8 USCC, *Findings and Recommendations,* p. 16.
9 Oliver, *Planning Micronesia's Future,* p. 48.
10 United Nations, Trusteeship Council, *Report of the United Nations Visiting Mission to the Trust Territory of the Pacific Islands, 1961,* p. 12.
11 For a description of NSAM 145 and the report (Solomon Report) that it engendered, see Gale, *The Americanization of Micronesia,* pp. 102–110.
12 *Report by the United States Government Survey Mission to the Trust Territory of the Pacific Islands,* p. S-1.
13 Ibid., 1:53; p. S-26.
14 Ibid., 1:4, 9.
15 Ibid., 2:48.
16 Ibid., p. 131.
17 Robert R. Nathan Associates, *Economic Development Plan for Micronesia,* pt. 4, p. 731–732.
18 Ibid., pt. 1, pp. viii, 3, 62.
19 Ibid., pt. 2, pp. 283, 210.
20 Ibid., pt. 1, pp. 47, 51, 110–111, 55.
21 Ibid., p. 58.
22 Ibid., p. 90; pt. 3, pp. 508, 511, 686–687.
23 Ibid, pt. 4, p. 630.
24 Ibid., pp. 695–696, 705, 693.

25 United States Trust Territory of the Pacific Islands, Microfilmed Archives, "Individual Comments on the Nathan Report Regarding Economic Development Planning for the Trust Territory," TTA, reel no. 674, frame no. 0000, item no. 12145. An executive history and summary of the review also exists; see "Evaluation, Analysis, and Summary of Objectives of Program to be Undertaken by R. R. Nathan and Associates"; also "Report on Actions Taken to Implement Recommendations of the Trust Territory Economic Development Plan," both to be found on reel no. 551, frame no. 0154, document no. 9294.

26 Peter Wilson's evaluations, like those of Dr. Luke A. Howe, G. P. Daniels, Peter Hill, W. A. Forest, Peter Coleman, and Francis B. Mahoney, can be found in TTA, reel no. 674, frame no. 0000, document no. 12145.

27 Robert R. Nathan Associates, *Economic Development Plan for Micronesia,* pt. 1, pp. 96–100.

28 For a summary of modernization theory, both classical and revisionist, see Alvin Y. So, *Social Change and Development,* pp. 17–87.

29 Marshall Sahlins, *How Natives Think,* p. 14.

30 Robert L. Heilbroner and Lester C. Thurow, *The Economic Problem,* p. 617.

31 Elbert V. Bowden, "The Theory and the Practice of Economic Development Planning in the Scattered Tropical Islands of Micronesia," paper presented at the Pacific Regional Science Conference, East-West Center, Honolulu, Hawai'i, 27 April 1969, p. 16, in TTA, reel no. 0140, frame no. 0082, document no. 2296.

32 A copy of the ICA's *Human Development Project for the Marshall Islands,* along with related correspondence and other documents, can be found in TTA, reel no. 0237, frame no. 0084, document no. 4008.

33 Carpenter to High Commissioner Edward E. Johnston in "File on the Marshalls Human Development Project on Socio-Economic Development for the Marshall Islands—Institute for Cultural Affairs," TTA, reel no. 0237, frame no. 0084, document no. 4008.

34 Wayne C. Thiessen, "How About Team Work," in TTA, reel no. 0383, frame no. 0199, document no. 6211.

35 "Micronesia: An Alternative Description," TTA, reel no. 1376, frame no. 0002, document no. 21597.

36 Fred K. Fox and Ralph O'Connor, "A Proposal for Micronesian Development," Western Islands Development Enterprises, TTA, reel no. 0093, frame no. 0018, document no. 1556.

37 Cited in Trust Territory of the Pacific Islands, "Country Programme for the Trust Territory, January 1977–December 1981," TTA, reel no. 0356, frame no. 0060, document no. 5796.

38 Following final approval of the draft by the Congress of Micronesia, the high commissioner endorsed the five-year indicative economic development plan as law with his signature on 5 November 1976. For an overview of the United Nations' role in the drafting of the indicative development plan for the Congress of Micronesia, see H. S. Wanasinghe, "Report to the Congress of Micronesia on Administrative Changes to

Support the Five-Year Indicative Plan, 1977–1981," 24 March 1976, TTA, reel no. 0166, frame no. 0028, document no. 2813. See also "Report to the Congress of Micronesia: Background Paper on Major Issues to be Considered in Drafting the Micronesia Indicative Development Plan, 1976"; TTA, reel no. 1523, frame no. 0169, document no. 25703.

39 Palau District Planning Office, "Planning in Palau," 22 September 1975, TTA, reel no. 1295, frame no. 0071, document no. 20876.

40 Sam Falanruw, Director of Resources and Development for Yap, 11 February 1980, cover letter for the "Indicative Development Plan for Yap State," TTA, reel no. 0348, frame no. 0036, document no. 5596.

41 "This Is a First Background Paper of Yap Economic Development Plan, F/Y 1981–1986," TTA, reel no. 2151, frame no. 0174, document no. 30528. Neither the author nor the reviewer of this first draft is identified.

42 See "Consultants' Reports Index," n.d., TTA, reel no. 0418, frame no. 0000, document no. 7820. For a brief overview and history of the UNDP efforts in the Trust Territory, see Robert J. Trusk, "United Nations Development Programme: Assistance in Development Planning (TTP 75/001)," FY 1978 budget hearings, March 1977, TTA, reel no. 295, frame no. 0007, document no. 20830.

43 UNDP, *Policies and Procedures Manual,* 1 December 1973, pp. 6–17, TTA, reel no. 221, frame no. 0164, document no. 3676.

44 Graham Hancock, *Lords of Poverty.*

45 Dan Perin, "Gross National Accounts, The Federated States of Micronesia, April, 1980," pp. 8–11, TTA, reel no. 3863, frame no. 0083, document no. 35968. Perin's report is provided under a cover letter to Andohn L. Amarich, the chairman of the Committee on Future Political Status and Transition, and dated 7 April 1980. Though outside the immediate time period of this chapter and authored for a Federated States of Micronesia government office, Perin's criticisms address problems that had developed over the preceding five years as a result of UNDP studies and statistics gathering.

46 Perin to High Commissioner Janet McCoy, 3 March 1982, in "Correspondence and Other Information on the United Nations Development Program," TTA, reel no. 0892, frame no. 0035, document no. 14860.

47 M. Falanruw to Benzeevi, 6 November 1978, TTA, reel no. 0213, frame no. 0054, document no. 3725.

48 Christopher Goss, "Assessment of the Palau Development Planning Workshop," in "Files on Workshop of the Palau Indicative Development Plan, 13–16 December 1976," TTA, reel no. 1295, frame no. 0054, document no. 20868.

49 For a summary of the decision leading to the placement of the Peace Corps in Micronesia, see Hezel, *Strangers in Their Own Land,* pp. 311–312.

50 My account of the Peace Corps' first years in Micronesia draws from Gale, *The Americanization of Micronesia,* p. 119. See also the extensive file labeled "Correspondence, Reports, and News Clippings on Planning and

Utilization of Peace Corps Volunteers in Micronesia, May to November, 1976," TTA, reel no. 0579, frame no. 0012, document no. 10103.

51 Cited in Hezel, *Strangers in Their Own Land,* p. 311.

52 U.S. Department of State, *20th Annual Report on the Trust Territory of the Pacific Islands* (1967), p. 99. Of these 452 volunteers, 265 worked in education.

53 Hezel, *Strangers in Their Own Land,* p. 312.

54 Dirk A. Ballendorf, "Remarks to the High Commissioner and His Cabinet," 1968, TTA, reel no. 0500, frame no. 0000, document no. 08193.

55 Hezel, *Strangers in Their Own Land,* p. 314; editorial cited ibid.

56 David Platt, "Breathing In and Breathing Out," n.d., p. 2, TTA, reel no. 2108, frame no. 0005, document no. 29653.

57 Jack Sidener, "Observations on Strategies of Planning in the Western Carolines," 21 April 1971, p. 4, TTA, reel no. 0909, frame no. 0207, document no. 15815.

58 Peace Corps Micronesia, "A New Peace Corps Volunteer Placement Proposal Prepared by the Peace Corps Office and Host Agency, 1977," TTA, reel no. 0350, frame no. 0061, document no. 5641. Similar job descriptions for Peace Corps programs projected for the period from 1978 to 1980 can be found in TTA, reel no. 0350, frame no. 0070, document no. 5644.

59 Jack Vaughn, "The Peace Corps and the Shrinking Man," speech given at Columbia College, New York, New York, 14 February 1968, TTA, reel no. 0500, frame no. 0000, document no. 08193.

60 Francis X. Hezel, S.J., "A Brief Economic History of Micronesia," pp. 61, 36. The figures on fisheries can also be gleaned from the U.S. Department of State's annual reports on the Trust Territory of the Pacific Islands.

61 Ronald Powell, "Progress Report: Inshore Fisheries," November 1971, p. 1, TTA, reel no. 0544, frame no. 0055, document no. 9587.

62 Ibid., pp. 7–8.

63 Ibid., p. 15.

64 Michael D. Lieber, *More Than a Living.* In my recounting of Lieber, I draw on my published review of the book that appeared in *The Contemporary Pacific* 7, 1 (Spring 1995): 206–209. For fishing techniques and fish species, see Lieber's appendix 1, pp. 213–218, and appendix 2, pp. 219–229, respectively; for fishing's significance, p. 8. For another ethnology of fishing that examines the tension between subsistence economies and development projects, see Margaret C. Rodman, *Deep Water.*

65 Lieber, *More Than a Living,* p. 6.

66 Ibid., p. 49.

67 For Lieber's history of twentieth-century changes in fishing and in the social organization of Kapingamarangi, pp. 141–154.

68 A history of developmental efforts in agriculture can be extrapolated from James T. Hiyane, *The Role of Agriculture in Economic Development*

(Saipan: Trust Territory Department of Resources and Development, Department of Agriculture, 1970), TTA, reel no. 2110, frame no. 0143, document no. 3677; and the *Report on Agriculture,* jointly produced by the UNDP and the UNFAO, 1976, TTA, reel no. 1293, frame no. 0178, document no. 1989. Helpful also are the U.S. Department of State's annual reports on the Trust Territory.

69 Hezel, "A Brief Economic History of Micronesia," p. 53.

70 U.S. Department of Agriculture, *Survey of Agriculture in the Trust Territory of the Pacific Islands,* 1975, TTA, reel no. 0210, frame no. 0163, document no. 3679.; quotation, appendix A, p. 2.

71 Hezel, *Strangers in Their Own Land,* p. 267.

72 U.S. Department of State, *27th Annual Report on the Trust Territory of the Pacific Islands* (1974), p. 145.

73 As an example of this line of analysis, see the general thematic thrust of the collected essays in Richard Salisbury and Elizabeth Tooker, eds., *Affluence and Cultural Survival.*

74 Glenn Petersen, "Some Pohnpei Strategies for Economic Survival," p. 185. Tim O'Meara describes the complex but ultimately culturally reaffirming play between development and custom; see his "The Cult of Custom Meets the Search for Money in Western Samoa," pp. 135–155. There is also his larger work, *Samoan Planters.*

75 Petersen, "Some Pohnpei Strategies for Economic Survival," p. 187. On the distinctive, decidedly anticapitalist features of Pohnpeian agriculture, consult Petersen's "Ponape Agriculture and Economy."

76 Petersen, "Some Pohnpei Strategies for Economic Survival," pp. 190–191.

77 Ibid., p. 191.

78 Ibid., p. 192.

79 Roland Force, *Historic and Prehistoric Sites: Preservation of Culture and Cultural Tourism in the Trust Territory of the Pacific Islands* (Paris: UNESCO, UNDP, 1977), p. 71, TTA, reel no. 0320, frame no. 0172, document no. 4697.

80 "Tourism and Planning: Seeking Agreement of a Joint Venture," prepared for the Micronesian Planning Conference, June 1973, TTA, reel no. 1523, frame no. 0165, document no. 25701.

81 Mike Ashman, "Micronesia Tastes Tourism," paper presented to the Regional Development Planning Seminar, East-West Center, Technology and Development Institute and Culture Learning Institute, Honolulu, Hawai'i, 20–31 May 1974, p. 1, TTA, reel no. 0472, frame no. 0163, document no. 0171.

82 U.S. Department of State, *28th Annual Report on the Trust Territory of the Pacific Islands* (1975), p. 32; also, Hezel, "A Brief Economic History of Micronesia," p. 44.

83 Ashman, "Micronesia Tastes Tourism," p. 3.

84 Ibid., p. 5, 7.

85 Joab to Johnston, 30 July 1971, TTA, reel no. 0021, frame no. 0169, document no. 0331. The two-page letter is part of a larger file labeled

"Correspondence Regarding the Plan for Building the Continental Hotel in Ponape District."

86 A copy of the resolution can be found in the "Correspondence" file, ibid.

87 Director of Economic Development (William C. Rhyne) to High Commissioner, 11 July 1968, TTA, reel no. 0222, frame no. 0140, document no. 3883. The two-page letter is part of a larger file titled "Correspondence, Resolutions, Acts, and Information Guides Relating to Tourism (Yap Tourist Commission) in the District of Yap Islands."

88 Copies of the petition against the Yap Nature Life Garden and the Charter of the Council of Map are contained in the file titled "Reports and Other Information on Yap Economic Development Plan, 1975–1976," TTA, reel no. 1296, frame no. 0054, document no. 21399. An account of a conversation with Bernard Gaayan, the president of the Chiefs in Council, is also contained in this file and provides added details on the "Battle of Map"; the recorder of the conversation is not identified.

89 This phrase comes from an addendum that explains the outcome of the "Battle of Map"; it can be found with multiple copies of the petition and the Council of Map charter in TTA, reel no. 1296, frame no. 0054, document 21399.

5: Congressing over Development

1 In October 1978, the Congress of Micronesia was reconstituted into the Interim Congress of the Federated States of Micronesia in anticipation of the dissolution of the Trust Territory government. This action followed the 12 July 1978 plebiscite in which the Marshall Islands and Palau rejected the FSM draft constitution and opted instead to form their own separate governments. Chuuk, Kosrae, Pohnpei, and Yap remained together as the Federated States of Micronesia.

2 Antonio Gramsci, *Selections from the Prison notebooks*, p. 12. There is also *The Open Marxism of Antonio Gramsci.* For a variety of scholarly analyses and interpretations of Gramsci's work, see Carl Boggs, *The Two Revolutions;* Joseph Femia, "Hegemony and Consciousness in the Thought of Antonio Gramsci"; Teodoros Kiros, *Toward the Construction of a Theory of Political Action;* Thomas Nemeth, *Gramsci's Philosophy;* and Luciano Pellicani, *Gramsci: An Alternative Communism?*

3 James C. Scott, *Weapons of the Weak*, p. 318.

4 For an interesting qualification on the concept of "dominant ideology" in Marxian analysis, see Nicholas Abercrombie, Stephen Hill, and Bryan S. Turner, *The Dominant Ideology Thesis*. The authors argue against the likes of Althusser, Gramsci, and Habermas that it is not ideology but the "dull compulsion of economic relations" that effects the subordination of one class to another. There is nothing dull, however, about the attempted compulsion of economic relations involved in the remaking of Micronesia and the variety of local responses to that remaking. It is the contest around the imposition of new systems of economy that makes colonial theaters intriguing sites of resistance.

5 This point is made convincingly by Scott in *Weapons of the Weak*, pp. 316–318.
6 See especially Guha's early volume, *Elementary Aspects of Peasant Insurgency in Colonial India*, pp. 333–334.
7 On the origins of the Congress of Micronesia and the many, intricate, and legal issues concerning its charter, see Meller, *The Congress of Micronesia*.
8 For an account of the earliest efforts at American-style representative government, see Hezel, *Strangers in Their Own Land*, pp. 276–282.
9 Ibid., pp. 279, 280.
10 Ibid., pp. 295, 305.
11 A copy of this secretarial order with three subsequent amendments issued between 10 June 1965 and 29 July 1967 can be found in Meller, *The Congress of Micronesia*, pp. 406–416.
12 V. S. Naipaul, *The Mimic-Men*. Homi Bhabha, "Of Mimicry and Man." Bhabha's article appeared first in *October* 28 (1984), pp. 125–133.
13 Pierre Bourdieu, *Outline of a Theory of Practice*, pp. 37–38. See also his *Distinction*.
14 For Norwood's speech, see Congress of Micronesia, *Journal of the House of Representatives*, Second Congress, third regular session, 10 July 1967–8 August 1967, Saipan, p. 21. (meetings on Saipan unless otherwise noted).
15 For the comments of Haruo, Mangefel, Nimwes, and Silk, see ibid., Third Congress, second regular session, 14 July 1969–27 August 1969, p. 221.
16 Ibid., Fourth Congress, first regular session, January–February 1971, p. 286.
17 Ibid., Fourth Congress, second regular session, January–February 1972, Koror, p. 124.
18 Ibid., Fifth Congress, first special session, July–August 1974, p. 119.
19 Ibid., Sixth Congress, first special session, June–July 1975, p. 114.
20 Congress of Micronesia, *Journal of the Senate*, Sixth Congress, second special session, July–August 1976, p. 20. Delayed by a variety of logistical and bureaucratic complications, the Five-Year Indicative Development Plan, originally required for submission to the Congress by 31 December 1975, was presented to the House and Senate at this session; see also *Journal of the House of Representatives*, Sixth Congress, second special session, p. 17.
21 Congress of Micronesia, *Journal of the House of Representatives*, Seventh Congress, first regular session, January–February 1977, p. 138.
22 Ibid., Fourth Congress, fourth special session, May 1971, p. 78.
23 Congress of Micronesia, *Journal of the Senate*, Fifth Congress, first regular session, January–March 1973, p. 293.
24 Ibid., Fourth Congress, second regular session, January–February 1972, Koror, p. 5.
25 Congress of Micronesia, *Journal of the House of Representatives*, Seventh Congress, second regular session, January–February 1978, Kolonia, pp. 303, 304.

26 Ibid., p. 508.

27 Congress of Micronesia, *Journal of the Senate*, Second Congress, fourth regular session, 10 July 1968–8 August 1968, pp. 443–446.

28 Ibid., Fourth Congress, first regular session, January–February 1971, pp. 99–102.

29 Congress of Micronesia, *Journal of the House of Representatives*, Third Congress, third regular session, July–August 1970, p. 189, 227, 233–234.

30 Ibid., Fourth Congress, second special session August–September 1972, Kolonia, p. 61.

31 Ibid., second regular session, January–February 1972, Koror, p. 60.

32 Congress of Micronesia, Joint Committee on Future Status, *Hearings of the Eastern Districts Subcommittee (Truk, Ponape and the Marshalls)* (Saipan: Trust Territory Government Press, November 1973), p. 121.

33 Congress of Micronesia, *Journal of the Senate*, Fifth Congress, first regular session, January–March 1973, pp. 95–96.

34 Congress of Micronesia, *Journal of the House of Representatives*, Fifth Congress, first regular session, January–February 1973, pp. 140 (quotation), 182, 360.

35 Ibid., Sixth Congress, first special session, June–July 1975, pp. 77–78.

36 Ibid., Third Congress, third regular session, July–August 1970, pp. 150–151.

37 Ibid., Fifth Congress, first special session, July–August 1974, pp. 98–99.

38 Ibid., Seventh Congress, first regular session, January–February 1977, p. 232. The passage of this law involved a series of events that included a veto by the high commissioner, an override of that veto by the Congress, and negotiations between representatives of both parties that led to an effective and satisfactory legislative compromise later in 1977.

39 Congress of Micronesia, *Journal of the Senate*, Second Congress, third regular session, 10 July–8 August 1967, p. 160.

40 Congress of Micronesia, *Journal of the House of Representatives*, Seventh Congress, first regular session, January–February 1977, p. 498.

41 Ibid., Fourth Congress, second regular session, January–February 1972, Koror, p. 270.

42 Congress of Micronesia, *Journal of the Senate*, Sixth Congress, First Regular Session, January–March 1975, p. 215.

43 Ibid., Sixth Congress, second regular session, 12 January–1 March 1976, pp. 212–213.

44 For more on the possibilities of counterethnographies, see Hanlon, "Magellan's Chroniclers?"

45 Congress of Micronesia, *Journal of the Senate*, Sixth Congress, second regular session, 12 January–1 March, 1976, pp. 224, 143.

46 Ibid., Sixth Congress, second special session, 19 July–2 August 1976, p. 36.

47 Ibid., p. 37.

48 Congress of Micronesia, *Journal of the House of Representatives*, Fourth Congress, second special session, August–September 1972, Kolonia, p. 24.

49 Congress of Micronesia, *Journal of the Senate,* Seventh Congress, first regular session, January–February 1977, p. 79.

50 Congress of Micronesia, *Journal of the House of Representatives,* Seventh Congress, second regular session, January–February 1978, Kolonia, p. 453.

51 Ibid., p. 509.

52 Congress of Micronesia, Joint Committee on Future Status, *Hearings of the Eastern Districts Subcommittee,* p. 82.

53 Hezel, *Strangers in Their Own Land,* p. 343.

54 The title and text of this section draw heavily from Marshall and Marshall, *Silent Voices Speak.*

55 See, for example, Strathern, *The Gender of the Gift;* Jocelyn Linnekin, *Sacred Queens and Women of Consequence;* Annette B. Weiner, *Women of Value, Men of Renown;* idem, *Inalienable Possessions: The Paradox of Keeping-While-Giving;* and Maria Lepowsky, *Fruit of the Motherland.*

56 DeVerne Smith, *Palauan Social Structure;* and Lynn B. Wilson, *Speaking to Power.*

57 Jane Margold and Donna Bellardo, "Matrilineal Heritage," p. 135.

58 Kihleng, "Women in Exchange," p. 381.

59 dé Ishtar, *Daughters of the Pacific,* p. 46.

60 On this point, see Jane Dibblin, *Day of Two Suns.*

61 Marshall and Marshall, *Silent Voices Speak,* p. 1.

62 Ibid., p. 10.

63 See Mac Marshall and Leslie B. Marshall, "Opening Pandora's Bottle"; and idem, "Holy and Unholy Spirits."

64 Marshall and Marshall, *Silent Voices Speak,* p. 35.

65 Ibid., p. 66.

66 Ibid., p. 38.

67 See, for example, Goodenough, *Property, Kin, and Community on Truk,* pp. 120–128; Gladwin and Sarason, *Truk: Man in Paradise,* pp. 118–130.

68 Marshall and Marshall, *Silent Voices Speak,* p. 55.

69 Ibid., p. 43.

70 Quoted ibid., p. 44.

71 U.S. Department of State, *Thirty-second Annual Report to the United Nations on the Administration of the Trust Territory of the Pacific Islands* (1979), pp. 42, 18.

72 Marshall and Marshall, *Silent Voices Speak,* p. 40. For facts and figures cited in the remaining pages of this chapter, see pp. 69–90 passim. Letter to the editor quoted p. 72; for "carrying out the wishes of the people," see p. 74.

6: Dependency? It Depends

1 Hezel, *Strangers in Their Own Land,* pp. 361, 357 (quotation).

2 David Nevin, *The American Touch in Micronesia,* p. 94.

3 P. F. Kluge, *The Edge of Paradise,* pp. 240–42.

4 John Connell, *Sovereignty and Survival,* pp. 2–3; see also his "Island Microstates." John Cameron, "Economic Development Options for the Federated States of Micronesia at Independence," pp. 66, 36.

5 See Andre Gunder Frank, *Capitalism and Underdevelopment in Latin America;* also his *Latin America: Underdevelopment or Revolution.* For a survey of classical dependency theory, see So, *Social Change and Development,* pp. 91–165.

6 Theotonio Dos Santos, "The Structure of Dependence"; also idem, "The Crisis of Development Theory and the Problem of Dependence in Latin America." Whereas Dos Santos examined the structure of dependence, Samir Amin explained the transition to peripheral capitalism; see his *Unequal Development.* On dependence, see also Paul Baran, *The Political Economy of Growth;* and Martin Landsberg, "Export-Led Industrialization in the Third World." In contrast as representative works of the school of analysis that sees a U.S. need to bind the islands through a long-term political arrangement, see Gale, *The Americanization of Micronesia;* Roff, *Overreaching in Paradise.* See also Dibblin, *Day of Two Suns;* Donald McHenry, *Micronesia, Trust Betrayed;* Harold Nufer, *Micronesia under American Rule;* Gary Smith, *Micronesia;* and Roy H. Smith and Michael C. Pugh, "Micronesian Trust Territories—Imperialism Continues?"

7 Students of anthropology and history in the Pacific will recognize the subtitle of this section as taken from the work of Marshall Sahlins, who writes of the primacy of economic values in American culture; see his *Culture and Practical Reason,* p. 6.

8 Esteva, "Development," p. 18.

9 Gudeman, *Economics as Culture,* p. 69.

10 Esteva, "Development," p. 19. Stephen Gudeman makes this same point in his *Economics as Culture;* see especially the chapter "Ricardo's Representations," pp. 48–70. Gudeman argues that, despite claims to the contrary, the economic laws derived by Ricardo and the classical economists were never universal truths, but rather the products of a particular cultural logic expressed through the process of modeling; they seemed to carry the force of truth for a time because of their explanatory powers. Gudeman adds that in this the West is no different from other cultures that seek to construct their own models of livelihood. Problems result, however, when an imbalance of power gives undue weight and influence to one culture's badly flawed, self-serving translation of another's economic rational and logic. In this century, those problems lie embodied in the word "development."

11 Christopher Herbert, *Culture and Anomie,* p. 77. Adam Smith, *An Inquiry into the Nature and Causes of the Wealth of Nations,* pp. 15–16. Malthus cited in *Culture and Anomie,* Herbert, p. 122.

12 E. P. Thompson, *The Making of the English Working Class,* p. 362.

13 Ibid., pp. 199, 202–03.

14 Escobar, *Encountering Development,* pp. 65–66. For an extended treatment of the forces and events of the twentieth century that led to greater governmental intervention in the economies of the West, see Karl Polanyi, *The Great Transformation.* Polanyi's work is cited extensively by both Arturo Escobar and Gustavo Esteva.

15 Oliver Zunz, *Making America Corporate, 1870–1920,* p. 1.

16 C. Wright Mills, *White Collar,* p. xv.

17 It is Zunz, in *Making America Corporate*, p. 2, who interprets Biff's speech as a protest against the dehumanization brought on by the rise of modern business culture in America.

18 Charles Beard, *The Idea of National Interest.*

19 Martin J. Sklar, *The United States as a Developing Country*, p. 16.

20 Ibid., p. 19.

21 Sahlins, *Culture and Practical Reason*, pp. 166–167.

22 I borrow the title for this section of the chapter from Dire Straits' 1985 song, "Money for Nothing and Your Chicks for Free." The song spoofs the popular conceptions of rich, indulged, pampered, talentless, long-haired rock musicians who get their money for nothing and their women for free. Assumptions about the nature of dependency in Micronesia, and the mindless "savage" consumerism said to accompany it, strike me as similar in that island peoples are said to get their "money for nothing and their frozen chickens for free."

23 These figures are gleaned from U.S. Department of State, *Annual Report to the United Nations on the Administration of the Trust Territory of the Pacific Islands* (1948–1980). For a concise but effective history of economic development in American Micronesia, see Hezel, "A Brief Economic History of Micronesia," pp. 11–62.

24 Hezel, "A Brief Economic History of Micronesia," pp. 35, 37.

25 Ibid., pp. 37–41.

26 Doris Kearns, *Lyndon Johnson and the American Dream*, p. 210.

27 Ibid., pp. 210–11. A full text of Johnson's speech can be found in Marvin E. Gettleman and David Mermelstein, eds., *The Great Society Reader*, pp. 15–19.

28 Hezel, "A Brief Economic History of Micronesia," p. 41.

29 U.S. Department of the Interior, *Federal Programs Available to the Territories*, Report to Congress, 95-134, Title IV, section 401 (Washington, D.C.: U.S. Government Printing Office, 1978), 1:16–17. A copy of this report can be found in TTA, reel no. 794, frame no. 0000, document no. 13226.

30 Ibid., p. 1.

31 These figures come from the Micronesian Seminar, *U.S. Federal Programs in Micronesia: A Report on a Conference Sponsored by the Micronesian Seminar*, Kolonia, 12–14 March 1979, p. 5. A copy of this report can be found in TTA, reel no. 1353, frame no. 0068, document no. 21514.

32 Ibid., pp. 6–8.

33 A summary of CETA programs in the Trust Territory can be found in U.S. Department of Labor, *Report of Audit, Trust Territory of the Pacific Islands, CETA Grants, October 1, 1977 to March 31, 1979*. A copy of this report is in TTA, reel no. 3737, frame no. 0085, document no. 32789.

34 Office of Economic Opportunity (OEO), "The Mission of the Community Action Agency," Washington, D.C., 16 November 1970. A copy of this statement of purpose, authored by Donald Rumsfeld, then director of the OEO, is in TTA, reel no. 3784, frame no. 0000, document no. 33789.

35 William C. Rhyne, "Memorandum for Record," 4 December 1968, TTA, reel no. 3784, frame no. 0000, document no. 33789. Rhyne was director

of economic development for the Trust Territory government at the time of this memorandum.

36 Micronesian Seminar, *U.S. Federal Programs in Micronesia,* p. 6.

37 Juan Lizama and William Jackson, "Joint Report on Federal Regional Hearings on Aging, Administration on Aging, followed by Administration on Aging Workshop for Program Participants," 11 August 1971, p. 4, TTA, reel no. 1393, frame no. 0043, document no. 22248. At the time, Lizama was assistant administrator of the Trust Territory Department of Aging, while Jackson served as the territory's grant administrator.

38 Office of the Budget, Federated States of Micronesia, *U.S. Federal Programs Under the Compact of Free Association,* pp. 21, 117–121.

39 Hezel, "A Brief Economic History of Micronesia," pp. 40, 31, 36.

40 Cameron, "Economic Development Options," p. 38, shows figures that put total food, beverage, and tobacco imports for the islands that became the Federated States of Micronesia (Chuuk, Kosrae, Pohnpei, and Yap) at 43 percent and 48 percent of total imports for the years 1977 and 1978, respectively.

41 Hezel, *Strangers in Their Own Land,* p. 321.

42 U.S. Department of State, *25th Annual Report on the Trust Territory of the Pacific Islands* (1972), pp. 296–297.

43 Quoted in Hezel, *Strangers in Their Own Land,* p. 324.

44 Ibid., p. 322.

45 Fox Butterfield, "The Improbable Welfare State."

46 Ibid.

47 *Report of the Food Service Officer, Trust Territory of the Pacific Islands and Commonwealth of the Northern Mariana Islands, Pursuant to Section 20 of Public Law 94-105,* submitted to the Program Manager, Food and Nutrition Service, United States Department of Agriculture, circa 1977, p. 1, TTA, reel no. 0512, frame no. 0126, document no. 8701.

48 Trust Territory of the Pacific Islands, Food Service Office, "State Plan of Nutrition Operations under the Provisions of the National School Lunch Act and the Child Nutrition Act of 1966 as Amended," 1979, p. 1, TTA, reel no. 0512, frame no. 0128, document no. 8702.

49 These statistics are contained in a letter from Ruth G. Van Cleve, director of the U.S. Department of the Interior's Office of Territorial Affairs, to Trust Territory High Commissioner Adrian P. Winkel, 25 October 1978, in TTA, reel no. 0071, frame no. 0161, document no. 1137.

50 Ibid., p. 2.

51 Bossy's remarks are recorded in a cable of 13 November 1978 from the District Administrator on Pohnpei to the High Commissioner; a copy of that cable an be found in TTA, reel no. 0071, frame no. 0161, document no. 1137; see also *Journal of the Senate, Interim Congress of the Federated States of Micronesia, October 1978–February, 1979,* Kolonia, 11th day, 10 November 1978, pp. 46–47.

52 Innocenti to Moses, 8 November 1978, TTA, reel no. 0071, frame no. 0161, document no. 1137.

53 Apis' remarks are contained in a cabled press release from the Congress

of Micronesia, meeting on Pohnpei, to the High Commissioner in Saipan. The cable is dated 10 November 1978; a copy of it can be found in TTA, reel no. 0071, frame no. 0161, document no. 1137. The congressman's remarks are also recorded in the *Journal of the House of Representatives, Interim Congress of the Federated States of Micronesia, October 1978–February 1979*, Kolonia, 9th day, 10 November 1978, pp. 81–82.

54 *Journal of the Senate of the Congress of Micronesia, Seventh Congress, second special session, August to October 1978*, 27th Day, 28 October 1978, pp. 100–02.

55 Akapito to Moses, 26 November 1978, TTA, reel no. 0071, frame no. 0161, document no. 1137. In his letter, Akapito made note of the strong feelings of many in Chuuk that opposition to the Needy Family Feeding Assistance Program was ultimately motivated by strong anti-Chuukese sentiment in other islands and within certain government offices.

56 Bussell's remarks appeared in an article by Frederick H. Marks entitled "U.S. Food for Micronesia Debatable," *Honolulu Star Bulletin*, 22 October 1978. Bussell's comments drew the ire of many Micronesian congressmen and inspired a joint resolution (HJR 7-143) by the Congress of Micronesia requesting that he be "promoted" to some new position outside the Trust Territory.

57 Craley to Norwood, 11 February 1980, TTA, reel no. 1532, frame no. 0215, document no. 25573.

58 Moses to Mangefel, 2 November 1978, TTA, reel no. 0071, frame no. 0161, document no. 1137; a copy of the petition is in TTA, reel no. 0071, frame no. 0161, document no. 1137.

59 Moses to Akapito, 30 June 1970, TTA, reel no. 0071, frame no. 0161, document no. 1137; a copy of Salii's review is in TTA, reel no. 0071, frame no. 0161, document no. 1137.

60 *National Enquirer*, 21 May 1978; a copy of the brief article by Paul Corkery can also be found in TTA, reel no. 1494, frame no. 0070, document no. 25236.

61 U.S. Government Comptroller for Guam and the Trust Territory of the Pacific Islands, *Audit Report on the Federal Grants Management of the Trust Territory of the Pacific Islands*, Report no. RTT79-1, December 1978, pp. 5–8, TTA, reel no. 0213, frame no. 0000, document no. 3716.

62 See, for example, Van Cleve to Winkel, 25 October 1978; Van Cleve to Winkel, 2 November 1978; Van Cleve to Winkel, 9 November 1979; Van Cleve to Snyder, 15 November 1978; and Winkel to Straus, 31 October 1978. Copies of all letters are in TTA, reel no. 0071, frame no. 0161, document no. 1137.

63 Office of the Budget, Federated States of Micronesia, *U.S. Federal Programs under the Compact of Free Association*, p. 21.

64 Urban Systems Research and Engineering, *Grant Consolidation for the U.S. Territories* (Cambridge, Mass.: September 1981), pp. i–xii, TTA, reel no. 0775, frame no. 0156, document no. 13350.

65 See Ambassador Peter R. Rosenblatt's concerns over the detrimental effects of some federal programs in Micronesia in his letter to High

Commissioner Winkel, 11 December 1978, TTA, reel no. 0071, frame no. 0172, document no. 1138. Rosenblatt was the head of the Department of State's Office of Micronesian Negotiations during the administration of President Jimmy Carter.

66 Micronesian Seminar, *U.S. Federal Programs in Micronesia*, pp. 4, 27.

67 Ibid., pp. 12, 15, 16, 26. The basis for Borthwick's presentation was a paper entitled "Assessing the Impacts of Technological Projects and Evaluating Social Programs in Micronesia"; a copy can be found in TTA, reel no. 1353, frame no. 0068, document no. 21514.

68 A summary of Haruo's comments are contained in a cable from the District Administrator on Pohnpei to the High Commissioner on Saipan dated 10 November 1978 and found in TTA, reel no. 0071, frame no. 0161, document no. 1137; see also *Interim Congress, Federated States of Micronesia, October 1978–February 1979, Kolonia, 9th day, 10 November 1978*, pp. 85–86.

69 Thomas, *Entangled Objects*, esp. chap. 3. James G. Peoples, *Island in Trust*, p. 185. Glenn Petersen, "Brilliant Island, Swaying in Soft Motion," p. 23. DeVerne Smith, *Palauan Social Structure*, p. 313.

70 Office of the Governor, Truk State, FSM, *Sudden Impact: Social and Economic Consequences of U.S. Federal Program Withdrawal, Truk, Federated States of Micronesia* (1985), pp. 1–2, TTA, reel no. 3851, frame no. 0161, document no. 35725.

71 Ibid., p. 9.

72 Walter Bagehot, *Physics and Politics*, p. 468.

73 Maurice Godelier, "Infrastructures, Societies and History." Inga Clendinnen, *Ambivalent Conquests*, p. 161. Raymond Williams, *Culture and Society, 1780–1950*, p. 376.

7: Dumping on Ebeye

1 The published histories of American nuclear testing in the Marshalls and its effects include Dibblin, *Day of Two Suns;* Stewart Firth, *Nuclear Playground;* Robert C. Kiste, *Kili Island;* idem, *The Bikinians;* Giff Johnson, *Collision Course at Kwajalein;* and Jonathan M. Weisgall, *Operation Crossroads.* For a consideration of the sexist politics that surround nuclear testing, militarism, and tourism in the Marshalls and the larger Pacific, see Teaiwa, "bikinis and other s/pacific n/oceans."

2 Dibblin, *Day of Two Suns*, p. 5.

3 Ivan Brady and Greg Dening, "History's Politics," p. 13.

4 Robert D. Bullard, *Dumping in Dixie*, p. xiv.

5 Nicholas B. Dirks, ed., *Colonialism and Culture*, p. 3.

6 Though all of the Marshall Islands had been claimed by Germany in 1885, the forces of German colonialism did not directly or extensively affect daily life in the Kwajalein Atoll complex.

7 Said, *Culture and Imperialism*, p. 8. Said makes this point with special reference to the United States and its denial of the imperialism that is a large part of American history.

8 An effective summary of developments on Ebeye from 1944 through

1966 can be found in Francis B. Mahoney, "The Ebeye Problem—Background, Issues and Recommendations," 1 August 1966, TTA, reel no. 0610, frame no. 0036, document no. 10892. For historical summary, see also "The Ebeye Housing Problem," circa 1966, TTA, reel no. 0863, frame no. 0089, document no. 14374.

9 Both statements are cited in Hezel, *Strangers in Their Own Land*, p. 274.

10 For an early description of conditions on Ebeye, see Jack Tobin, "Ebeye Village." A copy of this report can also be found in TTA, reel no. 0282, frame no. 0172, document no. 4221.

11 On the relocation of the Roi-Namur people, see Johnson, *Collision Course at Kwajalein*, p. 19. Johnson discusses the 1960 terms of compensation for the U.S. Navy's use of Roi-Namur and the controversy surrounding it on p. 29. For Lib, see "Record of a Conference Held on 18 November 1960 in the Office of Captain Gordon"; High Commissioner to Acting District Administrator, Marshalls, 29 November, 1960; and High Commissioner to Assistant District Administrator, Marshalls, Kwajalein, "Meeting with Libese," 2 August 1965. All of these materials can be found in TTA, reel no. 0511, frame no. 0000, document no. 8639.

12 Government documentation on the relocation of the Mid-Corridor peoples is extensive. See, for example, "Report of Joint Study Group: Impact of Nike-Zeus and Nike-X Planning on Marshallese Population on Kwajalein Atoll," 6 December 1963, TTA, reel no. 0511, frame no. 0008, document no. 8686; "Conference on Relocation of Marshallese and Ebeye Island Development Plan," 25 June 1964, TTA, reel no. 0511, frame no. 0051, document no. 8640; Attorney General to High Commissioner, "Conference at Honolulu Re Ebeye," 4 May 1964, TTA, reel no. 0486, frame no. 0188, document no. 8271; District Administrator, Marshalls, to High Commissioner, "Mid-Atoll Relocation—Ebeye," 28 April 1965, TTA, reel no. 0511, frame no. 0000, document no. 8639; Hicom Representative to High Commissioner, "Mid-Corridor Problem," 31 March 1967, TTA, reel no. 0511, frame no. 0051, document no. 8640; and William V. Vitarelli, "Outline of Procedures That Were Used to Investigate the Mid-Corridor Problem and Suggested Approach for the Final Negotiations in Dealing with All Present Claimants," 31 August 1967, TTA, reel no. 5011, frame no. 0051, document no. 8640.

13 Hezel, *Strangers in Their Own Land*, p. 325.

14 Johnson, *Collision Course at Kwajalein*, p. 19.

15 Distad Representative, Ebeye, to High Commissioner, "Political Development in Ebeye," 23 June 1967, TTA, reel no. 0142, frame no. 0097, document no. 2317. The observation of Ebeye as a slum can be found in Hawaii Architects and Engineers, *Ebeye and Carlson Islands, Marshall Islands District*. A copy of this development plan, prepared for the United States Army and the Trust Territory government, can be found in TTA, reel no. 0108, frame no. 0142, document no. 1749. For "affluent paupers," see P. F. Kluge, "Micronesia's Unloved Islands: Ebeye," p. 32. William V. Vitarelli, "What Is Ebeye?" 22 August 1967, p. 3, in TTA, reel no. 0142, frame no. 0097, document no. 2317.

16 The opinion of the UN mission is cited in the report "The Ebeye Housing Problem," n.d., TTA, reel no. 0863, frame no. 0089, document no. 14374. The "disaster waiting to happen" is quoted in John Connell, *Marshall Islands,* p. 24. For the polio epidemic, see Greg Dever, *Ebeye, Marshall Islands,* pp. 10–11. For the 1966 report, see Mahoney, "The Ebeye Problem, TTA, reel no. 0610, frame no. 0036, document no. 10892.

17 Mahoney, "The Ebeye Problem"; see also High Commissioner to All Assistant Commissioners, Department Heads, and District Administrators, "Ebeye Improvement Program," 14 April 1966, TTA, reel no. 0238, frame no. 0119, document no. 4026.

18 "Ebeye Improvement Program Moves Ahead," 30 November 1966, Press Release no. 200-66, in TTA, reel no. 0142, frame no. 0097, document no. 2317.

19 Hawaii Architects and Engineers, *Ebeye and Carlson Islands, Marshall Islands District,* TTA, reel no. 0108, frame no. 0142, document no. 1749.

20 Mahoney, "The Ebeye Problem," p. 4, TTA, reel no. 0610, frame no. 0036, document no. 10892.

21 Ibid.

22 Ibid., p. 5; see also Johnson, *Collision Course on Kwajalein,* p. 27.

23 Cited in Johnson, *Collision Course on Kwajalein,* p. 21.

24 Vitarelli, "What Is Ebeye?" p. 3.

25 Paul Jacobs, "The Natives Are Forbidden to Shop on a U.S.-Administered Pacific Isle."

26 Dever, *Ebeye, Marshall Islands,* p. 8.

27 Ray Yuen, "Litter, Overcrowding, Illness."

28 Quotation in Dever, *Ebeye, Marshall Islands,* p. 1.

29 Recounted in Johnson, *Collision Course on Kwajalein,* p. 25.

30 Dever, Ebeye, Marshall Islands, pp. 9, 1.

31 Jacobs, "Forbidden to Shop."

32 Dever, *Ebeye, Marshall Islands,* pp. 10–11.

33 Ibid., p. 2.

34 For a sense of life on the Kwajalein Missile Range, see the United States Department of the Army's *A Visitor's Guide to Kwajalein* (1982). A copy of this guide can be found in TTA, reel no. 0637, frame no. 0048, document no. 11673.

35 Giff Johnson, "Ebeye and Kwajalein."

36 Jacobs, "Forbidden to Shop."

37 Ibid.

38 Johnson, *Collision Course on Kwajalein,* pp. 23, 24.

39 Jacobs, "The Natives Are Forbidden to Shop."

40 Quoted in Firth, *Nuclear Playground,* p. 66.

41 Giff Johnson, "Ebeye: Apartheid, U.S. Style."

42 On this point, see Thomas, *Colonialism's Culture,* p. 2.

43 A summary on the initial phase of Operation Exodus can be found in Hicom-Distad Rep, Ebeye, to High Commissioner, "First Report on Accomplishments of Operation Exodus," 20 July 1967, TTA, reel no. 0142, frame no. 0097, document no. 2317.

44 High Commissioner to Director of the Office of Territorial Affairs, U.S. Department of the Interior, "Issue Analysis: Redevelopment of Ebeye," 4 September 1979, TTA, reel no. 0886, frame no. 0074, document no. 14671. E. V. Bowden to Mr. Norwood, High Commissioner, "Summary of Findings and Recommendations Regarding Economic Problems of Ebeye," 17 January 1967, TTA, reel no. 0863, frame no. 0089, document no. 14374.

45 Bowden to Norwood, "Summary of Findings," p. 2.

46 Emmett Rice, "Proposed Actions to Alleviate Ebeye Problems," 1 March 1977, TTA, reel no. 0227, frame no. 0192, document number not given.

47 *U.S. Army Report of Fact-Finding Team on Kwajalein-Ebeye* (1977), TTA, reel no. 0323, frame no. 0113, document no. 4719; quotation on p. 1.

48 Johnson, *Collision Course on Kwajalein*, p. 24.

49 I am extrapolating a bit from Nicholas Thomas' notion of "savage commerce," a notion I have dealt with more literally elsewhere in this manuscript; see his *Entangled Objects*, p. 11.

50 A copy of this editorial can be found in TTA, reel no. 0334, frame no. 0041, document no. 5228.

51 William V. Vitarelli, "Ebeye in Transition: A Community Development Study," n. d., p. 8, TTA, reel no. 0526, frame no. 0085, document no. 9106.

52 "Attachment to Memorandum of 2/25/77," TTA, reel no. 0334, frame no. 0053, document no. 5230.

53 District Administrator, Marshalls, "Ebeye-Kwajalein Report," 19 July 1972, TTA, reel no. 1568, frame no. 0155, document no. 26814. The American anthropologist Jack Tobin is the actual author of this report released through the district administrator's office.

54 Quoted in Johnson, *Collision Course on Kwajalein*, p. 20.

55 Peter R. Rosenblatt, memorandum to Ruth Van Cleve, 2 November 1978, TTA, reel no. 0886, frame no. 0074, document no. 14671; quotation on p. 2.

56 Quoted in Johnson, *Collision Course on Kwajalein*, p. 23.

57 U.S. House of Representatives, "Current Problems in the Marshalls," pp. 3–6. Part of Balos' testimony is also reproduced in Dever, *Ebeye, Marshall Islands*, p. v–vi. quotation on p. vi.

58 Assistant District Administrator, Marshalls, Kwajalein, to High Commissioner, "Meeting with Libese," 2 August 1965, TTA, reel no. 0511, frame no. 0000, document no. 8639.

59 District Administrator, Marshalls, to High Commissioner, "Mid-Atoll Relocation—Ebeye," 26 April 1965, TTA, reel no. 0511, frame no. 0000, document no. 8639.

60 Special Committee of the Congress of Micronesia on the Mid-Corridor Problem to the Honorable Betwel Henry, Speaker of the House, 26 August 1969, TTA, reel no. 0511, frame no. 0000, document no. 8639. The report is in the form of a five-page letter.

61 District Attorney, Marshalls, to District Administrator, Marshalls, "Minutes of the First Meeting, Ebeye Ad Hoc Committee," 7 January 1976, TTA, reel no. 0334, frame no. 0053, document no. 5220.

62 Copies of both the Nitijela's resolution and Emergency District Order no. 76-1 can be found in TTA, reel no. 0323, frame no. 0113, document no. 4719.

63 Guha, *Elementary Aspects of Peasant Insurgency in Colonial India,* pp. 333–334. A copy of Dribo's suit and the Trust Territory government's earlier petition for the condemnation of Dribo's land through a declaration of eminent domain can be found in TTA, reel no. 0511, frame no. 0000, document no. 8639.

64 This summary of protest and of struggle between the Kwajalein landowners and the governments of the Marshalls and the United States draws heavily from Johnson, *Collision Course on Kwajalein,* pp. 27–38.

65 Cited in Firth, *Nuclear Playground,* p. 67.

66 Cited in Johnson, *Collision Course on Kwajalein,* p. 33.

67 Dribo makes this statement in Adam Horowitz' film *Home on the Range.* A copy of the 55-minute film can be found in the Wong Audio-Visual Center, Sinclair Library, University of Hawai'i at Manoa, Honolulu, Hawai'i.

68 Arnold H. Leibowitz, *Defining Status,* pp. 611, 653.

69 Kabua's statement is made before the camera in Horowitz, *Home on the Range.*

70 I play in this section on the title of David Lowenthal's *The Past Is a Foreign Country,* p. XVI. Citing L. P. Hartley, who initially coined the phrase, Lowenthal underscores the chasm between contemporary popular presumptions and uses of the past and the quite different reality that was the past. The Republic of the Marshall Islands' willingness to consider as a legitimate source of national income the dumping of other nations' nuclear waste material within its territory would seem to make the future of the islands a foreign country against the stark nuclear realities of the past and present.

71 Republic of the Marshall Islands, *Marshall Islands Guidebook,* p. 43, 44.

72 Kluge, *The Edge of Paradise,* p. 49.

73 David North, "Cashing in on Nuclear Waste." An even more recent proposal to build a nuclear waste storage facility on the atoll of Erikub is reported by David Waite, "Marshalls May Allow Nuclear Site," *Honolulu Advertiser,* 31 May 1997.

74 Dibblin, *Day of Two Suns,* pp. 123 and 83, respectively.

75 Carucci, "The Source of the Force in Marshallese Cosmology," pp. 91–92.

76 Ibid., p. 92.

8: The End of History for the Edge of Paradise?

1 Firth, *Nuclear Playground,* p. 49.

2 Francis Fukuyama, *The End of History and the Last Man.* For an encapsulation of Fukuyama's argument, see pp. XI–XXIII. Among the critical assessments of Fukuyama's work are Michael S. Roth, "Review of The End of History and the Last Man by Francis Fukuyama," Alan Ryan, "Professor Hegel Goes to Washington."

3 Fukuyama, *The End of History*, pp. 55–57 for "History." An exposition of Fukuyama's very limited and particular notion of culture can be found in pp. 211–222.

4 For a summary of the Micronesian status negotiations, see Hezel, *Strangers in Their Own Land*, pp. 331–344. Quotation in McHenry, *Micronesia: Trust Betrayed*, p. 103.

5 Quoted in Hezel, *Strangers in Their Own Land*, p. 333.

6 For a summary of the Northern Marianas movement toward commonwealth status with the United States, see ibid., pp. 335–337.

7 Works on this prolonged, tortuous period for Palau include Robert C. Aldridge and Ched Myers, *Resisting the Serpent;* Roff, *Overreaching in Paradise;* Sue Rabbitt Roff and Roger Clark, *The Problem of Palau;* and Donald R. Shuster, "Palau's Constitutional Tangle."

8 The United Nations Security Council officially dissolved the trusteeship agreement for what had become the Commonwealth of the Northern Mariana Islands, the Federated States of Micronesia, and the Republic of the Marshall Islands in December 1990. In 1991, the headquarters for the Trust Territory government moved from Saipan to Koror, Palau.

9 Fukuyama, *The End of History*, p. 71.

10 A recent academic statement of this position can be found in Edward J. Michal, "Protected States." Michal, using the nineteenth-century notion of protected states in consensual security agreements with larger metropolitan nations, argues that the Compact of Free Association recognizes both the sovereignty and independence of the FSM and the Marshalls. Michal takes issue with Stewart Firth's belief that the compact undermines rather than recognizes the national integrity of the two Micronesian governments. See Firth, "Sovereignty and Independence in the Contemporary Pacific."

11 For a thorough, detailed, and critical assessment of the terms of the Compact of Free Association and what they mean for the governments of Micronesia, see Henry J. Schwalbenberg, S.J., *Memos on the Draft Compact of Free Association.* The quoted phrase is taken from testimony found in U.S. House of Representatives, "Approving the Compact of Free Association with the Marshall Islands and the Federated States of Micronesia and Approving Conditionally the Compact of Free Association with Palau," p. 4.

12 The compact exists as *Public Law 99-239: Compact of Free Association Act of 1985 between the United States and the Governments of the Federated States of Micronesia and the Republic of the Marshall Islands;* it was signed into law on 14 January 1986. The compact between the United States and the Government of Palau was approved separately by the United States Congress and was signed into law on 14 November 1986 as Public Law 99-658. Because of major differences between the constitution of Palau and the security provisions of the compact, actual implementation was delayed for reasons cited in the text. On 30 November 1987, the United States Congress passed a joint resolution authorizing the implementation of Public Law 99-658 at a mutually agreeable time between

the governments of Palau and the United States and after the differences between the compact and Palau's constitution had been reconciled. That time proved to be 1 November 1994.

13 These figures are estimates drawn from the dollar amounts specified in the compact and approved as Public Law 99-239. An earlier, somewhat more modest set of compact expenditure projections can be found in the 1 July 1985 report of the House's Committee on Foreign Affairs entitled "Approving the Compact of Free Association with the Marshall Islands and the Federated States of Micronesia and Approving Conditionally the Compact of Free Association with Palau," pp. 11–14.

14 For a summation of these objections by other U.S. territories, see the statement of Roger Mintz, deputy assistant secretary for tax policy with the United States Department of the Treasury, in U.S. Senate, *Hearing Before the Committee on Finance*, pp. 1–2.

15 U.S. House of Representatives, "Approving the Compact of Free Association with the Marshall Islands and the Federated States of Micronesia and Approving Conditionally the Compact of Free Association with Palau," p. 5.

16 Leibowitz, *Defining Status*, p. 643; see also Smith, *Micronesia: Decolonisation*, p. 10.

17 Quoted in U.S. House of Representatives, "The Proposed Compact of Free Association: The Federated States of Micronesia," p. 155.

18 Quoted ibid., p. 19.

19 U.S. House of Representatives, "On The Proposed Compact of Free Association: The Marshall Islands," p. 15.

20 Salii's remark is recorded in Kluge, *The Edge of Paradise*, p. 32. Andohn's assessment is cited in David L. Hanlon and William Eperiam, "The Federated States of Micronesia," p. 103.

21 Quoted in U.S. House of Representatives, "On the Proposed Compact of Free Association: The Marshall Islands," p. 183.

22 Cited in U.S. Senate, "On S. J. 286—A Resolution to Approve the Compact of Free Association and for Other Purposes," p. 185.

23 Roberts' and Clark's remarks can be heard in the film *Strategic Trust: The Making of a Nuclear-Free Pacific*. A copy of this film is in the Sinclair Library's Wong Audio-Visual Center on the campus of the University of Hawai'i at Manoa. Leibowitz, *Defining Status*, p. 596.

24 Roberts in the film *Strategic Trust*.

25 Catherine Lutz, "The Compact of Free Association, Micronesian Non-Independence, and U.S. Policy," p. 26.

26 Henry Schwalbenberg, S.J., *Memos on the Draft Compact of Free Association*, no. 7: "American Military Needs in Micronesia: Valid Perceptions or Unnecessary Contingencies?" p. 25. See also memo no. 9, "The FSM and Denial."

27 Henry J. Schwalbenberg, S.J., "Compact of Free Association.

28 A copy of Buckley's letter can be found in U.S. House of Representatives, "Approving the Compact of Free Association between the United States, the Marshall Islands, and the Federated States of Micronesia," pp. 23–34.

29 U.S. House of Representatives, "The Impact of the Proposed Compact of Free Association on Economic Development in Micronesia," pp. 111–112, 118.

30 Personal communication from Mr. Dan Perin, formerly national planner for the Federated States of Micronesia, Kolonia, Pohnpei, 4 June 1991.

31 I am not aware of any provisions within the compact or its enabling legislation, PL 99-658, that mandate or authorize the conduct of audits in Palau by any agency of the United States government.

32 Speaking before the House Committee on Interior and Insular Affairs' Subcommittee on Public Lands and National Parks on 21 May 1984, Ms. Patricia Krause of the U.S. General Accounting Office acknowledged the stringency of the planning and auditing requirements in the compact but added that their effectiveness would depend on the cooperation of the American and Micronesian governments to monitor the appropriate expenditure of compact monies. This statement aside, the potential for American intervention and control in the process of government in Micronesia remains formidable.

33 Kluge, *The Edge of Paradise,* pp. 3, 5. For two very different reactions to Kluge's book, see Robert C. Kiste's review in *The Contemporary Pacific* and that of Glenn Petersen in *Isla.* My own assessment is close to Petersen's.

34 Kluge, *The Edge of Paradise,* p. 16.

35 For an official report on alleged instances of corruption, see U.S. General Accounting Office, *U.S. Trust Territory: Issues Associated with Palau's Transition to Self-Government.* Quotations from Kluge, *The Edge of Paradise,* pp. 44, 45.

36 Kluge, *The Edge of Paradise,* p. 174.

37 Ibid., p. 189.

38 Ibid., p. 87.

39 Ibid., p. 242.

40 On this point, see, for example, David Ludden, "India's Development Regime."

41 Hezel, *Strangers in Their Own Land,* p. 366.

42 I allude here to John H. Bodley's liberal but dated critique of anthropology's relationship with tribal peoples, *Victims of Progress;* see also the highly pessimistic assessment of Pacific Islands' futures offered in Rodney V. Cole, ed., *Pacific 2010.*

43 Smith, *Micronesia: Decolonisation,* p. 77, describes the United States as trying to use the Republic of the Marshalls government as a "political buffer to shield itself from the direct repercussions" of its nuclear and military activities in the island group. The Kwajalein landowners' disputes with Majuro can be seen then as a reflection of this situation.

44 On this point, see Glenn Petersen, "The Federated States of Micronesia's 1990 Constitutional Convention."

45 James Clifford, *The Predicament of Culture,* p. 17.

Bibliography

Abercrombie, Nicholas, Stephen Hill, and Bryan S. Turner. *The Dominant Ideology Thesis.* London: George Allen and Unwin, 1980.

Addo, Herb. "Beyond Eurocentricity: Transformation and Transformational Responsibility." In *Development as Social Transformation: Reflections on the Global Problematique,* edited by Herb Addo et al., 12–27. Boulder, Colo.: Westview Press in Association with the United Nations University, 1985.

Aldridge, Robert C., and Ched Myers. *Resisting the Serpent: Palau's Struggle for Self-Determination.* Baltimore: Fortkamp, 1990.

Alexander, William J. *Ebeye: Report and Recommendations to the District Administrator.* Honolulu: Micronesian Support Committee, 1977.

———. "Wage Labor, Urbanization, and Cultural Change in the Marshall Islands." Ph.D. dissertation. New School for Social Research, 1978.

Alkire, William. *An Introduction to the Peoples and Cultures of Micronesia.* Second edition. Menlo Park, Calif.: Cummings, 1977.

———. *Coral Islanders.* Arlington Heights, Ill.: AHM, 1978.

Amin, Samir. *Unequal Developments: An Essay in the Social Transformation of Peripheral Capitalism.* New York: Monthly Review Press, 1971.

Appadurai, Arjun, ed. *The Social Life of Things: Commodities in Cultural Perspective.* New York: Cambridge University Press, 1986.

Aseniero, George. "A Reflection on Developmentalism: From Development to Transformation." In *Development as Social Transformation: Reflections on the Global Problematique,* edited by Herb Addo et al., pp 48–85. Boulder, Colo.: Westview Press in Association with the United Nations University, 1985.

Bagehot, Walter. *Physics and Politics.* In vol. 4 of *The Works of Walter Bagehot,* edited by Forrest Morgan. Hartford, Conn.: Travelers Insurance, 1889.

Bailey, Gilbert. "Freedom on Kwajalein." *Asia* 44 (October 1944): 437–440.

Baran, Paul. *The Political Economy of Growth.* New York: Monthly Review Press, 1957.

Barnett, Homer G. *Anthropology and Administration.* Evanston, Ill.: Row, Peterson, 1956.

———. *Being a Palauan.* New York: Henry Holt, 1960.

Beard, Charles A. *The Idea of National Interest.* New York: Macmillan, 1934.

———. *An Economic Interpretation of the Constitution of the United States.* New York: Macmillan, 1935.

Behar, Moises. "Nutrition: A Social Problem." *Micronesian Reporter* 24, 2 (1976): 15–19.

Bérubé, Michael. "Pop Goes the Academy: Cult Studs Fight the Power." In "Cult Studs," *VLS: The Village Voice Literary Supplement,* no. 104 (April 1992).

Bhabha, Homi K. "Sly Civility." *October,* no. 34 (Fall 1985): 71–80.

———. ed. *Nation and Narration.* New York: Routledge, 1990.

———. "Of Mimicry and Man: The Ambivalence of Colonial Discourse." In *October: The First Decade,* edited by Annette Michelsen, Rosalind Krauss, Douglas Crimp, and Joan Copjec, 318–322. Cambridge, Mass.: MIT Press, 1987.

———. "The Other Question: Difference, Discrimination and the Discourse of Colonialism." In *Out There: Marginalization and Contemporary Culture,* edited by Russell Ferguson et al., 71–87. New York: New Museum of Contemporary Art, 1990.

———. *The Location of Culture.* New York: Routledge, 1994.

Biersack, Aletta, ed. *Clio in Oceania: Toward a Historical Anthropology.* Washington, D.C.: Smithsonian Institution Press, 1991.

Blomstrom, Magnus, and Bjorn Hettne, eds. *Development Theory in Transition: The Dependency Debate and Beyond: Third World Responses.* London: Zed Books, 1984.

Bodley, John H. *Victims of Progress.* Second edition. Menlo Park, Calif.: Benjamin/Cummings, 1982.

Boggs, Carl. *The Two Revolutions: Antonio Gramsci and the Dilemmas of Western Marxism.* Boston: South End Press, 1984.

Boserup, Ester. *Women's Role in Economic Development.* New York: St. Martin's Press, 1970.

Bourdieu, Pierre. *Outline of a Theory of Practice.* Translated by Richard Nice. Cambridge: Cambridge University Press, 1977.

———. *Distinction: A Social Critique of the Judgement of Taste.* Translated by Richard Nice. London: Routledge and Kegan Paul, 1984.

Bowen, R. N. *CIMA Bibliography.* Honolulu: Pacific Scientific Information Center, Bernice P. Bishop Museum, 1963.

Bowers, Neal M. *Problems of Resettlement on Saipan, Tinian, and Rota, Mariana Islands.* CIMA Report, no. 31. Washington D.C.: Pacific Science Board, National Research Council, 1950.

Brady, Ivan, and Greg Dening. "History's Poetics: An Interview with Greg Dening." *In Dangerous Liaisons: Essays in Honour of Greg Dening,* edited by Donna Merwick. Melbourne University History Monograph, no. 19. Melbourne: Department of History, University of Melbourne, 1994.

Brantlinger, Patrick. *Rule of Darkness: British Literature and Imperialism.* Ithaca, N.Y.: Cornell University Press, 1988.

Brewer, Anthony. *Marxist Theories of Imperialism: A Critical Survey.* London: Routledge and Kegan Paul, 1980.

Bullard, Robert D. *Dumping in Dixie: Race, Class and Environmental Quality.* Boulder, Colo.: Westview Press, 1990.

Butterfield, Fox. "The Improbable Welfare State." *New York Times Magazine,* 27 November 1977.

Cameron, John. "Economic Development Options for the Federated States of Micronesia at Independence." *Pacific Studies* vol. 14, 4 (December 1991): 35–70.

Carr, E. H. *What Is History?* New York: Vintage Books, 1961.

Carrier, James G., ed. *History and Tradition in Melanesian Anthropology.* Berkeley: University of California Press, 1992.

Carucci, Laurence Marshall. "The Source of the Force in Marshallese Cosmology." In *The Pacific Theater: Island Representations of World War II,* edited by Geoffrey M. White and Lamont Lindstrom Pacific Islands Monograph Series, no. 8. Honolulu: University of Hawai'i Press, 1989.

Clendinnen, Inga. *Ambivalent Conquests: Maya and Spaniard in Yucatan, 1517–1570.* Cambridge: Cambridge University Press, 1987.

Clifford, James. *The Predicament of Culture: Twentieth-Century Ethnography, Literature, and Art.* Cambridge: Harvard University Press, 1988.

Clifford, James, and George Marcus. *Writing Culture: The Poetics and Politics of Ethnography.* Berkeley: University of California Press, 1986.

Cole, Rodney V., ed. *Pacific 2010: Challenging the Future.* Pacific Policy

Paper 9. Canberra: National Centre for Development Studies, Research School of Pacific Studies, Australian National University, 1993.

Comaroff, Jean, and John Comaroff. *Of Revelation and Revolution: Christianity, Colonialism, and Consciousness in South Africa.* Vol. 1. Chicago: University of Chicago Press, 1991.

———. *Ethnography and the Historical Imagination.* Boulder: Westview Press, 1992.

Congress of Micronesia. *Journal of the House of Representatives.* Saipan: Trust Territory Government Press, 1965–1978.

———. *Journal of the Senate.* Saipan: Trust Territory Government Press, 1965–1978.

———. Joint Committee on Future Status. *Hearings of the Eastern Districts Subcommittee (Truk, Ponape, and the Marshalls).* Saipan: Trust Territory Government Press, 1973.

Connell, John. *Marshall Islands.* Country Report no. 8, Migration, Employment, and Development in the Pacific. Noumea: South Pacific Commission, 1983.

———. *Sovereignty and Survival: Island Microstates in the Third World.* Research Monograph, no. 3. Sydney: Department of Geography, University of Sydney, 1988.

———. "Island Microstates: The Mirage of Development." *The Contemporary Pacific* 3, 2 (Fall 1991): 251–87.

Cooper, Frederick. "Colonizing Time: Work Rhythms and Labor Conflict in Colonial Mombassa." In *Colonialism and Culture,* edited by Nicholas B. Dirks, 209–245. Ann Arbor: University of Michigan Press, 1992.

Croce, Benedetto. *History, Its Theory and Practice.* Translated by Douglas Ainslie. New York: Harcourt, Brace, 1923.

Decker, J. A. *Land Problems in the Pacific Mandates.* Issued under the auspices of the Institute of Pacific Relations. Shanghai: Kelly and Walsh, 1940.

Dening, Greg. "Review of *Marists and Melanesians* by Hugh Laracy." *New Zealand Journal of History* 12 (1978): 82.

———. *Islands and Beaches: Discourse on a Silent Land, Marquesas, 1774–1880.* Honolulu: University Press of Hawai'i, 1980.

———. *The Bounty: An Ethnographic History.* Melbourne University History Monograph Series, no. 1. Melbourne: History Department, University of Melbourne, 1988.

Dever, Greg. *Ebeye, Marshall Islands: A Public Health Hazard.* Honolulu: Micronesia Support Committee, 1978.

Diaz, Vicente. "Simply Chamorro: Telling Tales of Demise and Survival in Guam." *The Contemporary Pacific* 6, 1 (Spring 1994): 29–58.

Dibblin, Jane. *Day of Two Suns: U.S. Nuclear Testing and the Pacific Islanders.* New York: New Amsterdam Books, 1988.

Diggins, John Patrick. *The Proud Decades: America in War and Peace, 1941–1960.* New York: W. W. Norton, 1988.

Dirks, Nicholas B., ed. *Colonialism and Culture.* The Comparative Studies in Society and History Book Series. Ann Arbor: University of Michigan Press, 1992.

Dirks, Nicholas B.; Geoff Eley; and Sherry B. Ortner, eds. *Culture/Power/History.* Princeton, N.J.: Princeton University Press, 1994.

Dos Santos, Theotonio. "The Structure of Dependence." In *Readings in U.S. Imperialism,* edited by K. T. Kan and Donald C. Hughes, 225–236. Boston: Extending Horizons, 1971.

———. *Unequal Development: An Essay in the Social Transformation of Peripheral Capitalism.* New York: Monthly Review Press, 1971.

———. "The Crisis of Development Theory and the Problem of Dependence in Latin America." In *Underdevelopment and Development,* edited by H. Bernstein, 57–80. New York: Monthly Review Press, 1973.

Embree, John F. "Micronesia: The Navy and Democracy." *Far Eastern Survey* 5 (June 1946): 164.

———. "Report on Field Trip to Micronesia, Dec. 14, 1945–Jan. 5, 1946." Manuscript. Hawaiian and Pacific Collection, Hamilton Library, University of Hawai'i at Manoa.

Emerson, Rupert; Lawrence S. Finkelstein; E. L. Bartlett; George H. McLane; and Roy James. *America's Pacific Dependencies.* New York: American Institute of Pacific Relations, 1949.

Epstein, Judith. *Deceptive Distinctions.* New Haven, Conn.: Yale University Press, 1985.

Escobar, Arturo. "Planning." In *The Development Dictionary: A Guide to Knowledge as Power,* edited by Wolfgang Sachs, 132–145. London: Zed Books, 1992.

———. *Encountering Development: The Making and Unmaking of the Third World.* Princeton Studies in Culture/Power/History. Princeton, N.J.: Princeton University Press, 1994.

Esteva, Gustavo. "Development." In *The Development Dictionary: A Guide to Knowledge as Power,* edited by Wolfgang Sachs, 6–25. London: Zed Books, 1992.

Falgout, Suzanne. "From Passive Pawns to Political Strategists: Wartime Lessons for the People of Pohnpei." In *The Pacific Theater: Island*

Representations of World War II, edited by Geoffrey M. White and Lamont Lindstrom, 117–148. Pacific Islands Monograph Series, no. 8. University of Hawai'i Press, 1989.

Federated States of Micronesia. Interim Congress. *Journal of the House of Representatives, October 1978 to February 1979*. Kolonia, Pohnpei: Trust Territory Government Press, 1979.

———. *Journal of the Senate, October 1978 to February 1979*. Kolonia, Pohnpei: Trust Territory Government Press, 1979.

———.Office of the Budget. *U.S. Federal Programs under the Compact of Free Association:* A Report of the Status of U.S. Federal Programs under the Compact of Free Association. Kolonia, Pohnpei: Federated States of Micronesia Government, 1987.

Femia, Joseph. "Hegemony and Consciousness in the Thought of Antonio Gramsci." *Political Studies*, 23, 1 (March 1975): 29–48.

Ferguson, James. *The "Anti-Politics" Machine: "Development," Depoliticization, and Bureaucratic Power in Lesotho.* Cambridge: Cambridge University Press, 1990.

Firth, Stewart. *Nuclear Playground.* South Sea Books, no. 1. Pacific Islands Studies Program, Center for Asian and Pacific Studies, University of Hawai'i. Honolulu: University of Hawaii Press, 1987.

———. "Sovereignty and Independence in the Contemporary Pacific." *The Contemporary Pacific* 1, 1 and 2 (Spring and Fall 1989): 75–96.

Fischer, John L. *The Eastern Carolines.* New Haven, Conn.: Human Relations Area Files Press, 1957.

Flinn, Juliana. *Diplomas and Thatch Houses: Asserting Tradition in a Changing Micronesia.* Ann Arbor: University of Michigan Press, 1992.

Force, Roland W. *Leadership and Cultural Change in Palau.* Fieldiana Anthropology, A Continuation of the Anthropological Series of the Field Museum of Natural History, vol. 50. Chicago: Chicago Museum of Natural History, 1960.

Foucault, Michel. *Discipline and Punish: The Birth of the Prison.* Translated by Alan M. Sheridan. New York: Vintage Books, 1979.

———. *Power/Knowledge: Selected Interviews and Other Writings, 1972–1977*. Edited by C. Gordon; translated by C. Gordon et al. New York: Pantheon Books, 1980.

Frank, Andre Gunder. *Capitalism and Underdevelopment in Latin America.* New York: Monthly Review Press, 1967.

———. *Latin America: Underdevelopment or Revolution.* New York: Monthly Review Press, 1969.

Fuentes, Annette, and Barbara Ehrenreich. *Women in the Global Factory.* Boston: South End Press, 1983.

Fukuyama, Francis. *The End of History and the Last Man.* New York: Free Press, 1992.

Gale, Roger W. *The Americanization of Micronesia: A Study of the Consolidation of U.S. Rule in the Pacific.* Washington, D.C.: University Press of America, 1979.

Gettleman, Marvin E., and David Mermelstein, eds. *The Great Society Reader: The Failure of American Liberalism.* New York: Random House, 1967.

Gladwin, Thomas. "Chief Petrus Mailo." In *In the Company of Men,* edited by Joseph Casagrande, 41–62. New York: Harper, 1960.

———. *East Is A Big Bird: Navigation and Logic on Puluwat Atoll.* Cambridge: Harvard University Press, 1970.

Gladwin, Thomas, and Seymour B. Sarason. *Truk: Man in Paradise.* Viking Fund Publications in Anthropology, no. 20. New York: Wenner-Gren Foundation for Anthropological Research, 1953.

Godelier, Maurice. "Infrastructures, Societies and History." *Current Anthropology* 19 (1985): 763–771.

Goodenough, Ward H. *Property, Kin, and Community on Truk.* Hamden, Conn.: Archon Books, 1966.

Goodenough, Ward H., and Hiroshi Sugita, in collaboration with Boutau K. Efot et al. *Trukese-English Dictionary/Pwpwuken Tettenin Foos, Chuuk-Ingenes.* Memoirs of the American Philosophical Society, no. 141. Philadelphia: American Philosophical Society, 1988.

Goodman, Mike. "Jet-Setting Promoter, Ford Appointee Push Port." *Los Angeles Times,* 1 February 1977.

Gramsci, Antonio. *Selections from the Prison Notebooks.* Edited and translated by Quinten Hoare and Nowell Smith. London: Lawrence and Wishart, 1971.

Gregory, C. A. *Gifts and Commodities.* London: Academic Press, 1982.

Gronemeyer, Marianne. "Helping." In *The Development Dictionary: A Guide to Knowledge as Power,* edited by Wolfgang Sachs, 53–69. London: Zed Books, 1992.

Gudeman, Stephen. *Economics as Culture: Models and Metaphors of Livelihood.* London: Routledge and Kegan Paul, 1986.

———. "Remodeling the House of Economics: Culture and Innovation." *American Ethnologist* 19, 1 (February 1992): 141–154.

Guha, Ranajit. *Elementary Aspects of Peasant Insurgency in Colonial India.* Delhi: Oxford University Press, 1983.

Hancock, Graham. *Lords of Poverty: The Free-Wheeling Lifestyles, Power, Prestige, and Corruption of the Multi-Billion-Dollar Aid Business.* London: Macmillan, 1989.

Hanlon, David. *Upon a Stone Altar: A History of the Island of Pohnpei to 1890.* Pacific Islands Monograph Series, no. 5. Honolulu: University of Hawai'i Press, 1988.

———. "Micronesia: Writing and Rewriting the Histories of a Nonentity." *Pacific Studies* 12, 2 (March 1989): 1–21.

———. "Sorcery, 'Savage Memories,' and the Edge of Commensurability for History in the Pacific." In *Pacific Islands History,* edited by Brij V. Lal, 107–128. Canberra: Journal of Pacific History, 1992.

———. "Patterns of Colonial Rule in Micronesia to 1942." In *Tides of History: The Pacific Islands in the Twentieth Century,* edited by Kerry R. Howe, Robert C. Kiste, and Brij V. Lal, 93–118. Honolulu: University of Hawai'i Press, 1994.

———. "Remaking Micronesia: A Reflection on the Cultural and Strategic Politics of Economic Development in American Micronesia, 1945–1968." In *Dangerous Liaisons: Essays in Honour of Greg Dening,* edited by Donna Merwick. Melbourne University History Monograph Series, no. 19. Melbourne: Department of History, University of Melbourne, 1994.

———. "Review of *More Than a Living* by Michael D. Lieber." *The Contemporary Pacific* 7, 1 (Spring 1995): 206–209.

———. "Magellan's Chroniclers?: American Anthropology's History in Micronesia." In *Proceedings of the Conference on American Anthropology in Micronesia, 20–23 October 1993, Honolulu, Hawai'i,* edited by Robert C. Kiste and Mac Marshall. Honolulu: University of Hawai'i Press, forthcoming.

Hanlon, David L., and William Eperiam. "The Federated States of Micronesia: Unifying the Remnants." In *Micronesian Politics,* edited by Roniti Teiwaki, 80–99. Revised edition. Suva, Fiji: Institute of Pacific Studies, University of the South Pacific, 1988.

Harris, Walter B. "South Sea Islanders under Japanese Mandate." *Foreign Affairs* 10 (1932): 691–697.

Hawaii Architects and Engineers. *Ebeye and Carlson Islands, Marshall Islands District.* Final Report, vol. 1. Trust Territory Physical Planning Program. Honolulu, 1968.

Heilbroner, Robert L., and Lester C. Thurow. *The Economic Problem.* Fourth edition. Englewood Cliffs, N.J.: Prentice-Hall, 1975.

Herbert, Christopher. *Culture and Anomie: Ethnographic Imagination in the Nineteenth Century.* Chicago: University of Chicago Press, 1991.

Hezel, Francis X., S.J. *The First Taint of Civilization: A History of the Caroline and Marshall Islands in Precolonial Days, 1521–1885.* Pacific Islands Monograph Series, no. 1. Honolulu: University of Hawai'i Press, 1983.

———. "A Brief Economic History of Micronesia." In *Past Achievements and Future Possibilities: A Conference on Economic Development in Micronesia.* Ponape, 22–25 May 1984. Majuro, Marshall Islands: Micronesian Seminar, 1984.

———. *Strangers in Their Own Land: A Century of Colonial Rule in the Caroline and Marshall Islands.* Pacific Islands Monograph Series, no. 13. Honolulu: University of Hawai'i Press, 1995.

Hezel, Francis X., and Mark L. Berg, eds. *Winds of Change: A Book of Readings in Micronesian History.* Omnibus Program for Social Studies and Cultural Heritage. Saipan: Trust Territory Government of the Pacific Islands, 1982.

Hobart, Mark, ed. *The Growth of Ignorance: An Anthropological Critique of Development.* New York: Routledge, 1993.

Hobsbawm, E. J. *Nations and Nationalism since 1780: Programme, Myth, Reality.* Cambridge: Cambridge University Press, 1990.

Horowitz, Adam. *Home on the Range.* Oakland, Calif.: The Video Project, 1991.

Hughes, Daniel T. *Political Conflict and Harmony on Ponape.* New Haven, Conn.: Human Relations Area Files Press, 1970.

Hughes, Daniel T., and Sherwood G. Lingenfelter, eds. *Political Development in Micronesia.* Columbus: Ohio State University Press, 1974.

Hunt, Lynn, ed. *The New Cultural History.* Berkeley: University of California Press, 1989.

Ishtar, Zohl dé. *Daughters of the Pacific.* North Melbourne: Spinifex, 1994.

Jacobs, Paul. "The Natives Are Forbidden to Shop on a U.S.-Administered Pacific Isle." *Newsday,* 13 February 1977.

———. "Attempting to Change Paradise." *Newsday,* 14 February 1977.

Jameson, Fredric. "Third World Literature in the Era of Multinational Corporations." *Social Text* 15 (1986): 65–88.

Johannes, R. E. *Words of the Lagoon: Fishing and Marine Lore in the Palau District of Micronesia.* Berkeley: University of California Press, 1981.

Johnson, Giff. "Ebeye: Apartheid, U.S. Style." *The Nation,* 25 December 1976, 22.

———. "Ebeye and Kwajalein: A Tale of Two Islands." *The Progressive* 43, 2 (February 1979): 47.

———. *Collision Course at Kwajalein: Marshall Islanders in the Shadow of the Bomb.* Honolulu: Pacific Concerns Resource Center, 1984.

Joseph, Alice, and Veronica Murray. *Chamorros and Carolinians of Saipan.* Cambridge: Harvard University Press, 1951.

Kardam, Nuket. *Bringing Women In: Women's Issues in International Development Programs.* Boulder, Colo.: Lynn Rienner, 1991.

Kearns, Doris. *Lyndon Johnson and the American Dream.* New York: Harper and Row, 1976.

Keesing, Roger M., and Margaret Jolly. "Epilogue." In *History and Tradition in Melanesian Anthropology,* edited by James G. Carrier. Berkeley: University of California Press, 1992.

Kihleng, Kimberlee S. "Women in Exchange: Negotiated Relations, Practice, and the Constitution of Female Identity on Pohnpei Island, Micronesia." Ph.D. dissertation, University of Hawai'i at Manoa, 1996.

Kiros, Teodoros. *Toward the Construction of a Theory of Political Action: Antonio Gramsci.* Lanham, Md.: University Press of America, 1985.

Kiste, Robert C. *Kili Island: A Study of the Relocation of the Ex-Bikini Marshallese.* Eugene: Department of Anthropology, University of Oregon, 1968.

———. *The Bikinians: A Study in Forced Migration.* Menlo Park, Calif.: Cummings, 1974.

———. "Review of *The Edge of Paradise* by P. F. Kluge." *The Contemporary Pacific* 5, 1 (Spring 1992): 208–210.

Kluge, P. F. "Micronesia's Unloved Islands: Ebeye." *Micronesian Reporter* 16, 3 (1968): 31–37.

———. *The Edge of Paradise: America in Micronesia.* New York: Random House, 1991.

Labby, David. *The Demystification of Yap: Dialectics of Culture on a Micronesian Island.* Chicago: University of Chicago Press, 1976.

Landsberg, Martin. "Export-Led Industrialization in the Third World: Manufacturing Imperialism." *Review of Radical Political Economics* 11 (1979): 50–63.

Leibowitz, Arnold H. *Defining Status: A Comprehensive Analysis of United States Territorial Relations.* Dordrecht: Martinus Nijhoff, 1989.

Lepowsky, Maria. *Fruit of the Motherland: Gender in an Egalitarian Society.* New York: Columbia University Press, 1993.

Lessa, William A. "Ulithi and the Outer Native World." *American Anthropologist* 52 (1950): 27–52.

———. *The Ethnology of Ulithi Atoll.* CIMA Special Report, no. 28. Washington, D.C.: Pacific Science Board, National Research Council, 1950.

———. "The Place of Ulithi in the Yap Empire." *Human Organization* 9, 1 (Spring 1950): 16–18.

———. "An Evaluation of Early Descriptions of Carolinian Culture." *Ethnohistory* 9, 4 (Fall 1962), 313–403.

———. *Ulithi: A Micronesian Design for Living.* Case Studies in Cultural Anthropology. New York: Holt, Rinehart and Winston, 1966.

Lieber, Michael D. *More Than a Living: Fishing and the Social Order on a Polynesian Atoll.* Conflict and Change Series. Boulder, Colo.: Westview Press, 1994.

Lingenfelter, Sherwood Galen. *Yap: Political Leadership and Culture Change in an Island Society.* Honolulu: University Press of Hawai'i, 1975.

Linnekin, Jocelyn. *Sacred Queens and Women of Consequence: Rank, Gender, and Colonialism in the Hawaiian Islands.* Ann Arbor: University of Michigan Press, 1990.

Lockwood, Viginia; Thomas G. Harding; and Ben J. Wallace, eds. *Contemporary Pacific Societies: Studies in Development and Change.* Englewood Cliffs, N.J.: Prentice Hall, 1993.

Lowenthal, David. *The Past Is a Foreign Country.* Cambridge: Cambridge University Press, 1985.

Ludden, David. "India's Development Regime." In *Colonialism and Culture,* edited by Nicholas B. Dirks, 247–287. Comparative Studies in Society and History. Ann Arbor: University of Michigan Press, 1992.

Lutz, Catherine A. "The Compact of Free Association, Micronesian Non-Independence, and U.S. Policy." *Bulletin of Concerned Asian Scholars* 18, 2 (April–June 1986): 21–27.

———. *Unnatural Emotions: Everyday Sentiments in a Micronesian Atoll and Their Challenge to Western Theory.* Chicago: University of Chicago Press, 1988.

Lutz, Catherine A., and Jane L. Collins. *Reading National Geographic.* Chicago: University of Chicago Press, 1993.

Mahony, Frank J. "The Innovation of a Savings System in Truk." *American Anthropologist* 62, 3 (June 1960): 465–482.

Maitland, Frederick W. *Selected Essays.* Edited by H. D. Hazeltine, G. Lapsley, and P. H. Winfield. Cambridge: The University Press, 1936.

Marglin, Frédérique Apfell, and Stephen A. Marglin. *Dominating Knowledge: Development, Culture and Resistance.* Oxford: Clarendon Press, 1990.

Margold, Jane, and Donna Belardo. "Matrilineal Heritage: A Look at the Power of Contemporary Micronesian Women." In *Women in Asia and the Pacific: Towards an East-West Dialogue,* edited by Madeleine J. Goodman. Honolulu: Distributed for the Women's Studies Program by the University of Hawai'i Press, 1985.

Marks, Frederick H. "U.S. Food for Micronesia Debatable." *Honolulu Star Bulletin,* 22 October 1978.

Marshall, Mac. *Weekend Warriors: Alcohol in a Micronesian Culture.* Palo Alto, Calif.: Mayfield, 1979.

Marshall, Mac, and Leslie B. Marshall. "Opening Pandora's Box: Reconstructing Micronesians' Early Contacts with Alcoholic Beverages." *Journal of the Polynesian Society,* 84, 4 (1975): 441–465.

———. "Holy and Unholy Spirits: The Effects of Missionization on Alcohol Use in Eastern Micronesia." *Journal of Pacific History* 11, 3 and 4 (1976): 135–166.

———. *Silent Voices Speak: Women and Prohibition in Truk.* Belmont, Calif.: Wadsworth, 1990.

Marzani, Carl, ed. and trans. *The Open Marxism of Antonio Gramsci.* New York: Cameron Associates, 1957.

Mason, Leonard E. "Research Problems and Ethics in Micronesia." Special Bulletin, American Anthropological Association (January 1967). Copy at Hawaiian and Pacific Collection, Hamilton Library, University of Hawai'i at Manoa.

Mauss, Marcel. *The Gift: Forms and Functions of Exchange in Archaic Societies.* Translated by I. Gunnison. Introduction by E. E. Evans-Pritchard. London: Cohn and West, 1970.

McHenry, Donald F. *Micronesia, Trust Betrayed: Altruism vs. Self-Interest in American Foreign Policy.* New York: Carnegie Endowment for International Peace, 1975.

Meller, Norman, with the assistance of Terza Meller. *The Congress of Micronesia: Development of the Legislative Process in the Trust Territory of the Pacific Islands.* Honolulu: University of Hawai'i Press, 1969.

Merwick, Donna, ed. *Dangerous Liaisons: Essays in Honour of Greg Dening.* Melbourne: University of Melbourne, Department of History, 1994.

Michal, Edward J. "Protected States: The Political Status of the Federated States of Micronesia and the Republic of the Marshall Islands." *The Contemporary Pacific* 5, 2 (Fall 1993): 303–332.

Micronesian Seminar. *U.S. Federal Programs in Micronesia: A Report on a Conference Sponsored by the Micronesian Seminar.* 12–14 March 1979. Kolonia, Pohnpei. TTA, reel no. 1353, frame no. 0068, document no. 21514.

Mies, Maria. *Patriarchy and Accumulation on a World Scale: Women in the International Division of Labour.* London: Zed Books, 1986.

Miguel, Lino. Interview, 15 May 1983. Ninseitamw, Kolonia, Pohnpei.

Mills, C. Wright. *White Collar: The American Middle Class.* New York: Oxford University Press, 1953.

Moore, Robert W. "Our New Military Wards, the Marshalls." *National Geographic* 88, 3 (1945): 325–352.

Murdock, George P. "Foreword." To Ward H. Goodenough, *Property, Kin, and Community on Truk.* Yale University Publications in Anthropology, no. 46. New Haven, Conn.: Yale University Press, 1951.

Naipaul, V. S. *The Mimic-Men.* London: Deutsch, 1967.

Nathan, Robert R. *Economic Development Plan for Micronesia: A Proposed Long-Range Plan for Developing the Trust Territory of the Pacific Islands.* 4 parts. Washington, D.C.: Robert R. Nathan and Associates, 1968.

Nemeth, Thomas. *Gramsci's Philosophy: A Critical Study.* Sussex: Harvester Press, 1980.

Nero, Karen L. "Time of Famine, Time of Transformation: Hell in the Pacific, Palau." In *The Pacific Theater: Island Representations of World War II,* edited by Geoffrey M. White and Lamont Lindstrom, 117–147. Pacific Islands Monograph Series, no. 8. Honolulu: University of Hawai'i Press, 1989.

Nevin, David. *The American Touch in Micronesia.* New York: W. W. Norton, 1977.

North, David. "Cashing in on Nuclear Waste." *Pacific Islands Monthly* 64, 6 (June 1994): 11–13.

Nufer, Harold F. *Micronesia under American Rule: An Evaluation of the Strategic Trusteeship, 1947–1977.* Hicksville, N.Y.: Exposition Press, 1978.

Oliver, Douglas L. *Planning Micronesia's Future: A Summary of the United States Commercial Company's Economic Survey of Micronesia.* Cambridge: Harvard University Press, 1951.

———. *The Pacific Islands.* Revised edition. Honolulu: The University Press of Hawai'i, 1961.

O'Meara Tim. *Samoan Planters: Tradition and Economic Development in Polynesia.* Case Studies in Cultural Anthropology. Fort Worth, Tex.: Holt, Rhinehart and Winston, 1990.

———. "The Cult of Custom Meets the Search for Money in Western Samoa." In *Contemporary Pacific Societies: Studies in Development and Change,* edited by Victoria Lockwood, Thomas G. Harding, and Ben J. Wallace, 135–155. Englewood Cliffs, N.J.: Prentice Hall, 1993.

Ong, Aihwa. *Spirits of Resistance and Capitalist Discipline.* Albany: SUNY Press, 1987.

Pacific Daily News. Editorial, 21 June 1972.

Palau Gazette. "Is It Belau, Palau or Both?" 19 February 1986.

Pagden, Anthony. *European Encounters with the New World from Renaissance to Romanticism.* New Haven, Conn.: Yale University Press, 1993.

Paterson, Thomas G. *American Foreign Policy: A History.* Lexington, Mass.: D. C. Heath, 1977.

Peacock, Karen. "'Badge of Shame,' Battle of Courage." Graduate Seminar Paper, University of Hawai'i at Manoa, 1981. Copy courtesy of author.

Pearce, Roy Harvey. *Savagism and Civilization: A Study of the Indian and the American Mind.* Revised edition. Berkeley: University of California Press, 1988.

Peattie, Mark R. *Nan'yō: The Rise and Fall of the Japanese in Micronesia, 1885–1945.* Pacific Islands Monograph Series, no. 4. Honolulu: University of Hawai'i Press, 1988.

Pellicani, Luciano. *Gramsci: An Alternative Communism?* Stanford, Calif.: Hoover Institution Press, 1976.

Peoples, James. *Island in Trust: Cultural Change and Dependence in a Micronesian Community.* Boulder, Colo.: Westview Press, 1985.

Perin, Dan. Personal communication. Kolonia, Pohnpei, Federated States of Micronesia, 4 June 1991.

Peter, Joakim. Personal communication. Honolulu, Hawai'i, 11 October 1996.

Petersen, Glenn. "Ponape Agriculture and Economy: Politics, Prestige, and Problems of Consumption in the Eastern Caroline Islands." Ph.D. dissertation. Columbia University, 1976.

———. "Brilliant Island, Swaying in Soft Motion." Paper prepared for the Symposium on Dependency and Development in Oceania, General Meeting of the Association for Social Anthropology in Oceania. Galveston, Texas, 1980.

———. "Review of *The Edge of Paradise* by P. F. Kluge." *Isla: A Journal of Micronesian Affairs* 1, 1 (Rainy Season 1992): 125–131.

———. "Some Pohnpei Strategies for Economic Survival." In *Contemporary Pacific Societies: Studies in Development and Change,* edited by Victoria Lockwood, Thomas G. Harding, and Ben J. Wallace, 185–196. Englewood Cliffs, N.J.: Prentice Hall, 1993.

———. "The Federated States of Micronesia's 1990 Constitutional Convention: Calm Before the Storm?" *The Contemporary Pacific* 6, 2 (Fall 1994): 337–369.

Polyani, Karl. *The Great Transformation.* Boston: Beacon Press, 1957.

Pomeroy, Earl S. *Pacific Outpost: American Strategy in Guam and Micronesia.* Stanford, Calif.: Stanford University Press, 1951.

Poyer, Lin. "Echoes of Massacre: Recollections of World War II on Sapwuahfik (Ngatik Atoll)." In *The Pacific Theater: Island Representations of World War II,* edited by Geoffrey M. White and Lamont Lindstrom. Pacific Islands Monograph Series, no. 8. Honolulu: University of Hawai'i Press, 1989.

———. *The Ngatik Massacre.* Washington, D.C.: Smithsonian Institution Press, 1993.

Pratt, Fletcher. *The Marines' War: An Account of the Struggle for the Pacific from Both American and Japanese Accounts.* New York: William Sloane and Associates, 1948.

Pratt, Mary Louise. "Scratches on the Face of the Country; or, What Mr. Barrow Saw in the Land of the Bushmen." *Critical Inquiry* 12 (Autumn 1985): 119–143.

———. *Imperial Eyes: Travel Writing and Transculturation.* New York: Routledge, 1992.

Price, Willard. *America's Paradise Lost.* New York: John Day, 1966.

Pryor, Larry. "Palau Islands Thrust into Superport Battle." *Los Angeles Times,* 1 February 1977.

Rabinow, Paul. *The Foucault Reader.* New York: Pantheon Books, 1984.

———. "Representations Are Social Facts: Modernity and Post Modernity in Anthropology." In *Writing Culture: The Poetics and Politics of Ethnography,* edited by James Clifford and George Marcus, 234–261. Berkeley: University of California Press, 1986.

Republic of the Marshall Islands. *Marshall Islands Guidebook.* Updated and revised. Majuro, Marshall Islands: Micronitor News, 1989.
Richard, Dorothy E. *United States Naval Administration of the Trust Territory of the Pacific Islands.* 3 vols. Washington, D.C.: U.S. Government Printing Office, 1957.
Riesenberg, Saul H. *The Native Polity of Ponape.* Smithsonian Contributions to Anthropology, vol. 10. Washington, D.C.: Smithsonian Institution Press, 1968.
Ritzenhaler, R. E. *Native Money of Palau.* CIMA Report, no. 27. Washington, D.C.: Pacific Science Board, 1949.
Rodman, Margaret C. *Deep Water: Development and Change in Pacific Village Fisheries.* Boulder, Colo.: Westview Press, 1989.
Roff, Sue Rabbitt. *Overreaching in Paradise: United States Policy in Palau since 1945.* Juneau, Alaska: Denali Press, 1991.
Roff, Sue Rabbitt, and Roger Clark. *The Problem of Palau.* London: Minority Rights Group, 1984.
Roth, Michael S. "Review of *The End of History and the Last Man* by Francis Fukuyama." *History and Theory* 32, 2 (1992): 188–197.
Roxborough, Ian. *Theories of Underdevelopment.* London: Macmillan, 1979.
Ryan, Alan. "Professor Hegel Goes to Washington." *New York Review of Books,* 26 March 1992, 7–13.
Sachs, Wolfgang, ed. *The Development Dictionary: A Guide to Knowledge as Power.* London: Zed Books, 1992.
Sahlins, Marshall D. *Culture and Practical Reason.* Chicago: University of Chicago Press, 1976.
———. *Islands of History.* Chicago: University of Chicago Press, 1985.
———. "The Economics of Develop-Man in the Pacific." *Res* 21 (Spring 1992): 12–25.
———. "Cosmologies of Capitalism: The Trans-Pacific Sector of 'The World System.'" In *Culture/Power/History,* edited by Nicholas B. Dirks, Geoff Eley, and Sherry B. Ortner, 412–455. Princeton, N.J. Princeton, University Press, 1994.
———. *How Natives Think, About Captain Cook for Example.* Chicago: University of Chicago Press, 1995.
Said, Edward. *Orientalism.* New York: Vintage Books, 1979.
———. *Culture and Imperialism.* New York: Vintage Books, 1994.
Salisbury, Richard, and Elizabeth Tooker, eds. *Affluence and Cultural Survival.* Washington, D.C.: American Ethnological Society, 1985.

Schaffer, Paul D. "Confess Therefore Your Sins: Status and Sin on Kusaie." Ph.D. dissertation. Stanford University, 1976.

Schoeffel, Penelope. *Women in Development: Federated States of Micronesia.* Country Briefing Paper. Manila: Asian Development Bank, Programs Department East, April 1993.

Schwalbenberg, Henry M., S.J. "Compact of Free Association: More Association Than Free." *Pacific Magazine* 7, 3 (32) (March–April 1982): 28–31; and 7, 3 (33) (May–June 1982): 28–31.

———. *Memos on the Draft Compact of Free Association, #1–#13.* Moen, Truk: Micronesian Area Research Seminar, December 1981–April 1984.

Scott, James C. *Weapons of the Weak: Everyday Forms of Peasant Resistance.* New Haven, Conn.: Yale University Press, 1985.

Shuster, Donald R. "Palau's Constitutional Triangle." *Journal of Pacific History* 15 (1980): 74–82.

Sklar, Martin J. *The United States as a Developing Country: Studies in U.S. History in the Progressive Era and the 1920s.* New York: Cambridge University Press, 1992.

Smith, Adam. *An Inquiry into the Nature and Causes of the Wealth of Nations.* Edited by Edwin Cannan. Chicago: University of Chicago Press, 1976.

Smith, Bernard. *European Vision and the South Pacific.* 2d ed. New Haven, Conn.: Yale University Press, 1985.

Smith, DeVerne Reed. *Palauan Social Structure.* New Brunswick, N.J.: Rutgers University Press, 1983.

Smith, Gary. *Micronesia: Decolonisation and U.S. Military Interests in the Trust Territories [sic] of the Pacific Islands.* Canberra: Pacific Research Centre, Australian National University, 1991.

Smith, Roy H., and Michael C. Pugh. "Micronesian Trust Territories—Imperialism Continues?" *Pacific Review* 4, 1 (1991): 36–44.

So, Alvin Y. *Social Change and Development: Modernization, Dependency and World Systems Theories.* Newbury Park, Calif.: Sage, 1990.

Spoehr, Alexander. *Majuro: A Village in the Marshall Islands.* Fieldiana Anthropology, A Continuation of the Anthropological Series of the Field Museum of Natural History, vol. 39. Chicago: Chicago Natural History Museum, 1949.

———. Saipan: *The Ethnology of a War-Devastated Island.* Fieldiana Anthropology, A Continuation of the Anthropological Series of the Field Museum of Natural History, vol. 41. Chicago: Chicago Natural History Museum, 1954.

Strategic Trust: The Making of a Nuclear Free Pacific. New York: Cinema Guild, 1984.

Strathern, Marilyn. *The Gender of the Gift: Problems with Women and Problems with Melanesian Society.* Berkeley: University of California Press, 1988.

Teaiwa, Teresia K. "bikinis and other s/pacific n/oceans." *Contemporary Pacific* 6, 1 (Spring 1994): 87–109.

Thomas, Nicholas. *Entangled Objects: Exchange, Culture and Colonialism in the Pacific.* Cambridge: Harvard University Press, 1991.

———. *Colonialism's Culture: Travel, Literature and Government.* Princeton, N.J.: Princeton University Press, 1994.

Thompson. E. P. *The Making of the English Working Class.* New York: Vintage Books, 1963.

Tobin, Jack. "Ebeye Village: An Atypical Marshallese Community." Majuro, 18 February 1954. Photocopy. Special Hawaiian and Pacific Collection, Hamilton Library, University of Hawai'i at Manoa, Honolulu, Hawai'i.

———. "To the District Administrator, Marshalls: Ebeye-Kwajalein Report, 19 July 1972." Photocopy. Special Hawaiian and Pacific Collection, Hamilton Library, University of Hawai'i at Manoa, Honolulu, Hawai'i.

Torgovnik, Marianna. *Gone Primitive: Savage Intellects, Modern Lives.* Chicago: University of Chicago Press, 1990.

Trumbull, Robert. *Paradise in Trust: A Report on Americans in Micronesia, 1946–1958.* New York: William Sloane, 1959.

United Nations. Trusteeship Council. *Report of the United Nations Visiting Mission to the Trust Territory of the Pacific Islands, 1961.* Supplement 20 Official Records, Twenty-seventh Session, 1 June–19 July 1961. New York: United Nations.

United States. *Report by the United States Government Survey Mission to the Trust Territory of the Pacific Islands* ("Solomon Report"), 1963. Summary and 2 vols. Honolulu, University of Hawai'i, Hamilton Library, Hawaiian and Pacific Collection.

United States. Department of the Interior. *Federal Programs Available to the Territories.* Report to Congress, 95-134, Title IV, section 401. Washington, D.C.: U.S. Government Printing Office, 1978.

United States. Department of State. *Annual Report to the United Nations on the Administration of the Trust Territory of the Pacific Islands.* Washington, D.C.: U.S. Government Printing Office, 1948–1980.

United States. General Accounting Office. *U.S. Trust Territory: Issues*

Associated with Palau's Transition to Self-Government. Report to Congressional Requesters, 89-182. 2 vols. Washington, D.C.: GAO, National Security and International Affairs Division, 1980.

United States. Office for Micronisian Status Negotiations. *Draft Environmental Impact Statement for the Compact of Free Association.* Washington, D.C.: Office for Micronesian Status Negotiations, 1984.

United States. Office of the President. *President's Message to Congress Transmitting a Draft of the Proposed Legislation to Approve the Compact of Free Association between the United States and the Government of Palau, 9 April 1986.* Washington, D.C.: U.S. Government Printing Office, 1986.

———. *President's Message to Congress Transmitting the Proposed Legislation to Approve the Compact of Free Association between the United States and the Federated States of Micronesia and the Republic of the Marshall Islands, and Other Purposes, 20 February 1985.* Washington, D.C: U.S. Government Printing Office, 1985.

United States. Trust Territory of the Pacific Islands Archives. Microfilmed Records of the Trust Territory Government, 1952–1986. Honolulu, University of Hawai'i, Hamilton Library.

United States. Trust Territory of the Pacific Islands. Office of Planning and Statistics. *Gugeegue and Carlson Island Development—Ebeye Redevelopment.* Saipan: Trust Territory Printing Office, 1978.

———. *Briefing Document for Ebeye Redevelopment and Gugeegue Development.* Saipan: Trust Territory Printing Office, 1984.

United States Commercial Company. *Summary of Findings and Recommendations.* Vol. 1 of *Economic Survey of Micronesia, 1946.* Honolulu, University of Hawai'i, Hamilton Library, Hawaiian and Pacific Collection.

United States Congress. *Public Law 99-239: Compact of Free Association Act of 1985 between the United States and the Governments of the Federated States of Micronesia and the Republic of the Marshalls, 14 January 1986.* Washington, D.C.: U.S. Government Printing Office, 1986.

———. *Public Law 99-658: Compact of Free Association Act of 1985 between the United States and the Government of Palau, 14 November 1986.* Washington, D.C.: U.S. Government Printing Office, 1987.

United States House of Representatives. "Current Problems in the Marshalls." *Hearings before the Subcommittee on Territorial and Insular Affairs: Oversight Hearings on the Marshalls District, Trust Territory of the Pacific Islands.* On Ebeye 13 July 1976 and on

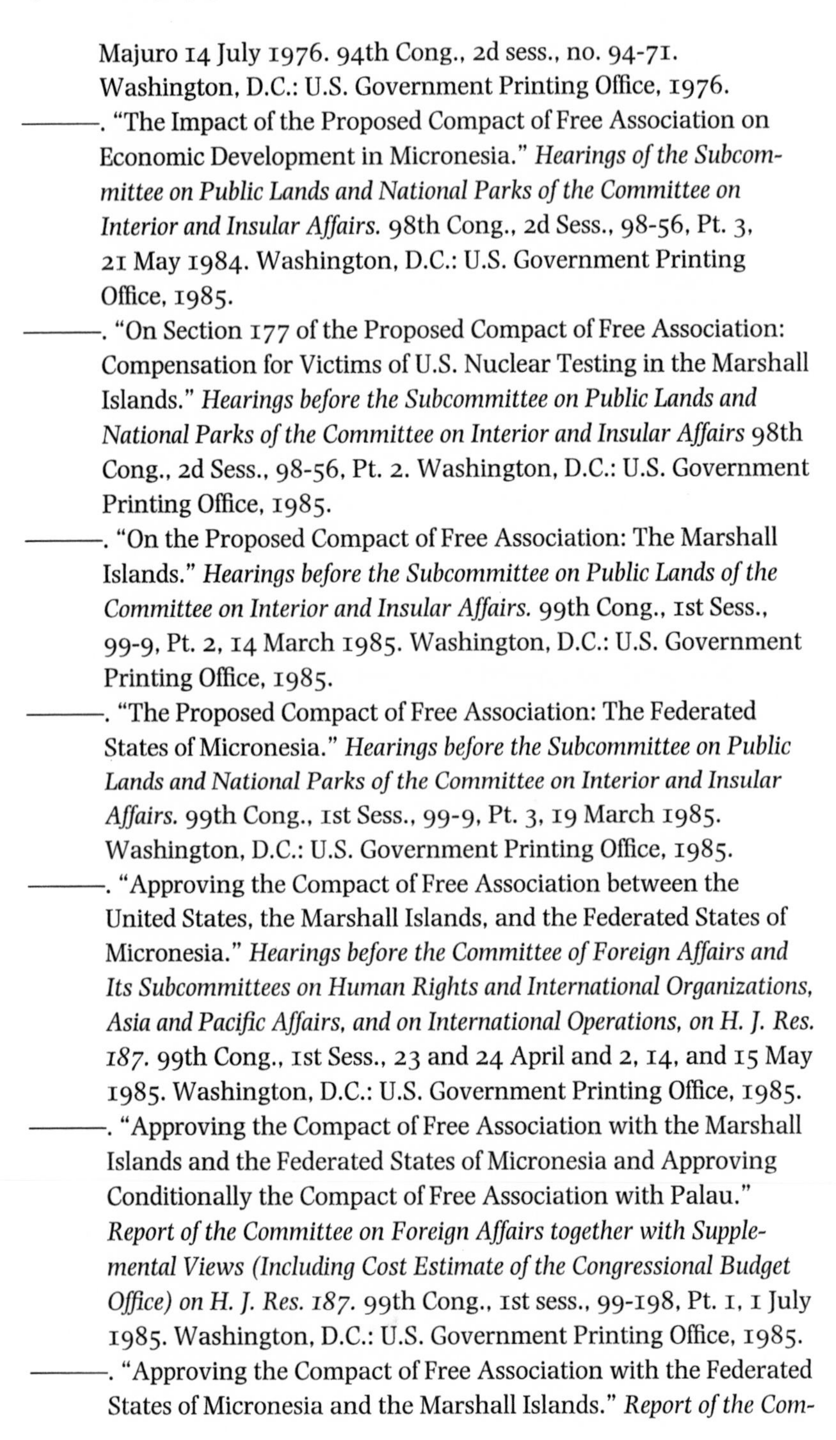

Majuro 14 July 1976. 94th Cong., 2d sess., no. 94-71. Washington, D.C.: U.S. Government Printing Office, 1976.

———. "The Impact of the Proposed Compact of Free Association on Economic Development in Micronesia." *Hearings of the Subcommittee on Public Lands and National Parks of the Committee on Interior and Insular Affairs.* 98th Cong., 2d Sess., 98-56, Pt. 3, 21 May 1984. Washington, D.C.: U.S. Government Printing Office, 1985.

———. "On Section 177 of the Proposed Compact of Free Association: Compensation for Victims of U.S. Nuclear Testing in the Marshall Islands." *Hearings before the Subcommittee on Public Lands and National Parks of the Committee on Interior and Insular Affairs* 98th Cong., 2d Sess., 98-56, Pt. 2. Washington, D.C.: U.S. Government Printing Office, 1985.

———. "On the Proposed Compact of Free Association: The Marshall Islands." *Hearings before the Subcommittee on Public Lands of the Committee on Interior and Insular Affairs.* 99th Cong., 1st Sess., 99-9, Pt. 2, 14 March 1985. Washington, D.C.: U.S. Government Printing Office, 1985.

———. "The Proposed Compact of Free Association: The Federated States of Micronesia." *Hearings before the Subcommittee on Public Lands and National Parks of the Committee on Interior and Insular Affairs.* 99th Cong., 1st Sess., 99-9, Pt. 3, 19 March 1985. Washington, D.C.: U.S. Government Printing Office, 1985.

———. "Approving the Compact of Free Association between the United States, the Marshall Islands, and the Federated States of Micronesia." *Hearings before the Committee of Foreign Affairs and Its Subcommittees on Human Rights and International Organizations, Asia and Pacific Affairs, and on International Operations, on H. J. Res. 187.* 99th Cong., 1st Sess., 23 and 24 April and 2, 14, and 15 May 1985. Washington, D.C.: U.S. Government Printing Office, 1985.

———. "Approving the Compact of Free Association with the Marshall Islands and the Federated States of Micronesia and Approving Conditionally the Compact of Free Association with Palau." *Report of the Committee on Foreign Affairs together with Supplemental Views (Including Cost Estimate of the Congressional Budget Office) on H. J. Res. 187.* 99th Cong., 1st sess., 99-198, Pt. 1, 1 July 1985. Washington, D.C.: U.S. Government Printing Office, 1985.

———. "Approving the Compact of Free Association with the Federated States of Micronesia and the Marshall Islands." *Report of the Com-*

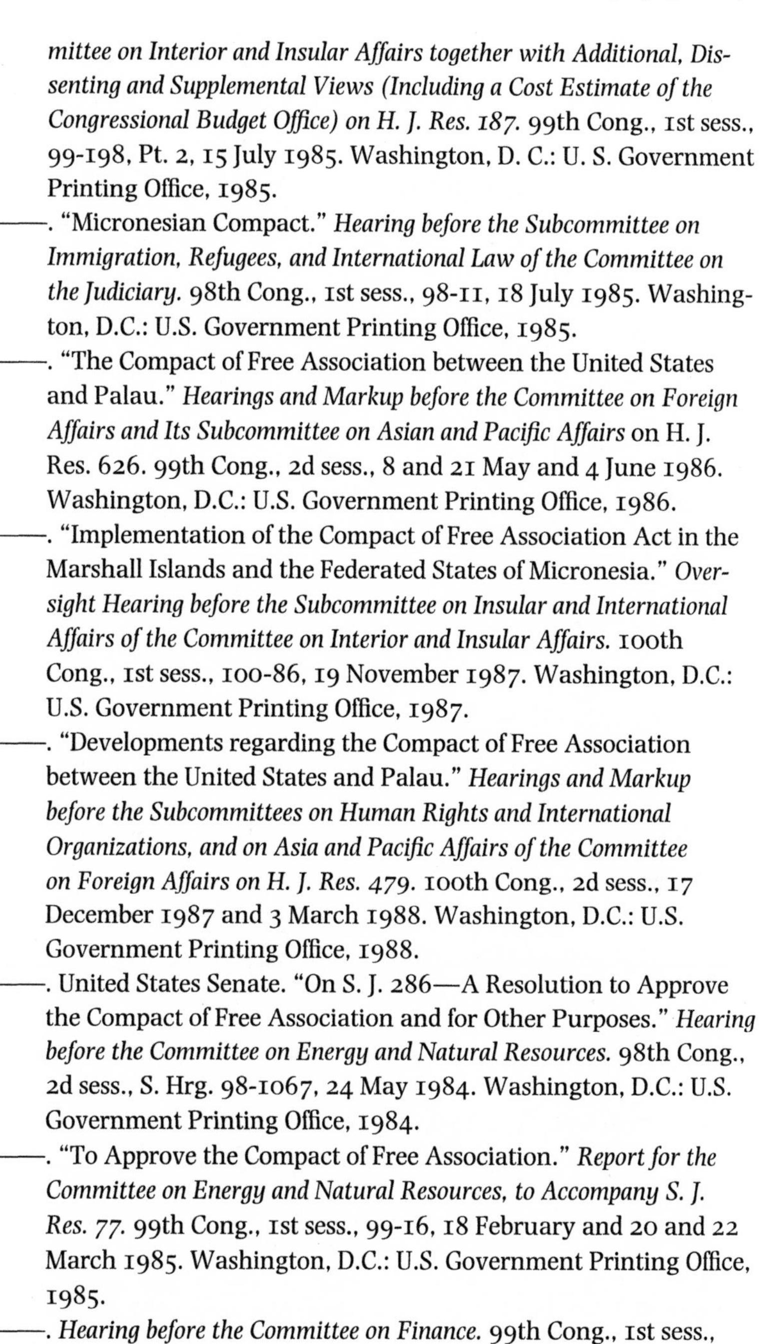

mittee on Interior and Insular Affairs together with Additional, Dissenting and Supplemental Views (Including a Cost Estimate of the Congressional Budget Office) on H. J. Res. 187. 99th Cong., 1st sess., 99-198, Pt. 2, 15 July 1985. Washington, D. C.: U. S. Government Printing Office, 1985.

———. "Micronesian Compact." *Hearing before the Subcommittee on Immigration, Refugees, and International Law of the Committee on the Judiciary.* 98th Cong., 1st sess., 98-11, 18 July 1985. Washington, D.C.: U.S. Government Printing Office, 1985.

———. "The Compact of Free Association between the United States and Palau." *Hearings and Markup before the Committee on Foreign Affairs and Its Subcommittee on Asian and Pacific Affairs* on H. J. Res. 626. 99th Cong., 2d sess., 8 and 21 May and 4 June 1986. Washington, D.C.: U.S. Government Printing Office, 1986.

———. "Implementation of the Compact of Free Association Act in the Marshall Islands and the Federated States of Micronesia." *Oversight Hearing before the Subcommittee on Insular and International Affairs of the Committee on Interior and Insular Affairs.* 100th Cong., 1st sess., 100-86, 19 November 1987. Washington, D.C.: U.S. Government Printing Office, 1987.

———. "Developments regarding the Compact of Free Association between the United States and Palau." *Hearings and Markup before the Subcommittees on Human Rights and International Organizations, and on Asia and Pacific Affairs of the Committee on Foreign Affairs on H. J. Res. 479.* 100th Cong., 2d sess., 17 December 1987 and 3 March 1988. Washington, D.C.: U.S. Government Printing Office, 1988.

———. United States Senate. "On S. J. 286—A Resolution to Approve the Compact of Free Association and for Other Purposes." *Hearing before the Committee on Energy and Natural Resources.* 98th Cong., 2d sess., S. Hrg. 98-1067, 24 May 1984. Washington, D.C.: U.S. Government Printing Office, 1984.

———. "To Approve the Compact of Free Association." *Report for the Committee on Energy and Natural Resources, to Accompany S. J. Res. 77.* 99th Cong., 1st sess., 99-16, 18 February and 20 and 22 March 1985. Washington, D.C.: U.S. Government Printing Office, 1985.

———. *Hearing before the Committee on Finance.* 99th Cong., 1st sess., S. Hrg. 99-182, 29 July 1985. Washington, D.C.: U.S. Government Printing Office, 1985.

———. "Compact of Free Association." *Hearing before the Committee on Energy and Natural Resources, on S. J. Res. 231.* 100th Cong., 2d sess., 28 January 1988. Washington, D.C.: U.S. Government Printing Office, 1988.

———. "Palau Compact of Free Association Implementation Act." *Hearing before the Committee on Energy and Natural Resources on H. J. Res. 175.* 101st Cong., 1st sess., 26 September 1989. Washington, D.C.: U.S. Government Printing Office, 1989.

Useem, John. "The American Pattern of Military Government in Micronesia." *American Journal of Sociology* 51, 2 (September 1945), 93–102.

———. "The Changing Structure of Micronesian Society." *American Anthropologist* 47, 4 (October–December 1945): 567–588.

———. "Americans as Governors of Natives in the Pacific." *Journal of the Social Sciences,* 2, 3 (1946): 39–49.

———. "Military Government on Saipan and Tinian." *Applied Anthropology: Problems of Social Organization* 5, 1 (Winter 1946): 1–39.

———. *Report on Yap and Palau.* United States Commercial Company Survey. Washington, D.C.: United States Commercial Company, October 1946.

———. "Applied Anthropology in Micronesia." *Applied Anthropology: Problems of Social Organization* 6, 4 (Fall 1947): 1–14.

Waite, David. "Marshalls May Allow Nuclear Site." *Honolulu Advertiser,* 31 May 1997.

Wallerstein, Immanuel. *The Modern World-System: Capitalist Agriculture and the Origins of the European World Economy in the Sixteenth Century.* New York: Academic Press, 1974.

Weber, Max. *The Protestant Ethic and the Spirit of Capitalism.* New York: Scribner and Sons, 1948.

Weiner, Annette B. *Women of Value, Men of Renown.* Austin: University of Texas Press, 1976.

———. *Inalienable Possessions: The Paradox of Keeping-While-Giving.* Berkeley: University of California Press, 1992.

Weisgall, Jonathan M. *Operations Crossroads: The Atomic Tests at Bikini Atoll.* Annapolis, Md.: Naval Institute Press, 1994.

White, Geoffrey M., and Lamont Lindstrom, eds. *The Pacific Theater: Island Representations of World War II.* Pacific Islands Monograph Series, no. 8. Honolulu: University of Hawai'i Press, 1989.

Wilber, Charles K., ed. *The Political Economy of Development and Underdevelopment.* Fourth edition. New York: Random House, 1988.

Williams, Raymond. *Culture and Society, 1780–1950*. London: Chatto and Windus, 1958.

———. *Marxism and Literature*. Oxford: Oxford University Press, 1977.

Wilson, Lynn B. *Speaking to Power: Gender and Politics in the Western Pacific*. New York: Routledge, 1995.

Wolf, Eric R. *Europe and the People without History*. Berkeley: University of California Press, 1982.

Wright, Rear Admiral Carleton H. "Let's Not Civilize These Happy People." *Saturday Evening Post*, 3 May 1947, 23, 149–150.

Yanaihara, Tadao. *Pacific Islands under Japanese Mandate*. London: Oxford University Press, 1940.

Young, Robert. *White Mythologies: Writing History and the West*. London: Routledge, 1992.

Yuen, Ray. "Litter, Overcrowding, Illness Plague Tiny Island of Ebeye." *Honolulu Star Bulletin and Advertiser*, 22 January 1978.

Zunz, Oliver. *Making America Corporate, 1870–1920*. Chicago: University of Chicago Press, 1990.

Index

About the Author

David Hanlon is associate professor of history at the University of Hawai'i and editor of *The Contemporary Pacific: A Journal of Island Affairs.* His previous book, *Upon a Stone Altar: A History of the Island of Pohnpei to 1890,* won the 1989 Erminie Wheeler-Voegelin Prize for ethnohistory.

LaVergne, TN USA
05 May 2010
181669LV00002B/7/P